Taking Flight with OWLs

Examining Electronic Writing Center Work

Taking Flight with OWLs

Examining Electronic Writing Center Work

Edited by

James A. Inman
The University of Michigan

Donna N. Sewell
Valdosta State University

 LAWRENCE ERLBAUM ASSOCIATES, PUBLISHERS
2000   Mahwah, New Jersey   London

Lawrence Erlbaum Associates, Inc., Publishers
10 Industrial Avenue
Mahwah, NJ 07430

Cover design by Kathryn Houghtaling Lacey

Library of Congress Cataloging-in-Publication Data

Taking flight with OWLs : examining electronic writing center work / edited by James A. Inman, Donna N. Sewell.
    p.   cm.
Includes bibliographical references and index.
ISBN 0-8058-3171-1 (acid-free paper). — ISBN
0-8058-3172-X (pbk. : acid-free paper)
1. English language—Rhetoric—Study and teaching—Data
processing. 2. Report writing—Study and teaching—Data
processing. 3. English language—Computer-assisted instruction. 4. Report writing—Computer-assisted instruction. 5.
Online data processing. 6. Writing centers. I. Inman, James
A. II. Sewell, Donna N.
PE1404.T24   1999
808'.042'0285—dc21
                      99-21630
                         CIP

Books published by Lawrence Erlbaum Associates are printed
on acid-free paper, and their bindings are chosen for strength
and durability.

Printed in the United States of America
10 9 8 7 6 5 4 3 2 1

For Ralph and Sandra Inman

For Wes Sewell and Hilda Cox Newberry

Contents

About the Authors and Editors

Eileen Apperson-Williams received her MA in nonfiction prose and will receive her MFA in poetry in the spring of 1999 from California State University, Fresno. Although her academic focus has been creative writing, she is devoted to the teaching of composition and is supportive of the roles of tutors in the writing process. While collaborating with Carlson, Apperson-Williams was Assistant Director of CSU, Fresno's extensive Writing Center that employs approximately 35 tutors and enrolls approximately 500 students.

Randall L. Beebe is Director of Composition at Eastern Illinois University, where he teaches courses in technical writing, composition theory, and British Romanticism. He is currently studying the impact of technology on literature and composition courses and is preparing a book-length rhetorical study of British women novelists of the late 18th and early 19th centuries.

Mary J. Bonevelle completed her master's degree in English at Eastern Illinois University, where she tutored in the university's writing center. She received her bachelor's degree from Siena Heights University, and she teaches English part-time at Baker College in Muskegon, Michigan. Her main intellectual interests are American maritime disasters of the early 1900s, Middle Eastern culture, and composition theory.

Lady Falls Brown directs the University Writing Center at Texas Tech University. A former president of the National Writing Centers Association, she has also served as South Central Representative and At-Large Representative to the organization. She is owner and moderator of wcenter (1991-present), a listserv devoted to the discussion of writing center theory and practice. She received the National Writing Centers Association award for Outstanding Service in April 1994 and currently serves on the editorial board for *Writing Center Journal*.

Wayne Butler earned his PhD in English Education from the University of Texas at Austin. Between 1992 and 1997, he taught at the University of Michigan's English Composition Board, serving in various capacities including Lecturer, Director for the Peer Tutoring program, Associate Director for Instruction, and Acting Director. He coauthored with William Condon *Writing the Information Superhighway* (Allyn & Bacon, 1997), a writing textbook to help students use the Internet in the writing process. Currently Butler is CEO of the Daedalus Group, Inc., an educational consulting and software firm and publisher of the Daedalus Integrated Writing Environment.

David A. Carlson has a BA from California State University, Fresno, and will receive an MA in English Literature with a Certificate of Advanced Composition Studies from California State University, Fresno, in the spring of 1999. His thesis work is on reactions from a few British 19th century novelists to Wordsworth's influence on education. Carlson was the lead designer of the online tutoring program, writer of the Website, and a tutor and supervisor for the CSU, Fresno, writing center.

Joanna Castner is a PhD candidate, graduate part-time instructor, and online writing consultant in the Technical Communication and Rhetoric program at Texas Tech University. She is currently researching online classroom discourse patterns for her dissertation. Her publications include articles in *Computers and Composition, The Writing Lab Newsletter*, and *CCTE Studies*.

Michael Colpo has recently completed his MA in Literature and Environment at the University of Nevada, Reno, where he has also served as an instructor of English composition, a tutor and Web consultant for the campus Writing Center, and a member of the UNR Web Development Team. Although still actively involved in the academic community, he is presently self-employed as a computer consultant and Website developer.

William Condon is Director of Washington State University's (WSU) Campus Writing Programs. In addition to supervising campuswide assessment and writing across the curriculum programs, he supervises WSU's Writing Center. He also participates in the development of online learning environments. Condon is co-author of *Writing the Information Superhighway* (Allyn & Bacon, 1997), and—with Liz Hamp-Lyons—*Assessing the Portfolio: Principles for Practice, Theory and Research* (forthcoming from Hampton Press).

Eric Crump is (officially) the Website Manager and (unofficially) the NetRat in Residence for the National Council of Teachers of English. He is the cofounder of the University of Missouri's Online Writery and the editor and chief instigator of *RhetNet, a Dialogic Publishing (Ad)Venture* or *CyberJournal for Rhetoric and Writing* (depending on which you prefer). He gets paid to play on the net so sees no need for hobbies and such stuff.

Gail Summerskill Cummins is Director of the Writing Center and an Assistant Professor of English at the University of Kentucky. She teaches courses on writing, tutoring, and teaching composition and writes about these topics. An advocate of service learning, she is involved in a variety of technological literacy exchanges between the University of Kentucky and the Kentucky public schools. She is founder of the Kentucky Writing Center Association and the Appalachian Partnership of Peer Tutors.

Andy Curtis is Assistant Professor in the Department of English at the Hong Kong Polytechnic University in the China Special Administrative Region (SAR) of Hong Kong. One of his main responsibilities there is the design, delivery and development of English language-related support programs for postgraduate research students, an increasing number of whom are from Mainland China. He has worked with teachers and students in the United Kingdom and elsewhere in Europe, in the United States and Canada, Indonesia, Thailand, Korea, and elsewhere in Southeast Asia.

Danielle DeVoss is a graduate student in the Rhetoric and Technical Communication program at Michigan Technological University. Her interests include women's resistances to computer technologies, computer-related literacies, and the performance of gender in online realms.

Joel A. English is an Assistant Professor at Old Dominion University. He manages the OWL-Shop resources and listserv for online writing labs. He is a member of the Instructional Technology Committee of National Council of Teachers of English and the editorial board of *Kairos: A Journal for Teachers of Writing in Webbed Environments*.

Shawn Fullmer is a doctoral candidate in composition and rhetoric at the University of Nevada, Reno (UNR), where he teaches undergraduate courses in composition, works as an administrator for the Core Writing Program, and is a consultant at UNR's Writing Center. He is the 1996 recipient of the Robins Awards Teaching Assistant of the Year. His interests include computers and composition, qualitative research methodologies, and literary nonfiction.

Mark Hara is currently working toward an MA in Rhetoric and Composition at Arizona State University (ASU), where he teaches in the Electronic Classroom Composition program. Prior to attending ASU, he was employed for 3 years at the Michigan State University Writing Center, consulting with students and faculty on composition and technology issues while working toward his teaching certification in English and computer science. His interests include teaching, computer-assisted instruction, and class issues.

Muriel Harris is Professor of English and Director of the Purdue University Writing Lab. She founded and continues to edit the *Writing Lab Newsletter* and founded and continues to coordinate the development of the Writing Lab's OWL (http://owl.english.purdue.edu). Her publications—including *Teaching One to One: The Writing Conference* and the *Prentice Hall Reference Guide to Grammar and Usage* (soon to appear in a 4th edition)—focus on writing center theory, practice, and pedagogy and advocate the writing center as a uniquely effective setting in which to work collaboratively with writers. She and the OWL staff continue to explore the uses of technology in the writing center as well.

James A. Inman was Spencer Fellow at the University of Michigan, where he studied in the Joint Doctoral Program in English and Education. He currently serves as News Editor for *Kairos: A Journal for Teachers of Writing in Webbed Environments*, Cocoordinator of the Netoric Project, and Chair of the Computer Research Section of the Midwest Modern Language Association, and he is a member of NCTE's Committee on Instructional Technology. Inman is now Assistant Professor and Director of the Center for Collaboration and Communication at Furman University.

Jennifer Jordan-Henley is an Assistant Professor of English and Director of the Oak Ridge Writing Center at Roane State Community College in Tennessee. In addition to composition, she has also taught an online class in technical writing and recently developed a Writing Center Practicum. Her work has been published in *Computers and Composition*, the *Writing Lab Newsletter*, and Longman's *Online English Pages*. She is the administrator of the RSCC OWL, located at http://www2.rscc.cc.tn.us/~jordan_jj/OWL/OWL.html.

Jason Lambert recently graduated from Utah State University with an MA in the Theory and Practice of Writing. He participated in USU's Online Beginning Composition program as an instructor and is currently a technical writer in Logan, Utah. His research interests include the impact of technology on technical communication practice and pedagogy.

Jane Love participated in the development of the Networked Writing Environment at the University of Florida (UF), where she also codesigned and cotaught, with Anthony Rue, the first graduate practicum in electronic pedagogy for the Department of English. She holds a PhD in literary theory from UF, where she currently teaches in the Center for Women's Studies and Gender Research.

Brad E. Lucas is a doctoral candidate in composition and rhetoric at the University of Nevada, Reno, where he teaches various undergraduate courses in composition and the humanities. He is a member of the UNR Web Development Team and serves on the Board of Directors for the Center for Holocaust, Genocide, & Peace Studies. His research interests include research methodologies, critical theory, oral history, and testimony.

Mark Mabrito is Associate Professor of English at Purdue University, Calumet, where he has been a faculty member since 1989. He teaches courses in the professional writing program, business technical writing, as well as writing courses delivered via the Internet/Web. His research interests and publications focus on computers and writing, writing in the workplace, and writing apprehension.

Barry M. Maid is a Professor of Rhetoric and Writing at the University of Arkansas at Little Rock. He currently teaches courses in technical communication and computer-mediated communication. His most recent published work is on computer-mediated communication, program administration, and personality theory.

Eric Miraglia is Assistant Director of the Writing Program at Washington State University. His work in recent years has focused on the creation of interactive community-centered spaces for teaching and learning, including Washington State University's Online Writing Lab (http://owl.wsu.edu) and the Speakeasy Studio & Cafe (http://morrison.wsu.edu/studio). Miraglia's scholarly work has appeared in the *Journal of Basic Writing,* the *Journal of Advanced Composition,* and elsewhere; he is also the coeditor of a forthcoming NCTE volume on Writing Across the Curriculum, entitled *WAC for the New Millennium.*

Barbara J. Monroe, a codirector of the English Composition Board's Peer Tutoring Program at the University of Michigan (UM), directed the high school OWLs to Detroit and Bay City and will be directing the statewide expansion of OWL, cosponsored by UM's Academic Outreach and Ameritech. She is also heading up the campuswide implementation of *eNotebook*, a Web-based integrated environment she codeveloped with Gonzalo Silverio, an effort sponsored by UM's Sweetland Writing Center as a WAC initiative.

Joel Norris is Coordinator of a small group writing tutorial course, General Education 302, at Washington State University. He also directs WSU's Online Writing Lab (http://owl.wsu.edu) and teaches technical writing. Besides his work with OWLs, Joel is researching the benefits writing tutors derive from their tutoring experiences and is writing a book on small group tutoring.

Rebecca Rickly is a Visiting Assistant Professor at Texas Tech University where she teaches Technical Communication and is Associate Director of the Composition Program. Previously, she codeveloped and coordinated the University of Michigan's Online Writing and Learning (OWL). Rickly currently chairs National Council of Teachers of English Instructional Technology Committee. Her publications include *The Online Writing Classroom* (with Susanmarie Harrington and Michael Day, Hampton Press, forthcoming), and her work has appeared in *Computers and Composition*, CMC *Magazine*, and *Kairos*.

Tim Roskams has his master's degrees in Applied Linguistics, Business and Engineering. He currently teaches professional communication and is a course coordinator in the English Language Centre of the City University of Hong Kong. His previous jobs in Hong Kong have involved designing and teaching university language and business courses. His research interests are second language writing instruction, implicit vocabulary acquisition, teacher development through action research, and teaching evaluation. Before working in Hong Kong, he designed and taught English language preparatory courses for Asian students in Australia.

Donna N. Sewell is Assistant Professor of English at Valdosta State University, where she directs the Writing Center in addition to teaching writing and literature. Recently a Governor's Teaching Fellow, Sewell has been working on several technology projects, including investigations of MOO-based tutoring and electronic collaboration and mentoring. Sewell earned a PhD in English, specializing in Rhetoric and Composition, from The Florida State University in 1995.

Mark Shadle, Associate Professor of English Writing and Writing Lab Director, teaches a wide range of courses at Eastern Oregon University in La Grande, Oregon. His current teaching involves the use of multigenre, multidisciplinary, multicultural and multimedia student projects. He has published works of journalism, criticism, scholarship, and fiction on a variety of subjects, including writing tutoring and counseling; Wendell Berry; Ishmael Reed; multicultural literature; jazz/blues; and environmental literature. More complete information can be found, via the World Wide Web, at http://www.eou.edu/~mshadle/.

Jake Shewmake recently completed an MA in the Theory and Practice of Writing program at Utah State University (USU). His research interests include the effective design and use of Internet-based learning environments to teach creative writing, professional writing, and first-year composition. He is currently consulting with the developers of a new Internet-based learning environment at USU and is working as a freelance writer from his home in Cedar City, Utah.

Sharon Thomas is currently Associate Chair of the Department of American Thought and Language at Michigan State University (MSU), where she has also recently been both Associate Director and Acting Director of the Writing Center. Her chapter resulted from a collaborative project designed both to advance the use of technology to support writing on campus and to provide professional development for the undergraduate and graduate students employed in the MSU Writing Center.

Jamie Thurber is a recent graduate of the University of Alaska, Fairbanks, receiving his MFA in Creative Writing. During his degree work, he developed the Internet Tutoring Program with Professors Susan Blalock, Pete Pinney, and Rich Carr, and fellow student Jeff McAllister. He is also a graduate of the US Air Force Academy and uses his engineering degree to work in Information Systems, moonlighting as a Technical Writing instructor and writer and daylighting as father to Talia, husband to Deidre, and whatever else he can think of.

Denise Weeks is an Assistant Professor of English at Weber State University. She served as Writing Center Director for 1 year and currently teaches the university's Methods and Practice in Tutoring Writing course for new writing center tutors. She also teaches courses in Professional and Technical Writing, composition, and literature.

PREFACE

The Hatching of *Taking Flight with OWLs*: Promise and Possibilities

James A. Inman
University of Michigan
Donna N. Sewell
Valdosta State University

Taking Flight with OWLs examines computer and other technology use in writing centers. Its purpose is to move beyond anecdotal evidence for implementing computer technology in writing centers, presenting carefully considered studies that theorize the move to computer technology and examine technology use in practice. The need for such a collection is evident: Writing center practitioners have long discussed their roles in relation to their supporting institutions; now, they are challenged to explore—even reinvent—their roles as computer technologies transform centers and institutions.

The move to computer technology has occurred so rapidly that center staff and administration, despite putting forth a strong effort, have not had much opportunity to study how and when to infuse computer technology. Some excellent articles in such print journals as *Writing Center Journal*,

Computers and Composition, College Composition and Communication, and
Writing Lab Newsletter and in such online journals as *Kairos: A Journal for
Teachers of Writing in Webbed Environments* and *RhetNet: A Dialogic Publishing (Ad)venture* have addressed the tension between the pressure to
adopt computer technology and the time needed to consider carefully such
adoption. Hobson's (1998b) *Wiring the Writing Center* and Blythe's (1998)
chapter in *The Writing Center Resource Manual* also begin to work through
these issues. In exploring varied stages of computer and other technology
infusion through field-based accounts, *Taking Flight* offers readers an important and unique resource.

Taking Flight with OWLs begins with chapters that examine and engage
the potential of technology in writing centers. Central to the first section's—toward a Definition and Context for Electronic Writing Center
Work—focus is that computer technology and its potential impact must be
considered thoroughly before it can successfully be incorporated into the
writing center. Beginning this volume, Shadle (chap. 1) offers "The Spotted
OWL: Online Writing Labs as Sites of Diversity, Controversy, and Identity," in which he reports and analyzes the results of a recently administered
survey designed to study the diversity and success of technology use in online writing labs. Brown, owner and moderator of wcenter, follows Shadle
with chapter 2, "OWLs in Theory and Practice: A Director's Perspective,"
which traces the development of *OWL* as a term and the development of
Texas Tech University's OWL as a way to describe the challenges and rewards of integrating computer technology into writing centers. Taking a different approach, Curtis and Roskams present chapter 3, "Language
Learning in Networked Writing Labs: A View from Asia," which analyzes
the reactions of English as a Second Language (ESL) students to computer
technology in writing labs. In "The Culture of Technology in the Writing
Center: Reinvigorating the Theory–Practice Debate," the section's final
chapter, Beebe and Bonevelle (chap. 4) examine the impact computer technology has on the culture of a writing center.

The second section—Narratives of Experience—offers five narratives of
experience, each exploring a different stage in writing centers' adoptions of
computer technology. In "Theories Before Practice(s): Proposing Computers for Writing Centers," Weeks (chap. 5) outlines her experience writing a successful grant to acquire computers for her center, suggesting that
the grant writing process naturally produces theory before practice. In the
second chapter of this section, Thomas, Hara, and DeVoss (chap. 6) offer
"Writing in the Electronic Realm: Incorporating a New Medium Into the

Work of the Writing Center," a chapter that details the experiences of Michigan State University writing tutors and writing center administrators in moving to technology and in working to improve the quality and diversity of their electronic and traditional services. Next is "Emerging (Web)Sites for Writing Centers: Practicality, Usage, and Multiple Voices Under Construction," by Fullmer, Lucas, and Colpo (chap. 7), which discusses a study conducted at UNR to gauge student reactions to their first OWL and the subsequent revisions; the authors describe how they created their assessment tool and how they evaluated the results. The fourth chapter of this section, "Cyberspace and Sofas: Dialogic Spaces and the Making of an Online Writing Lab," authored by Miraglia and Norris (chap. 8), examines the process by which Washington State University's OWL was created, focusing on the construction of dialogic spaces, both amongst the development team and for the potential clients. In "Advice to the Linelorn: Crossing State Borders and the Politics of Cyberspace," this section's final chapter (chap. 9), Jordan-Henley and Maid, pioneers of synchronous tutorials, describe the politics involved with their creation of a cross-institutional tutoring environment.

"The Asynchronous, Online Writing Session: A Two-Way Stab in the Dark?" begins section III—Asynchronous Electronic Tutoring; Castner (chap. 10) studies dialogue as a feature of e-mail tutoring. This section's second chapter, "The Anxieties of Distance: Online Tutors Reflect," by Carlson and Apperson-Williams (chap. 11), evaluates the role distance plays in formulating productive discourse in online tutorials; using examples from their own practice, the authors suggest ways that any potential limitations imposed by distance may be overcome. Mabrito's (chap. 12) "E-mail Tutoring and Apprehensive Writers: What Research Tells Us," the last chapter of this section, explores the potential of e-mail as an accessible and promising site of writing assistance for apprehensive writers, sharing examples from his own work.

Section IV—Synchronous Electronic Tutoring—begins with "Synchronous Internet Tutoring: Bridging the Gap in Distance Education," by Thurber (chap. 13), which investigates the use of audio-visual computer technology to conduct real-time tutoring sessions; Thurber grounds his discussion in specific examples of his work at the University of Alaska at Fairbanks. The second chapter of this section, "The Real(Time) World: Synchronous Communications in the Online Writing Center," by Shewmake and Lambert (chap. 14), explores ways in which chat environments assist tutors. English details his efforts at using MOOs in "Putting the

OO in MOO: Employing Environmental Interaction" (chap. 15), analyzing transcripts of cybertutorials and considering the role of metacognition in MOOing. In "Ethics, Plugged and Unplugged: The Pedagogy of Disorderly Conduct," the section's final chapter, Love (chap, 16) engages the role of professional ethics and subversions of authority in making real-time, MOO-based encounters between tutors and students as productive as possible for both parties.

The final section is titled Looking to the Future. In "Making Up Tomorrow's Agenda and Shopping Lists Today: Preparing for Future Technologies in Writing Centers," this section's first chapter, Harris (chap. 17) describes how computer technology may affect instruction, administration, institutional mission, and research in writing centers. The second chapter, "Centering in the Distance: Writing Centers, Inquiry, and Technology," by Cummins (chap. 18), emphasizes that a consideration of community, with an emphasis toward a critical perspective that enables the observation of these communities, allows new and productive alliances to be formed. In "The Near and Distant Futures of OWL and the Writing Center," Monroe, Rickly, Condon, and Butler (chap. 19) explore the future of OWL, which they define in several different and productive ways, focusing on issues of institutional politics, the transformation of higher education, and potential partnerships with corporate and other sponsors. In the section's final chapter, "How Many Technoprovocateurs Does It Take to Create Interversity?" Crump (chap. 20) speculates about the role of writing centers in educational progress; in particular, he engages and extends the writing center metaphor into an uncertain future, arguing that we should not have our feet on both the accelerator and the brake at the same time.

ACKNOWLEDGMENTS

Assembling *Taking Flight with OWLs* has been a project that incorporated the outstanding work, generous support, and timely assistance of many people. Although we name a few people who have helped us along the way, we mean this effort also as a general acknowledgment for anyone who has assisted us; there have been so many people. We are grateful.

The authors have been generous with us at every stage of the process: authoring and submitting excellent chapters, industriously revising whenever asked, and speedily responding to any additional needs, like additional citation information or biographical statements. We are proud to be associated with such a terrific group.

At our respective universities, we have received support. At the University of Michigan, James Inman frequently consulted with his mentor, Anne Ruggles Gere, who helped with ideas during all stages of the negotiation and submission process; he also received valuable support from his cohort colleagues, Jeff Buchanan, Shawn Christian, and Cathy McFaul. At Valdosta State University, Donna Sewell wants to thank the graduate and undergraduate tutors, far too numerous to name, who have willingly helped her think through uses of technology in the Writing Center. Diane Howard eagerly shared new ideas and technologies, and Susan Barron, Susan Seyfarth, and Sandra Giles (now at Abraham Baldwin College) read Donna's writings carefully and thoughtfully. We both wish to thank Thomas Dasher, John Hiers, and especially Patricia Marks for their support throughout this project.

No project as large as this one could be accomplished without the support of family and friends, and we are both grateful for the involvement of many people. For James, his parents, Ralph and Sandra Inman, to whom he dedicates this book, have been his strongest supporters, and he also has enjoyed the involvement of his grandparents, Ralph and Ellen Inman. Donna wants to thank Wes Sewell for everything he took over to allow her to finish this project. Also, her family kept her sane through the process by refusing to let her forget about the rest of the world while working on this volume. Helen Daniels Sewell deserves a special hug for her assistance during the most frantic period.

Finally, we want to acknowledge the support and assistance of Lawrence Erlbaum Associates, particularly Naomi Silverman, Lori Hawver, and Sara T. Scudder. They have been very helpful throughout the entire process; we are pleased to have this work in such capable hands.

INTRODUCTION

Reeling in the Horizon: OWLs and Perspective in Writing Center Work

Donna N. Sewell
Valdosta State University
James A. Inman
University of Michigan

She pulled in her horizon like a great fish-net. Pulled it from around the waist of the world and draped it over her shoulder. So much of life in its meshes! She called in her soul to come and see.

—Zora Neale Hurston

Among writing teachers, writing center personnel often have been at the vanguard of the move to online instructional applications, developing a range of variations on tutorial and consulting services that translate to the unique conditions of electronic/computer mediated communications.

—Eric Hobson, 1998a

As writing center professionals, we are now at a challenging moment in our history, a space wherein the very nature of our work is being fundamentally altered by the rapid and successful growth of computer and other technologies, and especially the often, equally rapid and uninterrogated implementation of these technologies in education. In our work, we must begin to think through the issues raised in the previously cited quotations: we must, as Hobson (1998a) described, continue to occupy positions "at the vanguard of the move to online instructional applications," and we must as Hurston (1937) so beautifully described, reach out to the horizon, attempt to reel it in, and bring it closer to our lives and work.

A HISTORICAL VIEW

In 1984, North challenged writing centers to answer a vital question: "What happens in writing tutorials?" (p. 29); although his call has been answered in part (Davis, Hayward, Hunter, & Wallace, 1988; Hynds, 1989; Wolcott, 1989), he and those who responded could not foresee the radical changes that computers and other technologies would bring to writing center practice. These innovations have not just changed writing center practice; they have rewritten it.

By 1986, tutors and directors found pedagogically sound uses for computers, focusing mostly on revision strategies rather than on skills and drills software (Luchte, 1987; McKenzie, 1989; Serico, 1986). Based on interviews with tutors and writer, Farrell (1987) stated that these two groups

> see the computer acting as a third party or neutral ground, giving immediate feedback and ease of revision, inviting more writing, opening dialogue between writer and tutor, acting as a learning device, and giving writers pride in their work. (p. 29)

As writing center administration and staff became technologically savvy and began effectively communicating, important developments occurred. For example, Kinkead's (1988) article, "The Electronic Writing Tutor," argues for writing centers to establish an e-mail presence. In examining the rapid proliferation of technology, Selfe (1989) emphasized that technological writing centers are valuable in helping us "inform and update our notion for literacy as it is practiced in computer-supported communication environments" (p. 3). We now have many variations of computer literacy, including Ulmer's (1997) *electracy* and what others have termed *technoliteracy* (Carlacio, 1998; Inman & Howard, 1996; Miller, 1995), but the principal idea is that computer users must have some awareness of computer operations and of their own role in utilizing technology.

Even given the progress and critical discussions of the 1980s, scholarly attention to computer technology use in writing centers has been delayed, perhaps because of practical matters, such as obtaining grants, finding space for computers, locating people with technical expertise, and weighing expense against perceived results. Despite developing Purdue University's Online Writing Lab and participating regularly on wcenter, Harris (1990) did not mention computer technology as a trend or tradition in "What's Up and What's In," suggesting that as late as 1990 many writing centers had not adopted computers and those that had were not far beyond word processing and invention software. Some scholars directly challenged technological innovations in writing centers; Summerfield (1988) warned writing centers to be wary of technology: "Watch out for computer terminals. Watch out for all evidence of attempts to break down the gathering of minds" (p. 68).

Although Summerfield's (1988) concern that technology "CAN threaten the community of the writing center" is justified given the number of self-help programs in existence in the late 1980s (when she authored her essay), computer technology can also connect people who would not otherwise gather (p. 67). Many of us already value such connections as they allow us to correspond through electronic lists, such as wcenter and acw-l; attend online conferences, such as the Teaching in the Community College Online Conference, which was started 3 years ago; and gather together on MOOs, such as Connections and LinguaMOO. Although more writing centers are moving toward electronic communication with students via asynchronous and synchronous technology, and although many writing center professionals are becoming more comfortable with technology, much more research is needed to move everyone confidently into what surely will be a high-tech future.

In terms of technology, the field of computers and composition is generally ahead of writing centers, but we can benefit from the research of its practitioners, just as our work in writing centers can benefit compositionists. One example of significant research in computers and composition is Haas' (1989) "Seeing It on the Screen Isn't Really Seeing It," in which she discussed four problems computer users have reading the screen: "formatting, proofreading, reorganizing, and critical reading or getting a sense of the text" (p. 20). This article suggests "that student writers (1) would not recognize that writing on-line had drawbacks which might affect their reading of their own texts, and (2) would not use hard copy to supplement their computer writing the way experts do" (p. 27). These findings indicate that tutors and students need to move back and forth between printed text and online text; Haas' work is only one example of the wealth of available research. Other scholars in computers and composition (Eldred & Hawisher, 1995; Mabrito, 1991) and in distance education (Cohen & Riel, 1989l; Feenberg, 1989; Harasim, 1989) have much to offer as well.

With the increased demand for scholarly examinations of computer technology use, several studies have examined asynchronous and synchronous communication in writing centers. Coogan (1995) emphasized the ways in which e-mail tutorials differ from walk-in tutorials:

> By replacing talk with asynchronous writing, e-mail disrupts the most familiar boundaries in the writing center: shared space and limited time. As a result, e-mail changes the conference's discipline by slowing it down (from 30 minutes to several days), and by collapsing the self into text where it becomes a rhetorical construct, not a social given. (p. 171)

Discussions of e-mail tutoring occur frequently on wcenter and owl-shop, and many writing centers have adopted e-mail, although policies differ as to who may submit an essay for review by tutors. Like asynchronous tutoring, synchronous work has improved and expanded significantly in recent years. The cyberspace tutorial project between Jordan-Henley's school and Maid's school, which serves as the basis for their chapter (chap. 9) in this collection, resulted in students expressing "a much greater interest in revision than that which normally occurs in a composition class" (Jordan-Henley & Maid, 1995b, p. 213).

One constant realization is that incorporating computer and other technologies has, of course, advantages and disadvantages. As part of a focus on OWLs in the inaugural issue of *Kairos: A Journal for Teachers of Writing in Webbed Environments*, Blythe (1996) presented a thorough overview of these issues. One of the most obvious advantages is the accessibility that students, and indeed everyone, gain to writing centers through technological media (Nelson & Wambeam, 1995; Selfe, 1995). Challenges include increased training time for staff, the development of online materials, and the cost of technology.

The most recent examinations of computers and other technologies' impact on writing center practice are collected in Hobson's (1998) *Wiring the Writing Center*. In Hobson's collection, important chapters by Monroe and Rickly work to describe not just the possibilities of online tutoring, but also the actual dynamics of online tutoring work and how cybertutors might best be trained; these treatments represent a more mature fieldview—whether adopting technology for writing center work continues to become less of a choice and more of a requirement. Another chapter, "Email 'Tutoring' as

Collaborative Writing," by Coogan, builds on his earlier writing about e-mail tutoring as a "new way to do work," this time suggesting that such work requires working together.

Wiring the Writing Center also offers a more mature perspective of technology-based writing centers by demonstrating that such work redefines the very idea of a writing center. In her chapter, "WAC on the Web: Writing Center Outreach to Teachers of Writing Intensive Courses," Kimball suggested that a Web-based writing center can support Writing Across the Curriculum (WAC) initiatives, and similarly, Gardener, in "Have You Visited Your Online Writing Center Today?: Learning, Writing, and Teaching Online at a Community College," reminds us that community colleges are important sites for electronic writing center work. Finally, Childers, Jordan and Upton described the promise of online writing center work for high schools in their chapter, "Virtual High School Writing Centers: A Spectrum of Possibilities."

What *Wiring the Writing Center* also included was a series of chapters that took a more critical stance toward online or electronic writing center work. Wallace, for example, in his "Random Memories of the Virtual Writing Center: The Modes-to-Nodes Problem," described how technological advancement and university of institution-based advancement often work at very different rates; and he explored how this generates a problematic tension for writing center professionals. Additionally, Carino offered what he called "A Cautionary History," in which he explored institutional concerns for the adoption of computer technologies: the blurring of lines, for instance, between computer labs and writing center. Taking these views a step further, Lerner examined the development of electronic writing center work in a larger context, that of education's progress in general toward instructional technologies. Where Lerner seemed particularly critical was in his conclusion: "Writing Center professionals can be a skeptical lot, experienced in carefully reading texts and uncovering hidden agendas; when it comes to our future with technology, that skepticism may be our greatest asset" (p. 136). Although our own critical perspective on technology use is not as skeptical, we do acknowledge and respect the stances that these three scholars are taking.

CONCLUSION: A CHALLENGE

Writing centers occupy a dynamic position at the crossroads of computers and composition, distance education, and composition theory, pulling ideas, theories, and pedagogies from each. Simpson (1985) reminded us to celebrate changes in writing centers and to work to ensure that changes are beneficial:

> Writing centers unquestionably will continue to change. We must be careful to use the structure we have built as a way of detecting those changes, of evaluating them and of adjusting to the changes that represent improvement and working to prevent those we consider harmful (p. 57).

Quite naturally, some scholars, including several in this collection, may disagree with Simpson's suggestion that we "use the structure we have built." Regardless of future directions, however, Simpson correctly argued that writing centers will continue to evolve, and we believe that the next evolution necessarily involves computer technology, whether by choice or by force.

In this rapidly changing sphere of progress, many challenges exist for writing center thinkers, but with these challenges come exciting opportunities. Undeniably, computers have internationalized writing center work, and the possibilities of electronic communication have significantly broadened our audience. Writing centers should continue to celebrate their diversity, taking advantage of the opportunities that computer technology presents. In publishing *Taking Flight With OWLs*, we implicitly, if not overtly, extend North's (1984) landmark work and offer a new call: Research into technology use in writing centers is needed now more than ever. It will take innovative thinkers and critical attention for writing centers to continue to be centers of influence for their campuses and beyond and for writing center professionals to have the courage and the vision to adapt their missions to the new and progressive institutions and work contexts that no doubt await us just beyond the horizon. We need to reach out for the horizon and, like Hurston's Janie, reel it in.

I

Toward a Definition and Context for Electronic Writing Center Work

1

The Spotted OWL: Online Writing Labs as Sites of Diversity, Controversy, and Identity

Mark Shadle

Eastern Oregon University

In the summer of 1997, I received a stipend from Eastern Oregon University to research Online Writing Labs (OWLs). Although listserv conversations, conference presentations, and informal discussions with other writing center directors provided some information, I waded into the netstream to survey OWLs. I sent a survey to various national listservs, including the two catering to members of the National Writing Centers Association (NWCA): wcenter (wcenter@ttacs6.ttu.edu) and owl-shop (owl-shop@bsu.edu). Also, I visited OWLs, particularly those accessible from the NWCA site run by Bruce Pegg at Colgate University (http://departments.colgate.edu/diw/NWCAOWLS.html), and then e-mailed the survey to the Webmasters of those OWLs. During the fall of 1997, I revisited many survey participants via e-mail and the telephone and reviewed OWL research in appropriate journals, such as *The Writing Center Journal* and *Computers and Composition* (see their World Wide Web site at http://www.cwrl.utexas.edu/~ccjrnl/toc.html). Finally, to gain a deeper perspective on OWLs, I traveled to a large university very interested in developing an OWL and a small liberal-arts college uninterested in having an OWL.

The rather lengthy survey consisted of 17 central questions about the purposes, audiences, and uses of existing OWLs, whereas 11 supplemental questions explored technical matters. Knowing the overwhelming schedules of writing center directors, I accepted whatever respondents could provide, receiving partially completed responses, as well as extremely lengthy ones. The comments in this chapter come from 67 complete surveys from over 39 states, representing small private schools with only 60 students to large public universities with over 33,000 students. Further information about the entire survey is posted on the Eastern Oregon University Web pages, (http://www.eou.edu/~mshadle/stipend97.html).

In certain circles, this often anecdotal and incomplete data might seem a failure. Even the writing center community occasionally debates the value of surveys, usually as part of a larger quantitative versus qualitative discussion. These survey results are offered as a still life of OWLs, allowing OWL administrators to tell their stories essentially in their own words; these sometimes incomplete or even contradictory accounts create a context for later chapters in this volume that explore individual centers' uses of technology. The comments from OWL administrators are purposely anonymous to protect respondents, but readers familiar with writing center literature and lore will no doubt recognize particular people or sites. These comments and the perspectives they reveal should help other schools as they create, maintain, and/or revise an OWL.

ONLINE WRITING LABS

The growth rate for OWLs has been steadily accelerating. Although 4% of schools do not have an OWL or have had one for 5 years or more, 20% have had one for 3 years, 24% for 2 years, and 40% for 1 year or less. Because defining an OWL is tricky, the respondents wrote more about what they had, rather than about what an OWL should be. Almost all had home pages on the World Wide Web, and over one half used group or tutor e-mail or online resource materials. About one fourth of respondents employed listservs. Some also had searchable databases, asynchronous courses, MOOs, newsgroups, Multi-User Domain (MUDs), or e-mail links. The following OWL functions appeared more rarely: a grammar hotline archive, an interactive net forum, general links, links to other schools, an e-mail link with area high schools, critiques of student Web pages, an online survey about writing attitudes, information on summer institutes, and classroom presentations on technology and synchronous courses. These functions are discussed more fully in the section on creating and revising an OWL.

Most OWLs target students (seven-eighths) and faculty (three-fourths). About one half of the OWL include staff or distance learners in their audience. One third of OWLs mentioned community members. The following list ranks intended audiences from most common to least common: students, faculty, staff, distance learners, community, administrators, people all over the world, high schools, other colleges, and middle schools.

Almost all OWLs were created to provide greater access to resource materials, and at least one third of OWLs hoped that posting frequently asked questions (FAQs) online would allow tutors to spend less time answering routine questions and more time tutoring. One half of respondents emphasized the growth of distance learning and one third noted the importance of more flexible tutoring through e-mail or synchronous chat software as reasons for their creation. Ironically, a few directors reported that the OWL came first and was being used to develop or create face-to-face tutoring. The following list ranks the reasons for creating an OWL from most common to least common: continuous access to information about the center, growth of distance learning, efficiency from answering FAQs online, a more flexible schedule for tutoring, development of face-to-face tutoring, improved computer literacy and collaboration for students, and preference of computer screen to live tutee.

Resistance to OWLs

The basic resistance to OWLs included the following concerns: philosophic disagreement with the idea of an OWL; lack of equipment, money, and/or personnel; resistance of faculty, staff, or tutors to online tutoring; and the usefulness of existing OWLs. Although the testimony received here was not lengthy, it was often passionate. In a century when most people believe in the geometric acceleration of technological change (whether true or not), responses like the following are unsurprising:

> I'm a Luddite who considers computer technology a scourge! My view on learning is that it is an embodied experience, that we gain from each other's physical presence, and new technology that renders us even more abstract than we already are to each other is dangerous.

Other writing center directors have resisted an OWL based on the location, image, mission, and student population:

Philosophically, I question the emphasis placed on online writing labs ... .
We have a residential campus, fairly small, and the writing center is centrally
located, so there's no logistical problem with students actually coming to the
writing center.

Some responses complained about lacking staff, money, computer equipment, or sufficient time to supervise online tutorials and indicated that tutors preferred face-to-face tutorials anyway. One center director talked
about giving up on an OWL: "I've tried, unsuccessfully, to get local faculty
interested in doing something like this [creating an OWL]. Their lack of interest has made me somewhat reticent to extend my time, effort and money
into creating an OWL." Others felt the quality of existing OWLs was the
best argument for not making their own.

Writing Center Practice

About one sixth of respondents felt that their OWL did not affect tutor
training or writing center practice, arguing that OWLs do not substitute for
face-to-face tutoring and that tutors resist online consultations. Others felt
OWLs bolstered existing practice by directing students to face-to-face tutoring, providing resource materials, forcing tutors to customize handouts,
increasing access, using tutors' time more efficiently, improving and increasing communication among writing center staff, and easing accreditation. One director found middle ground:

I don't think the online services change the face-to-face tutoring, but tutoring changes a little when you tutor online. For example, you have to work
harder to create a dialogue; since you can't see who you're tutoring, you don't
bring prejudices ... to the tutorial as much; it's a little more difficult to be
non-directive.

About one sixth of respondents felt OWLs dramatically affected writing
center practice by providing their audience with exciting e-mail encounters; focusing upon issues outside face-to-face tutoring; helping tutors collaborate more in pairs and triads; offering tutors unique MOO or MUD
environments for their multiple roles; increasing resources from other
schools; creating online archives of listserv comments; enhancing learning
beyond the classroom; providing new kinds of support for Writing-Across-the-Curriculum (WAC), Writing-Intensive Classes (WIC),
and distance-education courses; and changing thinking processes in many
ways.

Overall, OWLs affect tutor training in complex and sometimes contradictory ways. With computer technology constantly changing, pedagogy moves to take advantage of new opportunities for teaching and tutoring. Writing centers enact this constant struggle to adapt to new possibilities. Although some respondents alluded vaguely to the uniqueness of online tutoring, others clearly stated how their OWL integrates writing center theory and practice. This respondent discusses the collaboration and diversity of tutors' work with a very sophisticated MOO:

> It [our OWL] has greatly enhanced the conferencing capabilities … . Our TAs have to share a suite of two connecting offices …, so they frequently prefer to log onto the MOO and meet their students online … . Teachers (and tutors from other schools) may also record any tutoring session and e-mail themselves and the student a copy of the logged session. They may use the MOO to paste in text from a word file to go over specific parts of the paper … they are working on. They may archive the paper itself as an object in the MOO and edit it online just as they would in their word program. They may assign access privileges for reading the text to others, or they may encrypt the text so only they can read it, or only those they grant reading privileges to. There is an in-MOO e-mail system, so actually tutors and students may do all their synchronous and asynchronous work in the MOO without using e-mail. Collaborative/group tutoring is also possible in our moderated rooms where one group may sit at a virtual table and converse with only those at their table, at the same time as other groups are in that virtual room. Those who want the whole room to see what they say, like the teacher or tutor, for example, may "speak up" to the room at large. Again, all of this may be recorded.

OWLs such as this one that have effectively integrated computer technology in philosophically and pedagogically sound ways can serve as models for beginning OWLs.

Writing centers on campuses with effective WAC, WIC, and computer-assisted instruction (CAI) programs reported that their OWLs have fostered workshops that not only train tutors, but also help students and faculty:

> We have an OWL that is a Web site, but our interests lie more in the use of technology by students and faculty to support writing through extending classroom conversations, conducting research on the Internet, publishing Web pages. To that end, we have developed several classroom presentations on these topics that include how to use search engines, how to evaluate Web

sites, how to cite material from the Internet, how to put up a Web page, how to design Web-based assignment .... We also have a group of undergraduate writing consultants who work as Internet Writing Consultants who are available to work one-on-one or with small groups of students working on Web-based writing assignments. This past summer, we did a two-week faculty technology project for faculty in our college (Arts and Letters) and will do a half-day, campus-wide workshop for faculty this fall as part of the Provost's faculty development program. We have added a technology component to all our summer institutes as well—our national writing project institute, our high school students' summer institute, and our faculty writing project summer institute.

Although many OWLs are not (yet) receiving a lot of use, one center director seemed to speak for many: "Although the use [of our OWL] is not yet extremely great, the Online Writing Center is changing how we think of the Writing Center."

Evaluation of OWLs

Successful OWLs. Approximately seven eighths of respondents assessed their OWLs as successful. Some directors had no physical writing center, and others noted that the OWL publicized their face-to-face tutorials. The advent of OWLs redefined success for some centers to include praise from administrators, a prominent position on school Web pages, a high number of hits, or many online tutorials. User input often created a perception of success. One MOO director, for example, claimed 500 regular users and countless guests. Several administrators cited complaints from students when they tried to move the OWL or take it down for repairs, as well as positive responses from students, faculty, and outside evaluators. Success also meant students regularly using the OWL, especially to download resource materials or follow links to other labs and sites. Being overwhelmed by requests for workshops or online tutoring indicated success for some centers, whereas the quality of online tutorials impressed others.

Alterations in tutor training proved important, but reaching distance-education students and receiving praise from the community and region were equally important. Established OWLs noted that they served other OWLs by providing resources, although they wanted other sites to ask permission. One administrator described the overall and multifaceted success of her writing center's well-known OWL:

Our Web site got about 1.5 million hits last year. We've won numerous awards from Internet services, have been mentioned in numerous magazines and journals in the U.S. and around the world, ... have licensed some of the materials for other sites, gotten university grants and serve as good university publicity, have many requests for a screen capture in books, have published articles and made conference presentations on our OWL, and had one of our OWL Coordinators write a dissertation on OWLs that won an NWCA scholarship.

Unsuccessful OWLs. Respondents most commonly judged their OWLs as failures because of little or poor use. One OWL handled only two questions per semester! Some directors felt the OWL's location contributed to low use: "Truthfully, I don't think there is an audience. How could there be? The site is so deeply buried I can't imagine anyone finding it." Quite a few respondents felt the poor location or use of the OWL could be attributed to administrators who do not value the Internet.

Unsurprisingly, some OWLs had difficulty attracting students, either because of poor advertising or because special student populations presented additional challenges. As Curtis and Roskams show with their chapter (chap. 3) in this collection, we still have much to learn about online work with the ESL population. One school that responded to my survey enrolls 95% ESL students; the director explained that these students' cultural focus on face-to-face communication makes them uncomfortable on the OWL.

Another set of responses suggests that local issues affect OWL practice. Some respondents did not believe, for example, that their tutors had the technological skills necessary to be excellent both online and face to face; without increasing the budget and improving access, directors could not offer additional training. Others pondering the demise of their OWL pointed to unanticipated problems with hardware and software, believing that their students were better served by conversation offered face to face and via mail, phone, and fax.

Constructing an OWL

OWL Builders. About 60% of OWL builders were writing center directors and just over one third were writing center staff. Other students or computer-center staff assisted one sixth of respondents. English and writing teachers, WAC faculty, writing program administrators, outside consultants, and a Chair of Humanities also helped construct OWLs. Besides attending campus workshops and working on their own or with the help of colleagues, OWL builders also mentioned the usefulness of online tutorials. A fairly typical response came from a director who said:

> We offer workshops for students and faculty on using the Internet to support writing through extending classroom conversations, conducting research, and publishing Web pages. We also have Internet writing consultants who can meet with faculty and/or students to work on Web sites that are part of class writing projects. We train each other. We have no extra funding.

Nearly 90% of OWL builders reported that they lacked the necessary equipment, training, and support. Almost as many lacked the computer literacy or funds to create an OWL, and one half argued passionately that they lacked time more than anything else. However, one respondent claimed that even computer-challenged OWL builders should quit whining and put up an OWL:

> When I received initial funding, I subcontracted with a student to design the gif files for the Website. The whole thing cost $40. My word processor converts straight text to HTML. I had the Website and service up and running less than a week after the personnel funding was approved. University Luddites who use their technical ignorance as an excuse for not establishing such services should hang their heads in shame.

Some center directors are clearly angered by an OWL adding more responsibility to an already overwhelming schedule; one said her major obstacle was

> Lack of release time and/or support or understanding from my department. I taught three courses per semester and ran the writing center and computer lab while I was developing this OWL, and finally had to learn HTML and Web design from scratch on my own time to complete it.

Funding. A few OWLs were highly funded for staff and/or equipment, but most were not. A clear majority either had no permanent funds for the OWL or had to juggle discretionary or tutoring funds. Graduate-student support and some course-release time were possible in some places, although the English department budget had to be used elsewhere. These approaches were often combined with the use of work-study students, student tech-fee support, and/or grants from industry. One administrator of a large OWL indicated tremendous school support: "We've actually had a lot of funding for this—over $400,000. The university is making a long-term commitment as well, but we could use significantly more funds to meet our goals."

Connections and Servers.   All but several schools reported having high speed (usually 10base T, but a few 100base T) Ethernet connections instead of modems for their OWLs. Twice as many OWLs were hooked into a campus server instead of owning their own. Most respondents felt their servers were medium or fast with mediocre or excellent maintenance of the center computers.

Hardware.   About twice as many OWLs were built with IBM-compatible personal computers (PCs) as with Macintoshes. However, directors strongly petitioned administrators to include both platforms in their centers. Although some OWLs were judged successful without many decent computers, the most successful OWLs usually reside at universities featuring updated computer labs or CAI programs. The number and quality of computers varied enormously. One center limped along with a lonely IBM 386 and another with two tired Mac II Sis. Other centers boasted 55 Pentium PCs or 45 new Power Macs. The vast spectrum of varying brands and computer capabilities—from old text browsers to multimedia machines with huge memories and Random Access Memory (RAM)—reminds us how fast the technology changes.

Software.   Software installed on center computers varied even more—in both brand name and generation—than the computers, including word processors, Web browsers, Hypertext Mark-up Language (HTML) editors, tutoring software, spreadsheets, graphics programs, presentation programs, repair and disk doctoring programs, and (sometimes searchable) databases. Some OWL builders handcoded the HTML whereas others used packaged editors. Other key software included programs for scanning graphics (e.g., PhotoShop) and compressing images (e.g., clip2gif).

Revising an OWL

Access.   Many directors felt the need to allow efficient access from even low-end computers with text-based browsers. Some centers achieved this goal by avoiding split screens or frames or big graphics (unless compressed). Nearly one half of the responding OWL supervisors insisted that "less is more":

We avoid frames, multimedia, and lots of graphics for download times in part. We try to design for the broadest use of browsers—and to make a point about not needing glitz to provide good stuff.

However, others emphasized the importance of balancing aesthetically pleasing Web design and download time:

> I did try to consider the whole range of browser capabilities, but didn't avoid nice graphics to accommodate slow modems. I used "alt img" alternatives to images and am constructing a very simple split-screen e-mail page for those whose browsers don't support the Common Gateway Interfaces (CGI) "live chat" room on our interactive page.

About 98% of respondents had graphics like photos, tables, graphs, or logos on the Web pages of their OWL, believing that graphics humanized the OWL. One was willing to think in an interesting and utopian way: "I think look and feel are important. I think ideally a Website should have a team consisting of a graphic artist, a Java programmer, and a content provider/editor." Most compromised by keeping some graphics but minimizing download time by using compression software (e.g., clip2gif or graphic converter) to reduce the image size. The following list ranks graphics from the most common to the least common: tables, graphs, or logos; photos; animated gif(s); image maps; original artwork; unusual background colors/textures; graphics linked with usage or evaluation; and custom-designed headers. A few reported that campus Webmasters removed all graphics from their pages!

Multiple Audiences.   Audiences for OWLs include on-campus and distance-education students, faculty and staff, members of the community, and surfers from far afield. In revising for multiple audiences, directors planned to focus on the needs of the audience, include resources on nonacademic writing, offer alumni access for better publicity, and encourage conversation with faculty.

Resource Materials.   Some respondents wanted to customize handouts or generate material as different as FAQs and writing center philosophy. Although some yearned to expand common features like a grammar hotline, others leaned toward WAC-based handouts. One respondent argued passionately for putting samples of students' written work online, "both for the edification of the writers and the possible future benefits of other student writers and composition researchers." Administrators wanted their revised OWL to clarify writing center philosophy and policies, improve resources for documenting sources, create an online consultation schedule, share campus-specific materials, and advertise the writing center.

Interactive Features. Adding interactive features to OWLs such as the following ranked high: real time chat forum; synchronous learning for distance learners; online services; asynchronous learning; searchable database; video conferencing; VRML-based MOO; support for CAI and other courses; interactive tutorials (e.g., CGI script); e-mail as suggestion box or for contact; listservs; links to other sites; MOO book and journal archive; and a better search engine for the site. Only half of reporting OWLs had asynchronous teleconferencing classes on their campuses. Software used for such conferencing in classes or via the OWL included both browser-based (e.g., Netscape Chat) and independent systems (e.g., First Class).

TUTOR TRAINING

Many respondents use OWLs to provide general information about tutoring services and to initiate conversations about the theory and practice of tutoring. OWLs have sometimes preceded physical writing centers or have prompted the creation of a tutor-training class. Certainly, tutor-training materials can be dispersed more quickly with the advent of the OWL, and individualized tutor home pages demonstrate the new kinds of opportunity that demand changes in training.

CHECKLIST FOR CREATING AN OWL

In my work with this project, I've maintained an ideas list. The following is a checklist of sorts for anyone interested in building and maintaining OWLs:

- Decide who is in charge of creation, maintenance, and supervision.
- Explore funding sources and settle on budget.
- View other OWLs, using NWCA and other directories.
- Discuss electronic writing with others interested at your site or campus.
- Discover and negotiate specific audiences.
- Discover and negotiate purposes and features with all audiences.
- Storyboard all features.

- Choose computer platform.
- Decide whether to link to campus server or to use own server.
- Choose kind of server and access.
- Check speed of server and links to Internet.
- Choose HTML editor(s) and software for creation and maintenance.
- Test low- and/or high-end creations on several computers early on.
- Test all features and functions with a local audience first.
- Ask other OWL administrators to review site using national listservs.
- Post site address and request for listing to Colgate University's NWCA site.

OWLs AS DIVERSITY, CONTROVERSY AND IDENTITY

OWLs are part of the identity of writing centers. Some smaller schools have become national leaders online, whereas others have OWLs rather than physical writing centers. Many OWLs support current trends toward virtual education, and the rapid rise of distance education may be the same kind of revolution that created community colleges and adult education programs earlier in the century. Online writing and tutoring have clearly begun to test how strong our desire is to define education as convenient or efficient. OWL materials and services that can be accessed around the clock change the ways we live and use our time.

The Western Governors University and the University of Phoenix are just two schools that emphasize virtual learning. One administrator explained how enormously the OWL had changed education:

> Synchronous online individual and small group mentoring seems crucial here. We are a multi campus institution with a ninety percent commuter population and an increasingly visible population of students with disabilities. These technologies offer us possibilities for addressing the issues raised by these characteristics of our university. The university itself is investing over forty million dollars in the coming five years in state of the art technology—especially encouraging distance learning. If we're not on this bandwagon, it will run right over us (and lots of faculty and students as well).

Yet, many OWL administrators, teachers, and tutors question the price of more computer time and less face-to-face conversation. Are we an increasingly collaborative society via the World Wide Web or a nation of lonely electronic individuals? Has our long battle for privacy allowed us to enjoy the idiosyncrasies of particular selves online, or do our networked, virtual lives represent the loss of a rewarding face-to-face interaction? We have answers to these questions that apply to the work of writing centers, but no clear consensus.

As the trends of lower budgets, fewer trained teachers, and more students converge, OWLs offer at least temporary solutions to assisting students and faculty. The diverse kinds of OWLs and their range of purposes help chart the larger course of education in America, while allowing writing centers to redefine their emerging identities online. OWLs are constantly evolving. One of my favorite comedians, Stephen Wright, once mentioned the man who bought a puppy and immediately walked it 2,000 miles so he would never have to walk it again. I believe this story is speaking to all OWL administrators who believe they can build an OWL and leave it alone: Prepare to keep walking your OWL!

2

OWLs in Theory and Practice: A Director's Perspective

Lady Falls Brown
Texas Tech University

From: VAXB:uf7063   16 April 1986 9:49
To: @comp.dis
Subj: Do you need writing help?

Hi,

I am the "electronic tutor" for the Writing Center. If you have questions about your writing, you can ask me, and I will reply within 24 hours. What kinds of questions can you ask? Just about anything about writing: punctuation, paragraphs, organization, transitions, content, editing—the list could go on and on.

How do you ask questions? My username is uf7063. The instructions for using mail are included in your manual. I'm looking forward to "talking" to you. Write back!

—Kinkead, 1987, p. 340

Sound familiar? Sounds like many of us who read and respond to writers via our OWLS. Look at the date, however—16 April 1986. In addition, look at the source of the message—VAXB:uf7063, a VAX-based, e-mail address.

In "Computer Conversations: E-Mail and Writing Instruction," Kinkead (1987) explained:

> The electronic tutor was created a year after we began using E-mail in writing classes when we found through instructor/student conferences that some students were unwilling to go to the Writing Center for additional help because they were "afraid to go through the door" (pp. 339–340).

E.T., as the electronic tutor at Utah State was called (Kinkead, 1987, p. 340), may have been the first writing center consultant to respond electronically to student writers as Hawisher, LeBlanc, Moran, and Selfe (1996) in *Computers and the Teaching of Writing in American Higher Education, 1979–1994: A History* pointed out: "To our knowledge, this article on e-mail or computer-mediated communication is the first article on this subject to appear in a mainstream composition journal" (p. 146). In "The Electronic Writing Tutor," Kinkead (1988) acknowledges that "establishing a 'wired' writing center tutor may seem like a lot of work, but it taps an audience that might not ordinarily use the writing center because of time conflicts, distance problems, second language problems, or simply shyness" (p. 5). Kinkead concluded, "Although the electronic tutor cannot duplicate the comprehensiveness of the writing center tutorial or the value of face-to-face dialogue, the service offers an additional way for helping writers write" (p. 5).

Ten years later, writing center directors and consultants continue to discuss the work involved in establishing an online writing center, the reasons for establishing such a center, and the effectiveness of tutors working in electronic environments as opposed to working in face-to-face situations. According to the NWCA Web page (Pegg, 1998), last reviewed on May 12, 1998, some 237 directors have created online writing centers or OWLS, suggesting that they believe virtual writing centers can help writers improve their writing.

This chapter, then, provides a brief history of OWLs and shares information about creating and operating OWLS, information derived from my personal experience and from the experiences of other writing center folks as reflected in the print and electronic literature. Readers considering establishing an OWL can apply what we have learned to their own situations.

SOURCES OF INFORMATION

I reviewed archived wcenter discussions as well as print and Web articles containing key words such as *OWLS, online writing centers, computers in writing centers, computer-mediated instruction,* and *e-mail conferencing.*

ORIGIN OF THE TERM *OWL*

Although online writing centers originated as early as 1986, the term *OWL* did not enter our vocabulary until the early 1990s. Harris (1996), editor of *The Writing Lab Newsletter* and director of both the writing lab at Purdue University and the award-winning Purdue OWL, said that long before the Web or even Gopher existed, she and Manley coined the term when they established an e-mail version of their services: " ... the first guru who set up our e-mail service years ago pounced on OWL as an easy acronym for our e-mail address: owl@cc.purdue.edu." Harris provides this information in response to Camille Langston (personal communication, June 3, 1996), who suggested that "since we are no longer calling writing centers 'writing labs,' maybe we should no longer call online writing labs OWLS. We could change the name to 'COWS' (Centers of Online Writing)." Langston closed her post with "Moo, Camille Langston." Langston's response prompted Crump (1996) to agree that another term might be appropriate and to offer "WIOLE (writing intensive online learning environment)"; Gardner (1996) suggested "VWC [Virtual Writing Center]. " Harris began her post concerning the origin of OWL by pointing out:

> ... some of us aren't in that "no longer" group you mention. We still have a "lab" at Purdue, and it's got a great connotation that I wouldn't change for anything. Students here have "help labs" in all kinds of fields, and such labs are places to mess around, ask questions, and do hands-on stuff in very informal settings. We also have a bunch of "centers" on campus ... "Center for Instructional Services," "Psychological Services Center," the "Computing Center, " and other such places that most students can't/don't relate to easily and that have lots of bureaucratic red tape involved. Nope, not all of us have become "centers" ... or least we hope we haven't here. I'd say it matters a lot as to what words mean locally.

... Besides, any Midwestern land grant institution like this place is pretty touchy about being yet one more "MOO U," especially since that great novel MOO nailed us so well. ;)

So the term *OWL* came into existence, although the NWCA Web page indicates that not all directors use the term in naming their virtual writing spaces.

COMPUTERS IN THE COMPOSITION CLASSROOM AND IN THE WRITING CENTER

OWLs are an outgrowth of computer technology, composition theory and practice, and writing center theory and practice.[1] My relationship with computers, writing, and eventually OWLs began during the years Hawisher, LeBlanc, Moran, and Selfe (1996) designated as "1983–1985: Growth and Enthusiasm."[2] I started graduate school in 1982, when Jeanette Harris established the writing center at Texas Tech. As a graduate student, I drafted papers for my courses on yellow legal pads and typed final copies on an antiquated IBM electric (not Selectric) typewriter. After typing numerous revisions of a paper for publication, I bought a Kaypro because Jeanette used one and I thought I could learn from her.

My interaction with computers increased in 1988 when Fred Kemp, codeveloper of *Daedalus Integrated Writing Environment* (DIWE) software, accepted a composition position at Texas Tech. Kemp brought with him an enthusiasm for computers and writing, a respect for writing centers, and a generous spirit. When I was named interim director of the writing center in 1988–1989 and then director in 1989–1990, I became an ex-officio

---

[1]*Computers and the Teaching of Writing in American Higher Education: 1979–1994: A History* focuses on the impact of computers on composition theory and practice, but readers learn that writing center people, such as Muriel Harris, have been involved since the earliest stages because of their work in writing and computer labs (p. 29). In response to my query about whether writing center people attended the first 1982 Computers and Writing Conference held at the University of Minnesota, Lillian Bridwell-Bowles (personal communication, May 26, 1998) responded via e-mail: "Yes, I'm sure there were writing center people here. I don't think we kept the registration files, but my memory of the audience is that it was made up of about 1/3 computer people (some of whom were also in rhet/comp) and about 2/3 instructional or writing lab people. Best I can do. My colleague Donald Ross may remember more."

[2]Hawisher et. al. (1996) organized the information into five chapters—"1979–1982: The Profession's Early Experience With Modern Technology"; "1983–1985: Growth and Enthusiasm"; "1986–1988: Emerging Research, Theory, and Professionalism"; "1989–1991: Coming of Age—The Rise of Cross-Disciplinary Perspectives and a Consideration of Difference"; "1992–1994: Looking Forward." I included the titles of the chapters so that readers can place their own experiences with computers, composition, and writing centers into this continuum.

member of the composition committee, listening to Kemp discuss computer-based instruction and collaborative writing theory. That fall, when Tech became a beta test site for the Mac version of *Daedalus*, I volunteered to be one of the instructors. I also joined Megabyte University (MBU-L), a discussion list for people interested in computers and writing.[3] My interest in developing an online writing center grew as a result of tutoring in the writing center, observing students respond to one another's texts, and reading the discussions about computers and writing on MBU-L by such people as Fred Kemp, Cynthia Selfe, and Eric Crump. Inspired by what I was learning, I asked Kemp in 1990–1991 to set up an online writing center, which he did by linking our site to the computer classrooms in the English department.

In that early OWL, first-year composition students placed their papers in an electronic folder named *WCenter*. Performing online tutorials was difficult because the plodding speed made opening documents tedious, and the 9-inch monitor on the Mac Plus limited what we could see of a text. Because the writing center did not have an e-mail address, we could only offer our services to students physically present in the computer classrooms. We were an English department OWL at best. During that period, the writing center staff reflected on what we were doing and debated the ethics of responding to papers online, concerned about what kinds of comments to make, where to place the comments, how many comments to make, and whether online responses violated the principle of face-to-face interaction. In spite of the value we saw in online tutorials, we reluctantly ended the project because of the difficulties caused by inadequate technology (i.e., small screens and limited speed).

THE INTERNET AND THE OWL

In addition to establishing an online writing center, Fred Kemp also helped me develop a listserv for writing center people, creating wcenter in 1991.

---

[3]In an e-mail message, Fred Kemp (personal communication, May 20, 1998) wrote, "Lady, I started MBU when I got back from the CCCC meeting in Seattle in 1989, probably in early April. Cindy had delivered a socko presentation about 'online universities' and I was all fired up. I went over to Stephen Downing (whose cousin Jan and I had known in Commerce) and asked for a university account. He put me onto some character whose name I forgot who told me that 'e-mail is a trivial resource.' Oooo, blood boiled, for I had been using national e-mail for three years with Michael Spitzer's PARTI project out of New York Institute of Technology. I got the account (I was the first in the English department) and started learning about the Internet. I began MBU as a distribution list where I would get e-mail from somebody and distribute it to the group. Each time. By hand. In September of 1989 I brought down the Rice bitnet entry into Texas for four hours, and Downing asked me to use listserv (which nobody had told me about earlier), and I did, and the rest is history. Boring history, but history."

My interest in electronic tutoring continued because wcenter list members discussed computers in writing centers and electronic tutoring (Crump, 1992; Hobson, 1993; O'Donoghue, 1992). By 1993, designated "the Year of the Internet" by Hawisher et. al., (1996, p. 242), list members were talking about getting online. Harris (1993) wrote in a February 5th post to wcenter: "We are planning to get online on our campus to offer some electronic tutoring ... " Coogan (1994) started an online writing center at SUNY Albany in 1993. Although most OWLs sprang from physical writing centers, Ericsson (1994) at Dakota State University established an OWL independent of an on-site center. In addition to e-mail addresses to which writers could send drafts for asynchronous conferencing, the Internet made possible real time conferencing through MUDs and Multi-User Shared Hallucinations (MUSHes). In "Online Writing Labs (OWLs): A Taxonomy of Options and Issues" Harris and Pemberton (1995) presented a helpful model of interactive or reactive computer interactions occurring on a time continuum ranging from "timedisplaced" to "real time" (p.147).[4]

By summer 1994, announcements of OWLs began to appear on wcenter. Maid (1994) invited list members "to attend the grand opening of one of several Cyberspace Writing Centers [created by Maid and Jennifer Jordan-Henley] to be held at DaedalusMoo" in August 1994. On November 29, 1994, Kimball reports that the Undergraduate Writing Center at University of Texas, Austin is developing a MUD, and in March 1995, Menzer, also of UT-Austin, announced a MUSH. Faster, more powerful computers with larger screens and more sophisticated software programs encouraged writing center people to develop Websites advertising a variety of on-site and online services.

Inspired by what other writing centers were doing and by my belief that writers need readers, whether physically or virtually present, we established an e-mail address for our OWL in November 1995. The following spring, graduate students in Patricia Goubil-Gambrel's document-design course created a Website for us. Like all OWL Websites, ours was informational, including who (staff), what (on-site and online center), when (hours), where (location), and why (the mission statement). One link enabled users to access our handouts and those at the Purdue OWL; another link enabled users to access our online writing center address. Recently, we added an

---

[4]People new to the concept of types of possible interactions should find this article especially helpful. In addition to the model for types of OWL interactions, Harris and Pemberton (1995) also defined terms such as automated file retrieval (ARF), Gophers, World Wide Web, e-mail dropboxes and newsgroups, chat systems, and so forth.

interactive MOO in which tutors and clients meet by appointment to discuss writing projects. To date, the university writing center OWL has performed over 1,200 electronic tutorials.

ISSUES TO CONSIDER
WHEN ESTABLISHING AN OWL

Funding

Adding an OWL component to a writing center requires funds to purchase the necessary equipment if a center does not already have computers and Internet access. Writing Center directors should look for national, state, and local funding sources. The Office of Educational Technology (http://www.cd.gov/Technology/) sponsored by the U.S. Department of Education lists numerous grant opportunities. At Texas Tech, the Office of Research Services Website (http://www.ors.ttu.edu/) provides links to public and private funding agencies. Our writing center had Internet access, but the one Mac Plus was pitiful, so we received Higher Education Assistance Funds (HEAF) to purchase four Power Macs, one of which we designated as our OWL. We use Eudora Light to collect submissions, which the OWL director distributes to the consultants.

Technical Support

If directors are not well versed in computer technology, they need access to knowledgeable and sympathetic technical support people. As Nelson and Wambeam (1995) noted, campus computer-support groups sometimes do not understand that "relationships among students, teachers, and machines are interactive and collaborative" and require kinds of support different from what they provide for administrative computing (pp. 137–138). Strand (1994) suggested that directors should get a friend in the computer field: "I had relatively few problems setting up our mailing address and Gopher site because I went right to the man in charge and his team. it [sic] helps that the man in charge is married to a friend of mine." Although none of my friends married a computer expert, I have excellent technical support. In addition to Kemp, one of my advisers has been Joseph Unger, the English department's computer technology specialist at the time. Unger, who has a master's degree in English, has taught in the computer classroom, understands collaborative learning environments, and possesses encyclopedic knowledge of computers, software, and the Internet. Not only did Unger help me prepare the HEAF proposal for computers and software, but he also connected our computers to the Ethernet and installed all the software. Unger and I agreed that the writing center would pay him to set up the computers in our center, but he would not charge for later services because the university writing center has a symbiotic relationship with the Computer-Based Writing Instruction Research Project. Helping the writing center benefits the project.

Staffing

Without consultants an OWL will not fly, so the director must decide how to staff the OWL, a decision tied to funding. Many OWLs are staffed by on-site consultants, but that practice proved problematic. Our fledgling OWL became operational in early November 1995 when Jeff Williams, an on-site consultant and teacher, encouraged his students to use the newly created OWL. Initially, the staff and I took turns responding to papers when we had no appointments. However, we stopped online tutorials to work with on-site clients. Frequently, we could not return to the online tutorial for 1 hour or so, requiring us to begin again because we had lost our train of thought. Realizing that we needed uninterrupted time to read and respond online, we scheduled 30-minute appointments for online submissions as though the writers were physically present. However, we continued to privilege drop-ins. Toward the end of the semester, we frequently did not have time during the day to perform the OWL tutorials. Despite the difficulties, our experiment seemed worthwhile, especially when we received the following message from Wendell (1995):

> I just wanted to tell everybody at the writing center "thanks." Ya'll [sic] have been a big help. If I would've had access to a writing center in high school, my English grade would not have shot up. Thanks, I plan on using the writing center my next 3 years in college. Thanks again!!

In December 1995, Lynnea Chapman King volunteered to develop a real OWL. In keeping with King's increased duties and responsibilities, I named her assistant director in charge of the OWL. Deciding to create an online staff, I negotiated with the director of graduate studies to hire five additional graduate teaching assistants to serve 5 hours a week as online writing consultants. To gain the director's support, I pointed out that being an OWL consultant is an excellent *curricula vitae* line, that graduate students need the money, and that the position could reward excellent graduate students.

Now, as then, OWL consultants neither work in the on-site writing center nor attend the weekly colloquia for the on-site tutors. King created a distribution list for the group, and she and her staff conducted their weekly colloquia on a MOO. King also devised a rotation system so that the tutors responded to an equal number of papers. Taking advantage of the research opportunities afforded by this experience, several consultants presented papers at regional and national conferences. Joanna Castner, an OWL consultant, authors a chapter (chap. 10) in this volume.

Staffing an OWL is expensive but no more expensive than staffing an on-site center. For three semesters (Spring 1996, Fall 1996, and Spring 1997), the staff consisted of five consultants plus the assistant director. For the 1996–1997 academic year, the OWL cost approximately $13,600, a sum that included fringe benefits figured at approximately 15% of the staff's salary. Because submissions did not justify five tutors, in the 1997–1998 academic year, I reduced the number of tutors to three. Several days this spring, however, we received more submissions than the online staff could respond to within our 24-hour turnaround time. Although on-site tutors helped when they were available, some days we were completely booked in the center. Rather than hire an additional tutor at .125 FTE or ask tutors to work overtime for no pay, we established OWL by the Hour (OBTH). Those tutors willing to work overtime are sent two tutorials at a time (the equivalent of two 30-minute tutorials), and they are paid $14.70 an hour to read and respond to the texts. OBTH provides several benefits: the readers are trained consultants, they are paid for their extra work, and their hourly wage does not increase their fringe benefits.

Responding to Submissions

Both the on-site and the online tutors have experimented with ways to respond to submissions. For record-keeping purposes, we save a copy of the text we receive. The assistant director then forwards the paper to the tutor. Some tutors respond holistically, writing their comments at the end of the paper; others make comments between paragraphs. Occasionally, we insert remarks within a sentence. Most important, we remember that we are talking to a person. I encourage the consultants to limit each tutorial to approximately 30 minutes, although I frequently exceed that length.

Advertising

Just because a director establishes an OWL does not mean that students will use it (Coogan, 1994). Although writing center Websites may receive numerous hits (in March 1998, our Website received 3,052 total hits, whereas our OWL received 109 submissions), students must learn that an OWL is available and, more important, how to use it. To advertise our OWL, we include our e-mail address and our Website address on bookmarks and brochures that we place in the library and in the study-skills center. We also distribute flyers with instructions on how to submit texts to the OWL to students, and we advertise our on-site and online services once a week in *The University Daily*, the student newspaper.

Keeping Statistics

Once an OWL exists, a director must monitor its flight and evaluate it. Just as we keep detailed statistics concerning the number of clients, the number of tutorials, and the length of tutorials for the on-site writing center, King, the assistant director in charge of the online writing center, also keeps a spreadsheet in which she records the date of submission, the author's name, the tutor, the date the tutorial is returned to the writer, and the length of time spent on the tutorial. In addition, King tracks the OBTH tutorials. During the 1997–1998 academic year, the OWL staff performed 773 tutorials.

During the first few semesters, the spreadsheets indicated that almost all the students who submitted online had been required to do so by their instructors who were teaching in the computer classrooms. Recently, we see an increasing number of submissions from other students. This change may result from the students' growing familiarity with technology. Some students continue to use the OWL semester after semester.

LOOKING AHEAD: PROMOTING DISTANCE LEARNING AND OUTREACH THROUGH OWLS

Directors should consider the role an OWL may play in the mission of their institutions. Here at Texas Tech, President Donald Haragan is committed to technology, to distance education and learning, and to recruitment. Situated on the South Plains of West Texas, Lubbock, a city of 194,000, is encircled by numerous small communities. Although the majority of students who attend Texas Tech live in Lubbock, many commute from their homes in Shallowater, Brownfield, Idalou, Crosbyton, Ropes, and so forth. As

Kinkead suggested in 1988, not only can our OWL provide interactive learning situations for students, but it can also enable commuters to access our services.

OWLs can assist outreach efforts. For the past 3 years, I have been working with students and faculty in surrounding schools.[5] Having taught in the public schools, I know that English teachers do not have time to read multiple drafts of student writing because most teach five classes a day, each class containing 20 to 25 students. As a pilot project, the university writing center OWL has begun offering online tutorials to students in area schools. In 1996, we worked with an advanced placement class at Muleshoe High School, 70 miles northwest of Lubbock. Although wired internally, the school did not have Internet access, so the administration applied for a Telecommunications Infrastructure Fund (TIF) grant to acquire a T1 line. In the meantime, the assistant superintendent copied essays from the students' disks and pasted them into e-mail messages addressed to us. We returned tutorials to him, which he then copied onto the students' disks. This attempt taught us that effective OWLs should respond within 24 hours so that writers can use the suggestions. We also learned that the process of sending submissions and receiving comments must be easy.

The first area school to write a successful TIF proposal, which included our letter promising online tutorials, was Southland Public Schools, a tiny school 30 miles southeast of Lubbock. Kemp, Unger, King, and I helped them establish a computer classroom and a high school writing center. We also supported Lockney Independent School District (ISD), located 70 miles northeast of Lubbock. Twenty-three students in the AP English class sent papers to our OWL. Lori Satterwhite, (personal communication, May 12, 1998), the instructor, wrote:

Lynnea,

Thank you so much for responding to my students' papers. I think they really were impressed with the Writing Lab staff. As we only have 1 ½ weeks of school left including finals, I doubt that we will submit any more papers this school year. However, we look forward to using your service next year. I will not be here next year; however, I will see to it that Charles Keaton, our technology director, has the names of the upcoming juniors and seniors so that he can go ahead and begin working on their e-mail addresses.

---

[5]Monroe, Rickly, Condon, and Butler describe aspects of a similar project between the University of Michigan English Composition Board and a Detroit inner school with their chapter (chap. 19) in this collection.

Again, thanks for your service. I think it will be very helpful.

Lori Satterwhite
Lockney High School

Based on students' and teachers' responses, the OWL benefits students who submit papers. Perhaps if these students have positive experiences working with the Texas Tech OWL, they will attend our university. If the teachers have positive experiences, perhaps they will encourage their students to consider Texas Tech as well. The program is growing; in Fall 1998, we will work with five area schools: Southland ISD, Lockney ISD, Frenship ISD, Floydada ISD, and New Deal ISD.

In addition to working with area students, we have received queries and papers from writers in other states and in other countries. One of our previous online consultants taught school in her native country, Argentina, last fall, and we read and responded to her students' papers.

CONCLUSION

Is the OWL worth the effort? If the purpose of a writing center, physical or virtual, is to help writers become better writers, then the answer is yes because we can assist writers who might not otherwise have access to our services. Is an OWL worth the expense? Can we justify the technology required and the salaries of the consultants? In other words, can we justify the expense of operating an OWL in terms of the number of submissions? To date, we have not reached 100% capacity each week, although some weeks we have exceeded 100%. The OWL is neither more nor less cost effective than the on-site writing center; we are not booked 100% of the time there either. Is online tutoring as effective as on-site tutoring? The two types of tutoring are similar yet different. We work one to one with writers, just not face to face. Sometimes, I wish the writers and I were in the same physical space so I could show them what I mean and see their responses. Instead, we must rely on written language rather than body language to understand and convey meaning. As director of the University Writing Center, I am committed to the OWL because I believe that it has an important role to play within the university community as well as in interactive distance learning and in the university's outreach efforts.

3

Language Learning in Networked Writing Labs: A View From Asia

Andy Curtis
Hong Kong Polytechnic University
Tim Roskams
City University of Hong Kong

The move to computers in writing centers seems inevitable. Crump (1994) believed that in the future students will do most of their writing online. Healy (1995), Jordan-Henley and Maid (1995a), and Kinkead (1988), among others, have pointed out the advantages of creating virtual spaces for writing centers. Nelson and Wambeam (1995) encouraged writing centers to lead in developing and using computers for writing; they warned that writing centers avoiding technology may face resource reductions, marginalization, and the abrogation of decision-making power to nonexperts.

This chapter addresses what we see as a significant gap in scholarship about electronic writing center work. At the Chinese University in Hong Kong, we work with Asian students seeing networked computer technology affect writing for the first time. Our work exists primarily in a hybrid environment, the combination of a writing center and a networked writing lab, and in that space, we have carefully studied our students' interactions with computers.

Although most computers and writing research has a first-language orientation, Sullivan and Pratt (1996) pointed out that "networked computers may have more advantages for the ESL writer than for the native speaker writer," for many reasons, including that networked classrooms offer "the less proficient speaker more time to think about what to 'say,' thus reducing anxiety and the probability of error" (p. 492). Kivela (1996), in one of the few papers on networked writing in Asia, found a decrease in Hong Kong university learners' anxiety through using networked computers over time.

Much research focuses on student behaviors, often in terms of student–student and student–teacher interaction and observable learning outcomes. Recent studies have used the written record of students' exchanges, such as Pratt and Sullivan's (1994) comparison of conversational turn taking in electronic and oral discussions and Chun's (1994) analysis of students' statements and questions to each other and to the teacher during computer conferences. Again, such data is clearly useful and, not coincidentally, relatively straightforward to collect. However, we also need data on students' affective reactions and perceptions of these environments, particularly as these change over time. Such information could provide important insights into the success, or lack thereof, of networked computers in the classroom and in the writing center.

Given this scarcity of research on computer-based writing in Asia, we wanted to study the benefit and limitations of networked writing laboratories from the students' perspectives. Writing center administrators who have to make decisions about installing and using networked computer technology should find this information useful. This chapter explores the following questions:

- How students rate their feelings before and after using networked computers in a writing course? What reasons would they give for any changes that occurred?
- How useful students find networked writing labs in developing their English academic writing skills?
- How might this data be of use to tutors, students, and writing centers when designing, teaching, and evaluating such courses?

SUBJECTS AND SETTING

At the Chinese University of Hong Kong (CUHK), our computer writing classes and writing center are complementary, but independently planned, managed, and financed. The writing laboratory consists of 23 networked computers—22 for students and 1 teacher console. Students at the CUHK can develop their writing skills by enrolling in courses offered by the English Language Teaching (ELT) Unit, by using self-access writing programs, and by scheduling appointments at the writing center. Both the self-access materials and the writing center are provided by the university's Independent Learning Center (ILC), which works very closely with the ELT unit; unit staff volunteer with ILC activities such as the writing center, and our Introduction to Academic Writing (IAW) courses are held in the ILC's networked writing lab.

The students in this study were in four classes of approximately 20 students per class (total = 74) attending a 13-week IAW course at the CUHK. The IAW course aims to develop informative and persuasive writing skills in English based on library research; the students analyze audiences, write summaries and paraphrases, and conduct library research. The major course tasks consist of revising successive drafts of essays, based on peer and teacher feedback. Students submit a piece of writing every week, usually a summary of an article or a draft of an academic essay based on relevant reference material. They use the network to provide feedback on other students' drafts and to exchange ideas for assignments (e.g., working titles and tentative thesis statements) with the teacher and classmates.

During the writing lab classes, teachers joined various group conferences, often responding online to students' comments, but also moved around the class, talking to the students about their work. This arrangement provided face-to-face interaction as well as feedback via the network. Students submitted portfolios (hard copy and electronic) of all their work (including several transcripts of online class discussions) with marks awarded for final drafts, essay improvements, and responses to other students' work.

EXPLORING METHODOLOGICAL OPTIONS

In order to gauge student perceptions of the integrated writing environment, we examined students' affective reactions to networked computers and their reasoned evaluation of the system's effect on their academic writing. Students were surveyed in the penultimate week of the term using the following questionnaire.

The following questions are designed to help us, your teachers, to learn more about your experience and impressions of using computers in this *Introduction to Academic Writing* course. Please answer the following questions, accurately and honestly. As you can see, your identity will be kept completely anonymous. Thank you.

Introduction to Academic Writing: ELT 2402 A B C D (tick one)

1. So far, 10 double sessions have been held on this course in the computer writing lab in the ILC. How many of the 10 sessions have you attended?
   Number _____

2. Had you ever used computers *before* taking this course?
   Yes No   (tick one)
   If your response is "No," go to item 4.

3. If you had used computers before this course:

   a. *Where* had you used computers before? (tick as applicable)

   Home   College
   School   Work
   Other_____

   b. During *a typical week*, how frequently did you use computers? (tick one)

   less than once
   one to two times
   three to four times
   five to seven times

   c. For what purposes did you usually use computers? (tick as applicable)

   Playing Games
   Word Processing
   Internet/E-mail/WWW
   Other_____

4. Approximately how long have you been using computers?

_____

5a. When you *first started* this Introduction to Academic Writing course, what were your <u>initial</u> feelings of using networked computers in the writing laboratory ?

Circle the number which most accurately reflects your <u>initial</u> impressions.

1 = no feeling   6 = strong feeling

Curious	1 2 3 4 5 6
Confused	1 2 3 4 5 6
Disappointed	1 2 3 4 5 6
Enthusiastic	1 2 3 4 5 6
Excited	1 2 3 4 5 6
Surprised	1 2 3 4 5 6
Worried	1 2 3 4 5 6
Hopeful	1 2 3 4 5 6
Unhappy	1 2 3 4 5 6

5b. Please give reasons for your <u>initial</u> impressions of using networked computers in the writing laboratory on this course?

_____

_____

_____

_____

6a. This course is now in its 10th week. What are your <u>present</u> impressions of using networked computers in the writing laboratory on this course?

Circle the number which most accurately reflects your <u>present</u> impressions.

1 = no feeling   6 = strong feeling

Curious	1 2 3 4 5 6
Confused	1 2 3 4 5 6
Disappointed	1 2 3 4 5 6

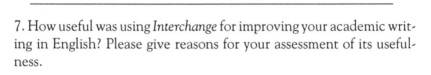

Enthusiastic   1 2 3 4 5 6
Excited   1 2 3 4 5 6
Surprised   1 2 3 4 5 6
Worried   1 2 3 4 5 6
Hopeful   1 2 3 4 5 6
Unhappy   1 2 3 4 5 6

6b. For any feelings which have *changed since the beginning* of the course, please explain *why* you think they have changed.

_____
_____
_____
_____

7. How useful was using *Interchange* for improving your academic writing in English? Please give reasons for your assessment of its usefulness.

Usefulness   1 2 3 4 5 6

Reason

_____
_____
_____
_____

Thank you for completing this questionnaire.

Regarding their affective reactions to the networked writing environment, students rated the strength of seven feelings about using the networked computers in the writing laboratory on a 6-point Likert scale, ranging from a 1 (*no feeling*) to a 6 (*strong feeling*), at the start of the term and after 12 weeks. The seven feelings were *confusion, disappointment, worry, unhappiness, enthusiasm, hope,* and *excitement*. We also requested reasons for their initial reactions and for any changes in feelings. Regarding the perception of the network for improving their academic writing in English, students rated the usefulness of *Interchange* on a similar 6-point Likert scale and provided reasons for their ratings.

Because participation was voluntary, we received a total of 64 responses from the 74 students (86% return rate). We calculated simple descriptive statistics and bivariate correlations for the numerical values from the Likert scores and analyzed student comments.

Students' Affective Reactions to the Online Writing Laboratory

Students' initial impressions of the writing laboratory varied. Some were curious, excited, and enthusiastic, but many were worried; still others experienced mixed emotions. The Likert responses showed that students new to computers were significantly more likely to be confused ($r = 0.39, p < .005$) and worried ($r = 0.36, p < .005$) at the start of the term, but not more likely than others to feel confused or worried at the end of term ($p = .05$).

Generally, students' affective reactions became less intense over the course as they grew more accustomed to using the networked computers (see Table 3.1). A reduction in the strength of positive emotions was balanced by a reduction in the strength of negative emotions. Reductions in excitement were larger than reductions in other positive emotions. There were also larger reductions in the negative emotions of worry and confusion than in disappointment and unhappiness.

A *t-test* analysis showed that there were no significant differences ($p = 0.05$) on the change of any emotion between the two classes taught by each teacher ($n1 = 33, n2 = 31$). Thus, a teacher effect creating a difference between the classes is unlikely.

Changes in emotional state seemed to measure what was happening more clearly than did affective student comments, and the Likert scores provided a numerical measure to assist in the interpretation of the

Table 3.1
Average Likert Scores for Seven Emotions at Start/End of Course

Emotion	Type	Mean Before	Mean After	Mean Change
1 Enthusiasm	Positive	3.63	3.28	-0.35
2 Excitement	Positive	3.56	2.70	-0.86
3 Hope	Positive	3.56	3.08	-0.48
4 Disappointment	Negative	1.91	1.86*	-0.05
5 Worry	Negative	2.84	1.69*	-1.15
6 Confusion	Negative	2.83	1.75*	-1.08
7 Unhappiness	Negative	1.70*	1.56*	-0.14

comments by indicating both *direction of change* and *magnitude of change* of the seven emotions. We considered both reductions in negative emotions (*confusion, disappointment, worry,* and *unhappiness*) and increases in positive emotions (*enthusiasm, hope,* and *excitement*) as positive change. Numerical differences in the Likert scales of four negative emotions (*disappointment, worry, confusion, unhappiness*) and three positive emotions (*enthusiasm, excitement, hope*) were added to produce a total affect change (TAC) to the use of the computers in the writing laboratory between the start and end of the course. These TAC scores classified the students into three groups: *those who had an overall neutral, overall negative,* or *overall positive affect change.*

The 18 students with a negative TAC generally made more specific comments. For example, comments included initial feelings of excitement dampened by finding the networked lab "not interesting at all." Others complained about the quality of peer feedback or unprepared classmates: "I am quite disappointed because computer usage is not as convenient and efficient as I initially think;" "The repeated processes are quite boring to me;" " ... my classmates have not been making full use of the computers for interchange, due to the lack of preparation, slow typing speed, etc."

Of those 25 students who had a positive TAC, many were positive mostly due to decreases in confusion, disappointment, unhappiness, and/or anxiety. Some students, however, believed interacting in writing to be valuable: "Interchange ... forces us to think in English, type in English. If only verbal discussion, we will all speak Cantonese;" "Because after the lessons, I recognized learning English could be funny and not boring."

Overall, the TAC classification showed 25 students (39%) were more positive and 18 (28%) more negative about the online writing laboratory at the end of the course than at the start. However, in reflecting on the causes of their affective reactions, no student commented explicitly on the use of the technology to improve their writing. Although we as teachers were concerned about putting the technology to best pedagogical use, students' affective reactions seemed to be more influenced by concerns such as worries about typing speed, their interest level in interacting with others in the class, and the ability of the network as a medium to exchange ideas, comments, and suggestions.

Students' Perceptions
of the Usefulness of Online Writing

Finally, we asked students if the networked writing system had improved their academic writing in English. Again, the students used a 6-point Likert scale to indicate usefulness. This question asked the students to link the computer technology and their writing improvement. Approximately 85% of the students felt that the *Interchange* sessions were either moderately useful or very useful: Very Useful (5 or 6; 21.9%), Moderately Useful (3 or 4; 62.5%), Of Little or No Use (1 or 2; 15.6%). These data, although encouraging, are insufficient. We need to know why the students rated it as they did.

The majority of students, 57 out of the 64 (89%), answered this question with responses that can be grouped under five headings: *Collaborative Learning (CL)*, *Time (T)*, *Thinking Skills (TS)*, *Interesting or Boring (I/B)*, *General Comments about Writing (W)*. Table 3.2 demonstrates this organization.

Most responses could be easily classified. Some comments, however, were more difficult: "Actually very few response from others. Still quite useful as I can read others' writing and learn from that." This comment was treated as two statements, as a negative comment related to CL and as a positive CL comment. Some comments could fall into two groups; for example, "My partners can give me comments immediately" refers to CL as well as T. When this happened, we categorized by the statement's emphasis, in this case on the feedback's immediacy. Of the 78 statements making up the answers given by the 57 students who responded to this question, 67 (86%) were classifiable. An example of an unclassified statement is "This function is the most useful one among the network," as no reason for usefulness is given. The percentages of student responses can be seen in Table 3.3.

Positive comments about the benefits of collaborative learning and writing in networked labs dominated the responses. This information, along

Table 3.2
Examples of Students' Answers and Their Classification

Type	Positive	Negative
CL	Other classmates can give me suggestions	Actually very few responses from others
T	We can discuss with different members at the same time	Sometimes there is not enough time
TS	Can force us to think in English	(none)
I/B	Using Interchange can also make the lessons more interesting	Students are not very interested in it
W	We write more and practice more	(none)

Table 3.3

Students' Answers Grouped by Type of Reason Given for Usefulness

Type of Comment	Positive % (n = 67)	Negative % (n = 67)
CL	37.3	7.25
T	10.4	17.9
TS	6.0	0
I/B	4.5	7.5
W	9.0	0

with the few negative CL comments, demonstrates that the students' views of such environments do match those of the teachers. Time garnered nearly 30% of the responses when positive and negative references are combined. The negative comments express that too much time was spent on certain activities or that too little time was available. Although similar, these points differ in that the former relates to the nature of the task, whereas the latter concerns how lab time is managed. The sheer number of negative time comments has important implications for tutors. More time should be allowed for reading and responding to other students' drafts and comments, given slow typing speeds and heavy traffic on the Internet.

IMPLICATIONS

This study should contribute to an ever-growing dialogue about the impact of electronic media on language learning. Our students' reactions highlight that using networked computers raises a number of issues. Based on our findings, the issue of how tutors and students can improve learning in such environments falls into three categories: expectations, knowledge, and experience/skills.

In light of the impact of students' initial and changing expectations, tutors should help to minimize any mismatching between tutors' and students' expectations. With written information flowing simultaneously from various sources, perceptions of roles and responsibilities need to be clarified in the networked writing lab environment. In Asian writing contexts, for example, some students feel that the majority of the information should be coming from the teacher, perhaps using more traditional teacher talk (correction-oriented approaches), or they may feel that the feedback given by the teacher is better than that given by other students (e.g., Arndt, 1992; Garratt, 1995) or elicited from themselves. In this case, such networked sessions, with less teacher talk, may be seen by the students as initially confusing or chaotic.

Tutors can minimize disappointment, and subsequent demotivation, by, for example, making explicit to students the benefits and limitations of such writing environments. The technology can facilitate particular writing processes, such as brainstorming and exchanging feedback, while providing practice for typing and using the language. However, the students should be prepared for possible information overload and time shortages that may accompany synchronous interaction. If students know that initially the process may be slow until everyone learns the system, but that everything subsequently speeds up, they can adjust their time-related expectations. Although nearly 90% used computers for an average of 3 years, many became anxious about using computers in a teaching and learning mode. Therefore, some time and resources may need to be spent training students.

Similarly, explicit instruction should be given in how to give and receive peer feedback (Brock, 1994; Cheung & Warren, 1996; Garratt, 1995; Mangelsdorf & Schlumberger, 1992). Exchanging feedback in a networked writing environment may require tailored instruction. For example, students need to know that the short and chatty e-mail exchanges they are used to sending differ from the helpful and constructive feedback they need to provide. Also, they must realize the importance of giving tactful criticism, taking into account the absence of the usual nonverbal cues.

We believe, as does Blythe (1997), that networked computer technology will have a significant impact on the writing center, necessitating a reevaluation of the long-term consequences of computer technology on writing center work. In particular, students' perceptions can show us ways to make effective use of networked computer technology. Writing centers should not expect computer technology to provide sudden successes, to serve more students on the same resources, or to decrease client contact time. A quick or easy move from traditional to high-tech writing centers probably will not occur; should the move occur at all, it may happen without the blessing of all tutors and students. However, if writing centers can allocate time and resources, train staff and students, commit technical support, and regularly renegotiate roles and responsibilities, networked writing centers may fly.

4

The Culture of Technology in the Writing Center: Reinvigorating the Theory–Practice Debate

Randall L. Beebe
Eastern Illinois University
Mary J. Bonevelle
Baker College

If recent developments in theoretical physics, popularized for nonspecialists under the rather vague term of *chaos theory*, have taught us anything, they have shown us that the more local, or particular, our observations become, the more varied and complex objects appear to be, whereas more global observations, although more hazy and indistinct, reveal form and order. We begin with this local–global dichotomy in order to make an analogy, albeit somewhat crude, to the recent concern in writing center literature about the apparent inconsistencies between writing center theory and practice. The local–global model tries to account for the disparities between two otherwise valid perspectives: what seems ordered and predictable on closer inspection appears in disarray—unpredictable, unmeasurable, or chaotic. Such a model relates to the discrepancies between writing center theory and practice: However ordered and complete our theories are, the more closely we look at our practice, the more we find that theory cannot account for—that is, cannot order and make sense of—the particularities of what we do locally.

Such a model might also be useful as we consider the impact of technology on writing center theory and practice. Although technology, generally conceived, is unified and ordered, the local application of technology is multifaceted, limitless, and idiosyncratic. Introducing technology into the writing center environment complicates the theory–practice divide even more. To better understand the complexity of technology and its local and global integration into writing centers, this chapter explores three fundamental questions:

1. How does the integration of technology widen or bridge the divide between practice and theory in writing centers?
2. In what ways can examining recent technologies help writing center professionals better understand and analyze the theory–practice gap? (Is technology merely a tool, or does it represent a new kind of culture that demands a new practice?)
3. Do theorists know enough about the future of technology in composition (and learning studies) to understand how that technology might ultimately correlate with writing center practices and theories?

Implicit in these questions is the assumption that writing centers are places where a delicate balance exists between perceptions and strategies. Integrating technology into writing centers necessarily affects this balance. Although this chapter offers some ways to rethink the inconsistencies between theory and practice—as well as some ways to think through the integration of networked and Web-based technologies into writing centers—our thesis is a rather simple one: Technology needs to be understood as a complex of issues and relations, which can both augment and offset current educational cultures and practices.

Technology, in other words, assumes agency (a practice); an agent applying technology implies a goal (a theory). Integrating technology effectively into writing centers demands a thorough and honest rethinking of where and how the gap between theory and practice most sharply affects any given writing center. Although difficult, such rethinking can push writing centers both to determine what they most want to retain as they integrate technology and to clarify—perhaps enhance—their role in educational institutions. Therefore, the remainder of this chapter, explores the controversy between theory and practice in the writing center while considering the impact of technology on theory and practice.

THE STATE OF THE ART:
NEGOTIATING THEORY AND PRACTICE

In her introduction to *Intersections: Theory/Practice in the Writing Center*, Mullin (1994) suggested that writing center theories have not fully accounted for students and thus need to be reexamined: "Reassessment will enable us to articulate our theories and to review practices that may not be engaging our changing student populations" (p. vii). She admitted that "those in writing centers also represent academic culture which excludes individual voices and privileges its own language" (p. xiii). Many of these exclusions and privileges can be eliminated if writing center theorists acknowledge the need for continual reassessment—leading to changes occurring at a discursive level rather than simply bringing more computers into writing centers.

One of the most direct but least recognized courses of action for reconsidering writing center work is thoroughly examining how student expectations influence theory and practice. Writing center theorists are not out of touch with practice; indeed, the most prominent scholars in writing center theory have been involved for many years with the day-to-day operations of writing centers at their institutions; because of their administrative status, however, most are concerned with training tutors, gaining institutional support, and trying to keep writing center theories consistent with current composition theories. Where and how technology fits into this mix is still very much in question. What seems clear is that although many may perceive technology as a way to bridge the gap between theory and practice, technology often complicates matters by bringing its own matrix of theory–practice dichotomies. Technology is theory writ large: it is always possible and always potential but always needs human agency to make it work locally and toward a specific, and usually context-dependent, situation.

The very word *theory* is so formidable to some that they feel it is too established to change. Current writing center practice is based on theory derived from composition theory. Conflicts between tutors' and students' perceived roles in tutorials have indicated that theory needs to be revised based on practice. As Hobson (1994) convincingly argued, "we must reshape theory to fit our particular needs in the particular historically located situations in which writing center practitioners find themselves" (p. 8). Languishing in the actual gap between theory and practice are the tutees, caught between their own expectations and tutors who are motivated by theory. Tutorials seldom mirror the ideal expressed in a majority of the predominant theory.

Bruffee (cited in Gillam, 1994) stated, "What peer tutor and tutee do together is not write or edit, or least of all proofread" (p. 43). He was right. What peer tutor and tutee do together is struggle to reach common ground concerning the direction each expects the tutorial to take.

The current theory and basis for tutor training only compound the expectation conflict. Just as the literature and research have tended to disregard student expectations, so have tutor-training techniques. As tutors realize that their training provided insufficient strategies for countering conflict with students, they developed a dialogue of their own, dialogue that occurs, primarily, in the "Tutor's Column" of *The Writing Lab Newsletter*. Whereas tutors address problems and propose solutions to expectation conflict, administrators and theorists continue on their own separate path, one that bypasses central issues of tutorial tension. Writing center theory, based on composition theory, has been established. Now, theorists should use insight from actual practice, especially tutors' insights, to refine this theory.

Yet, current theory does not accommodate the flexibility needed in practice, especially the flexibility that allows tutors to work effectively with students whose expectations conflict with theory. The theory behind writing centers assumes that practice is static rather than dynamic. DeCiccio, Rossi, and Cain (1995) pointed out that theories "have a way of becoming stripped of complexity, rigidified, and rendered monolithic as they become popularized" (p. 26). When students expect a different approach to tutoring than that presented by tutors, either theory breaks down completely as tutors reluctantly, and almost guiltily, defy tutoring doctrine, or a high degree of tension occurs between tutors and students. Writing center theory must endorse flexibility in tutor training. If theories appear less rigid, tutors can function better in the dynamic environment of the writing center and diffuse expectation conflict to a certain extent.

The other main problem in tutor training, and an overall problem in writing centers, is that tutors are instructed in methods that are unfamiliar both to them and to the students they tutor. Collaborative learning, which most writing centers heartily embrace, dictates many ideals that can enhance and improve the learning process. Unfortunately, until academe as a whole adopts collaborative learning, the concept remains an ideal. In principle, the writing center can easily employ collaborative learning techniques. However, as Lunsford (1995) so courageously observed, it is difficult to create a collaborative environment in writing centers because "the students', tutors', and teachers' prior experiences may work against it" (p. 112). Undoubtedly, current experiences also work against collaborative learning.

Classrooms at all levels still maintain hierarchical structures in which teachers impart wisdom to students with little self-guidance from students. Collaborative learning can create effective tutorials. However, that most students lack even the most basic familiarity with the concept of collaborative learning creates confusion more than it leads to common ground.

College students rely heavily on instructors dictating the subject matter. Because didactic, hierarchical, noninteractive classrooms are familiar to students, they are comfortable in such environments and expect them. Students expected to control the progress of the writing center tutorial often experience an uncomfortable, unfamiliar role. Trimbur stated that writing center professionals "must teach tutors to 'unlearn' the traditional hierarchical academic model in order to resocialize tutors as collaborative learners within student culture" (cited in Bushman, 1991, p. 32). Current tutor-training methods attempt to do this, but what about resocializing tutees? Again, tutor-training methods create expectation conflict by presenting students with unfamiliar environments. Tutors should help students understand that writing centers do not operate under the dominant academic model.

Writing center literature has noted that peer tutoring is a contradiction in terms, revealing another conflict between theory and practice. How can tutors act as peers and collaborators when they know more about writing than tutees (Cogie, 1995, p. 166)? When writing tutors refuse to claim authoritative positions, students become confused. Students come to the writing center seeking experts in writing rather than struggling classmates. To avoid conflict, writing centers should reexamine the notion that tutors are just readers, a notion that undermines writing centers' missions by causing students to question tutors' qualifications. Acknowledging and addressing student expectations can help writing centers clarify their image and avoid misconceptions. This process also results in something much more important—the long sought-after, and so far elusive, connection between theory and practice, or at least the basis for a connection.

TECHNOLOGY'S ROLE IN ADDRESSING THE THEORY–PRACTICE GAP

How can technology help us rectify the inconsistencies between writing center theory and practice—or, at least, how can it help us work within the inevitable constraints of theory and practice? Clearly, technology manifests itself most prominently in writing centers in the form of an OWL, a potentially useful feature of the contemporary writing center. Within the writing center and within the local community, OWLs serve practical and performative ends. Globally, OWLs can reach place-bound clients and, along with other OWLs, form an infrastructure to support students and teachers. Yet OWLs are not without limits; many factors can make OWLs problematic or simply not useful. This section discusses how to assess the feasibility of OWLs, how their implementation addresses certain problems concerning writing center theory and practice, and how technology may hinder more than help writing center goals.

While designing, implementing, and maintaining an OWL consume tremendous time and resources, especially in the earliest stages, the process itself provides a useful opportunity for writing center administrators and tutors to discuss the purpose and layout of the OWL—in other words, a chance to enact the theory–practice dichotomy. To implement an OWL, writing center administrators and tutors must theorize the center's presence, space, and identity on the Web and then find a way to make that identity real. The most pressing and difficult question is that of purpose. Should the OWL reflect as closely as possible the physical writing center in scope and purpose? In asking the question, a writing center staff must virtually try to make theory and practice coexist. Where the two break down is as important to understand as where they work together.

In addition, writing center staff members are probably at various stages of computer literacy. In order to foster a collaborative environment, the center's administrator must help the computer phobic overcome their fears while reeling in the cyberjunkies. Requiring all to participate in moving the writing center online encourages theoretical praxis and practical theory. The OWL is more than a tool for making handouts and other materials readily available; the writing center's virtual form becomes a literal focal point for discussion and debate.

Maintaining the Website is yet another example of where theory and practice necessarily collide in that maintenance requires both mechanics and creativity. Maintenance is similar to the thankless task of making sure that enough handouts are in stock and that tutor logs and schedules are in order. Once one knows where everything is and how to discard the old and make the new, the task itself is unproblematic, requiring no advanced skill. Website maintenance, however, invariably leads to rethinking design and content. In the very best way, such updates always involve authorship, creativity, and performance, matters too important to exclude any staff. In this respect, the practice and theory of OWLs exist both virtually and physically: OWLs do not become the responsibility of only the "techies" on staff, nor does the writing center itself fall into stasis, divided between those who theorize and those who practice.

Assuming that the writing center has appropriate computer hardware and Internet access, creating a Website for advertising the writing center and its services is relatively easy. Web publishing is becoming easier to do as word-processing applications, Web browsers, and HTML editors merge into a single, unified tool. However, despite the relative ease of Web publishing, we need to question the purpose of doing so and consider a diverse range of answers. For example, if the writing center's goal is to advertise itself and offer materials that a user can download, then that goal can be accomplished quickly with little maintenance. However, that kind of goal—however useful it might be for a local community—is limited, perhaps even retrograde.

Time and training are major problems associated with OWLs, hardly surprising given that lack of time for developing computer literacy and for continual retraining echoes throughout the educational technology literature. More and more, tutors need advanced computer literacies; they need to be quite skilled in manipulating network technologies, designing Web pages, and answering computer-application questions. Because most tutors are overworked with face-to-face tutorials, adding another dimension to their job description hardly seems fair; many writing centers are already understaffed without the resources to provide extensive training. Computer technology has been sold as a time saver, and in regard to repetitive tasks, this claim rings true. Yet, anyone who has taught in a computerized classroom, created Web pages, or participated in electronic conferencing knows that time is just about the last thing saved. A commitment to technology in a writing center unequivocally means a greater expenditure of time for administrators and tutors. To be sure, this expenditure is not in itself a problem, for technology training is fast becoming a common practice in writing centers. If the time spent in training and developing OWLs can be seen as part of the overall theory of the center, then the often enormous expenditure of time can be justified.

Although one may receive training for a particular software application, the competence that comes from the training is almost always a competence in general use, not in applying the application to a particular discipline or support service. Designing a Web page or navigating through a chat room does not teach me how to apply that skill toward solving writing center problems. Do I have theoretical knowledge about an application and need to find a practice for implementing that knowledge, or do I have a practical skill without a theoretical foundation? In the last few years, we have been more successful as a writing center by using technology to solve local problems first. In other words, our first goal in designing our Website was to meet the needs of our own students and faculty rather than assume that a Website (and, thus, a potentially global audience) puts us in competition with well-established and well-funded sites like Purdue's OWL. We also discovered that our intranet, created via economic and easy conferencing software, has provided us with an easier way to connect our tutors to each other and to their tutees than the Internet does. Our practice, therefore, has become to resist technology as a theory (as only potential and possibility) and harness it toward very practical ends.

Committing a writing center to go online requires support from the educational institution, and that support should be in two forms—money and expertise. If the first great myth about technology is that it saves time, the second is that technology is cheap. The kind of technology necessary to implement synchronous online tutorials or the kind of writing center envisioned by Crump (1995) and Johnson (1996), for instance, requires institutional support. For many writing center administrators, however much they may want to change the culture of learning and the theoretical premises underlying writing centers, institutional support in money and computer expertise does not exist. Here, we meet another place where practice and theory collide; perhaps better said, the lack of financial and technical support does not allow a writing center to experiment with technology and thereby reinvent itself in this changing educational climate.

The last area that poses problems for writing centers as they flirt with technology is assessment. Simply put, do OWLs work? How do we know? To date, very little research discusses this problem or demonstrates results. Yet, for any kind of learning support unit, certainty about what we are doing and being able to document it are crucial issues. The anecdotal information that has been published provides some encouragement, if only by demonstrating that writing center practitioners continually look for new ways to reach their clients even without adequate time, training, money, and technical support.

CYBERTUTORS: TECHNOLOGY AND THE PROBLEM OF TRAINING TUTORS

Addressing student expectations involves conceptualizing the roles that tutors can play in minimizing this conflict. Roderick (1982) rightly asserted,

"Tutors are, indeed, the heart and soul of the writing center experience" (p. 39). Thus, in mending expectation conflict, tutors are the heart and soul of the solution. Writing center administrators must teach tutors skills for clarifying expectations, managing the tension of expectation conflict, and modifying various approaches to tutoring.

Advancing technology affords new opportunities for strengthening tutor training. Conferencing software, online interactive journals, and even electronic mail allow ongoing education. The writing tutors at the University of Richmond use *Daedalus Interchange* to teach new tutors about the complexities of tutoring (Essid, 1996, p. 45). Groups of three to five tutors meet online biweekly to discuss problems they encounter. Then, tutors log onto an *Interchange* conference in which a fictional tutoring scenario is described, detailing a fictional tutee's questions and attitudes. Through this program, tutors discuss ways to work with each scenario presented (p. 46). The University of Richmond tutors found the simulations realistic and helpful in preparing them to deal with actual tutoring problems (p. 41). Electronic conferencing's main benefit over face-to-face tutor meetings is that the software can be programmed to allow tutors to participate in discussions anonymously. Many people are less reluctant to engage in discourse when they can do so in anonymity. Even in cases where tutors' identities are apparent, conferencing software enables more participation from everyone; one or two individuals who may dominate verbal discussions struggle to do so online where everyone's comments are relayed without interruption.

The Merrimack College writing tutors use online interactive journals. Unlike conferencing software, online journals are asynchronous and similar to an e-mail discussion group. Tutors record their journal entries and then read and discuss each other's perceptions, receiving advice and sharing experiences. The primary purposes for the interactive journals are to "engage in discussion designed to work through the thorny issues [tutors] address in scholarly journals and conferences" and to "attempt to determine the relative merits of adhering to theory as opposed to conceding our service role ..." (DeCiccio et al., 1995, p. 33). Essid (1996) found that transcripts of conferences can be quite useful to future tutors, especially when those transcripts bring out important points or issues (p. 51). The University of Richmond tutors agree that the conferencing software and the transcripts from the conferences helped them accomplish more effective training and tutorials throughout the year (p. 52). Conferencing software, online interactive journals, and transcripts of these dialogues give tutors previews of the types of conflicts and attitudes they may encounter and provide a forum for tutors to discuss the best ways for dealing with all types of conflicts and misconceptions.

Tutor training should also include how to use software while tutoring. When tutors and tutees sit side by side in front of a monitor, verbal interaction is minimized, often unintentionally. The dynamics of tutorial sessions change when a computer becomes partly responsible for assisting the tutee. To what extent should tutors rely, and indirectly teach tutees to rely, on programs such as spelling and grammar checks? The flaws of these programs as proofreaders are well-known. Likewise, the benefits of rereading a document to find errors are clear. During tutor training, tutors must be taught to help tutees balance the use of technological applications with eyesight and human reasoning.

Other problems arise with tutees who lack basic operational knowledge of software programs. Do writing center tutors assume an increasing share of responsibility to teach software as more composition classrooms become computerized? When tutees who lack software skills come to writing centers, tutors definitely need to teach basic software operations or no progress can be made. Tutors who take responsibility for computing work in tutorials, hoping to keep sessions focused on writing rather than on technology, undermine their own efforts, taking tutees away from their own texts. Clearly, tutor training should emphasize that teaching tutees about relevant software applications is appropriate. Equally important, writing tutors need to know the various programs being used by their institution's composition classes. The more tutors know about the software programs that their tutees use, the more effectively tutors can help tutees.

In terms of student expectations, integrating technology into writing centers brings new concerns for tutor training. To begin with, students expect tutors to be familiar with the software programs used in composition classes. Tutees who are less familiar or more intimidated by software may expect their tutors to take more control of tutorials and likely even to take control of the actual software and hardware. In such cases, tutors may inadvertently end up doing a greater portion of tutees' work. Tutor training not only needs to teach tutors to understand writing center technology, but also to use the technology without disregarding the collaborative principles of tutoring. Because many students are unfamiliar with collaborative instruction, these students may benefit more from a modified collaborative approach, especially if these students are also unfamiliar with the predominant composition technologies. Teaching tutors flexibility allows them to use varying degrees of collaboration depending on the needs of their tutees.

Online writing centers that invite individuals to e-mail papers to online tutors, such as the University of Michigan OWL, create more issues in tutoring. How can tutors who are only communicating with a writer through e-mail teach tutees about the writing process in the same way allowed by face-to-face communication? Tutors frequently assess tutees' body language and tone of voice to determine the success of their tutorial strategy. These indicators are practically nonexistent in electronic media. In addition, the idea of a service where students can send in their papers (electronically) and receive comments through e-mail at a later time appears to go against the collaborative foundation of writing center theory.

II

Narratives of Experience

5

Theories Before Practice(s): Proposing Computers for Writing Centers

Denise Weeks
Weber State University

It is getting easier to cite reasons why more and more educational institutions are investing so much money in technology. A headline in *The New York Times* (1995) reading "Connecting Every Pupil to the World" tells us that computer access and Internet connections have achieved dramatic results for inner-city, at-risk students (p. A14). President Clinton urges us to let technology whisk us into the 21st century on Internet II. In higher education, we hear that state-of-the-art computer facilities are valuable selling points in student (and faculty) recruitment efforts, and we recognize that basic computer literacy is essential for students' professional development and workplace preparation. We hear more ominous claims, too, about the "inevitable, irreversible, and unpredictable" nature of this technological transformation (Gilbert, 1996, p. 58), and we hear barely veiled threats from proponents of online universities that "if the [traditional] universities do not reform quickly, they will decline into irrelevance" (Pelton, 1996, p. 17). But how do these plans and predictions for the future affect writing centers? Writing centers are often not included in statements about "the University"; they are more likely to be left out of planning meetings than, say, athletic departments, and they are not typically included in mission statements that describe the university's goals.

This marginalization has given writing centers a valuable freedom, in many cases (North, 1984); it allows them to carry out their subversive activities (Lunsford, 1995, p. 42) and to be liberatory (Warnock & Warnock, 1984) in their (often) subterranean corners of the university. Literally out of sight of administrators, writing centers offer inviting and nonthreatening resources for student writers. As outsiders, however, writing centers have not always been able to command much attention from financial backers and are often dependent on already tight English department or student services budgets.

Because of this lack of secure and plentiful funding, writing center directors, like enterprising business professionals, learn to watch for promising grants and write convincing proposals. Perhaps not surprisingly, in this climate in which "most schools are already footing substantial bills for their computer systems" (Collins, 1996), writing centers now have a unique opportunity to cash in on the support being given to technology. In some instances, large amounts of money are available to those who can successfully argue a need for technology. We find ourselves in the unusual (if temporary) situation of having more resources for technology initiatives than our administrators know what to do with: "There is no longer any question about whether or not information technology will become an integral part of education. There are only questions about when and how" (Gilbert, 1996, p. 2). Is writing a proposal to get computers for a successful traditional writing center, then—at a time when funding opportunities seem rich—just a reflexive grab for money and machines? Can we predict the consequences of making these bids for computers? Do we know what we are getting into when we attract administrators' attention to our typically out-of-the-way centers? Most importantly, in making our case for technology, do we remain true to our own conceptions of what a writing center should be?

In this chapter, I discuss the discoveries I made while writing two different proposals for writing center computers, and in doing so, I challenge the assertion that practice always precedes theory in writing centers. Sometimes we theorize based on expected or hoped for outcomes and begin the hard work of establishing practices after we get the funding to proceed.

THE PROPOSALS

Two opportunities for funding presented themselves to me in the spring of 1997. The first was a request for proposals (RFP) from the Utah System of Higher Education (USHE), and the second was from my own institution's Academic Resource and Computing Committee (ARCC), whose goals each year include funding student labs as well as discipline-specific and faculty-computing needs. The most interesting part of the proposal-writing process was discovering a rationale or justification for the use of computers in the small, noncomputerized writing center and assessing how much of my argument was based on my own and others' speculations about the future.

In the first proposal, written collaboratively by the director of the Teaching and Learning Forum on my campus, the forum's secretary, the director of WAC, and myself, we borrowed the language of the RFP and invoked the picture of the cyber-universities that regents (and governors) in the West love so well, hypothesizing our connection to that future by showing how an online writing center could serve the clientele that the online university is banking on. Part of the resulting proposal read as follows:

> The new educational paradigm supported by USHE, the Western Governor's University, and the new Weber State Online requires that educators support "new modes and methods of teaching and learning for both on-campus and off-campus learning environments." Part of the challenge in making full use of the technologies is to provide education that is not bound by place, space, or time. Students enrolled in "virtual" classes still need support systems, however. They need to have access to the "human" element of education as well as the text resources often hard to access from remote sites. (USHE Proposal)

In this bid for computers, we also called on one of the first tenets of the writing center: that "the better the relationship, the better the interaction; the better the interaction, the better the learning" (Tiberius, cited in Murphy & Sherwood, 1995b, p. 6).

Although this proposal ultimately failed to get us any computers, the proposal-writing process itself turned out to be very valuable because it forced me to investigate what I thought computers might do to our small, noncomputerized writing center. Did I want our center to provide any-time, any-place tutoring? Could it? On the other extreme, would computers in the writing center serve simply as writing tools that would not significantly alter tutor–client relationships? With the material made available through the National Writing Center Association (NWCA) Web page—including its over 200 links to online writing centers—and excellent articles by pioneers in this emerging field (Collins, 1996; Coogan, 1995; Jordan-Henley & Maid, 1995a), I had ample evidence that others had made this move before me. Yet, as each writing center exists in a unique context, coming into being in response to various administrative, programmatic, budgetary, and personnel decisions and configurations (Kinkead & Harris, 1993), I could not reasonably assume that several computers would transform our center into a copy of the writing center at Purdue University, the one at the University of Missouri, or the center of our nearest neighbor: Salt Lake Community College. Nor did I think computers should effect such a transformation of our center.

In the process of revising the first proposal and submitting it to my on-campus funding organization, then, I began thinking less about expected applications and more about appropriate applications of computers in our writing center. The failure of the first proposal was disappointing, but it gave me the opportunity to move away from my notion of what computers should do in a writing center (based on the terms and expectations of the USHE) and forced me to look at what they probably would do, given the unique features of our academic context. The resulting, winning proposal made this short statement of rationale:

> Computers purchased to implement an on-line writing center will be used to assist all Weber State students improve their writing. More specifically, writing center tutors will use the computers to conduct asynchronous on-line tutorials with students working from their homes, offices, or on-campus computer labs; assist walk-in students who need help with papers, preparing oral presentations, or designing attractive documents; and create and maintain a writing center Web page that will link to helpful online resources and will advertise the writing center's services. The computers will also be available to students on a walk-in basis when tutors are not using them to assist student "clients" or work on student publications.

> The writing center's on-line service will help non-traditional and distance students by providing another avenue through which they can get help with their writing assignments. Our writing center, which already serves students from all disciplines (we conducted 504 tutoring sessions in the Winter 1997 quarter alone, where 40% of those students were from departments other than English), could serve an increased number of students whose schedules preclude their spending extra time on campus seeking assistance. Additionally, on-line tutoring and the availability of computers in the writing

center will help students whose instructors in all disciplines are already re-quiring on-line submission of homework. We believe that increased access to tutoring in writing—made possible by computers—will help students achieve academic success across disciplines. (AARC proposal)

To directors of writing centers that are already equipped with computers, to tutors who have already conducted online tutoring sessions or met with a client whose draft was on a disk, to anyone who has designed a writing center Web page, my proposal will seem mundane. The proposal did not ask for a radical revisioning of the traditional writing center, nor did it conceive of a use for computers that others had not already incarnated. Its scope was quite modest, requesting only three high-speed computers to be connected to the campus network. I still included in my rationale plans to use the computers to conduct asynchronous, online tutoring (a remnant from the first proposal), and I pointed to hypothetical students who would be enrolling in online writing classes as early as the fall of 1997. I also added a component inspired by my experience teaching Professional and Technical Writing: Computers would enable tutors to work with students on different kinds of writing assignments, including slides and documents that require a consideration of their design and layout. This expansion of services was really at the heart of my goals for the writing center: I hope that computers will supplement, rather than replace, the face-to-face tutorials at which we are already proficient.

LESSONS LEARNED

What informed my second proposal was less virtual university hype and more concrete consideration of what I had read, heard, and experienced. I took into consideration the support I could count on from organizations like WAC and the Teaching and Learning Forum—intellectual if not financial support—and I drew on information I gathered from articles and presentations on valuable, practical, and even challenging uses of computers in writing centers. Coogan's (1995) thoughtful analysis of one tutorial exchange via e-mail, for example, described the insecurities a virtual tutor has when the writer is not there, in person, to respond to comments and suggestions. Notwithstanding this impediment to an easier rapport, however, Coogan (1995) wrote favorably of the conversational style his responses took in this new media. I also heard encouraging reports from the field while attending the 1997 Rocky Mountain Peer Tutoring conference. There, I heard a discussion of how a stand-alone computer in the writing center at the University of Idaho was used to assist students whose papers were on diskette. Tutor Marjanna Hulet (1997) explained that when students work with soft copy rather than hard copy, they are able to initiate the cutting, pasting, and reorganizing that the tutor might suggest during the tutorial, and they can leave the meeting with a neater draft to work with and a better sense of how to use the word processor to its potential as a writing aid. At the same conference, I saw examples of student drafts submitted via e-mail to tutors working at the Salt Lake Community College online writing lab, and I heard the tutors discuss the parameters of a productive session. What both talks suggested is that computers can make the writing tutorial more effective and educational for both tutor and client, but that successful interactions require considerable forethought and preparation, especially for online tutoring. The same things we want to see in face-to-face conferences (the assignment, the student's understanding of that assignment, and the student's immediate writing goal) need to be presented in virtual tutorials as well.

Also informing my request for computers for the writing center were the experiences I had with technology while in graduate school at the University of Texas at Austin. There, in the Division of Rhetoric and Composition's Computer Writing and Research Lab, I participated in experiments similar to the ones Fitzgerald (1994) described in "Collaborative Learning and Whole Language Theory": "There [in a computer writing lab/writing center], ... we found solutions by talking, reading what each had suggested, listening to each other and to students, and writing together on the screen" (p. 16). It was an environment where students and faculty shared ideas for projects and solutions, helped each other with disks and drafts, and negotiated computer, as well as composition, crises. We were informed, for the most part, by theories coming out of rhetoric and composition, and we were able to practice many of them via computer-assisted collaboration; real time, online conversation; and computer-assisted drafting, revising, and editing. With and around computers, professors and teaching assistants shared their own work while they shared teaching ideas and strategies. The computers, and the small basement room that housed them, helped genuine writing communities cohere. But in terms of my proposal, and justifying my request for computers to the funding organization on my campus, these largely anecdotal accounts were not the kind of evidence that mattered most. The more important question was theoretical in another sense: The committee was not so interested in how the computers would help us assist students as they were in how many students the computers would enable us to serve.

What I had not considered when I first thought about incorporating computers into the writing center, but what became an important point in the college-level review of this proposal, was how these computers would be used when not serving the immediate needs of the center. Would they go unused? On our predominantly commuter campus, open labs are always crowded during peak hours (8am–1pm); rarely can students walk in and find a vacant machine. Students frequently cite "no room in the computer lab" as they ask for extensions on their papers, and there are always long lines of students waiting at the printers. The idea of three computers sitting idle in the writing center obviously struck some on the committee as wasteful, so the suggestion was made that the writing center forego having its own computers and instead share computers with the open lab next door to it. According to this plan, the writing center computers would be open lab computers until a tutor needed to use the machine. A sign on the computer would inform students that their use of the computer was contingent on tutors not needing it, and they could be asked to vacate at any time. My argument against this suggestion was that the computers would then not be part of the writing center, that tutors could not work as easily with online drafts or student clients, and that students working in the open lab would resent being asked to vacate a computer for a tutor—no matter what the reason. The idea of tutors going to another room to do online tutoring or work with students on their drafts did not fit with my notion of an online writing center. But more convincing than my argument against this sharing of resources was the argument of a colleague, who reasoned that putting three computers in the writing center actually added to the total number of computers available to students on campus. Getting the computers in the center was my main priority; conceding that they could be used by students on a walk-in basis (when writing center tutors were not using them for writing center business) was not difficult, although it did give me some concern. I never wanted the writing center tutors to become technology assistants, answering more computer than composition questions. However, as writers become more dependent on technology, the availability of writing tutors who can answer technical questions that support revision (like how copying and pasting works or how "Save As" facilitates drafting) will, it seems, help to create better writers and not just better texts (North, 1984). Again, I let hypotheses shape my claims. Will computers actually serve this purpose?

I detail this negotiation process with the proposal committee because, again, it helped me discover some of my own notions about, and biases toward, the use of computers in the writing center. I wanted computers, but I did not want an open computer lab. I wanted technology to facilitate document sharing, but I did not want students to use e-mail to simply drop off their drafts to be edited by our tutors. I hoped that computers would enhance the production of writing center documents (e.g., handouts, flyers, and publications), but I did not want them to be used only as stand-alone word processors. I was sensitive, too, to the concerns of the existing tutors who looked at this move toward computerization with suspicion. They were, in fact, almost unanimously against it, holding to a North-inspired, purer vision of the writing center as a place where people go to talk—not type—about writing. I did not dismiss their fears or concerns; instead, I took them seriously as I designed my syllabus for the next tutor-training course that would include a section on "Computers in the Writing Center."

SPECULATIONS FOR THE FUTURE

The question that this chapter set out to explore (and invert)—"Why has practice preceded theory in writing centers, and is this problematic?"—requires a follow-up question: problematic for whom, or for what? Problematic for our tutors? for our budgets? for the centers?

If many writing center directors are beginning to incorporate computer technology into their daily operations before understanding the clear theoretical justification for doing so, it is probably because they receive more assistance to buy computers than to theorize. Those of us who use computers in our classes, read student drafts submitted via e-mail, or make assignments and syllabi available over the Internet might still be asked to conduct empirical studies to evaluate differences between traditional and computer-assisted learning environments, but fewer of us will be challenged outright to prove that computers are worthwhile. It seems, in fact, that we have reached a point of no return. Our administrators have made up their minds about technology, but in many cases, they have not gathered their evidence from us. Our (largely) anecdotal evidence about increased participation, greater collaboration, and students' new enjoyment of writing has not been all that persuasive. Instead, administrators' enthusiasm and support for technology appears to derive from ideas they received from industry advocates: that technology will help us (and them) increase productivity.

Governor Mike Leavitt (1993), a major proponent of the Western Governor's University, said in a speech entitled "Gearing up with Technology":

> I'm not just talking about an expansion of television courses, but an expansion into every available medium. Entire courses should be obtainable on compact disk. For that matter—entire majors could ultimately be placed on disk ... courses could be offered with regularly-scheduled labs or discussion, or tests. Groups may meet once a week rather than 3 or 5 times a week. This multiplies the productivity of the instructor. (p. 4–5).

Former Speaker of the House Newt Gingrich made a similar equation between technology and an (apparently) limitless availability of educational resources when he said that "[w]e could do so much to make education available twenty-four hours a day, seven days a week, that people could literally have a whole different attitude toward learning" (cited in Oppenheimer, 1997, p. 46). I do not deny that technology will help us make resources available in new, different, and exciting ways, but I question the simple formulas being applied to technology and learning. At the same time that Governor Leavitt (1993) claimed that a virtual university would allow instructors to increase their productivity, for instance, he also claimed that the Internet would help us make a return to the golden era of Socratic, dialogue-based, one-to-one education. "Technology-delivered education brings Socrates back," Leavitt (1993) claimed, adding that the "spirit of Socrates will be everywhere, teaching our citizens the critical thinking skills that prepare them for tomorrow" (p. 6). The important factor that Leavitt and many administrative technology advocates leave out of the formula is the amount of time it takes instructors, departments, and colleges to find intelligent uses of technology. Just because the Internet makes resources available does not mean that teaching and learning will occur at information-rich sites. Socratic dialogue cannot be burned onto a CD-ROM and sold in a course packet. Even if it does occur online, that kind of personalized education takes time.

If introducing computers (and computer-assisted tutoring) into the writing center encourages more misguided notions about increased productivity, then we are running a risk by encouraging their use. Already the tutors who work in the writing center at Weber State University are very concerned about computers creating a sterile environment, a center unable to provide the "personal touch" that they feel characterizes their sessions with student clients. They are suspicious, too, as I am, of the any-time, any-where, 24-hours-a-day rhetoric of virtual university proponents. What does it mean, in practice, to provide feedback any time? Do tutors no longer work set hours? Do they work on an on-call basis? Will they still meet in our bricks-and-mortar center? My answer to this last question is a definitive "Yes." Yes, they will still meet in the center, still hold face-to-face tutorials, and still talk to their peers about writing. A virtual writing center should draw more students to our services and provide another medium for writing support; it should not replace the physical writing center.

Another possible problem resulting from the introduction of computers into our centers could be an increased strain on our budgets. Proposals or grants may have given us the windfall to purchase the computers, but do we have enough in our annual allotment to maintain them? Do we trade out a tutor for a technical support assistant? Do we assign tutors the role of troubleshooting and fixing machines, or do we just spend another 5 hours of our own time working on computers? Ultimately, do these new claims on our time and attention deprive the center—and the students who frequent it—of our energy? These are the questions that need to be answered in practice. The theories that persuaded the committee to fund the computers cannot answer these questions. The theories can only excite our imaginations and give us hope for increased community, greater collaboration, and new ways of assisting students. The practice that we initiate next year will begin to answer our concerns.

6

Writing in the Electronic Realm: Incorporating a New Medium Into the Work of the Writing Center

Sharon Thomas
Michigan State University
Mark Hara
Arizona State University
Danielle DeVoss
Michigan Technological University

In the past few years, like many others in the world of writing centers, we have sought to incorporate technology into our practices. Buffeted by conflicting claims—online consulting radically changes the practice of consulting; online consulting is not much different from face-to-face consulting—we have struggled to find ways to determine for ourselves and for our own situation the benefits and drawbacks of the technologies invading our campus. Most problematic for us as practitioners in a relatively young writing center (established 1992) has been the lack of opportunities to pay attention to whether or not these new technologies are congruent with our own emerging pedagogical and theoretical stances. Like many writing centers, our practices are built on a particular set of beliefs, and, at times, the rapid influx of technology has threatened to transform our

65

practices in ways that were both uncomfortable and incompatible with our underlying beliefs.

BECOMING AN OWL

Three years ago, we followed Purdue University's lead and went online. Our original World Wide Web site resembled many other early writing center Websites. Most of the written materials available at the center were put online. The site had limited graphical content, was created using basic HTML, and could be viewed using most of the browsers available at the time. In the summer of 1996, the site was reconceived and reborn as the Writer's Retreat. That summer, two undergraduate writing consultants (UWCs) and two graduate students worked together to revamp the site. Operating on the premise that talk is a useful intervention into the writing process, these four students initiated a conversation about the new Website using our in-house listserv. Out of the many suggestions, we settled on a "Writer's Retreat," an online country cottage to which writers could go for writing resources. Next, the team posted a paper floorplan of the retreat in our writing center and invited comments from visiting faculty, clients, and our consultants. Based on the suggestions that soon covered the model, we searched for appropriate materials on the Internet and, eventually, compiled over 100 links to resources for writers.

Our first venture into using technology to support our work was entirely congruent with our North-inspired (1984) pedagogical stance that our goal was to support the efforts of students to become better writers, not to fix their papers. When we assessed our efforts in light of our beliefs, we agreed that using technology to provide resources that writers could use on their own seemed eminently appropriate to our particular writing center philosophy. However, our next foray into using technology—online consulting—was an entirely different story.

CONSIDERING ONLINE CONSULTING

While developing our OWL, we began to investigate online consulting. Not only were we attracted to the possibilities of using e-mail to reach students at remote locations, but we were also curious to see how our consultation sessions would function when we changed the medium from face-to-face response to written response. Because students at our university have been required since the fall of 1993 to participate in e-mail discussion groups as part of a required 200-level course, most of them are comfortable with this medium; the students' e-mail experience encouraged us to start consulting via e-mail.

Working with an instructor in a first-year composition course, we invited her students to e-mail their papers to our writing center account. When the papers were received, we scheduled a UWC to respond by e-mail, using a regularly scheduled appointment time (50 minutes). We experimented with this design three times during the semester. Each time about ten students e-mailed their papers, and four or five UWCs responded.

Despite Coogan's (1995) statement that online tutoring allows for a new openness and flexibility in consulting, the UWCs quickly fell into a far more evaluative mode, one they described as acting like a teacher. Because they were not face to face with the student writers and could garner no feedback, the hierarchical structure of the interactions, rather than dissolving, became more rigid. Coogan (1995) claimed that in online consulting, "interpreting student text, rather than the student, becomes [the] centerpiece" of the consultation (p. 171). This type of interpretation posed a difficulty for our UWCs. In this case, the introduction of technology substantially altered the consulting sessions. In retrospect, the UWCs preferred to retain the model of conventional face-to-face consultation because they did not want to respond to a text; they wanted to respond to a student about a text.

Perhaps, as Coogan (1995) argued, the online writing tutorial can become a continually evolving discussion in writing if tutor and writer continue their conversation over an extended period of time—if the consultant makes some general comments, waits for a response, answers, responds again, and so on (p. 175). Given the funding and time restraints of our writing center (and possibly other writing centers as well), we do not have that kind of flexibility.

The next semester, we piloted a study of online consulting using an Internet Relay Chat program that allowed for synchronous conversations. Even though the synchronous format allowed for an interactive conversation in real time, both the UWCs and the student writers preferred face-to-face consultations. As Blythe (1996) pointed out, in the online journal *Kairos* (http://english.ttu. edu/kairos/1.1/owls/owlfront.html), online conversations may mask some important nonverbal cues such as facial expression and tone of voice. Those UWCs who participated in this project missed facial expressions and tone of voice. As a result, we decided to shelve online consulting until we needed to work with students in remote locations.

At this point, we thought we had made our peace with technology and the choices we were being forced to make. Providing online resources did not disrupt our practices; however, consulting online did, so we would choose to do the former but not the latter. Then, a significant event occurred on our campus.

TURNING TO THE INTERNET

In May 1996, our president, Peter McPherson, declared that Michigan State University (MSU) had entered "a new age of access" and presented the MSU Technology Guarantee to the university community. The guarantee (available online at http://www.msu.edu/events/techinfo/) is composed of six promises, each emphasizing access to knowledge, and includes the promise of an intensive, quality-based technological experience for undergraduate students with affordable lifelong technological access for MSU alumni. When students returned to campus for the fall 1996 semester, they discovered they could use their e-mail accounts to access four megabytes on the university server for their own use; faculty discovered they had 10 megabytes. How the members of our university community communicate, conduct research, and publish began to change even more rapidly, and we began to ask ourselves, once again, how we might best support the emerging electronic literacy we were observing.

In the summer of 1996, we began to work on ways to support computer-based student writing. Using earlier classroom presentations as models, we developed interactive sessions that demonstrated the use of computer technology to support writing. Creating these presentations helped us articulate the assistance our staff could offer.

Extending Classroom Conversations

Because of the heavy e-mail use on our campus, we looked for examples of using e-mail to support writing. Many faculty, we discovered, were already using e-mail at least to contact students, and several had devised more ingenious applications.

In a required 200-level course taken by around 3,000 students each semester, the instructors created an electronic shared journal that allowed group members to access a shared e-mail forum at any time. One instructor used this approach in her first-year composition course. She still invited students to work in small groups to discuss the course reading assignments on e-mail, but she also, each week, chose one or more of the e-mail discussions and posted them to her class Website, making use of her recently acquired space on the university server. In this manner, the students could see what other groups were discussing, and the instructor provided good models for discussion groups. Then, she took the conversation one step further. She invited the authors of some of the texts that these students were reading and discussing to join these conversations. Amazingly enough, several agreed, and she posted those interactions to the Website as well.

When we started our workshops on using technology to support writing with this example, the conversations that ensued helped us understand the importance of engaging in conversations with authors. We had already understood that extending discussion in this manner supported student writing because it invited students to share and learn from each other's responses to the reading assignments. We also found that it provided a forum for trying out ideas, and it gave students an audience of peers to respond to their developing arguments. Looking back, though, we see that the opportunity to receive responses from the authors made the most significant impact on faculty and students alike.

Conducting Research on the Internet

In addition to using technology to support writing through extending opportunities for discussion, we were also interested in the Internet as a place for students to increase their knowledge about a topic and, therefore, their ability to write confidently about it. For this part of our new session, we showed them various search engines on the Web, such as *Lycos*, *Altavista*, and *Yahoo!*, including information on identifying the most appropriate search engines for particular topics.

During the first semester of this project, we did not advertise these presentations but piloted them with several groups of faculty, graduate students, and classes. Some faculty members engaged their students in complex, Web-based research assignments. A religious studies professor, for example, had students work in groups to research a Hindu deity using Web resources. Students analyzed the history of the deity, constructed a list of links to related sites, and gathered textual and graphical content to supplement their research—all of which they, eventually, posted to the course home page.

Other faculty members, however, complained that they knew how to teach students to evaluate the information they found in the library, but they did not know how to teach students to evaluate Internet sources. Books were written by authors with reputations and journal articles had been refereed, but anybody could post to the Internet. With so little control over what could be posted to the Internet, how would students determine the authenticity of the information found there? These questions sent us searching for information to help students critically evaluate Internet sources and resulted in yet another handout on assessing author credibility and information reliability.

Publishing on the World Wide Web

Even before MSU provided all students, faculty, and departments with server space for Web page construction, we had developed a presentation on publishing on the Web. Some writing faculty almost immediately saw the possibility of giving their students a wider audience for their work. Instead of the audience of one (the professor), students could now write for a potentially worldwide audience. Instead of imagining their audience, students could actually post their work to that audience, which significantly changed the way they viewed the composing process. When we introduced students enrolled in a writing center-based, linked course to issues of content and design of existing Web pages, of navigation and use of Web editors and HTML, and of the possibility of using hypertext document design techniques, we discovered they were far more willing to spend time revising, shaping, editing, and discussing their work.

The Need for Further Support

Soon after we began doing these presentations, faculty and students began to request further support, especially for Web publication. We responded by encouraging those consultants interested in hypertext and Web publication to prepare themselves to consult with students and faculty working on such projects. Soon, we had a corps of Internet Writing Consultants (IWCs) who established their own listserv and held biweekly meetings similar to those of our regular consultant meetings; in these meetings the IWCs not only discussed the specifics of hypertext mark-up language, but also of composing issues, techniques to evaluate Websites, and methods for doing research on the Web. In preparing themselves to consult with students and faculty on Internet-supported writing projects, they reflected on past issues, problems, or concerns. These meetings provided a space for stimulating discussions of practical and theoretical issues.

The Problems of Internet Consulting

When our new IWCs began consulting, however, we found that they were not, in fact, as well prepared for and comfortable with this new kind of consulting as we had thought. Based on a survey conducted in the spring of 1997, most IWCs indicated that they had no trouble understanding the relationship between technology and writing, but they did have difficulty integrating Internet consulting into their conceptions of the Writing Center and its goals (Hara, 1997). One consultant wrote that "Internet Consulting brings forth this new type of writing (not so linear, not so textual, but more technical) which requires us to tailor some of the strategies and specific theory behind the overarching goals [of the Writing Center] to accommodate" (Hara, 1997). This "tailoring of strategies" gave many consultants trouble, though, when they began consulting. Once again, technology was disrupting our practices, threatening to disconnect our practice from our underlying theory and pedagogy.

Many IWCs indicated that their goals for Internet consultation sessions included helping clients understand the Web as a publication medium and preparing them to work on their pages. The consultants generally indicated, both in the survey and in discussion, that their favorite sessions were ones in which they were able to talk about large issues such as audience, publication, clarity, and coherence—many of the same issues addressed in conventional consultations. When they discussed their Internet consulting experiences, they generally used concepts drawn from their face-to-face sessions. As Bernhardt (1993) pointed out, "Electronic text does not create a totally new rhetoric but depends for its design on the strategies of paper texts" (p. 151). Apparently, consultations formed around electronic composition depend, for their design, on conventional consultations as well.

However, consulting about Internet writing had frustrations unique to the medium. Similar to their experiences with online consulting, several IWCs felt that the focus of their consulting sessions had changed, shifting from the client to the computer. As one consultant pointed out in a discussion at the 1997 East Central Writing Centers Association conference, "You can't exactly say to a client: 'You want an image in your page? Can you think of some ways you could do that?' You need to teach them the language to a certain extent before you can move on to whole-composition issues" (DeVoss, Hara, & Kik, 1997). Most IWCs were uncomfortable moving from peer consultants to teachers.

Revising the Internet Writing Consultancy

Based on the IWCs' observations, we began, at the weekly meetings, to discuss and revise the Internet Writing Consultancy. Together, we developed practical strategies to address the problems the IWCs had encountered: Start the session away from the computer; encourage clients to set goals; and create and encourage dialogue.

1. Start the Session Away From the Computer. IWCs often complained that their sessions focused on what could be termed *word-level issues* in face-to-face writing consultations. In other words, consumed with the mechanics of HTML, clients were resistant to discussing whole-composition issues, such as effective use of the medium and the development of ideas. To counter this tendency, IWCs often begin sessions at tables and ask clients to draw designs for their Web pages on paper, creating visual maps of their sites and planning the information for each page. IWCs then can engage clients in discussions of whole-composition issues and suggest ways to use hypertext to its fullest. When the consultations finally move to the computer, clients usually have clear ideas of how they want their sites to look. Although these ideas change during composition, clients focus less on mechanical HTML issues when sessions begin in this way. In addition, the IWCs can tailor the consultation to focus on issues that the client has indicated are important in the site map, resulting in increased responsiveness to clients' needs.

2. Encourage Clients to Set Goals. Many IWCs reported that their most frustrating sessions were ones in which clients seemed uninterested in the writing process and "just wanted to get something up and move on" (Hara, 1997). These sessions frustrated consultants and clients and produced mediocre Web pages. Now, IWCs encourage clients to do the following:

- Form concrete goals for their Websites.
- Be aware of and write for different audiences.
- Write within specific modes of rhetoric.
- Explore the possibilities of hypertext.

Establishing clear goals leads to more effective Web pages.

3. Create and Encourage Dialogue. One of the most important elements of a session, dialogue, was often lacking in Internet writing consultations, or the dialogue concerned the computer rather than writing.

Beginning the sessions away from the computer usually results in the establishment of a good dialogue as the IWC and the client discuss the client's goals and plan together how to achieve those goals. Once the dialogue begins, sustaining it is relatively easy when the consultation moves to the computer. Clients with clear goals readily take charge of the session, questioning IWCs as to the particulars of achieving their goals. Once this dialogue is established, IWCs begin to feel like responders to writers with works in progress, rather than instructors engaged in teaching technology.

COPING WITH TECHNOLOGY

Every time we have experimented with technology in our writing center, we have experienced some changes in our practices. Sometimes, as in the development of the Writer's Retreat, these changes neither disrupted our practices nor challenged our underlying philosophy about consulting. Other attempts to integrate technology into our work, such as experimenting with consulting online, caused changes so uncomfortable that we discontinued the activity. Our most recent encounter with technology also threatened to disrupt our practices. This time, however, we examined that disruption and were able to revise our consulting practices in ways that were compatible with our practices.

Continually researching our practices and examining how they fit our philosophy has been an ongoing routine in our writing center and one that often uncovers incompatibilities, whether obvious at first or not. Strategies for resolving such conflicts are not so easily uncovered, but we continuously try to reestablish compatibility between practice and theory by searching for the causes of our discomfort and introducing subtle, but acceptable, changes in our practices, changes that do not contradict the principles that guide our choices.

7

Emerging (Web)Sites for Writing Centers: Practicality, Usage, and Multiple Voices Under Construction

Michael Colpo
Shawn Fullmer
Brad E. Lucas
University of Nevada at Reno

While more universities construct wired classrooms and develop their Internet services for clients, many institutes of higher education remain far behind in the technology-development curve. Such was the case with the UNR. UNR's writing center had no Web presence other than a spare, text-only page with an address, a telephone number, and the director's name. Clearly, the site needed changes. We found ourselves faced with the seemingly facile task of building the nest of a Website.

We began our first year at UNR as English graduate students having all come from technology-rich universities where the writing center and departments across campus had active and developed Websites (Utah State University, the University of Delaware, and the University of Texas at Austin). Through a clarity made possible only by deprivation, we soon realized that e-mail was rarely used and that Internet access was available only to off-campus clients in text-only format (faculty and staff were permitted full-scale, graphics-enabled access through Point-to-Point Protocol [PPP] connections). The English department contribution to the UNR Web was a modest page, rarely updated and not very informative. Similarly, the writing center Web page would have been better left off the Web rather than stay in its present form. Having spent numerous hours exploring the Web, witnessing its potential, and even constructing Websites, we were immediately aware of the limitations of our site as a form of informational media. Having come from wired universities, we now found ourselves lost in an environment lacking technology. At a campus where Internet interest was just beginning to bloom, this lack of resources was of little importance to most administrators and faculty.

Up until this point at UNR's writing center, technology was, for the most part, still seen as something simply interesting—word processing was the only recognizable computer tool held in any high regard. We realized the advantages of the university's entrance into this technological movement, but were uncertain that our concerns would fall on sympathetic ears. How would we convince the writing center administration of the Web's growing importance and value to academic communities? Should we attempt such a change even if we received a negative response? In addition, if we were asked to provide evidence to support Web development, where would we turn? These questions faced us in our decision to approach UNR's writing center. Fortunately, our concerns fell on sympathetic ears. The director, Mark Waldo, although still unsure of the impact a Web presence would have on the writing center, trusted our intentions to enhance this presence, to develop our HTML skills, and to contribute to the technological momentum of the university.

The writing center at UNR adheres to the philosophy of a decentered writing center, one that is not simply an outgrowth of the English department, but serves the entire campus through tutoring and a strong commitment to WAC. The first version of the writing center Website consisted of no more than a scanned image of the writing center's informational flyer, visible only through a link from the emerging English department Website. As a matter of courtesy, we had asked the director of the writing center if he would mind our inclusion of the writing center on the developing English department Website. The reaction was surprisingly positive, although it did come with specific concerns—mainly those surrounding the image that our WAC-based center sought to convey.

UNR's writing center is somewhat of an anomaly: Nearly 90% of the tutors have at least a bachelor's degree. Waldo assumed directorship in 1989, and since then, over 50,000 clients from nearly 40 disciplines have come to the writing center to work on their papers. In an interview, Waldo recalled that "there was a small writing lab that was the editing arm of the composition program in the basement of Frandsen Hall, but the university felt the need for a fully functioning, cross-disciplinary writing center" (personal communication, May 7, 1998). The center operates on the belief that a writing center "should be the heart of composition on campus." Waldo noted, "we not only do tutoring, but we also do consulting with various departments to help teachers design effective writing assignments. We use an inquiry-based collaborative approach" (personal communication, May 7, 1998). This philosophy is described in the writing center pamphlet:

> The University of Nevada, Reno's Writing Center, one of the most comprehensive in the United States, offers a variety of services and programs to the university and community. The center's principle mission is twofold. First, it assists students in improving the quality of the academic writing they do for their courses. Second, it provides help to instructors who include writing assignments as part of their course requirements. (Waldo, personal communication, May 7, 1998)

UNR's writing center usually employs 30 tutors from a wide range of disciplines, typically engaging in 50 tutoring sessions per day from 20 different classes. Waldo observed that "any given day is a microcosm of what happens the entire year—students range from needing a lot of help with their writing to being brilliant writers—basic writers to grad students" (personal communication, May 7, 1998).

When we first approached Waldo, he was supportive, enthusiastic, and willing to do whatever was needed to get us started on the Website. Although unfamiliar with the intricacies of the Web, Waldo provided a clear vision of what the writing center Website should be—if we were to make the commitment to its continued development. Of nearly equal importance to the writing center's goal of existing as an independent academic entity was the desire not to stray from its fundamental approach to the tutoring of client papers. In an attempt to provide valuable online informational assistance, we decided from the outset that we would not attempt online tutoring or any other sort of direct assistance over the Internet. Subsequently, we were unsure what information to provide, considering that so many other OWLs had developed such rich resources. We were reluctant to reinvent the wheel and develop another one of the many clearinghouses of information already provided by OWLs across the country. In developing a first Website, we decided that a few simple links to resources and handouts would suffice, at least until we had time and materials to develop these at home. Harris and Pemberton (1995) explained that their similar aim, although Gopher-based, was "to assist students gathering information in preparation for writing research papers—to become their easy gateway out—a particularly important service for novices learning to surf the Internet" (p. 149). Indeed, the very concept of the information-based OWL is practically antithetical to the learning environment Waldo worked to create in this WAC-based community. Many months after the initial Website was completed, our director decided that the easy access we had provided to sentence-level handouts conveyed the wrong image for the writing center. In accordance with the philosophy of the writing center, we agreed it would be better to emphasize the writing process, highlighting the importance of tutoring and one-on-one interaction rather than relegating our assistance to a series of abstracted online handouts. Because the writing center's question-asking strategy of tutoring focuses on individual client projects, we chose to move the online handouts to deeper levels of the Website, reachable only by those persons aware of the tradeoff made by choosing online assistance over the traditional writing center appointment.

Our current Website reflects a philosophy of guidance through a series of panels that reflect our priorities, and it moves clients toward making tutoring appointments. Our aims were, and still are, to enhance the image of the writing center, offer basic logistical information, and in the process, provide useful resource material for clients seeking assistance with their writing. We envisioned the Website playing a complementary role, what Harris and Pemberton (1995) described as "yet another service offered by writing centers, which enhances and expands present work, but not as a service displacing what we find so valuable and effective in writing center tutorials" (p. 146). We had only one flyer, one pamphlet, and a tutor schedule to work with—the rest was for us to create or appropriate.

We conceptualized the Website as a billboard that would increase awareness of the writing center and encourage clients to come in for tutorials. After converting the information and images from the handouts to the Website, we decided to index the site according to the following categories: *Writing Resources, Writing Center Staff, Students, Faculty and Staff, Community*, and *Research*. Thinking in terms of what clients would use the most, we privileged the online materials, followed by information about the tutors and the weekly schedule. Other categories explained the philosophy, mission, and operations of the writing center. After we shifted from thinking what clients would use the most to what would be of most use to clients, this configuration changed to an emphasis on appointment-setting procedures and writing center philosophy. Our revisions incorporated the links to writing-assistance materials in the context of these discussions and then only as an option that followed as "For further information about mechanics, usage, etc. see our list of hyperlinks."

Ideally, we hoped that clients who might not otherwise find us would discover the center on the World Wide Web. In other words, we were sitting on what Lasarenko (1996) called "the bottom rung of the OWL evolutionary ladder" (online). Regardless of our infant status, each new addition, ranging from the touches of color to the hard-fought and highly valuable acquisition of a CGI-script counter, boosted our pride and confidence. The value of our work's stock continues to increase with each new click of the counter.

At this point, we felt rather self-assured. After all, the writing center now had a Website that was linked from the top of the university's *Academics* index page, and our director seemed pleased. Up until this point, Mike Colpo and Brad Lucas had made all hypertext design choices. We realized that our thinking had to expand to include the voices and visions of the writing center's lifeblood—the clients who used our services. Shawn Fullmer brought his research methodology skills to the project as we all worked toward obtaining feedback from the academic population and determining what everyone wanted out of a writing center Website.

Making the Website easy to use and accessible for everyone mattered, but we were more concerned with generating ideas about the site itself rather than studying client practices and usage. We decided that distributing a questionnaire to clients would be an efficient and manageable method for gathering feedback. Copies were made available in printed forms placed at various computing sites on campus and through a link installed on the main writing center page. Our primary concerns in developing and using the questionnaire were making it simple (not only for the clients filling out the questionnaire but also for us in compiling the data and interpreting the answers) and integrating the client suggestions into actual Website renovation. With these concerns in mind, we wanted the questionnaire to be as easy as possible to complete.

In addition to the inconvenience of finding the Website and then writing down comments on a paper questionnaire, we encountered some reluctance on the part of the clients to do what they perceived to be extra work.

This response came about despite the fact that several composition instructors requested completed questionnaires before the end of the first week of class—when students were excited to begin the semester and before they developed a concern for grades or excess work. In the end, a combination of the instructor's perseverance and the clients' enthusiasm helped to create a response that constituted the bulk of our completed questionnaires.

After much discussion and reflection, we constructed a questionnaire (see Appendix 7.A) with both quantitative, objectively scored questions and qualitative, subjectively answered questions. Despite agreeing with Lauer and Asher (1988) that it is best to "use questions that have been shown to be useful and non-ambiguous in prior studies," (p. 65) we knew that research into writing center Websites was a new area of inquiry and could provide only limited guidance; therefore, we compiled questions posed by Waldo and ourselves and, in keeping with Lauer and Asher's advice, edited them for "directness, simplicity, and clarity" (p. 65). The quantitative data gathered provided us with generalizations, trends, or patterns about the Website's major strengths and weaknesses, whereas the qualitative answers enabled us to gather individual client voices and visions about the Website.

APPENDIX 7.A:
WRITING CENTER WEBSITE QUESTIONNAIRE

http://www.unr.edu/unr/coll eges/artsnscience/wc/index.html

Please answer the following questions by circling the appropriate number: #1 is "Least" and #5 is "Most." Do not put your name on this. When you are finished, please return this questionnaire to the envelope posted outside room 211 in Ross Hall or to the front desk at the Writing Center.

1. How easy was it to navigate through this Website?
        1 2 3 4 5

2. How informative was the Website in explaining the purpose of the Writing Center?
        1 2 3 4 5

3. How helpful was the Website in setting up a Writing Center appointment?
        1 2 3 4 5

4. How helpful was the Website for finding online resources?
    1 2 3 4 5

5. In general, how appealing was the Website?
    1 2 3 4 5

Please answer the following questions in the space provided. If necessary, please feel free to continue on the back of this sheet.

1. What are some tools/features you would like to see on the Website in the future?

2. In general, what do you want to find on a Writing Center Website?

3. How did the Website influence your decision to visit the Writing Center?

As instructors in the Department of English at UNR, each of us distributed questionnaires in our classrooms. We also asked colleagues to tell their students about the Website and to give them questionnaires. Additionally, we placed questionnaires at various computer labs on campus, hoping to elicit responses from a diverse range of Website browsers. A total of 300 questionnaires were distributed. Of those, we received 93 completed questionnaires. Although a response rate of only 31% is rather low, achieving a higher rate entails some difficulties—particularly the need for clients to go online to visit the Website before answering the questionnaire. Thus, we faced a dilemma that other first-time writing center Websites may encounter. Namely, in order to make a site genuinely appealing and useful for its audience, good feedback is necessary. However, an active audience may not yet exist.

We approached interpreting the quantitative data in general terms, looking for major trends or patterns (see Table 7.1). These quantitative responses provided us with a basic impression of clients' thoughts about the Website. Based on the responses to Question 1, most clients found navigating the Website fairly easy (79% answered with a 4 or 5). Responses to Question 2 suggest that most clients (78% answered with a 4 or 5) found the Website informative in explaining the writing center's descriptive rather than prescriptive style of tutoring and philosophy strongly committed to WAC. Responses to Question 4 suggest that in terms of finding online resources, clients also found the Website helpful (76% answered with a 4 or 5). However, Questions 3 and 5 raised areas of possible concern. Question

Table 7.1

Quantitative Results Tabulated From Questionnaires

	Questions Asked	Least				Most
		1	*2*	*3*	*4*	*5*
1.	How easy was it to navigate through the Website?	2	3	14	33	41
2.	How informative was the Website in explaining the purpose of the Writing Center?	1	3	15	48	26
3.	How helpful do you think the Website would be in setting up a writing center appointment?	11	5	27	32	18
4.	How helpful was the Website for finding online resources?	1	2	20	50	20
5.	In general, how appealing was the Website?	6	9	27	32	19

3—which 16% of the clients answered with a 1 or 2—indicated that some students did not find the Website helpful in scheduling appointments. Interestingly, at about the same time we began receiving completed questionnaires, Waldo expressed similar concerns about posting instructions on how to make an appointment at the writing center. Waldo envisioned the Website as teaching clients the process of making an appointment at the writing center—providing the writing center's telephone number and the name of a contact person. The need for such basic information was echoed by a student who asked, "Would you tell me how to make an appointment? Just phone? or go to your office directly?" In Question 5, 15% of the clients responding expressed a dissatisfaction with the general physical appeal of the Website; this concern became even more evident in the qualitative data.

Client comments pointed to more specific concerns. The most obvious of these was the need for colorful graphics to enhance the Website's appeal, friendliness, and playfulness. Not surprisingly, these comments echo current critical thinking. Jameson (1984), in his characterization of postmodernity, noted the precedence of play over seriousness, simulation over real, and surface over depth. Turkle (1995) connected Jameson's characteristics of postmodernity with the qualities of the new computer aesthetic. Client comments about the writing center Website seemed to reflect these expectations of playfulness, simulation, and surface features: "Make it these expectations of playfulness, simulation, and surface features: "Make it [the Website] more user friendly. More pictures (fun ones) (cartoons) and more colors would make it seem a lot more enticing. Also, perhaps a download section where you could get more visual things like the map of UNR. Overall very informative." A litany of comments repeated clients' expectations for a catchy and colorful Website. One client recommended that we put "more color into the page," another wanted "more visual stimuli," and yet another wanted the Website "links in color, more color overall, perhaps in subject headings." Similarly, one client noted that "more pictures are always helpful," and another client's statement that the "graphics are crude" reminded us that Web designers need to create aesthetically pleasing sites.

Another pattern arising from the comments centered around the need for examples of both client and instructor writing. Many clients expressed a desire to browse "examples of good student work online." Comments such as "it would be nice to view examples of good essays or papers," "maybe different examples of student writings," "more author's writings," and "maybe some examples so I could see how you critique papers" led us to consider the Website as a means for publishing client writing. Clients also expressed the need for an online questionnaire, asking that we "make the writing center questionnaire answerable right on the Website" and that "perhaps [clients should] be able to do the questionnaire online."

Clients provided many words of encouragement, particularly about links to other resources. One client said, "the ability to link up to other sources is wonderful" and another "I love the links to other writing centers, more would be even better." Similarly, one client appreciated the "proofreading tips," which "were great!" However, comments such as these seemed to contradict the writing center's collaborative, personal approach to tutoring and Waldo's intent for the Website to promote contact rather than acting as a clearinghouse for information.

Nevertheless, the Website did provide the impetus for some clients to visit the writing center's physical location. One client said that "the Website is the reason I went to the Writing Center." Another client noted that the Website "made me feel more comfortable to visit [the writing center] just because I now know more about what [the writing center] has to offer." Through questionnaire feedback, we discovered that client expectations were higher than our own. As novice Web engineers (working with a highly restricted campus server), we were providing an adequate service, but were still far from meeting clients' practical needs and visual desires. Clients seemed to be enthusiastic but, quite simply, anticipated "more!"

We also wanted to know more. We found ourselves asking basic questions: Where does an OWL get its inspiration and developmental support? What guidebooks are available for local pioneers? Perhaps the largest obstacle we had to overcome was self-confidence: We asked ourselves again and again, "Is what we're doing worthwhile? Is it useful?" In our attempts to explore further the role of Websites in writing centers, finding that so few people had chosen to write about this subject discouraged us, but we saw it as an opportunity to further knowledge in the field. Through repeated discussions with clients and colleagues, we saw the landmarks that we were connecting for ourselves and our university community. We are certain that we added a useful service to the existing operations of the UNR writing center, and we hope that we also provided a general model for fledgling Websites. In a WAC-based writing center, the Website is a way to reinforce the various and overlapping interdisciplinary connections across the curriculum, while simultaneously encouraging and emphasizing the face-to-face interaction that adds to these connections the attention, value, and sincerity of human communication. Through a concerted effort between clients, tutors, and directors, writing centers can expand their horizons without closing their doors.

8

Cyberspace and Sofas: Dialogic Spaces and the Making of an Online Writing Lab

Eric Miraglia
Joel Norris
Washington State University

Among the many concerns confronted by designers and administrators of OWLs, one issue is critically important: the need to provide a virtual space in which learning dialectics can be enacted with both social and epistemological richness. The interpersonal and ideological exchanges of face-to-face tutorials are rich with opportunities for writing and rewriting new truths, but those processes, social in structure and expression, can represent a daunting object of translation for creators of OWL spaces. Even if we reject, as perhaps we should, the pessimism of Postman (1992) about the role of computers in opening a posttextual episteme and the sinister associations Birkerts (1994) would have us make with the cathode glow of workstation monitors, we can't help but be cautious. What will learning dialectics look like when our OWLs are fully feathered and ready for flight? Will we have created a portal through which our best proximal pedagogies can be exported into the cybersphere? Will we have created something different, but equally rich, a new environment that facilitates student writers' epistemological processes? Will our worst fears have come to fruition—a glitzy, expensive virtual space that makes cyber-anxious administrators coo with pride, another overhyped hypertext? This chapter is, at its heart, the story of the asking of these questions during the creation of WSU's second-generation OWL, the story of the dialogic spaces that opened up as we proceeded, and the story of the dialogic spaces that continue to emerge as our OWL begins taking its tentative first flights.

We emphasize dialogic spaces because they are central to what our physical writing lab embodies. In the WSU writing lab, garage-sale lamps illuminate a scene of 1970s vintage side tables and couches whose personalities consistently outperform their looks. It's a place where you're sure you'll find a lava lamp if you look around long enough, where you can almost smell the incense. It's a place for people to be comfortable, to make eye contact, to put their feet up and talk. When they talk about the stories they want to craft, the truths they want to tell and retell, the words that will help them make new meanings for self and audience, you have the real sense of what dialogue is when it is honed to dialectic—that place, as Richards put it, where we enact "the *continuing* audit of meaning" (cited in Berthoff, 1984, p. 15). There is a special feeling in a place like that, a special feeling about the discovery of previously unmade meaning and the discovery of mechanisms for auditing meaning's dynamism and organic change; epiphanies, as it turns out, and the mild euphoria they induce, are contagious.

We emphasize dialogic spaces, too, because conversations emerged during our progress that both challenged and energized us and, ultimately, that convinced us that the successful translation–transmogrification of learning dialectics to an online space was attainable only through our own ongoing dialectical processes. As we organize our story around those processes, we hope to articulate what for us are the central dialogic spaces for creative exchanges during an OWL's creation. In these exchanges, directions are established that impact in crucial ways the probability that an OWL's raison d'être will be realized. It is not so much, we suggest, the specific outcome of the conversations that increases or decreases this probability; rather, the exchanges themselves, the provisional truths that they generate, serve as an indispensable foundation and as an invaluable heuristic for the creative process.

The key dialogic areas that emerged for us and that, we think, are applicable to the development of OWLs generally are as follows:

- *Progress and Priorities.* A dialogue that considers the needs of the proximal writing lab space, the potentialities and promise of an OWL as well as the attendant costs, and the general budgetary context.

- *Architecture and Carpentry.* A dialogue between those theorizing the space, practiced in the pedagogy and discourse of the proximal writing lab, and those who will build the space, whose expertise lies in theorizing the internal elegance of the system and its interface.
- *Cyberspace and Sofas.* An ongoing, increasingly rich dialogue between tutors about student–client writing in the OWL, one that helps invigorate the proximal lab in addition to supporting the online pedagogical work.

PROGRESS AND PRIORITIES

The creation of a meaningful OWL involves considerable resources—financial and otherwise. Because writing labs are not generally graced with lavish budgets, committing resources to virtual spaces at the expense of physical ones requires a negotiation that embraces theoretically sound Luddism, practical conservatism, and a prescience for new, unproven possibilities. At WSU, the provisional truths generated by this conversation persuaded us to proceed, and indeed, left us with little option but to proceed; grant monies were available to support online initiatives, whereas no special funding existed for the physical lab.

The successful "Virtual WSU Program" (VWSUP) grant (authored by Bill Condon, WSU Writing Programs Director, and Gary Brown, Associate Director of WSU's Center for Teaching and Learning) was itself at the crux of some debate. The VWSUP grant reviewers awarded $16,000 to the project from a fund contributed to the university by the Boeing Corporation—an amount that could purchase at least five modern workstations or a warehouse full of furniture nicer than what the writing lab had. Knowing that such an investment was allocated to the writing lab, but could not address the lab's most pressing needs, frustrated many for good reason: The start-up cost for the OWL equaled the annual operating budget for the physical writing lab. The writing lab community knew from the beginning that the grant, if awarded, wouldn't resolve pressing, proximal needs and would in fact broaden the lab tutors' responsibilities (they would serve both the physical lab and the new OWL); still, the grant budget made those proximal needs seem even more tangible, even more frustrating, and even more out of reach.

Developing online tutoring programs while maintaining the writing lab's proximal operations challenged us. The estimated budget for staffing the OWL's chatrooms 2 hours per day, Sunday through Thursday, for instance, exceeded $2,000 per semester—a prohibitive cost considering the writing lab's meager budget. Due to the writing lab's noise level and tutors' schedules, it was quickly deemed impractical, if not impossible, to cram a work-station dedicated to OWL interactions into the same small room where most of our writing lab's walk-in business occurs. Simultaneously, we worried that OWL tutoring (particularly chatroom discussions) might intrude on face-to-face discussions in the lab.

The dialogue that emerged from the tension between proximal needs and virtual promise helped shape the design strategies that characterized the process of creating the WSU OWL. We were all wary of the risk of reductivism; just because we could create an OWL, and just because someone would fund the project, didn't mean that it was a priori a good idea. The OWL's quality depended on its contribution to the lab's pedagogical mission; although the money had been earmarked for something new, the strings attached shouldn't prevent us from creating a space that demonstrably advanced the core mission of the writing lab proper. With this in mind, the team resolved early on to make the OWL serve the proximal lab in the following ways:

• **The OWL Would Broaden and Diversify the Writing Lab's Clientele**. By making the lab's services available to distant students and others who might not come to the lab in person, the client pool should increase; advertising and evangelizing would be geared to realizing this possibility. Moreover, the OWL would, we hoped, physically bring clients to the lab who otherwise might never have come; if the OWL experience was valuable, virtual visitors might become physical visitors. An increase in numbers could improve the lab's stature and its funding.

• **The OWL Would Help Strengthen the Writing Lab's Community of Tutors**. We envisioned two ways in which this might be accomplished. First, a significant portion of the OWL budget—half of it, in fact—would fund the salaries of OWL administrators, support tutor training, and purchase the computer hardware that would enable OWL administrators and tutors to access the site from the physical writing lab facility, all of which would tangibly benefit tutoring in the proximal space. Second, the OWL space would incorporate both public and private areas. For example, the Tutors' Private Parlor would house announcements of specific interest to tutors and provide a set of tutors-only chatrooms; customizable staff pages would help tutors add their own personal touches to the OWL, thus increasing, we hoped, their affiliation with the writing lab generally.

• **The OWL Would Help Stake Out Virtual Space as a Place Where Writing Lab Pedagogy and Values Have a Home**. We all know that designing and delivering multiple-choice tests and static syllaWebs via the Web is all too easy; computers lend themselves, as Aronowitz and Giroux (1993) put it, to replicating "the epistemological foundations of technological thinking that is rule, rather than context, driven" (p. 185). Writing labs are about nothing if not context; so, then, must be an OWL, and every small success we have in achieving that epistemological adherence moves the "foundations of technological thinking" ever so slightly in a positive direction. By creating a home in cyberspace for active, self-sponsored, and social learning, the writing lab would advance its own pedagogical values while simultaneously securing its position as the digital paradigm progresses. This last contribution of the OWL to the physical lab, although perhaps the least immediate and concrete, might prove to be the most important eventually.

These goals and commitments, in effect, describe a larger goal of making the OWL a true part of the writing lab itself, a human (as well as a virtual) extension thereof, and a project that explicitly benefits the entire writing lab community. The dialogic space spanning the tension between progress and priorities was crucial for us as we developed these goals; in some senses, it is a space we have yet to leave behind even as the WSU OWL is in production guise, entertaining guests and hosting active online interaction. We are still wrestling with strategies for making the OWL a more effective component of the writing lab of which it is a part.

ARCHITECTURE AND CARPENTRY

Our OWL-development team included both architects and carpenters: Writing lab staff, tutors, students, and learning technologies specialists knew what we needed to build, whereas graphic artists and programmers knew how to build it. So we thought. In many cases, team members wore more than one hat simultaneously, but a genuine diversity of creative stances was assembled. In the face of this heterogeneity, we discovered almost immediately something we already knew: Diverse professional positions were governed by diverse, sometimes incongruous, creative epistemologies. What we didn't already know, perhaps, was the degree to which our conversations in this dialogic space would lead to surprising, indispensable revisions to our overall conception of an OWL, nor the degree to which our collective epistemologies (as programmers, practitioners, etc.) would change in relation to this new pedagogical and technical medium.

The team assembled to design and build the WSU OWL brought experience and expertise to the table. Condon helped create the University of Michigan's OWL before coming to WSU, working on myriad learning technologies initiatives over the past 15 years. Brown, co-author of the grant with Condon, likewise ushered many learning technologies projects through planning and production. Johnson-Shull and Norris, respectively Director and Assistant Director of the Writing Lab, brought a sensitivity to the identity, mission, and history of the writing lab. Miraglia, Learning Technologies Specialist for the Student Advising and Learning Center, created the Virtual Classrooms Program on which the OWL was to be partially modeled; leading the tech team, the carpenters, he is also a compositionist—like Condon and Brown, a bridge between the architecture muse and the carpentry muse. Working with Miraglia, undergraduate Toby Taylor organized graphic design, and fellow undergraduate Pete Cihak worked with programming code; they represented both carpentry and a subset of the target (student) clientele. Others, too, contributed to the conversation, but this large, centrally concerned group indicates the range of voices.

We believed from the beginning that all members must be involved in the initial design of the OWL system; we wanted to avoid, if at all possible, the binarizing of the vision and development processes, even though different combinations of team members would be responsible for the two processes as they unfolded. That formative communication led, early and often, to divergent views about possible approaches. The dialogic roles adopted by the various team members contributed so much to this process that we began to notice ourselves adopting those roles habitually, with the explicit goal of generating productive dialogue.

Take, for instance, the issue of the OWL parlor, the page that welcomes users to the online space and directs their subsequent activity. Early on, the carpenters in the tech group (i.e., Miraglia, Taylor, Cihak) articulated varied design and programming options. Sensitive to an important rhetorical aspect of Web design, in which credibility among experienced Web travelers is often earned through successful, tasteful, and functional applications of advanced technologies, this group articulated rationales for embellishing the standard HTML fare; even javascripts or Shockwave elements could make the site's entrance visually and aurally impressive. Norris, Johnson-Shull, and others, thinking about novice Web travelers and about the range of potential OWL clientele, argued for a simpler approach. They realized that unnecessary paraphernalia could frustrate less-experienced and less-equipped users. Shockwave elements, for example, require a browser plug-in (something not all users know how to retrieve and install), often increase download time, and require additional RAM on the client's computer in order to function properly. Javascripts, although generally safe, can increase crashes. The pedagogical stakes, everyone realized, were extraordinarily high; a potential OWL client already uncertain about sharing writing, let alone sharing it online, might sustain very few dissuasive ripples in his virtual pond before rowing back to shore.

The parlor design that emerged from this conversation (see Fig. 8.1) emblematizes the philosophy we subsequently adopted in planning the remainder of the system. Simple and, we hoped, at least moderately elegant, this home page welcomes the user to the OWL and offers a series of doors into the OWL's other significant spaces.

This design philosophy attempts to get technology out of the way of what was really important: the social, interactive spaces in which patrons and tutors could interact. Moving beyond the e-mail paradigm meant making spaces accessible and unencumbered; to foster the many-to-many interactions we envisioned tutors and patrons needed straightforward, streamlined

FIG. 8.1. OWL Entrance or Parlor.

access to one another's writing with as little administrative overhead as possible. Although the administrative apparatuses were necessary—without log-ins and identification we could not track the usage and demographics crucial for sustaining long-term funding—we attempted to make the ingress into the social spaces as seamless as possible.

The dialogue between architects and carpenters continued as we designed and constructed these social spaces. The asynchronous Writers' Exchange, the primary interactive space in the WSU OWL, presented varied problems and opportunities. We had good, time-proven models on which to base our work (HyperNews and Usenet are two environments we considered), but we had a long shopping list as well:

• **Simplicity**. The Writers' Exchange, like the rest of the OWL, should rely on mainstream technologies—in this case, simple Web pages that required neither plug-ins nor other special software. The architects, again, emphasized consistency and ease of use.

• **Sophistication**. The system should accommodate the user's specific needs. The carpenters continually attempted to add power and functionality without compromising ease of use. The patron should not have to know, for example, that the Writers' Exchange looked different to a tutor, displaying more information; likewise, tutors do not need to know that an administrator would see links, buttons, and flags that were hidden to them. The pages could be customized without compromising the simplicity of the interface.

• **Publicness**. The writing lab already sported an online presence, an OWL that used e-mail for communications between tutors and patrons. The move to a Web-based social presence represented a move, too, to a more public forum; the social spaces therein, we thought, should constitute a one-to-many or many-to-many paradigm in place of the e-mail OWL's one-to-one paradigm; this publicness could encourage patrons to respond to one another's writing, encourage tutors to share their own writing with each other as well as with patrons, promote a culture in which the clients were as much an audience and a resource as the tutors. The spaces themselves would not create the activity or the culture, but they would invite such activity and provide a foundation for such a culture to develop.

• **Privacy**. Audience should always be a matter of choice, particularly in an academic environment; although use of the OWL might be self-sponsored, the writing shared in the OWL might not be, and we anticipated times when such writing might not be appropriate for public consumption. Patrons could choose to share their writing with the entire community or to limit the viewership to the OWL tutors.

• **Active passivity.** We wanted the Writers' Exchange to be a place where patrons came to share their writing and read the writing of others; in this sense, it would be a passive site. Responses to their writing would not be delivered to them (e.g., via e-mail), as this would tend to undermine the relation between the space and the people who inhabited it. On the other hand, the site should be smart enough to notify people when they received responses to their writing (if they wanted such a reminder). The passivity of the site should thus not be entirely inactive; the interactions within the site should generate active invitations to the community to return to the space, to reconnect with the conversation, and (we hoped) to engage the conversation further.

The Writers' Exchange, which evolved from this shopping list (see Fig. 8.2), negotiated between architects and carpenters, shares the warmth and simplicity of the parlor while providing community members access to one another's writing and collecting the necessary information to customize features and gather data for administrative analysis.

The organization, which employs tables, frames, and multiple pages to enable navigation through threads and conversations, had to handle much information: More than 400 shared pieces and responses were submitted to the OWL in its first 3 months of operation. Keeping the Writers' Exchange lean and navigable—keeping the apparatus itself as well as old conversations out of the way of new conversations and interactions—was a central concern.

The synchronous Talking Text spaces presented similar opportunities for technical sophistication or simplicity; simultaneously, it invited important questions about what kinds of discourse an OWL should foster. We questioned how and if synchronous chatrooms would enhance the OWL. Although we noted that chatroom discourse often failed to mirror the reflection that we thought appropriate, we recognized, too, that the synchronous exchange of the writing lab itself often derives its best energies from a lack of reflection, from the rapid and spontaneous exchange of ideas that could only happen online in a similarly synchronous space. Opting to provide such a space, we found ourselves in a familiar dilemma. The architects adhered to their doctrine of "simple is better;" the carpenters knew that simple Web pages, without the embellishment of other information-transfer protocols, do not lend themselves well to synchronous discourse. The compromise that emerged (see Fig. 8.3) adapted a frameset with two panels, wherein the top panel displayed the ongoing chat and the bottom panel provided a console for contributing to the conversation. The top panel, although consisting of a simple Web page, automatically refreshed every 15 seconds.

Believing that synchronous communication would only happen if we could make clients aware of one another's presence in the OWL, we created an interface on the OWL parlor to notify visitors of current chatroom activity. Moreover, we provided an interface for tutors to announce their presence in a chatroom; tutors' announcements, which would constitute an open invitation to visitors to discuss their questions synchronously rather than asynchronously, are also posted on the OWL parlor in addition to appearing in the Talking Text forum itself. This idea parallels our proximal writing lab space. Whenever possible, visitors to the lab are greeted by a tutor as they walk in the door, establishing immediate social contact. Although not staffing the OWL's Talking Text environment at all hours, we wanted to make sure that such contact was possible when tutors were available; because the

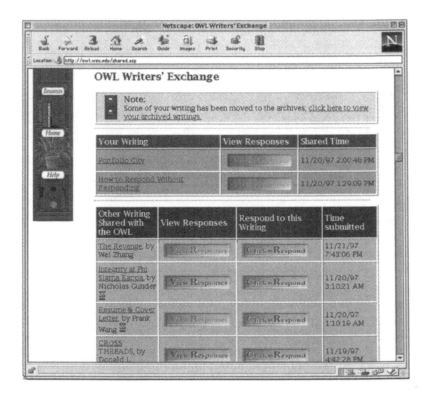

FIG. 8.2. The Writers' Exchange

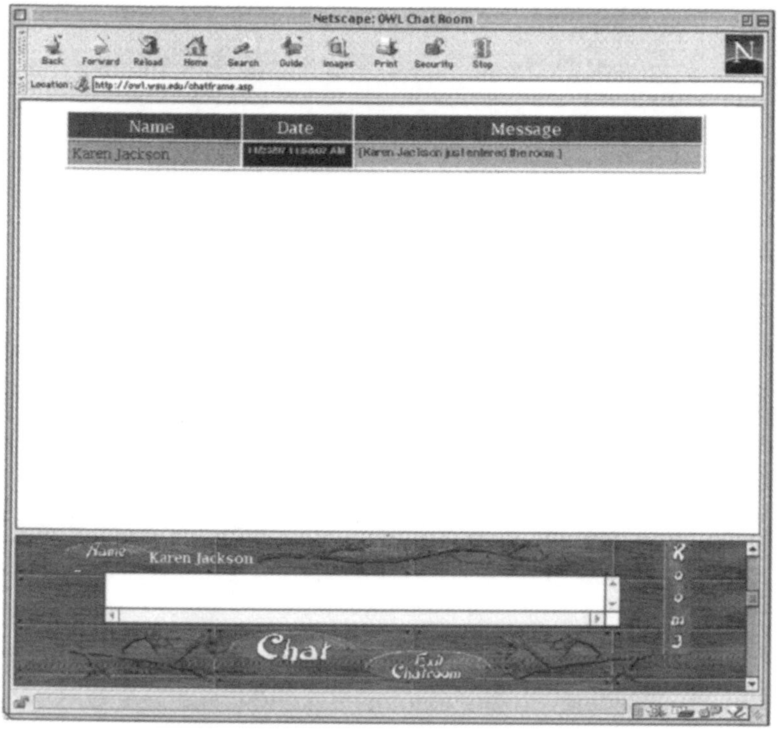

FIG. 8.3. Inside a Talking Text Environment (Chatroom).

writing lab is built on a foundation of social epistemology and social learning, we were committed to facilitating social interaction within the OWL in every way we could. (In Fig. 8.4, for example, the OWL entrance or parlor is seen with an indication that a tutor is present in Chatroom 3 and a further indication of activity in that chatroom. The graphical display of trees on the right side of the box offers direct ingress to the chatrooms[1]; "Hooey the Helpful Owl" is seen standing in the chatroom door of active rooms, helping users locate likely forums for so-

---

[1]Direct ingress from this interface, or from any other interface, is enabled only when the user is logged in. Our team determined in its development of the Talking Text space that we would not support anonymous chat interactions; rather, we would limit the use of chatrooms to individuals who had taken the time to create an OWL account and were currently "signed on." We hoped that this move would help us maintain a degree of accountability and respect in the synchronous spaces, where writers might be found sharing their thoughts and insecurities about writing. The tendency we had noticed in public, anonymous chatrooms toward less-than-respectful dialogue would, we felt, be detrimental to the project of the OWL in nourishing writers' enthusiasm for writing and being read.

cial interaction.) This functionality, too, seemed consistent with the principles which were opened up by our dialogue between architects and carpenters.

The parlor, which we wished to keep simple, would remain unencumbered by the chatroom announcements when they were inactive; when the possibility of synchronous contact existed, the parlor contains the announcement. No complicated work occurs by the visitor; the server decides what the page should look like based on current activity, but when synchronous contact is available, the OWL facilitates that contact.

CYBERSPACE AND SOFAS

Sustaining the spirit of peer tutoring within a technological framework is admittedly difficult. We wondered whether the collaborative episteme in our physical writing lab would translate virtually: Would the furniture of our tutoring methodology match our technological floor plan? From the outset, we

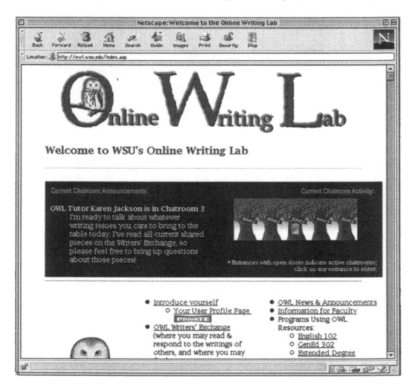

FIG. 8.4. Talking Text Announcements on the OWL Entrance Page.

wished to develop a conversational writing space through the OWL, a space, much like Ede's (1989) "Burkean parlor center," where dialogues of and concerning writing could continue even after the initial exchanges between OWL users and tutors ceased (p. 6). Although we feared that bringing such a space to fruition would be difficult due to our tutors' lack of experience responding to writing with writing (for the most part, our writing lab is a true peer tutoring center), we knew that our tutors were experts at deriving authority for themselves and the learning they promote through a paradigm of voluntary social interaction, organizing themselves—as Kail and Trimbur (1987) advocated more than 10 years ago—as co-learners with students in critical, knowledge-building conversations outside the hierarchical constraints of the academy (p. 9). We felt compelled, then, to avoid the authority-laden, monolithic responses of expert-to-novice e-mail exchanges in favor of more open-ended, discursive dialogues derived from multiple authorized and unauthorized voices. We wished to foster opportunities for tutors and students to express their ideas and concerns in writing, and to see them respond to each others' writing and to their processes of responding to writing. In short, we wished to see the collaborative, peer-to-peer dialogic spaces of our writing lab sofas interpenetrate the dialogic realm of the OWL, each informing, nourishing, and growing from the other.

The online written exchanges did not disappoint. Between October and December of 1997, more than 200 individuals shared their writing on the OWL, and more than twice that number responded to writing—an impressive debut, we thought, for such a fledgling space and such a protean online community. In sometimes extraordinarily short periods of time, students and tutors critiqued, questioned, and revised the OWL's shared writing. They shared essays, poems, reports, segments of dissertations, and even conference proposals. The dialogic interaction that we sought to achieve through the OWL occurred with great energy and activity, and the quality of the OWL interactions stunned us. A casual glance at the following response thread for one student's paper, for instance, yields considerable insight into the interior and exterior dialogues shaping the OWL participants' negotiations of their collaborative processes.

Response History for *I Haven't Decided Yet*

I haven't decided yet, by Matt (11/6/97 9:01:17 AM)

What is an argument?, by Kelly (11/6/97 3:48:09 PM) OWL TUTOR

A word on support, by Joel (11/6/97 3:51:19 PM) OWL TUTOR

Factual error, by Jennie (11/8/97 4:37:06 PM)

I KNOW!!, by Matt (11/9/97 9:26:15 PM)

Good!, by Jennie (11/11/97 6:46:38 AM)

"I Haven't Decided Yet," a clearly probationary title to a paper on the Equal Rights Amendment written by a student named Matt, attests to his consciousness of the online dialogue he is entering. The responses of tutors Kelly and Joel also are dialogic in nature; the first, "What is an argument?", invites Matt to respond to a direct question, and the second, "A word on support," suggests research paper conventions. Yet, it is Matt's retort to the third response that illustrates his willingness to establish authority over the emerging conversation. His "I KNOW!!" rejoinder to Jennie's matter-of-factly entitled, "Factual error," is clearly emotive, defensive, but it also indicates the kind of questioning and claiming of authority we wished the OWL to endorse for its patrons.

I KNOW!! by Matt (11/9/97 9:26:15 PM)

Dear Jennie,

I did know that the military goes to the house of these people who die in the military. But first of all that part was just a made up story. If that is okay with you. But I thought that the object of your response was to read the essay and give opinions on how to make the paper better. Although it is obvious that you can't look into a paper enough to find things other than the ones that are blatantly obvious. Please I would just like opinions to make my paper better. That was my rough draft and I was just thinking of some sort of an ending. That was not the ending I planned on using in my final paper. If you would suggest an idea that I could use that would be more helpful if you could.

Matt's response to Jennie (who questions whether the military would use an answering machine message, as in Matt's paper, instead of sending a personal representative to inform a family of a loved one killed in the line of duty) demonstrates how multivoiced dialogues can flatten hierarchical structures of authority. Jennie, correct as she may be, is not off the hook once she has posted her response. Matt feels more than comfortable, perhaps even compelled, to respond to her comment and clearly sees no transgression of etiquette in reminding his OWL respondents to recenter on his needs as an author.

This kind of full participation, we feel, is critical to the ongoing construction and authorization of knowledge necessary to sustain collaborative dialogues online. As Clark (1990) pointed out:

> If the consensus that contributes to the definition and direction of a community is to be the product of collaboration rather than of coercion, the written texts that address that community, like spoken statements, must be submitted to the very process of critical exchange that it is their nature to resist (pp. 51–52).

This full participation can only occur if the dialogue participants also subscribe to common social values and beliefs that coordinate their collective action. Tutors who respond to students online are responsible not only for providing thoughtful and constructive feedback, but also for encouraging safe and generative spaces for students' personal reflections to take on social expression. We have seldom seen Clark's admonition more explicitly enacted than in this early OWL exchange between Matt and his peer and tutor respondents. This interaction represents, for us, the successful movement of the discourse of writing lab sofaspace into OWL cyberspace; even if not all OWL patrons engage as full participants to the extent that Matt does here, the case can still be made that such participation is possible within the cyber-confines of the OWL's Writers' Exchange.

This thinking guided us as we prepared to introduce the OWL to our writing lab tutors. Although we wanted to promote and sustain democratic dialogues, we were not sure how to do so. After nearly 1 month of agonizing over guidelines, we decided to let the tutors figure it out for themselves, whittling our extensive material down to a single constraint: Our tutors can never post a response to the OWL until at least one other tutor reviews that response and signs it as co-author. This methodology has encouraged rich, ongoing dialogues between tutors on how to best achieve collaboration online and in face-to-face tutorials. The dialogues that occur on the sofaspace of our writing lab are often instigated and sustained by the challenges the tutors face in constructing their cyberspace dialogues. These ad hoc sofaspace symposiums on online conversations have led to fascinating metacritical dialogues within the OWL. Observe, for example, how two tutors, Jon and Sarah, respond to Eric, a student who critiques a paper written by his classmate Somer. Eric's response appears first followed by responses written by Jon and Sarah:

Thoughts on Somer's "The Lovepet" interpretation essay by Eric (10/14/97 5:47:50 PM)

Your introduction seems to be missing (you know, it ends with a thesis sentence and introduces the poem while going from a broad opening sentence). Without it, the reader gets lost quickly on the subject of what the essay is about.

I hate to be rude but what opinion are you trying to put forth? This is an essay, after all. Your essay seems more like an unassertive summary.

Cut to the Quick by Jon and Sarah (10/14/97 8:49:55 PM) OWL TUTOR

Ouch! In your response to the essay on "The Lovepet," I noticed little to no constructive, but a lot of criticism. Might you have included "just a spoonful of sugar" to help "the medicine go down?"

In addition to this comment, Sarah offers an example of how such constructive criticism might be written.

my response by Sarah (10/14/97 8:35:44 PM) OWL TUTOR

Dear Somer,

You have a lot of good ideas and I like your organization. A couple of ideas: You need an intro and a thesis. I don't see any here. If you do have one, you might want to make it a little more obvious. Your first paragraph would be great as a second paragraph, though. Also, although you have good ideas, you need to expand on them more. What makes these ideas significant? What do you think about them? What does the author want the reader to get out of this poem? These are just a few questions to help you.

You have a good framework for your essay. All you need to do is build on it. Keep up the good work!

When Eric tells Somer what's wrong with her paper, he engages her in a dialogue that instigates a subsequent sofaspace dialogue between Jon and Sarah about the nature of online tutorials. This secondary dialogue occurs outside of the OWL as Jon and Sarah negotiate the expectations of the collaborative community. In this case, as in so many we have witnessed in the OWL's early months, the sofaspace conversation moves back into cyberspace, this time in the form of the tutors' metacritical response to Eric. This secondary dialogue can be asynchronous and virtual, as writers attempt to meet the demands of producing knowledge (as was the case between the tutors Jon and Sarah and the patron Eric), or it can occur face to face, as was the case with Jon and Sarah as they discussed Somer's work and Eric's response. The latter dialogue led not only to the tutors' comment to Eric about the art of responding, but also to a further contribution to the conversation: Knowing that Eric probably did not realize his response to Somer's paper would be misconstrued as abrasive or terse, Sarah and Jon modeled a more sensitive and productive response.

As our tutors have become more familiar with online tutoring, they have engineered new, innovative ways to solicit tutoring assistance from their peers. Although it is not uncommon for a pair of tutors to read and respond to a student's paper simultaneously, some tutors, especially for longer essays, print a paper posted to the OWL and share it with their writing lab peers for review. The tutors may then choose to either write their individual comments on the paper or simply advise the tutor who printed the paper how to best respond to the writer's needs. Thus, it is not uncommon for three or more tutors to review a student's paper, and the comments of their peers, before a response is posted online; because this process allows for so many points of view to be woven into the fabric of the OWL staff's response, students can often receive a great deal of feedback from tutors quickly. Tutors may also opt to respond to a student's paper and then ask a peer to review both the paper and the response before posting it to the OWL. Although tutors sometimes provide only a cursory signature to a response after reviewing the written comments of their peers, we often see tutors provide detailed feedback concerning the nature of responses before they are posted online. Occasionally, these conversations last up to 30 minutes or longer. These dialogic processes outside of the OWL—in the writing lab's sofaspace—offer tutors multiple opportunities to share ideas nonconfrontationally and productively. Whereas one tutor may pour over a student's paper in search of grammatical or mechanical errors, another tutor may simply ask a student for clarification about her thesis statement. Without rigidly enforced hierarchical restrictions on how best to respond to the writing shared on the OWL (other than the writer's questions or concerns), tutors can work from their strengths, developing and drafting comprehensive insights into student writing. Furthermore, the process allows tutors to observe their peers' response strategies for handling writing issues that they may feel uncomfortable dealing with alone.

Our tutors base their practice on a response heuristic of higher-order and lower-order concerns, much like those described by Leahy in the April 1998 edition of *The Writing Lab Newsletter*. Our response hierarchy, however, is based directly on the evaluative criteria for the WSU Writing Program's Freshman Placement Exam and Junior Writing Portfolio: Tutors review student writing for issues related to (in descending order of importance) focus, organization, support, and proofreading. However, as the volume of OWL postings increases, the need for more structured methods of tutor–patron interaction has become necessary. In this respect, the OWL has had a tremendous impact on tutor training. Tutors have created a database of Websites concerning writing mechanics and common writing problems; they have drafted handouts on Internet citation styles, proper punctuation, common sentence structures, and methods of supporting an argument; additionally, they have planned a tutor training handbook on higher- and lower-order concerns. For us, this has been one of the most surprising and most rewarding aspects of the OWL, a true enrichment of the sofaspace catalyzed by our work within cyberspace.

THE CONVERSATION CONTINUES

It is more than just a cliché to note that the WSU OWL itself, the communities that have formed within it or around it, and the processes of revising and interacting with it are works in progress. The nature of writing and writing instruction is changing dramatically with the advent of word processing, desktop publishing, hypertext and hypermedia, and—perhaps most importantly—widespread social and cultural penetration of networked computing environments. The tools that mediate our contact with cyberspace, personal computers in all their desktop, laptop, palmtop forms, are themselves changing with dizzying speed; the state-of-the-art in personal computing continues to befuddle, always disappearing chimera-like around the next bend in the infobahn. Moreover, our expectations about the role of digital technologies in the making of meaning change apace with these advancements, and, as the culture shifts, so do our expectations of the learning environments in which we refine our efforts to advance literacy broadly defined. Suffice it to say that next year's OWL, the next decade's OWL, will almost certainly be much different than what we imagine today. What we are proposing here is that the dialogic spaces that open up in the process of building online learning spaces like OWLs will continue to be inhabited by rich discourses, and those discourses will continue to be the primary energy that we will harness in shaping and maintaining tomorrow's virtual learning spaces.

As a result of the pedagogical challenges they confront, OWLs will continue to represent the cutting edge in designing online learning spaces. Exposing the private beliefs of written texts to critical public forums can be challenging and painful, even in the warmest, most supportive arenas. The critical spectrum of responses to which a student can be exposed through online tutoring environments, such as the Writers' Exchange, means tutors must closely watch these human issues and means the environment itself must provide a semantic depth that allows for the conveyance of interpersonal cues. OWL tutors must regularly perform close readings of writers' intentions, some of which will be explicit, others not. For example, we emphasize that although the surface exchange of ideas concerning texts is important, discussions of subject matter really underwrite a much more complex and socially dynamic dialogue, a dialogue of knowledge-producing selves seeking dialectical negotiation with the defining narratives that constitute their sociocultural milieu. Yet, this training, even at its most successful and with experienced tutors, means nothing if the environment we provide for online tutoring fails to allow for such interactive richness. The Writers' Exchange of the WSU OWL, because of its palimpsestic design and its warm visual representation of these textual conversations, offers tutors and students opportunities to learn how their writing will be received within their own milieu in ways that our previous e-mail efforts failed to do. Yet, the potential to do more, to create richer spaces with increasing sensitivities and increasing capacities for interactive immediacy, continues to send us back to the drawing board, wondering how we can improve on what works and how to revise those elements that do not work.

That negotiation process, like the processes we enact as tutors within the online spaces, can be quite difficult. Still, we are as encouraged by what we see on the road we have taken as we are enticed by the roads not taken (e.g., MOO–OWL models, live and/or streaming video, etc.) and the roads still unfolding before us (e.g., Web-based document sharing with trustworthy security models, bandwidth expansions opening up new possibilities for graphical and video-based representation of ideas and identities, etc.). The WSU OWL's Writers' Exchange has provided a space for reflection and discussion, generating wonderful, successful dialogues about tutoring in our physical writing lab as well as on the OWL. We hope OWLs will continue to encourage these ongoing conversations between teachers and designers, tutors and users, and tutors and tutors; the sofas of all our various Burkean parlors, virtual or otherwise, should continue to be well-worn.

9

Advice to the Linelorn: Crossing State Borders and the Politics of Cyberspace

Jennifer Jordan-Henley
Roane State Community College
Barry M. Maid
University of Arkansas at Little Rock

As we approach the 21st century and find ourselves electronically linked to the entire globe, having students in Arkansas tutor students in Tennessee should be as easy as driving across the I40 bridge from Arkansas to Tennessee. While the Internet eliminates many boundaries, state legislatures (which control funding of state institutions) and internal politics (which can exist both between schools and among departments and individuals at those schools) sometimes hinder students at either location from serving one another. Beginning the Cyberspace Writing Center Consultation Project, however, we gave little thought to such political boundaries.

THE PROJECT

The Cyberspace Writing Center Consultation Project was conceived online in the spring of 1994 after one of the Netoric Project's Tuesday Cafés on

105

MediaMOO. Prolific users of e-mail, we discussed how a combination of asynchronous communication and the synchronous communication of MOOspace could benefit our students. Brainstorming collaboratively on MediaMOO, we considered having Jordan-Henley's community college students e-mail their essays to Maid's graduate students, who would then comment on the drafts and arrange a MOO meeting for further discussion. The community college students receive writing consultations; the graduate students gain exposure to community college students and additional teaching experience. And all students encounter online learning and teaching, supplementing the traditional classroom experience with active learning. The emerging technologies provided both the impetus and the place to create the project.

Creating the project in the late spring and early summer of 1994, we primarily focused on meeting the needs of both sets of students. Our exhilaration caused both of us, initially, to remain unaware of the internal problems and politics at our respective institutions. Likewise, we never dreamed that working at different kinds of institutions in different states would continually threaten the project, regardless of results and educational value.

Internal Politics and Institutional Problems

We began planning enthusiastically, not realizing that insufficient Internet access might hinder our efforts. In the spring of 1994, Maid's office Macintosh IISI was hard-wired to the Internet, allowing him to access his campus VAX using Versaterm, to access e-mail using VAX mail, and to telnet to one MOO at a time. Using his 2,400-baud modem and Mac LCII, he could dial up from home, accessing his VAX account with Versaterm. Unless University of Arkansas at Little Rock (UALR) students had home computers with modems, they could access the Internet only through a computer lab, equipped with 25 DEC dummy terminals, in the UALR library. In addition, Maid needed students to participate as his first cybertutors.

Fortunately, the fledging UALR Department of Rhetoric and Writing was moving in the summer of 1994, a move that resulted in the department gaining an ethernet connection through an AppleTalk network. Although still stymied by VAX mail, Maid could now conduct multiple telnet sessions. He also got four of the UALR writing center's Mac Classics hooked into the net, but unfortunately, the insufficient memory of the Classics prevented students from having word processing and e-mail or MOO sessions running concurrently. As for staffing the cyberspace writing center, Maid enhanced the curriculum of his graduate seminar—Working With Writers—to include a unit on working with writers in cyberspace.

Jordan-Henley, meanwhile, used a Mac SE30 in her office and had one additional line installed on another Mac SE30, specifically for the project, in the Roane State Community College (RSCC) writing center she directs. The monitors were small, black-and-white affairs without the ability to scroll up and down while telnetting. She could telnet to one MOO at a time and had a similar capability at home, where she used a Compaq 286. Thus, Jordan-Henley's students shared one computer, standing in line to e-mail their essays to UALR and scheduling MOO discussions one at a time.

In some respects, RSCC, a small college with fewer resources than UALR, entered the project seriously disadvantaged. Because the Internet connection was new to instructors, no one taught courses that used online capabilities. The system administrator, although supportive, wondered how something called a MOO could be used in classes, and e-mail accounts were not yet assigned to students. The school was also aligned with another college's hub and therefore affected by its problems, operating whims, and slow access, and no money existed for new equipment. We both worked with others to overcome these problems and to ensure adequate access, but even after explaining the project thoroughly, we often caught confused looks from colleagues and administrators. People who had not visited a MOO struggled to make sense of our project. MOOing, like writing, is better learned by doing it than by listening to others talk about it.

On the other hand, the president of RSCC, Dr. Sherry Hoppe, supported new technologies and innovative teaching methods, specifically asking instructors to use the Internet. Tamsin Miller, Director of Community Services, under which Jordan-Henley's writing center falls, felt the same way and wanted to support the writing center's viability as it entered the 21st century. Additionally, because RSCC has seven locations in a 100-mile radius, all of the faculty, administration, and staff relied on e-mail. At the time, this was not the case at UALR, where close proximity meant that some of the campus offices Maid needed (such as the grants office) did not have e-mail themselves, making the sending of copies from Arkansas to Tennessee unnecessarily time-consuming.

With the four UALR writing center computers and a captive group of students, Maid could deliver, at a minimal level, his part of the project. However, both of us knew that we needed more resources, especially in the areas of hardware and networking to run the project at its full potential. The appropriate step at UALR would have been for Maid to request resources from his department chair. Interestingly, the UALR Department of Rhetoric and Writing was experiencing growing pains during the 1994–1995 academic year and had no department chair. Turning the chaos into an advantage, Maid drew on the personal contacts made during his 11 years in administration, beginning with the campus grants officer.

In preliminary talks with Andy Covington, the UALR Director of Research and Sponsored Programs, a good news–bad news scenario developed. The good news was that the project pushed the boundaries of emerging technologies and granting agencies liked that. The bad news was that it focused on the teaching of writing, an area that falls through the cracks. Maid also discerned from these initial conversations that most funding sources supported personnel more readily than equipment, and equipment was desperately needed.

Covington suggested that even though the project was conceived as a way to help first-year writing students at community colleges where writing centers may struggle to find and train appropriate peer tutors, the initial project could test the method and the technology. Then, we could search for grants that would broaden the project's scope, specifically in the areas of science. Currently, projects in science education are more fundable than those in teaching writing. That appears to be a political reality.

As a result, Maid's initial efforts for external funding were directed to two National Science Foundation (NSF) Grants, one for Teacher Enhancement, the other for Instructional Materials; both were begun before a single student went online. Neither grant application was successful; however, the Teacher Enhancement Grant proved valuable later. While planning to write these two grants, we faced other political realities.

When money is involved, two colleges may struggle to work together. When one of those colleges is a 4-year university and the other a community college and when the two institutions have no track record of collaboration, both sides look suspiciously at the other. As project administrators, we learned early on that we had to establish trust between us before expecting our institutions to do the same. We therefore sought to clarify our intentions regarding the project, agreeing that the project should benefit both sides equally. Had we known each other for years, this process might have been easier. But we had not even met in person, a situation we rectified before the summer ended. In writing, we also established ground rules and a method of sharing information and funding.

On her end, Jordan-Henley used UALR's grant applications to her advantage, keeping Dr. Hoppe, Miller, and even the system's administrator posted of its progress, simultaneously stressing the need for state-of-the-art equipment. Unfortunately, the grants officer left RSCC, and an interim employee took his place. After apprising this new person of the situation, Jordan-Henley backed off to give her time to adjust to her position. By the time the interim grants officer felt established, however, a permanent grants officer was hired, who is currently working on the project. Although frustrating, this was a matter over which Jordan-Henley had no control, so she turned her attention elsewhere.

At the same time Maid was writing the grants, Jordan-Henley wrote the necessary documents for the project, posting them first to the RSCC Gopher and later to the World Wide Web. These documents included the project's rationale; instructional information for the students, cybertutors, and other interested faculty; and evaluation material. She also verified that the project complied with Southern Association of Colleges and Schools (SACS) accreditation standards.

We presented a paper at the National Conference on Peer Tutoring in Writing (NCPTW) in Birmingham, Alabama, the same fall the project began. Again, keeping others posted helped smooth the way to deal with more specific problems, including access and equipment. But it also created problems. Understandably, administrators wanted to use the project in press releases. Although desiring to help our schools achieve their goals, we hesitated. The project had yet to begin. We held firm, deciding that we had to go through the process before highlighting it. Realizing that we were taking a professional risk with the project, we wanted to do so only if we felt comfortable with what we were doing. We were also concerned, however, with how the project and projects like it would be perceived. From that standpoint, discussing it before implementation seemed somewhat dangerous.

State Politics and Political Limitations

Despite these distractions, we actually built our virtual reality writing center (The WritingWorks) on both Daedalus MOO (logos.daedalus.com 7777) and CollegeTown MOO (galaxy.bvu.edu 7777) during the summer of 1994. We built the rooms, created objects, and programmed verbs. We fine-tuned procedures for both cybertutors and students. Maid also created *Cywrite*, a mail list for his tutors, so that we could communicate effectively and provide feedback.

As planned, our first cybertutoring sessions occurred in the fall of 1994. Despite a few problems, some of which were technology-based, we felt successful, and our students gave us high marks. By the end of the semester, we had been through two rounds of cybertutoring, and the project's success was evident. We expected responses from the academic community. We had presented at the NCPTW and had an article on the project coming out in *The Writing Lab Newsletter*. We talked about the project whenever we could and responded to inquiries, but we had to control the amount of time spent online as we accumulated e-mail from instructors nationwide. What we had not expected was potential support from the Arkansas State Legislature.

Unbeknownst to us, Arkansas State Representative Doug Wood of Sherwood had heard of our project from Jim Frazer, part-time lecturer in the UALR First-Year Composition program and full-time cyberjunkie. Early in 1995, while the Arkansas Legislature was in session, Wood visited the UALR campus where Maid showed him how the project worked. While looking over Maid's shoulder, Wood saw Maid and Jordan-Henley talk in real time on the MOO and toured the WritingWorks complex. The visit had an effect on Wood, as did our acceptance to deliver two more presentations, one at the Computers and Writing Conference in El Paso, Texas, and the other at the NWCA conference in St. Louis, Missouri. Seeing the technology's national implications, Wood requested a proposal that promoted collaboration between 2-year and 4-year campuses. However, Wood is an Arkansas legislator. The project he was willing to support would only include Arkansas schools.

Jordan-Henley did not have to remind Maid that this was a joint project and that RSCC must receive some kind of compensation, whether it be in training, dollars, or future gain. However, we both found that we would have to be creative, flexible, and firm to convince others. We also discovered that sharing the project equally did not mean that we had to do the same thing in different states. Our agreement changed accordingly.

Despite the volatile 1995 session of the Arkansas General Assembly, Representative Doug Wood placed a special line item in the UALR budget designating $125,000 for the Cyberspace Project. The budget was passed and signed by the governor. However, Arkansas has a balanced budget clause as part of its state constitution. After the budgets are passed and signed, a committee from the legislature and governor's staff prioritizes projects for funding. The project was placed in the C1 funding category, which usually means "nice try, come back next session." However, the strong Arkansas economy suggested that in January or February 1996, some C1 funds might be available. If even a small part of the project was funded, the legislature would want to see results for future funding to occur.

The problems this posed were immense. Although we initially conceived of training Arkansas Community College instructors in the summer, we had no funds to do this. Should any of this money be distributed throughout the year (and it might come as late as April with all funding to be spent by June 30), we would have to show that we used it appropriately. With this as a possibility, Maid secured a $9,000 grant from the Arkansas Department of Higher Education (ADHE) to train community college teachers in Arkansas. In August of 1995, Jordan-Henley joined Maid in Little Rock and team taught an intensive course to instructors from four targeted Arkansas community colleges: Westark Community College in Fort Smith, Garland County Community College in Hot Springs, East Arkansas Community College in Forest City, and Pulaski Technical College in North Little Rock. This summer course created a cadre of trained community college instructors who could then supervise Internet tutorial work on their campuses. Complicating matters, the ADHE, like other funding sources, is not interested in funding support for student writing, even when new technologies are involved. As a result, the grant Maid wrote was really a writing and computing-across-the-curriculum grant, which trained teams of writing- and math–science teachers to use the new technology in a collaborative effort between teachers of both disciplines on one campus and across the state. The workshop was successful, and the mix of teachers led to interesting discussions that could be continued using these new technologies. The training in Arkansas represents progress and suggests how our tutorial model might be used in other areas. Although we have the potential for an Arkansas network, nothing has been put into place yet.

As we wrote this, much still remained as uncertain as it was in 1994. We have identified and trained instructors in Arkansas community colleges, and Maid continues to work with two of the original community colleges. Because of UALR system politics, any other community colleges coming on board will be those recently aligned with the university system. Tennessee is going a different route, with an online consortium between community colleges from the very beginning.

HOW THE PROJECT HELPED US

We have learned a good deal about the pitfalls and pleasures of online teaching. It takes much more work and organizational skill to teach successfully online than in a traditional classroom, but the payoffs are worth it. We have developed more meaningful relationships with our students, who, in turn, are more prepared for the future. Our own interests have also changed focus.

We both support the ground swell for online teaching at our institutions. Jordan-Henley created an Online Writing Lab on the World Wide Web and an internal e-mail discussion group, *Compwrite*, for her composition classes. She developed and taught an introductory technical writing class entirely online, with students from as far away as Japan and Northern Canada. Her students actively use the Web, e-mail, the Cyberspace Project, and now RSCC's online library access. Maid developed and teaches a course in writing for the Web, which focuses not only on writing HTML, but also on the rhetoric of hypertext. He is working with compressed video to Fort Smith, Arkansas, and looking for ways to combine compressed video and computers. He now runs his own small educational MOO, ArkMOO (pathos.rhet.ualr.edu 8888).

In addition, we have published "MOOving Along the Information Superhighway: Writing Centers in Cyberspace" in *The Writing Lab Newsletter* (1995a) and "Tutoring in Cyberspace: Student Impact and College/University Collaboration" in *Computers and Composition* (1995b). We have given numerous workshops and presentations on the subject, together and individually. Although we are often considered experts in the field 50 miles or 5 minutes away, that is not always the case at our home institutions, where politics again affects day-to-day interaction. At different times we found ourselves in opposition with our physical colleagues; however, we believed in our project, in each other, and in our students.

During the first 2 years of the project, we made tremendous strides in our equipment and access. We both have more current desktop computers with ethernet access, and Jordan-Henley's writing center boasts eight new machines, all online and connected to an ethernet minihub of its own. The Cyberspace Project is largely responsible for making writing needs more visible in the RSCC community; Jordan-Henley's equipment has been upgraded while many other writing centers suffer from cutbacks or play second fiddle to science and mathematics. Next year, she moves into a new campus with a state-of-the-art center and new computers. Before the project, the architectural drawings placed the writing center in a tiny triangle lost amid a maze of faculty offices, but now it is much larger and located next to the library.

RSCC also serves as a larger hub itself, having broken away from the other college on which it once depended; all students have access to e-mail accounts. In 1994, RSCC had 3 networked labs and 9 modems connecting users to the system. In 1998, it featured 22 networked labs with full Internet and World Wide Web capabilities. Four multimedia electronic classrooms are complete, with more to come, and the campus has 38 modem lines available. One of the largest, most complex systems in the Tennessee Board of Regents system, RSCC rivals and even surpasses some 4-year colleges.

Things are also considerably different at UALR. In 1995, the new student microcomputer lab opened with 15 Power Macs and 18 Pentium machines. All of the machines have complete Internet access including World Wide Web capabilities. The spring of 1996 saw the opening of UALR's library computer lab, in which 26 Pentiums, all with complete Internet access, replaced the old dummy VAX terminals. Two of the library's Pentium machines and two of the microcomputer lab's Power Macs are equipped for the visually impaired. Finally, the old Mac SE's and Classics in the university writing center were replaced in the middle of the fall 1996 semester with a workgroup server and 18 low-end Power Macs, five of which were replaced with G3 Power Macs in 1998. Again, all machines have full Internet capability. UALR's dial-up capability increased in the spring of 1997 from 24 modem lines to 80 modem lines.

WHAT WE HAVE LEARNED

One of us hears, almost daily, cries for help from instructors whose institutions have not yet entered the online realm. The topic seems almost overwhelming, especially when instructors are learning a new teaching method at the same time they are learning how to use the technology, when they are being pressured to learn everything overnight, or when not enough system-support personnel exist to help all the people who need it. Our advice, then, is summarized as follows:

- Start something, anything, even if on a shoestring. Don't wait for the perfect access or the perfect computers. Prove that your project works first.
- Begin by adapting standard classes to new pedagogies and using online technology as a supplement. Don't decide to teach your class entirely online until your students work online on a part-time basis. More often than not, doing so creates failure, and students pay for the mistakes.
- Find supporters at your campus and keep them abreast of your work. Keep a history of the project, saving documents that outline the project in detail, including student evaluations. Post the information to a Gopher or to the World Wide Web. Hold firm if supporters want to help you too much, and ignore those who try to block your success.

- Pick your projects carefully, following the institution's mission. Write and publish whenever possible, realizing that you have to explain unfamiliar terms and give demonstrations constantly. Work locally by giving presentations to area high schools and related groups.

- Some people insist that any course is easily adapted to online technology. This is not the case. Although being flexible is important, use sound judgment as an instructor, knowing what works best with students and with your own teaching style. Courses usually fail when hastily created just so a department or school can add them to its new online curriculum. "Humanware" is just as important as hardware and software. Technology does not replace human beings; it makes the latter even more important.

- Online technology is labor intensive and poses problems in creation that do not occur in the regular classroom. Writing all the lectures for an online course, for instance, takes time no matter how well you know the material. Writing is different from speaking, and the instructor must consider making the coursework interesting without immediate discussion or feedback. Instructors frequently discover how much they depend on student questions and discussion to remind them of what they should cover or to clear up problem areas. If the instructors are also creating the Web pages (and they should to be able to make timely changes), the design process itself must be considered.

- If working with two schools, put key people in touch with one another, and ensure that everyone receives paperwork. Then follow up.

- Use chaos to your advantage.

- Seek grants and work around existing political realities. Work across the curriculum whenever possible, and work for change. Ignore matters over which you have no control, or point them out to someone who does. Check on accreditation standards.

- Discuss the ground rules with your partner, and create a contract. Be willing to modify the contract.

- Keep in mind that as an instructor, you must learn many new procedures yourself, including some programming, in order to run an online project successfully. Additionally, many of these procedures are outdated or updated quickly, making it difficult to stay current. Don't allow the tools or the seduction of new online avenues to interfere either with your current project or with the coursework itself. It is not necessary to become a heavy-duty programmer; it is more useful for you to communicate effectively with your system administrator and to foster a good relationship. Know what you want before you call for help, and try to figure it out yourself first. You will learn more that way.

- Remember your students. Be flexible, expecting the technology to fail from time to time. Prepare back-up procedures. Never expect your students to do something you have not done yourself. They will do so soon enough anyway.

The climate in which we work is complex and ever-changing. Those who work in it constantly fight the danger of drowning with each new wave. So do we, but anyone who regularly uses e-mail recognizes drowning as a distinct possibility. In truth, however, instructors interested in online technology can create their own rafts and life jackets by planning carefully, by anticipating problems, and by gasping for air at the right times. When those fail, as they will, and instructors find themselves snagged on political driftwood, then treading water and allowing the current to change their direction is a viable option. Who knows? Downstream may turn out to be even better.

III

Asynchronous Electronic Tutoring

10

The Asynchronous, Online Writing Session: A Two-Way Stab in the Dark?

Joanna Castner
Texas Tech University

New and multiple ways of interacting have been made possible by computer technology, and writing center consultants have been experimenting with ways to incorporate these new technologies into their practices for some time. It is becoming apparent, as Blythe pointed out in 1997, that these computer-mediated interactions fundamentally change the nature of the consultant–client relationship and that we are only beginning to discover how such changes affect writing center practice. This chapter contributes to this discovery process by describing some of the potential pitfalls of e-mail consulting.

The asynchronous nature of e-mail creates important advantages, especially for students who live off campus or who work most of their waking hours. Anyone can e-mail a draft at any time from virtually any computer and receive a response relatively quickly. Despite these advantages, however, e-mail does not seem to encourage sustained dialogue unless instructors make time for extended conversations. Jordan-Henley and Maid (1995b), for example, described a successful project in which graduate students at the University of Arkansas at Little Rock consulted with undergraduate students at Roane State Community College in Oak Ridge, Tennessee. Discussing their writing with consultants via e-mail and MOOs, many undergraduates felt the consultants helped them improve as writers, and many graduates found online consulting pedagogically useful because of its ability to sustain ongoing conversations about writing. Time for these online conversations was built into the class schedule, however, and participation was required.

Ongoing e-mail interactions between consultants and students do exist; Coogan (1995), in a *Computers and Composition* article, described such dialogue, and one of Texas Tech's online consultants has sustained dialogue with a client for almost 1 year now. Interestingly, both of the student examples above are graduate students, who may have bigger, yet fewer projects with more revision time than undergraduates. Such examples of e-mail dialogues are few, however. Out of 554 e-mail consultations over the course of 1 year at Texas Tech, only 12 resulted in continued dialogue, and 6 of those involved the graduate student previously mentioned. Although ongoing interaction is hard to maintain in any medium without institutional support, synchronous interactions involve dialogue at least during the consulting session. This is not true, however, of the one-time e-mail session.

A total lack of dialogue proves problematic for many reasons, especially if a writing center's online practices rely primarily on e-mail interaction. First, if a writing center aims to facilitate learning by believing in and acting on the social construction of knowledge, then failing to foster dialogue between consultant and client contradicts the center's guiding principles. Second, anyone who has consulted face to face knows that dialogue is necessary for consultant and client to understand the assignment, for the consultant to understand the client's questions, and for the client to understand the consultant's responses. Finally, a lack of dialogue between consultant and client promotes the wrong idea about the goal of writing centers and the nature of the writing process itself. Consultants do not want clients to perceive writing centers as fix-it shops for writing, places where writing can be repaired in one session. E-mail consulting without dialogue, however, may promote these ideas by giving the impression that clients can send off their texts to be fixed at the last minute by a voiceless editor.

WHY SO FEW DIALOGUES?

After finding that most e-mail consultations at Texas Tech's online writing center did not involve dialogue, I looked to students in my two sections of first-semester writing to find out why. I required these students to e-mail a draft of each essay to the online writing center for an e-mail response, which they did, but none of my students e-mailed any of the consultants with further questions or revised drafts. I wondered how many of those students had questions about consultants' responses. After printing each student's drafts and e-mail responses (two drafts and two responses per student), I asked the students to highlight or underline each part of the e-mail responses about which they had questions. Out of 29 students altogether, 13 indicated understanding everything in their e-mail responses, and 16 had questions. Perhaps many of the 542 students who used Texas Tech's online writing center did not respond after an initial online tutorial because they simply did not need to do so. On the other hand, my students' responses suggest that more than half of them may need extended dialogue.

The second part of the study attempted to discover why those with questions did not ask them by asking students one question: "Not very many students e-mail questions back to the writing consultant about the responses they receive, and I'd like to have your thoughts about this: Explain why you didn't e-mail questions to the writing consultant about the parts of the responses that were confusing." I conducted a content analysis of their answers after constructing categories based on their responses. After coding the responses, I waited 1 week and recoded for interrater reliability, agreeing with my first coding choices 100%. In addition, a second coder recoded the answers into the categories, with an agreement of 93%, using Holsti's (1969) formula for interrater reliability. The categories, along with the number and percentage of answers that fell into each, are discussed below; some students listed several reasons.

1. I did not e-mail questions because it takes too long to get an answer, failing to give me enough time to revise. Seven responses, or 41%, fell into this category, the largest by far. The time factor may be one of the biggest problems facing students who want to use e-mail consultations. Many times, once students have a draft, the project due date is near. For example, in the two sections of first-semester writing from which the participants of this study came, I pushed the due date of all projects back one class period to allow extra time for response. That semester, the online writing center had a 24- to 48-hour guaranteed response time. The first class project was due October 2nd, and we sent drafts to the online writing center September 23rd. That means the students would receive responses by the next period at the latest, September 25th, but they would have had to e-mail questions immediately to get a response by the next period, September 30th. Then they would have had only 1 night, 1 day, and 1 night to revise one more time. That tight schedule is hard to avoid on a semester schedule.

2. I did not e-mail questions because I am unfamiliar with e-mail and did not know how to e-mail questions to the consultant myself. This category held the second highest number of responses with three, or 18%. One student wrote, "I was still a bit intimidated by the e-mail system simply because I was unfamiliar with how it works." Another student wrote, "Many students, like myself, are not comfortable with the e-mail process. This discomfort can only be overcome by experience. Many students do not want to take the time to ask for help with e-mail." Those who send drafts to the online writing center on their own are most likely already familiar with e-mail; thus, this factor might only be a problem in classes where students are required to send drafts using e-mail.

3. I did not e-mail questions because it is too inconvenient to get to a computer to do so. This category tied with Category 4 for the third highest number of responses with two responses, or 12%. This problem increases for those students without computers who live off-campus. For on-campus students without computers, e-mail consultations are no more convenient than face-to-face or MOO consultations.

4. I did not e-mail questions because I chose other sources for help. This category tied with Category 3 for the third highest number of responses with two responses, or 12%. Two students listed friends as their readers, and the other one did not identify the source. As friends are readily available, they provide a good solution to students' time constraints. Perhaps other students who do not respond to online consultants ask friends for answers instead.

5. I did not e-mail questions because I did not know that I could. One student, making up 5% of the total responses, said that the nature of the response led him to believe that dialogue through e-mail was not customary: "I thought it was pretty much a done deal. They gave me their input, and I either used it or did not. There was no asking." This response occurred despite the consultant inviting this student to e-mail back any questions. Even so, perhaps e-mail consultants should more strongly encourage extended dialogue about revised drafts.

6. I did not e-mail questions because I was already so confused by the first response that I thought that asking questions would only add to my confusion. One student, 5%, explained that he believed further response would just confuse him more. Extended dialogue about writing, taking one or two aspects of the writing at a time, might help this student. Yet, again, this process can consume too much time given due date constraints and the 48-hour e-mail turnaround. Perhaps face-to-face or MOO consulting would be a better medium in this case. Both environments encourage immediate feedback, and in both media, the consultant can immediately address such confusion.

7. I did not e-mail questions because I did not view the response as help, but as a class requirement that did not help me revise my draft. One student, whose response made up 5% of the total responses, explained that sending drafts to the online writing center and receiving responses were hoops to jump through for class credit instead of activities that could help him become a better writer. Thus, he never considered asking further questions. This problem should not occur when students choose to use the online writing center.

This small study suggests that time constraints limit e-mail dialogues more than anything else. Unless the response time is extremely quick, students may be unable to engage in extended e-mail dialogues about writing. Thus, online writing centers may want to focus their services on immediate media such as MOOs, both to serve their students' needs better and to foster a social constructionist pedagogy.

DIALOGUE AND SOCIAL CONSTRUCTION THEORY

According to the *theory of social construction*, learning and creating knowledge requires dialogue. This theory guides the collaborative practices of many writing centers. Although collaboration can also be based on expressionist theory, the purpose, then, is to develop the individual genius of the client–student; collaboration based on social constructionist theory facilitates the negotiation of knowledge. Many writing centers in the 1970s and early 1980s based collaborative practices on expressionist theory, but by 1990, Hemmeter noted many centers' adherence to the principles of collaborative learning based on social construction (1990, p. 36).

Dialogue, whether it be face-to-face, online, or intertextual, is essential to a theory of social construction. Philosopher Mark Owen Webb (1995) described *social constructionist theory* as: "Beliefs of interesting and reflective kinds cannot be had without language; knowledge requires belief; and so knowledge requires language. Language is essentially social; so knowledge is essentially social" (p. 87). In short, people learn and create knowledge through interaction and negotiation with others. This theory has important implications for writing center pedagogy: People can learn a great deal about writing through dialogue of all types. Bruffee (1984) pointed out, "We can think because we can talk, and we think in ways we have learned to talk" (p. 640). Clients learn about writing by writing and discussing that writing with others. They learn to reshape their writing by discussing its effects on readers and potential readers.

Consultants should engage clients in dialogues about writing to facilitate the learning process. Academic writing conventions exemplify socially constructed knowledge about writing. Consultants act as a link between clients and knowledge about academic writing conventions. Clients learn to define and apply writing conventions, such as thesis statements and coherence, by discussing them in the context of their own writing with someone who understands those conventions already. Helping clients gain this knowledge and become proficient in using conventions allows consultants to empower students to write effectively within the academic community and models social negotiation.

Without dialogue, e-mail sessions may not always be pedagogically sound. I doubt that one exchange—client questions consultant, and consultant answers client—counts as dialogue. Although, clearly, some situations can be handled effectively through such an exchange, these encounters do not model writing center practices. For example, a question about whether a particular sentence is a comma splice can be answered effectively through this type of exchange, but the mission of many writing centers, as North (1984) wrote, is to make better writers, not to edit texts. Most writing sessions deal with issues much more complex than grammar. Is it possible to teach effectively and fully idea development or coherence through one e-mail response? Perhaps, although several years of consulting tell me this would be a rare occurrence. If a writing center uses e-mail as another writing resource, such as a grammar handbook, while using other environments such as MOOs for consultations, then e-mail without dialogue might be fine.

DIALOGUE AND THE WRITING CENTER SESSION

Writing center sessions, whether face-to-face or online, require dialogue. Clients and consultants confront many complex issues each session, and dialogue is the medium through which understanding happens. Client and consultant must communicate the purpose of the assignment, the client's questions, and the consultant's response. In e-mail sessions without dialogue, these issues may never become clear either to consultants or clients, a circumstance resulting in potentially useless and/or irrelevant sessions.

Understanding the Assignment

Writing assignments can be hard to understand, and many factors complicate them further, such as the goals of individual instructors and lack of clarity. Without dialogue between consultant and client, these complicating factors can keep the consultant from responding appropriately and/or keep clients from asking important questions. Ultimately, insufficient dialogue may result in clients failing to respond appropriately to the assignment and, consequently, failing to learn the writing strategies the assignment attempts to teach. Part of being an effective writer is accurately assessing the rhetorical situation giving rise to the writing task. Consultants can use dialogue to help students understand assignments.

Instructor Goals for the Assignment. Writing assignments may be hard or even impossible to understand out of context. Instructors hope their students learn specific writing strategies through completing an assignment, and these goals shape the nature of the assignment. In the e-mail, if the client does not include the assignment or provides a brief summary that omits the goals, those goals may go unaddressed and unlearned. Some clients do not connect the relevance of the goals to their questions about the text, and some clients do not connect the importance of the rhetorical situation to the effectiveness of their writing. When e-mail consultants do not understand the assignment's goals and give inappropriate or unhelpful responses, clients may recognize the response as unhelpful without knowing why. Believing consultations to be generally useless, they may stop using the writing center. When the client and consultant discuss an assignment face to face or online in real time, however, important information unfolds over the course of the exchange, many times when the consultant responds inappropriately, prompting the client to indicate confusion.

Unclear Assignments. Some writing assignments are not clearly written or articulated, leaving the client and consultant to sort out the assignment's goals as best they can. Depending on the relationship between teaching faculty and consultants, consultants may ask the client to discuss the assignment further with the instructor, or the consultant may ask the instructor about the assignment. Without this kind of dialogue, again, the consultant may respond inappropriately, helping the client create a text that meets neither the assignment nor the goals for learning particular writing strategies.

Understanding Clients' Questions and Consultants' Responses

Writing consultants spend much time talking about writing. Many writing center clients, however, have not had such experience and are still learning how to discuss their writing. Talking about academic writing requires knowing terms, such as *development, organization, focus, coherence,* and *style,* and being able to assess the effectiveness of those aspects for a rhetorical situation. Without much practice, clients struggle to articulate their writing-related questions. When visiting the face-to-face writing center, clients often ask me to edit their texts. After I explain that writing centers do not edit, many clients indicate confusion because they perceive editing as fixing, or at least identifying, whatever might be ineffective in the writing. Only through dialogue do we discover their real questions.

When clients ask me to edit their papers through e-mail, I always wonder if they have other questions, but cannot articulate them. I explain the kinds of things to which writing consultants respond and, if the assignment is included, give general feedback to the text, which provides an example of writing issues appropriate for response. By analyzing my feedback, clients might be able to use some of its language to ask other questions. Because a client has never returned more questions through e-mail, however, I fear that many students simply find the response confusing (because it does not mesh with their concept of writing and the writing center mission) and dismiss the writing center as being irrelevant to their needs. In order for clients to find sessions relevant and useful, the consultant must ensure that the client understands the response. Even when both the client and the consultant are experienced writers, the client often needs more explanation concerning the consultant's feedback. This situation mirrors face-to-face consultations, which generally require clarification as well.

DIALOGUE AND CLIENT CONCEPTION

E-mail sessions without dialogue may promote a faulty conception of the online writing center's goals and the process of writing itself. If clients send in a paper, request a response, receive a response, but never engage in further dialogue, many clients may believe that the consultant has given all necessary ingredients to fix that text. Many clients, especially first-year writing students, do not know how many revisions go into crafting an effective text. They may not realize that one response from a consultant should begin a conversation about shaping and reshaping the writing. Many clients send their texts to us as a final precaution before submitting them to instructors. These clients view the writing center as last-minute insurance against anything that might be wrong with the paper. Using a hospital metaphor, Pemberton (1992) explained that many clients believe that writing centers fix writing problems:

> Instructors and students often have only the vaguest notions of how writing skills are actually taught or what sort of epistemology grounds a writing center, so they tend to conceive of writing centers in metaphorical terms, as representations of other institutions which perform seemingly related functions (p. 12).

This view of writing centers promotes the belief that writing center staff can effect a quick cure after only one visit to the clinic. However, as Pemberton (1992) wrote, " ... writing skills are not learned or corrected overnight; there is some question about whether they can be assimilated even over the span of several semesters" (p. 14). The ability to send texts through e-mail for a response without dialogue may contribute to the endurance of the writing center-as-hospital metaphor, a metaphor that may damage learning.

CONCLUSION

Writing center consultants should ground their use of technology in the theory supporting their pedagogy and should examine the context of technology use. Even if technology supports the pedagogy, the context may restrict its possibilities. Although e-mail can easily support dialogues, the university context may limit dialogues by providing inadequate time for writing and revising. Online consultants in this position may want to focus on synchronous media, working to make the technology user-friendly and accessible. Perhaps clients should only participate in e-mail sessions if they cannot participate in synchronous sessions or if consultants work with instructors to establish plenty of time for revision. As Kinkead and Hult (1995) wrote about the online writing center, "Most important is that writing centers keep at the forefront the goals that have sustained them through the computerless years and the computer-integrated years: to keep writers at the center" (p. 132).

ACKNOWLEDGMENTS

Many, many thanks to Suzy Langford, who took a day out of her hectic schedule to be the second coder for this project, and to James Inman and Donna Sewell, whose comments on various drafts of this project helped me so much.

11

The Anxieties of Distance: Online Tutors Reflect

David A. Carlson
Eileen Apperson-Williams
California State University at Fresno

The premises for online tutoring are noble—to improve access to campus writing centers and to narrow distances between students and tutors. Time constraints, proximity, and introverted personalities often keep students from attending tutoring sessions. Computer technology can bring students and tutors closer together, overcoming the distance that may exist.

The desire to span this distance prompted the writing center staff at California State University at Fresno (CSUF) to develop an online tutoring program. However, thinking about how to overcome obstacles between tutors and students via the Internet opened new challenges. In particular, the idea of distance becomes more complex when writing centers support both face-to-face and online tutoring. As distance is lessened by increasing access, what happens to the relationship between student and tutor? What happens as tutors respond through a faceless, expressionless computer screen? For us, the face-to-face relationship is one of the joys, as well as a reason for success, in a tutoring session. With online tutoring, this relationship is severed. The tutoring table is replaced with a computer screen: cold, sterile, and, to many, uninviting.

METHODOLOGY

In this chapter, we listen to tutors who work in the CSUF writing center; we share dialogue with other tutors and dialogue with students seeking writing assistance online. Dialogue and distance complicate and complement one another. Philosopher David Bohm (1996) reminded us of how we might view the nature of dialogue:

> "Dialogue" comes from the Greek word *dialogos. Logos* means "the word," or ... we would think of the "meaning of the word." And *dia* means "through." ... The picture or image that this derivation suggests is of a *stream of meaning* flowing among and through us and between us. This will make possible a flow of meaning ... out of which may emerge some new understanding. It's something new, which may not have been in the starting point at all. It's something creative. And this shared meaning is the "glue" or "cement" that holds people and societies together. (p. 6)

In distance tutoring, particularly faceless tutoring, the nature of dialogue is especially pronounced. Traditionally, gesticulation, tone of voice, and facial expression contribute to meaning and understanding. In e-mail tutoring, almost all meaning is carried through words alone.

For tutors accustomed to gesticulation, tone of voice, and facial expressions as an aid to Bohm's "flow of meaning," becoming comfortable using e-mail may take time, but it can be done: E-mail is a medium that allows more than is readily apparent. As seen in the quotations throughout this chapter, e-mail incorporates both formal and informal styles of writing, often in the same messages. Chesebro and Bonsall (1989) explained that with the proliferation of personal computers and modems, "personal 'messaging' was the most popular choice of the personal computer owner.... In virtually every test, home-computer owners seem to enjoy communication with other users more than any other computer-using activity" (p. 100). E-mail has quickly become a medium of friendships and alliances; hence, informal styles of writing (e.g., personal letters with fragments, idiomatic expressions, inside jokes, and allusions) are standard. At the same time, e-mail is often used by academics, who are trained to communicate in formal styles. Without showing faces, perhaps without stating credentials, people form e-mail groups, which put people using varied levels of formality in dialogue with each other.

E-mail style, then, tends to be an amalgam of styles. Conveying meaning becomes more difficult as intentions can be easily misinterpreted. Chesebro and Bonsall (1989) expressed this difficulty as a problem of how to maintain an interpersonal relationship: "the development of a [relationship] typically includes physical intimacy as one of its most important features.... If computer users claim that they have developed [relationships] solely through electronic connections, how must interpersonal specialists readjust their conceptions of [relationships]?" (p. 103). As "interpersonal specialists," tutors must readjust their conceptions of how to develop interpersonal relationships when tutoring online.

Important principles can be learned from the numerous listservs that continue to form rapidly around various academic subjects. Casal (1998), the listowner of an e-mail discussion group, regularly reminded the group of the following rules:

- No personal attacks or flame wars.
- No lengthy discussion of movies or other nonprint media.
- No arguing about list policies on the list. (Address all concerns privately to list owner.)
- Clear labeling of messages.
- No gushing about or bashing of characters or authors.

Although most of these rules do not literally apply to online tutoring, the spirit of them indicates how to maintain relationships over e-mail between tutors and students. These rules emphasize the constant need to exhibit courtesy and patience in a medium that does not allow for physical gestures and tone of voice. Words alone can seem cold and distancing even when not meant as such.

Rules meant to promote courtesy in dialogue are developed through practical experience. Elvira Casal (personal communication, June 4, 1998) mentioned her experiences with the discussion group as revealing "[a]nother problem[:] ... online communications seem to encourage some people to imagine an 'ideal audience' that often isn't there.... [and that online audiences] also have expectations ... and we feel irritated when these expectations are not met." Casal noted that e-mail users can easily offend others unintentionally. Bohm (1996) reminded us that distance is an element of every discussion, even face to face, and, in particular, he suggested that "[t]he people who take part are not really open to questioning [these] assumptions" (p. 7).

Online writing labs need to study interpersonal communication. Tutoring is most successful when dialogue occurs: "[i]n a dialogue ... nobody is trying to win.... There is a different sort of spirit to it. In a dialogue, there is no attempt to gain points, or to [demand that] your particular view prevail" (Bohm, 1996, p. 7). Even though the tutor may have more knowledge and experience than the student, the student and tutor should engage in a dialogue about writing rather than have the tutor lecture the student about writing. Through e-mail tutoring, words may often seem cold and insistent. We should learn how to communicate over e-mail in such a way that courteous and patient dialogue becomes the norm when physical appearance and tone of voice cannot convey such qualities.

Because interpersonal communication differs from individual to individual, the study of how distance affects communication between tutors and students must focus on actual online dialogue between tutors and students. In the discussion that follows, we explore the interpersonal communication of our online tutors; our particular emphasis is on how distance transforms or otherwise affects the relationships among them and between them and their students.

A DIALOGUE OF TUTORS

The unnerving loss of face-to-face interaction keeps some tutors and writing centers from tutoring online. New and experienced tutors alike may feel anxious responding to an impersonal computer screen. This section demonstrates the anxieties of tutoring online as well as underscores that many of the skills used in face-to-face tutoring can aid online tutoring: "Solid writing center theory applies in cyberspace as it does in the traditional center. Students still need to be put at ease and made to feel comfortable. They still need special attention on particular writing problems" (Jordan-Henley & Maid, 1995b, p. 212). Although anxiety toward online tutoring is understandably daunting—it certainly has been for us—online tutoring is not an entirely new experience despite the different tutoring environment.

Tutors continually expressed concern about venturing beyond the familiar environment of the face-to-face tutorial, fearing that distanced relationships would inevitably result from geographic distances. The semester before we began online tutoring we e-mailed our tutors with this question: "What are your expectations and/or anxieties as you approach online tutoring for the first time?" The first person to respond was Ginny, a three-semester tutor: "I guess the only worry I have is that I think it would be easy to lose the personal touch you get when tutoring face to face. This kind of personal interaction, I feel, has really helped me and my tutees to become better at writing." The e-mail dialogue that followed Ginny's post indicates that most tutors agreed. Used to forming trusting relationships with their students, tutors worry about altering the situation. John, a four-semester tutor, offered his concerns:

> First of all, I rely HEAVILY on the interpersonal communication that tutoring offers me. I use my own personality to build a relationship with my students that enables me to push them farther and farther with their work as the semester progresses. I do agree that there is tone and voice in writing but I also think that they can be easily misinterpreted, misunderstood, or simply missed when talking online. The relationship I generally have with my students is one built on trust and one that takes more than just a 25 minute session to cultivate (personal communication, August 7, 1997).

John brought up an important aspect of face-to-face tutoring: the development of the tutor/student relationship. In a traditional tutoring session, the first challenge to this relationship involves agreement over interpersonal distance. Although many students welcome personal interaction with their tutors, others keep a safe distance, a distance that usually decreases with time. This agreement on space creates favorable working conditions. With online tutoring, however, this space is already defined. A computer screen not only becomes a shield for those who are wary, but also creates a safety zone by virtue of anonymity. Such students may find what a student in Jordan-Henley and Maid's study (1995b) reported: "the computer [seems] as just another 'appliance' like a 'telephone, TV, or VCR'" (p. 213). Although dialogue occurs, the separation of the parties allows each a sense of control (Jordan-Henley & Maid, 1995b, p. 215). Thought is transmitted, whereas the lack of physical presence promotes the sense that each party chooses to receive information. One chooses to log on to e-mail much the same way that one chooses to turn on a television.

Some distances are fiercely maintained in face-to-face tutorials. At what point does a paper pass from being the student's work to the tutor's? Although this same opportunity for issues of distance occurs with electronic tutoring, the computer's presence between tutor and student poses as a guard against becoming too close. The tutor only knows what the student decides to present; the tutor cannot see the look in the student's eye, hear the emotion in the student's voice, or read the student's body language. Such privacy can be empowering to the student. In "Online Writing Labs (OWLs): A Taxonomy of Options and Issues," Harris and Pemberton (1995) stated:

> All dialogue in online configurations will be text driven, eliminating the sub-tle voice and body clues to composing processes.... Although tutors, thus, have to learn to rely on other clues as to who writers are, meeting onscreen will also mean meeting in a world where gender, ethnicity, and race are not immediately evident except through lexical and social cues. Voices normally shy may be stronger and clearer, and stereotypes are less likely to impact the tutorial. (p. 156)

Although some tutors like John worry that tutoring without face-to-face presence increases misinterpretation and misunderstanding, Harris and Pemberton (1995) reminded us that face-to-face interaction is not free of misunderstanding. Online communication alleviates some of the baggage that accompanies physical bodies. Perhaps, then, embedded within anxi-eties about the effects of distance on online tutoring is a positive result: that discussions foreground students' texts instead of the mediated relationships between tutors and students.

Justin, a three-semester tutor, began searching for ways, not unlike Har-ris and Pemberton, of making the best of this new interaction:

> I just finished reading Ginny's mail and I do agree that it would be strange to not have the close personal interaction that we have dealt with in our groups, but at the same time, distance allows us to avoid our own biases, judgments, etc., at least to a point. I think that communication could also be aided if, in contrast to our groups, we did not intimately know the student, and therefore there would be no worries on their parts of embarrassment when asking questions or discussing topics. Sometimes it is easier to open up to someone when you know that you won't be seeing them on Thursday. (personal communication, August 9, 1997).

Here, Justin suggested that although distance may prevent the familiar per-sonal interaction, it can bring us closer to our goals and to the student's goals too. In traditional writing centers, relationships between tutors and students are often close, with tutors becoming coaches, confidants, and even friends. Without question, much can be gained by this type of relation-ship. However, this interpersonal relationship sometimes prejudices both the tutors' and the students' views of writing. Online tutoring, as a result of distance, can alleviate some of this prejudice. Tutors and students still work on student texts, but the absence of face-to-face interaction causes the in-terpersonal relationship to develop through words about the writing rather than through physical presence. Online distance is an advantage for stu-dents, too, allowing them to raise questions that they may feel uncomfortable asking face to face. Some aspects of the power dynamic between tutors and students are flattened online.

Another tutor, Libra, argues that online tutorials place more responsibility on students:

> No, there won't be face to face interaction, but there will definitely be something to work on (this isn't always true when you're face to face with your students). I hope online tutoring presses the importance of planning ahead of time. Maybe students will learn to be more aware of the writing process by observing how many times a paper can be changed or reworked. (personal communication, August 10, 1997).

Libra made good points. The Website requires the students, first, to include the prompts and, second, to pinpoint particular problems with the papers. This strategy forces students to begin assessing the writing and to reread the assignments after writing the drafts. In planning our online site, we wanted to adhere clearly to our writing center's philosophies. Harris and Pemberton (1995) stated, "[p]eople who configure or plan OWLs must also weigh other options and make decisions as to which aspects of writing center theory and pedagogy are to be retained and which cannot be replicated exactly" (p. 155). By requiring that students include the assignments and individual concerns with the papers, we attempt to keep the students in charge of their writing. As Libra implied, this situation ideally occurs in face-to-face sessions: The students come to tutorials fully prepared. Too often, however, students rely on tutors for criticism, creating unbalanced interaction. Online tutoring, then, offers a potential solution.

As our most recent semester began, so began our first attempts at online tutoring. Reactions from the tutors were mixed. Although some online tutors complained about difficulty in organizing their thoughts, in being concise and clear, and in envisioning geographically-distant students, others thought it more productive than face-to-face tutoring. Those who liked the situation felt that they could be more concise because they were tackling just one aspect chosen by the student. These tutors appreciated avoiding the rambling that goes on at a face-to-face session in trying to encapsulate a critical response. However, the main concern had been trying to make verbal language textual—to maintain a sense of informality while demonstrating standard English to a large degree.

Joanna, a three-semester tutor, said that online tutoring, for her, "opened the gate for frustration." She received an online submission from an ESL student who was concerned with her thesis, run-on sentences, sentence structure, and conclusion. The essay, for a freshman composition class, began as follows:

> Most of the juvenile delinquents happened in Americans underclass. That is, a social class having the lowest status in society. Underclass refers to the areas within a city where minority groups tend to live. The stay in that area because of social and economic pressure. In addition, unemployment, crime, drug addiction, teen pregnancy, school dropouts, and illiterates, are common in these neighborhoods. The peak times for juveniles offenses, especially of serious crimes, are in the hours immediately after school. The Department of Justice recently found that while adult violent crimes rates continue to drop, todays juvenile offenders are the fastest growing segment among violent criminals.
>
> The unprecedented increase in juvenile criminality is expected to result in a dramatic increase in the overall rate of violent crime as these juveniles approach majority. The reason juvenile are delinquent include watching violence on television, broken family, gang, and failure of juvenile justice system. (personal communication, September 23, 1997).

Joanna responded:

> Hi, Mai! Reading your introduction, I conclude that the main point of your paper (your thesis) is to discuss the different causes of juvenile delinquency. You do a good job of letting me know where delinquency occurs most often (America's underclass society), though be sure to make the distinction that the underclass are not "areas" in a city where minorities live, but actual "people" who live in these areas. At this point, I would like to concentrate on specific areas of your writing which need work in order to make your sentences more easily understood. The two areas that I'd like you to concentrate on are singular vs. plural, and noun possession. For example: the 5th sentence in your intro makes a list of things that are common in an underclass neighborhood. Notice the difference between singular and plural:
>
> *unemployment IS common ("unemployment" is singular)
>
> *School dropouts ARE common ("school dropouts" is plural)
>
> I suggest rewriting the sentence so that you are using all singular nouns or all plural nouns. Now let's look at noun possession using examples from your intro:
>
> *Americans underclass. Because the underclass belongs to the Americans, it is possessive. American's underclass.

*Juveniles offenses. The offenses belong to the juveniles. Therefore, it is the juvenile's offenses.

*todays juvenile offenders ... means the juvenile offenders of today. Therefore, today's juvenile offenders ...

Another example is your sentence, "the reason juvenile are delinquent ... " You list more than one reason, so it should be plural (reasons). More than one juvenile is delinquent, so it should also be plural: The reasons juveniles are delinquent.

I believe it is a good idea for you to check through the rest of your essay to make sure your sentences use possession and plural vs. singular correctly. Thank you for submitting your essay! Please feel free to submit this again once you've checked it, or use our walk-in times to look at your paper in person. (MW 8-4) (T-Th 8-8) (Fri 8-12)

      Sincerely, Joanna (personal communication, September 24, 1997)

Shortly thereafter, the student resubmitted her essay, a reaction that is not a regular occurrence in our limited online experience:

I have rectified the mistake that you mentioned. Hope to receive the final correction from you. Most of the juvenile delinquents happened in Americans underclass. That is, a social class having the lowest status in society. People stay in this area due to their economic condition. In addition, unemployment, crime, drug addiction, teen pregnancy, and school dropout, is common in these neighborhoods. The peak times for juveniles offenses are in the hours immediately after school. The Department of Justice recently found that while adult violent crimes rates continue to drop, todays juvenile offenders are the fastest growing segment among violent criminals.

The unprecedented increase in juvenile crimes are expected to result in a dramatic increase in the overall rate of violent crime as these juveniles approach majority. The reasons juvenile are delinquent include watching violence on television, broken family, gang, and failure of juvenile justice system. (personal communication, September 26, 1997).

The student's revised draft indicates that she did not understand Joanna's earlier message. In a face-to-face session, Joanna could act on a student's confused look or hesitation by proceeding with another approach, saving both parties time and frustration. As Harris and Pemberton (1995) wrote, "[T]here are losses as well in this faceless, disembodied world as the lack of the personal contact may seem to dehumanize a setting that writing centers have traditionally viewed as personal and warm" (p. 155). Joanna believed that meeting with this student face to face would have been more effective. This reaction, however, was not felt by all.

Gabriel, a first-semester tutor, had a very different reaction to online tutoring:

> Seated across a table, tutors try to impress upon students the importance and techniques of communicating clearly in writing. Ironically, this exchange most often occurs in dialogue rather than text. Perhaps the greatest advantage of online tutoring is that it is a dialogue concerning better writing that occurs in the form of writing. The exchange is more beneficial, as the message and the medium are self-referential. (personal communication, October 1, 1997).

Gabriel echoed a point made by Coogan (1995): "Online writing tutors ... situate themselves not as technicians of writing ... but as equals; writers responding to other writers" (p. 176).

A native-speaking student, also in freshman composition, submitted his paper to Gabriel with the following concerns:

> Questions: 1) I am uncertain that the paragraphs flow together smoothly. In paragraph 5 on page 2, the text doesn't seem to gel well with each other. I'm noit is my topic sentence, or that I have different ideas and they need to be separated in two different paragraphs. The end of the page has a sentaence thst felt akward, but I'm not sure. 2) Is my thesis statement clearly recognizable in both the beginning, and the end of the essay? Does the thesis ffollow through the text? (personal communication, September 29, 1997).

To these concerns, Gabriel responded with the following:

> I very much enjoyed reading your essay on language. I agree that there are a couple of sticky transitions, and I interjected some comments using the "***" symbol as a "flag." One place that it doesn't flow is from ex-girlfriend TO snap decisions. I can guess the link, but can you think of 1 or 2 sentences that can serve as a link, a transition? One thing to consider is: Your paper (to me, that is) seems to develop as "we speak different languages —> some people SEEM dumb —>Slang can affect how we see people." Perhaps you could try dragging section 3 to be between 1 and 2. Hence: we speak different languages —> slang affects how we see people —> Some people SEEM dumb. Maybe this simple "click and Drag" might help your paper "flow", and you might discover the transitions to more naturally "find themselves" (Or maybe not, just something to think about.)

Finally, yes, there is a consistent thesis. Your paper seems to me focused. I wonder though, if the thesis is "we speak different Englishes." which it seems the intro.is hinting. It seems that your paper's consistent thesis is more complex than this, such as what the "difference" DOES.

You have a wonderful start, and I hope that you send more. I would like to see a next draft. Keep at it.

Gabriel A. (personal communication, September 30, 1997).

ENGAGING THE DIALOGUE

Joanna's and Gabriel's different attitudes toward online tutoring may lie in many factors, including their students. One student is an ESL writer, and the other is a native writer. Working with grammar, as Joanna did, can be difficult, even face to face. Explaining grammar in everyday language over a computer screen can enormously challenge even the most experienced tutors. Another reason lies in the fact that Joanna is an experienced tutor who has spent several semesters tutoring face to face, gaining knowledge and skill along the way. Gabriel, on the other hand, being new, had an advantage stepping into online tutoring because he did not yet favor face-to-face tutoring. This does not mean that more experienced tutors do not bring tremendous tutoring skill to online tutoring. It does, however, offer a possible explanation for the anxieties Ginny, John, and Joanna felt that Gabriel did not.

As our online tutoring program develops, some are still bothered by the loss of face-to-face interaction. We suspect, however, that anxiety will pass with time and experience online. If the primary emphasis of tutoring writing is on the text and the writer's approach to the text, then surely online tutoring brings increased opportunity for this practice despite the change of venue. If we are to reach more students, online tutoring is a viable option despite the anxieties that accompany any new practice. Distance continues to be a central element of our online tutors' work. We envision that what provokes anxiety now about online tutoring will eventually become comfortable and familiar as tutors gain experience.

12

E-mail Tutoring and Apprehensive Writers: What Research Tells Us

Mark Mabrito
Purdue University Calumet

The last few years witnessed a growing number of online writing centers and an increasing number of college campuses gaining access to network technologies supporting electronic communication. The promise of using computer networks for tutor–student collaboration has become a reality. On the one hand, using electronic communication (most commonly e-mail) for tutoring writing students offers some practical advantages—easy access to tutors, an efficient medium for exchanging text, and a permanent written transcript of the discussion for later review. At the same time, it offers a substantially different learning experience for both tutor and student, one characterized by the absence of body language and other visual cues that can indicate acceptance or understanding of the discussion.

For some students, the experience of writing (both in the classroom and in the tutorial) potentially can become a frustrating experience. Student writers, who Daly and Miller (1975a) termed *high-apprehensive writers*, represent one such group. For these students, writing is an act to be avoided at all costs. They frequently express negative attitudes toward writing and reading. By avoiding situations that demand writing, apprehensive writers create a self-fulfilling prophecy: The less practice they have with writing, the more likely they are to receive lower evaluations, a result that strengthens their belief that they are poor writers. Research has shown that writing apprehension can have long-term consequences for students, often resulting in their choosing academic majors and careers thought to require less writing (Daly & Shamo, 1978, p. 122).

Although there are more than 20 years of research in the area of writing apprehension, only recently have researchers attempted to explore computer conferencing as a vehicle for teaching and tutoring high-apprehensive writers. To better understand what role the writing center should play in this area, three basic questions need to be addressed:

1. What does research in writing apprehension indicate are some of the constraints of tutoring high-apprehensive writers?
2. What does research in using computer networks to teach writing tell us about the challenges of teaching apprehensive writers online?
3. What are the benefits of tutor–student collaboration via e-mail for high-apprehensive writers?

RESEARCH IN WRITING APPREHENSION

Drawing on studies in communication anxiety, Daly and Miller (1975a) first coined the term *writing apprehension*, which has become a widely studied construct in writing studies, and developed a survey instrument for determining levels of writing apprehension—the Writing Apprehension Test (Daly & Miller, 1975b). *Writing apprehension* refers to a collection of behaviors that include a writer's tendency to avoid situations that involve writing, to experience a sense of anxiety when faced with a writing situation, and to experience frustration while in the process of writing (Daly & Miller, 1975a, p. 244).

On the one hand, the physical (face-to-face) writing center tutorial affords high-apprehensive writers a positive experience. The writing conference model used widely in writing centers today is based on the notion of tutor as facilitator, creating an atmosphere where students are free to explore their voices as writers, experiment with text, and develop as writers (Reigstad & McAndrew, 1984, pp. 4–5). Although such atmospheres may be created through peer review groups and instructor conferences, these exchanges take place in the larger context of the writing course, a place that ultimately results in the formal evaluation of one's writing. Evaluation of writing is something that the high-apprehensive writer seeks to avoid because, as some researchers theorize, these writers frequently have experienced a long history of negative criticism and evaluation; therefore, they avoid writing, fearing adverse consequences (Daly, 1977, p. 13). Similarly, the more public forum of the peer group is a place where apprehensive writers feel less comfortable sharing their writing because fear of writing for public display is a salient feature of writing apprehension (Daly & Miller, 1975a, p. 244).

The face-to-face tutorial is not without drawbacks for apprehensive writers. Although fostering perhaps a low-risk environment, the business of the tutorial is still about writing. Apprehensive writers are less likely to participate in a tutor–student collaboration whose very purpose invites discussion, examination, and exploration of the student's writing. To further compound matters, research has indicated a correlation between writing anxiety and communication anxiety (Daly & Miller, 1975c, p. 251), thus making the verbal exchange of the face-to-face writing tutorial even more intimidating to apprehensive writers.

Although no definitive cause has been documented for writing apprehension, some successful pedagogical approaches have been developed over the years. Such approaches include a process-oriented approach to writing, a reduction in the evaluation of student writing (with most of this evaluation occurring at the end of the composing process), clearly defined objectives for writing assignments, and an emphasis on small, peer response groups whose negative feedback is carefully monitored by the instructor (Clifford, 1981; Fox, 1980). Additional approaches have emphasized supplementing oral comments with written comments on student texts (Spear, 1988, p. 110). Because written comments are more private than the more public oral comments, this initial private viewing allows the writer time to deal emotionally with his or her aversive reactions to negative comments.

A common goal to all these approaches is to create an environment that deemphasizes formal evaluation and writing for public viewing; instead, the focus is on creating an environment where high-apprehensive writers feel free to explore and develop as writers. One such environment may be the computer conference.

RESEARCH IN COMPUTER CONFERENCING AND WRITING INSTRUCTION

Writing centers have just recently moved from using computers for individual computer-assisted instruction and word processing to computer conferencing about writing via e-mail (Coogan, 1995; Jordan-Henley & Maid, 1995b). More than 10 years of research, however, have focused on the uses and implications of e-mail collaboration both in the workplace and within the writing classroom. The e-mail environment may prove to be less threatening to the high-apprehensive writer because it is an environment characterized by a psychological distance (Hiltz & Turoff, 1978, p. 94) on the part of participants, a distance that promotes a less threatening environment. Within this environment, the hierarchy in social relationships and organizations becomes less pronounced (Kiesler, Siegel, & McGuire, 1984, p. 1129), promoting more equal participation on the part of group members as well as increased instances of uninhibited behavior and socioemotional responses among users (Rice & Love, 1987, p. 101).

Within the classroom, researchers have found that computer networking among students provides increased opportunities for collaborative writing and group participation due to the less threatening nature of this environment (Rice, 1987; Sirc, 1988). Because participants can send messages at will during computer conferences without the permission of the teacher, this situation tends to produce more equal levels of participation on the part of students (Batson, 1988, p. 56). Additionally, communicating via a network may promote an increase in the amount of writing that students do (Duin, 1990, p. 49).

This decentralization of the classroom is one of the key characteristics of the networked classroom. Models for networked classrooms displace the authority of the teacher, moving away from a model of top–down transfer of information from instructor to student (Barker & Kemp, 1990); instead, the networked classroom focuses on intensive exchanges of text among students and instructors (Peyton, 1990; Thompson, 1988). In this environment, the student enjoys a greater responsibility as writer and as responder to other students' writing. Within this change of structure, the act of writing becomes a social act (Eldred, 1989, p. 201), where students and instructors are equal collaborators working toward a common goal. Jennings (1987), after conducting an advanced composition course via an electronic bulletin board, aptly described the difference in authority–responsibility relationships in the electronic versus the face-to-face classroom: "They [students] were not required to submit in public and the teacher-in-charge didn't have to hand down rewards and punishments to the seated congregation" (p. 17). This model of decentralized instruction is not unique, however, to the networked classroom, for it has been one of the main principles behind the writing center tutorial since its inception.

The relation between writing apprehension and computer networking is an area of research that has not been greatly explored. Previous research here, however, has suggested that writing with a computer may help to reduce anxiety about writing (Daiute, 1985), yet may have little impact on writers with very high levels of writing apprehension (Phinney, 1991). Only a few studies, however, have examined high-apprehensive writers as members of online writing groups. In a study of the effects of using computer networks on teacher–student and student–student interactions in an undergraduate composition course, Hartman et al. (1991) showed that high-apprehensive writers interacted slightly more with teachers electronically than face to face (p. 111). In a study of freshman composition students, Mabrito (1991) found that high-apprehensive business writing students participated more frequently in revision sessions via e-mail than in face-to-face sessions, as well as making comments that were more directive and text-specific during these e-mail sessions (p. 527). Similarly, Mabrito (1992) found that e-mail writing conferences, because of their written and permanent nature, helped to demystify the act of writing for these high-apprehensive writers by allowing them to view more closely the writing process (p. 29).

Although clearly more research in the specific area of writing apprehension and computer conferencing needs to be conducted, initial findings suggest that communicating about writing via a computer network provides some interesting opportunities to high-apprehensive writers. Most notably, computer conferencing allows high-apprehensive writers to participate more fully in discussions of their own writing and provides them a chance to explore more closely their writing processes. Not only participation increases, but also high-apprehensive writers communicate about writing in different ways during these conferences. Because of the text-based nature of electronic communication, a discourse that is somewhere between speech and writing (Spitzer, 1986, p. 19), high-apprehensive writers spend their time online interacting about writing through writing; thus, they are provided with additional experiences in the very area they would normally seek to avoid.

E-MAIL TUTORING
AND HIGH-APPREHENSIVE WRITERS

To address better the needs of high-apprehensive writers, writing centers should consider e-mail tutoring as a viable option. The environment created by the e-mail tutorial is merely a logical extension of the writing tutorial's goals—to decentralize instruction and create a tutor–student collaboration characterized by a dialogue of equal collaborators. On a practical level, it is one way of drawing these students into the writing center, a place that they would most likely avoid, knowing the experience would force them to focus on a close examination of their own writing. Once the tutor–student collaboration has been established, however, there are some real benefits from e-mail tutoring.

The e-mail tutorial may prove to be less threatening to high-apprehensive writers because it is an environment characterized by a psychological distance (Hiltz & Turoff, 1978, p. 94) and also because the written conversation of e-mail provides a less threatening method of evaluation (Brown, 1984, p. 49). These less public written comments create some emotional and psychological distance for high-apprehensive writers by providing a less traumatic arena in which to examine and discuss their writing. Such an environment might reduce these writers' feelings of anxiety toward the evaluation process and make them more willing to participate in the process as writers.

When high-apprehensive writers must function as writers and evaluators of their own writing, they are placed in a situation of great cognitive stress. They must write for public viewing, and, at the same time, they must communicate about writing as well. During the face-to-face tutorial, this situation is somewhat exacerbated by the sheer physical presence of the writing tutor. The e-mail conference affords greater physical and psychological distance to the high-apprehensive writer, providing greater freedom to experiment with writing. The more opportunities high-apprehensive writers have to talk about and experiment with their writing, the more likely their feelings of anxiety about writing will be reduced. Because the e-mail conference is asynchronous, high-apprehensive writers have more time to formulate and consider carefully their responses, a luxury not afforded by the face-to-face conference.

In addition to being less threatening, the written dialogue of an e-mail session is more useful to high-apprehensive writers when they revise their texts. Studies have shown that student writers respond differently to oral and written response when revising texts. Students tend to remember less of what was said in a face-to-face conference than they remember after reading written comments (George, 1984, p. 322). Similarly, participants in computer conferences remember more from these conferences than they do from face-to-face meetings (Hiltz & Turoff, 1978, p. 431). The written transcript of an e-mail tutorial provides a permanent blueprint from which the high-apprehensive writer can work when revising his or her text. Not only will these written comments provide better direction to high-apprehensive writers, but they also provide a means by which these writers can witness their own writing process. By reviewing transcripts, high-apprehensive writers can see the evolution of their texts, as well as their own and their tutors' conversations about these texts. Such a feature may help to demystify the act of writing, one of the main objectives in treating writing apprehension.

Through enough of these electronic exchanges, high-apprehensive writers will eventually acquire a vocabulary about writing and problem-solving strategies for tackling writing tasks. Eventually, they may feel more comfortable sharing their writing in the face-to-face tutorial as well as the classroom. The act of writing will no longer be a self-fulfilling prophecy of failure for these writers, but rather a manageable task they can confidently achieve.

IV

Synchronous Electronic Tutoring

13

Synchronous Internet Tutoring: Bridging the Gap in Distance Education

Jamie Thurber
University of Alaska at Fairbanks

In Alaska, where distances between students and campus can reach up to 800 miles, the University of Alaska at Fairbanks (UAF) writing center needed a way to reach distant students. Through the use of existing computer equipment, the Internet, and a few brave tutors and students, we developed a method of collaborating with off-campus students. The University of Alaska system consists of three main branches containing 15 campuses stretched across an area equal to the distance from Washington, DC to Albuquerque, NM. Approximately 40% of residents live away from the main campuses, away from areas with face-to-face writing center support. The state has a population density of approximately 1 person per square mile, compared to the U.S. average of 71 per square mile, making for a widespread population. Of the approximately 100,000 native Alaskans, 77% live away from the three main campuses. One of the University's main missions is to reach these rural and native populations.

At the University of Alaska flagship campus in Fairbanks, the writing center director, Susan Blalock, determined that the center needed to increase access for rural and native populations. In studying center records, we noted a significant difference between how successful we were in reaching residential students (via our face-to-face sessions) and how successful we were in reaching off-campus students (via fax tutorials). The distance hindered the students' ability to receive quality support for their writing assignments. With these locations stretched over such large distances, the Center could not increase face-to-face sessions. However, the Internet reached many of the villages, representing a possible solution.

Using low-end Pentium 75MHz computers, the freeware program *Microsoft NetMeeting,* and a 33.6 kbps modem (or greater) for communication, the Center began conducting remote tutorials. Students at distant sites opened their text document in their own text editor and chose a collaborative function within the *NetMeeting* program. This action allowed both the tutor and student to work in a common visual and aural space—they could view and edit the paper on both their screens while conversing about the document using headsets. The program began in the fall of 1996 with a pilot project to tutor students at a local community college; if the technology failed, the tutors could drive to the location and fix the problem. During the first two semesters, the writing center tutored 17 students in 21 different sessions. Since then, the service has extended to four remote sites: Dillingham, Unalaska, Galena, and Bethel.

A CASE STUDY—ONE SESSION

UAF tutors teamed up with Professor Pete Pinney, who taught several sections of English 111, Methods of Written Communication, a core writing class at the University. Prior to a student's arrival, Pinney established the *NetMeeting* connection by double-clicking the desktop icon. The student, in this case Irene, had only to pick up the headset and insert her disk to begin the session. At the direction of the tutor, Irene started a wordprocessing program and chose the *Collaborate* function on the *NetMeeting* control panel. The tutor could now see what Irene saw: a blank wordprocessing screen. He took control of the mouse to demonstrate that they were in visual, as well as verbal, communication.

Irene's paper, about substance abuse and the family, would not open because she composed it on a Macintosh computer, so she retyped her one-page draft. Having been tutored twice before, Irene knew the procedure. On discovering that Irene wished to work on her introduction, the tutor highlighted the last sentence of the first paragraph and asked Irene if this sentence was her thesis statement. She stated she thought it was. The tutor then asked if she could state more specifically how substance abuse affects the family and why it has gained attention at this time. She highlighted the sentence, deleted a portion of it, and typed another idea. After several iterations of Irene asking the tutor how it looked, the thesis was more focused, although they both agreed she should further refine it as the paper developed.

On realizing that Irene was struggling with the assignment, the tutor opened a Web browser, planning to visit the instructor's Web page. The tutor could not find the instructor's Web address and wanted to reestablish visual communication with Irene quickly, so he talked her through the process. Irene opened a Web browser and choose the *Collaborate* function on the *NetMeeting* control panel. The program started with Pinney's syllabus on top; this process consumed about 5 minutes, during which time the tutor and student maintained constant verbal communication.

At this point the tutor took control of the mouse and navigated to the assignment page. There, they found an outline, a sample paper, and full instructions for the assignment. The two of them highlighted the sample paper's thesis statement, noted its format, and returned to Irene's paper, at which point she rewrote her thesis in light of the new information. Returning to the sample paper and instructions, Irene and the tutor discussed the second paragraph, which defined the problem. When Irene questioned how the two paragraphs differed, the tutor highlighted a portion of Pinney's (1998) instructions from the Web page: "Setting the stage is much like creating an extended definition of the situation and/or unfamiliar terms. Here is the place to introduce concepts and what they mean before the reader comes across the terms or concepts later in the paper" (online). The tutor brought Irene's paper to the foreground so that they could discuss possible changes. Regaining control of the mouse, Irene made a note in her document to include definitions in that section. The two agreed that perhaps she could include information on the prevalence of family-related substance abuse.

When Irene wondered where to find such information, the tutor mentioned Web search engines and the University's online catalog. From the *Excite* site, they practiced a few searches until Irene indicated that she could look up the information later; then, the tutor showed Irene how to surf to the UAF Library home page, correcting any incorrect maneuvers she made while manipulating the screen images. Noting that the session had lasted about 45 minutes, 15 minutes longer than established face-to-face guidelines, the tutor ended the session, and they agreed to meet the following week. Irene put down the headset, and the tutor waited to hear the creak of the door that would signify the next student's arrival.

Case Study: Lessons Learned

Several ideas central to the success of Internet tutoring arise in this example, the details of which are culled from journal notes of three sessions with this student, whose name has been changed.

Visual Communication.   Once a connection is made between the two computers, a quick visual communication will help the session begin smoothly. By opening *NetMeeting* and choosing the *Collaborate* function, tutor and student can communicate visually as well as orally. Such visual communication allows the session to supplement spoken language with visual reference.

Patience With Students and Electronics.   Opening a file can prove frustrating for the tutor, as in Irene's case. Because she had a Macintosh-formatted diskette, she could not use it in the PC's standard configuration. Remaining flexible and finding solutions are crucial. Patience helps keep the lines of communication open. This environment calls for a tutor to be well-versed in using the technology. Several practice sessions among tutors are warranted, in which a practice paper is used and tutors practice student and tutor roles.

This practice also aids in getting used to the walkie-talkie, half-duplex method of conversation. Irene experienced a fuzziness in her first session; if this problem had not been fixed prior to her next session, she might have given up on the tutorials. Getting used to working with the audio takes time. At first, having to wait for the other person to stop before speaking can be uncomfortable. Idle conversation at the beginning of the session helps prepare the student for the tutorial. In addition, background noise can key a microphone, keeping the other person out of the conversation. This challenge necessitates prior planning to create a quiet environment.

Tutoring: Session Focus.   More than in many face-to-face sessions, visual focus remains on the product throughout the session. While Irene discussed her essay, the tutor highlighted her thesis and directed the conversation to that sentence. Irene rewrote the sentence several times, receiving immediate feedback from the tutor during and after each rewrite. Rather than waiting for the student to rewrite the entire sentence prior to seeing it, the tutor can watch the student's formation process. In Irene's case, while she is developing her thesis, the tutor could redirect her to consider why substance abuse is a problem. Thus, the tutor is engaged with the student throughout the process.

This engagement can, however, lead to a focus on the mechanics of the paper rather than the big picture. Although Irene did not do so, often the student will ask more questions on grammar and punctuation because these problems are easier to solve. The student can highlight the comma and ask, "Is this correct?", and quick feedback from the tutor results in a deleted or moved comma. The students who start down that path, without redirect by the tutor, take to the immediate fix and do not want to discuss higher-order concerns. To combat this difficulty, a tutor can turn away from the screen and shift the visual focus momentarily. As in any writing center session, reading several paragraphs of the paper at the beginning of the session can create an agenda, which can be used to redirect the focus in such moments.

Tutoring: Using Web Resources. As seen in Irene's case, on-line teaching material can help a session past a stumbling point. By having her instructor's material immediately available and being able to switch between the sample essay and her paper, Irene could see how to strengthen her thesis statement. The material also reminded the tutor of the instructor's format and desired approach, allowing both Irene and the tutor to discuss the assignment and to reshape her essay to better meet the assignment goals. Online collaboration can benefit greatly if universities encourage and assist faculty to put such material online.

In addition, Irene learned how to research her topic via the Web through online search tools, a practice she had seen before but had not performed. Much of the initial research for her topic could be performed from home, using Web-based resources (the validity of which has to be determined) and using online library sources. Writing center tutoring can move from discussing research to practicing it, improving the student's ability to access pertinent material.

BUILDING ON TIME-PROVEN PRACTICES:
A TUTOR'S EXPERIENCE

As with most new ventures, the tutors need to adjust perceptions and approaches to tutoring in this electronic environment. As much as possible, the tutors try to duplicate techniques used in a face-to-face session. As a tutor, I initiate the sessions by asking the students what they would like to focus on and what problems they are having with the paper. We begin with higher-order concerns, such as content and organization, and work down to the lower-order concerns, or mechanics, of the paper. One of our guiding principles, as in many writing centers, has been to let the students correct the papers, allowing them to take ownership of any changes made. The technology may encourage participants to focus a tutoring session more on product-oriented concerns than in a face-to-face session.

For the student, this focus on "what can I do now" is a helpful tool, if used wisely. We use the computer screen as the medium to communicate ideas visually, thus spending more time in the session focused on the product. Because we can both take control of the mouse and direct the other person to an area of the paper (by highlighting or some such action), we are both rereading the same section of the paper throughout the session. This action has led to an increase in students' finding and correcting their own errors; as I page down and stop on a paragraph, the students read along and often state, "That really makes no sense, does it?" The students have engaged visually and mentally on the same portion of the text that I have, an experience missing in face-to-face sessions in which I have to orient students to an area of their paper and engage them mentally to remember their thought process at each point I question them.

A difficulty arises, however, when the student asks, "What can I do to fix it?" Since the cursor is blinking, we have highlighted the confusing passage, and we both can modify the paper, I am often tempted to fix the problem myself. I have to remind myself to keep the student in charge by asking questions and helping the student discover a solution. The guiding principle of allowing students ownership of the text and corrections remains in effect.

On a positive side, students are more likely to take notes in Internet tutorials than in face-to-face sessions, where I sometimes wonder, when they have not taken a single note during the session, what they will remember once they leave. In these electronic tutorials, the student discovers a problem, searches for a solution, and works on a passage until satisfied. This content focus is most evident in sessions in which students come to the conference at the beginning of the writing process, with no draft or idea of how to begin. In this case, the student and I could have simply used the Internet connection as a phone conversation, saving long-distance costs. Yet, combining this conversation with use of their text editor as a whiteboard proves most successful. As the students brainstorm aloud, I type their thoughts on the screen. When they finish, they type a sentence or two as a thesis or a guiding thought for later writing. Interestingly, I can watch their thought processes as they type and verbally encourage them to continue a line of reasoning and trust their own ideas when they become stuck. Although I follow these same patterns in a face-to-face session, I often disengage and let them write for 1 minute or 2 before I have any idea of their direction, losing insight into their creation process. In the Internet tutoring session, I am closer to the students in the creation of their ideas because I can watch them being formulated on the screen.

In some ways, in keeping with our center's philosophy, the dynamics of our sessions need to be refocused to ensure that we use a process model for writing, rather than a product model. Brainstorming offers a particularly useful stage in which we might foster collaborative work with students in which we can talk with them about higher-order concerns.

STUDENT FEEDBACK

The writing center has received positive feedback from the students. Although the sample size is small (16 students), the center received an average of 4.3 out of 5 (86%) on the question, "How would you rate the value of the session?" Fourteen out of 16 students stated they would use the service again (the other 2 did not answer the question). When asked how they rate the Internet tutoring session against a face-to-face session, seven responded; three stated they liked it better than a face-to-face session, three said they liked both methods, and one rated the face-to-face session better. Although acknowledging the limited scope of the survey, its results support the conclusion that Internet tutoring allows us to successfully reach more students and, perhaps more importantly, to serve a diverse range of students in pedagogically sound ways.

CHALLENGES

The writing center has faced challenges in reaching students in the remote locations. At remote sites, students talk with instructors via audio-conference telephone only and possibly meet only once per term. In essence, these students have limited in-person tutors or teachers. In these locations, student interest and retention in the Internet Tutoring Program have languished. In addition, as the invariable computer problem surfaces, the on-site computer support staff is often learning *NetMeeting* with the student.

The center has seen the most success when the class instructor has continually advertised and promoted the program, including offering class points to participate. A level of advocacy for the project is required to keep students interested in trying out a new method of learning. In situations where students are uncomfortable about both their writing and computing skills, they are often fearful to begin. To combat this challenge and build excitement in the program, the center is applying for NSF and Federal Funds for the Improvement of Post-Secondary Education grants, which include funds for on-site Technology Champions. These people will act as problem solvers and advocates for the program.

From a technology standpoint, Internet tutoring will benefit from the passage of time. Because *NetMeeting's* development arose out of business requirements to bring together employees in the offices of widespread, global corporations, universities can benefit from their continued investment. Bandwidth is crucial to the success of this project; as it increases with the development of solutions such as Internet 2, *NetMeeting* users should see improved performance and capabilities.

TECHNOLOGY LESSONS

A member of the tutoring team should have a strong interest in computers and a willingness to track down solutions to the glitches. The team should be aware of the following considerations:

- A faster Internet connection brings better communication. Sessions in which we had a T1 connection to the Internet had much higher voice quality and less visual lag than those on a dial-up connection. Although we tutored with one PC connected to an Internet Service Provider (ISP) on a 14.4 kbps modem, the voice quality dropped out much more readily. A minimum of 33.6 kbps connection to an ISP is recommended.
- Internet traffic disrupts even the best connections. During high-traffic Internet times, dropouts in audio will occur. Be patient. If possible during these times, contact the other party and conduct the voice portion over the telephone while conducting the visual portion of the session over the Internet.
- Check that the computer is working at least one half-hour before the session. Murphy strikes often.
- During a presession computer test, check how the microphone and headphones have been put into the sound card. The markings on the sound card are often confusing, and it is easy to put the plug in the wrong hole.
- Check, if possible before the session, the screen-size setting of the other computer—be sure that your pixel sizes match (e.g., 640x480, 800x600). Otherwise, the smaller screen scrolls in a confusing manner.

- Use a computer with at least 16MB of RAM. The voice cuts out when the computer accesses virtual memory on the hard disk.
- Get headphones that cover both ears. In a noisy room, it is tough to hear with a single earpiece.
- Get the students up on audio first. They can be talked through the rest of the set-up.
- Speak slowly and clearly, and wait for the other to complete speaking. With half-duplex, it is like talking into a walkie-talkie: Only one person can talk at a time.
- Make small talk with the student before launching into the paper. Given the lack of body language, personalizing the session is extremely important.
- Keep talking with the tutee when reading his or her paper; with silence, both sides think the other one has been disconnected.
- Do not type on their paper—even though you will be tempted. The session never recovers; they will want everything fixed.

LOOKING AHEAD

When the UAF writing center began this project, team members were filled with doubts. Yet, each of the questions—on technology, student technical ability, and our ability to communicate—has been answered positively. The center has begun tutoring students over great distances, wherever the Internet reaches. Tutors continue to learn how to communicate better in this environment, but most of the lessons learned in face-to-face tutoring are applicable. The biggest challenges lie in overcoming student unease with the technology and remaining patient with technology glitches. Although in Alaska we speak of long distances, the program works even more smoothly across town, where fewer hops are needed through the Internet.

As universities seek new ways of reaching nontraditional students and increasingly emphasize delivery of courses to remote sites, writing centers must increase student access to the instructional support they require. With the right mix of tutors, students, and technology, the capability to collaborate across towns, states, or countries exists now.

14

The Real(Time) World: Synchronous Communications in the Online Writing Center

Jake Shewmake
Jason Lambert
Utah State University

At USU, synchronous communications software has allowed us to create an effective learning environment for first-year composition students in our online writing lab that is easy for students and tutors to use, requires only basic hardware, and, according to our students, has proven to be very effective as a distance tutoring model. This chapter outlines the events that led to the creation of the OWL, provides an overview of how the system works, views student responses, and, finally, looks to the future of our OWL.

BACKGROUND

In the fall of 1995, Christine Hult, David Hailey, and Joyce Kinkead worked with faculty and administrators at two other state schools in Utah to secure a grant to create online first-year composition courses. The grant they received was part of the Higher Education Technology Initiative (HETI) designed to help faculty and administrators find effective modes of delivery for distance education. Armed with $1 million, these individuals set out to create distance learning models as part of the state of Utah's commitment to technology and distance education. In the beginning, the developers of this program imagined using technologies such as Ed-Net and Com-Net as the prime delivery mode because Internet technology was only beginning to show signs of being able to support distance learning fully. However, as Internet technologies emerged that allowed for effective synchronous and asynchronous delivery modes, our department began to explore using them as the prime mode of delivery. As a result, the department was offering 10 to 15 online sections of freshman composition each quarter during the 1997–1998 academic year.

Early in this development process, the department recognized a need to offer the same type of student support services to students in the online classes that students in the traditional classes were receiving. The department believed that an OWL was the natural extension of the online course offerings and wanted to be able to provide vital services to the students who were venturing into unknown territory. E-mail tutorials were unsuccessful because of compatibility and accessibility problems. However, in the fall of 1996, the department accepted Shewmake's proposal to create an OWL that would better serve the online freshman English classes. Shewmake wanted to create a synchronous environment that would effectively address issues of compatibility and access while also providing an effective document-sharing type of environment.

IN THE BEGINNING

Shewmake began exploring OWL theory and practice. Learning from pioneers in the field like Muriel Harris, Barry Maid, Jennifer Jordan-Henley, Lady Falls Brown, and Michael Pemberton, he quickly realized that the main challenges would be to create an effective system for tutors and students to communicate without seeing each other. All of the USU tutors are trained according to the techniques outlined in Harris' 1986 book *Teaching One-to-One: The Writing Conference*. Because we believe in the value of one-to-one conferencing, the center would need to offer students and tutors a document-sharing environment, which allows both students and tutors to see the text and discuss it in real time simultaneously. They needed to be able to make changes and post them for the tutor to see so that it could be clear that progress was being made. In addition, the software programs to support this type of synchronous communication could not require technologically advanced students, the downloading of anything onto students' PCs, or the limiting of access because of bandwidth problems. The program also had to operate entirely on a Web browser so that students and tutors were not required to learn another technology. Finally, there should be no additional cost to the student to access the system.

At this time, we believed we could increase access to students because more hours would be available to students than had previously been available in the on-campus writing center. Based on the results of the Cyberspace Writing Project conducted by Jordan-Henley and Maid (1995a), we also felt that students would enjoy the ease of use and the fun often associated with communicating in the online environment. The lack of a face-to-face experience, we thought, would have both positive and negative results; what we would lose in the ability to ascertain meaning from physical gestures we felt we would gain in increased time on task, focus on written communication, lower degrees of intimidation experienced by students, and clear records of the progress made (or lack of progress made) during each session.

TAKING SHAPE

Based on our research and goals, we began examining programs like *NetMeeting* and *CU-SeeMe* to find out if they were feasible options. What we liked about the programs were the document-sharing features and the real time chat functions. Of course, we liked the video-conferencing capabilities as well, but we quickly realized that these features were not viable because they required too much bandwidth, financial expenditure, and technical skill. We began exploring ways of emulating these environments by combining real time chat functions. By splitting the screen on a Web page and placing a chat function on the top half of the page and discussion forum on the bottom, we could develop an effective one-to-one synchronous tutoring environment. After some initial test runs, we developed what is still our current system. We have added a calendar feature to allow students to schedule appointments with a tutor, but our system is still basically the same system we developed in the late fall and early winter of 1996.

HOW IT WORKS

Writing center consultations require two steps. First, the students select a tutor whose schedule fits theirs, make an appointment with that tutor, post their paper to that tutor's Web page, and finally send an e-mail notifying that tutor that an appointment has been made. The second step consists of meeting the tutor in real time on the tutor's Web page to discuss the comments the tutor has made regarding the student's paper.

Before the Session

The software program that allows students to post their paper on the tutor's Web page is a discussion forum program called *Ceilidh*. Figure 14.1 provides a picture of the Web page where students complete this portion of the first step. This same screen becomes the bottom half of the screen shown in Fig.14 2.

In this portion of the consultation, the student and tutor meet on the tutor's Web page at the appointed time to discuss the comments that tutor made regarding the paper before the meeting. Figures 14.2 and 14.3 show the screen where this interaction takes place.

During the Session

During the session both student and tutor can open the paper with comments and even add comments or rewrite sections of the paper and repost

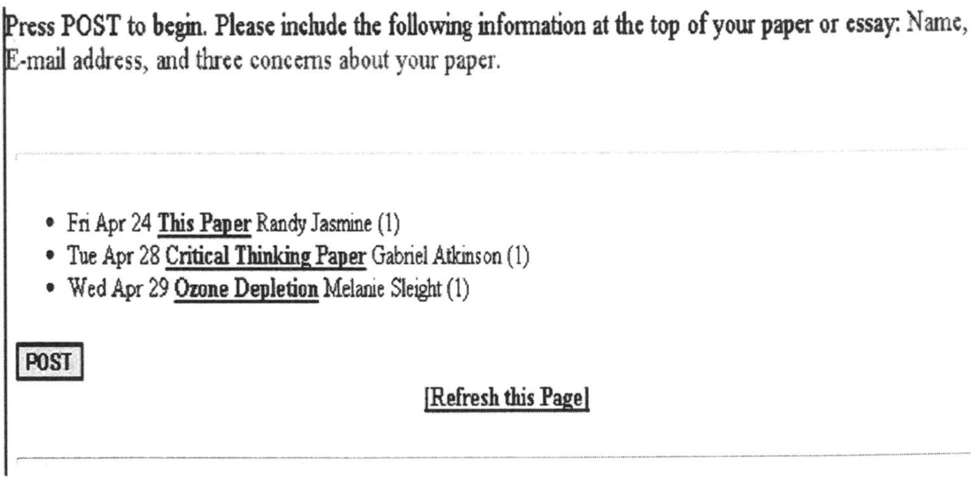

Press POST to begin. Please include the following information at the top of your paper or essay: Name, E-mail address, and three concerns about your paper.

- Fri Apr 24 **This Paper** Randy Jasmine (1)
- Tue Apr 28 **Critical Thinking Paper** Gabriel Atkinson (1)
- Wed Apr 29 **Ozone Depletion** Melanie Sleight (1)

POST

[Refresh this Page]

FIG. 14.1. Students post paper here and list concerns so that tutor can preview before appointment time.

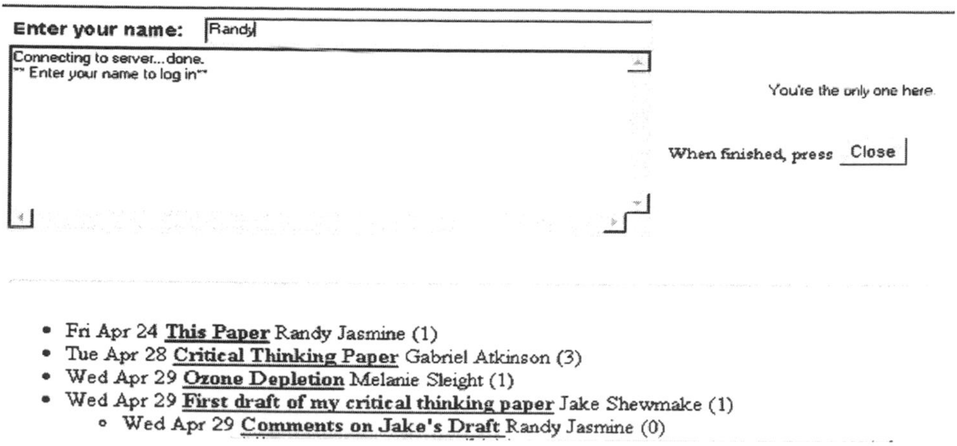

Enter your name: | Randy|

```
Connecting to server...done.
** Enter your name to log in**
```

You're the only one here

When finished, press Close

- Fri Apr 24 **This Paper** Randy Jasmine (1)
- Tue Apr 28 **Critical Thinking Paper** Gabriel Atkinson (3)
- Wed Apr 29 **Ozone Depletion** Melanie Sleight (1)
- Wed Apr 29 **First draft of my critical thinking paper** Jake Shewmake (1)
  - Wed Apr 29 **Comments on Jake's Draft** Randy Jasmine (0)

FIG. 14.2. Shows the screen that students first see when they arrive for the appointment. They just type in their comments and hit return. The space where you see the name Randy represents a tutor logging on. That is the same space where students type comments that appear in the dialogue box.

them so that the other individual can see the changes. Additionally, either party can copy and paste parts of the paper into the chat function for discussion.

After the Session

One of the most valuable aspects of the synchronous chat environment is the ability to record the session, which keeps notes of the session for the student and allows administrators to review student and tutor progress. In the physical writing center, someone must be present to observe tutorials for assessment purposes, but transcripts of electronic tutorials can be reviewed by people who were not present for the session. In this environment, we can maintain records of the session for evaluation and also share them with the students so that they may refer back to them when revising.

As can be seen in Figs. 14.1, 14.2, 14.3, 14.4, we have used a combination of a Web-based discussion forum and a real time chat function to create a very basic document-sharing environment. This environment allows for effective communication between student and tutor with very little computer hardware. In addition, this system does not require students to provide any software other than a Web browser. Essentially, this system has sidestepped many of the issues that keep students at other OWLs from tak-

Send a message: [   ]

```
** Enter your name to log in**
Randy enters the conversation.
Jake enters the conversation
Randy says, "Hello Jake!  How are you?"
Jake says, "Hi!  I'm great how are you?"
Randy says, "I am great too!  Listen let's get your paper open  Can you click on the link
  below called "Comments on Jake's Draft?  This will open the copy of your paper with
  my comments in it.  Then we can begin to talk!  Let me know when you have it open "
Jake says, "Okay Randy.  I have it open now!"
```

There are 2 people connected

When finished, press Close

```
>sl9t2
>Does my paper flow well?
>do my facts and arguments fit?
>have I used enough evidence and appeal?

> The pledge of allegiance is something that is no longer heard first thing in the morning when you walk into an elementary
classroom
JAKE HOW DO YOU FEEL ABOUT THIS AS AN OPENING SENTENCE?

Vocal prayers in schools and at the beginning of graduation ceremonies are quickly becoming a thing of the past. Anything that
makes mention of God or religious beliefs has almost become non-existent in our public school system. Is it really right that the
```

FIG. 14.3. Shows the screen on which the majority of the interaction takes place. The paper is open for both the student and the tutor to read while they discuss the work in the chat room at the top of the page.

Send a message: [   ]

```
Jake says, "Hi!  I'm great how are you?"
Randy says, "I am great too!  Listen let's get your paper open.  Can you click on the link
  below called "Comments on Jake's Draft?  This will open the copy of your paper with
  my comments in it.  Then we can begin to talk!  Let me know when you have it open."
Jake says, "Okay Randy.  I have it open now!"
Randy says, "Cool!  Did you have a chance to read my comments?"
Jake says, "Yes I did!  Thanks."
Randy says, "Great the let's talk about some of the questions you might have?"
Jake says, "Okay.  Well I wasn't sure why you were asking me that first question."
```

There are 2 people connected.

When finished, press Close

- Fri Apr 24 **This Paper** Randy Jasmine (1)
- Tue Apr 28 **Critical Thinking Paper** Gabriel Atkinson (3)
- Wed Apr 29 **Ozone Depletion** Melanie Sleight (1)
- Wed Apr 29 **First draft of my critical thinking paper** Jake Shewmake (1)
  - Wed Apr 29 **Comments on Jake's Draft** Randy Jasmine (2)
    - Wed Apr 29 **Copy of transcript from chat session** Randy (0)

FIG.14.4. Shows that the contents of the chat session have now been indexed as a message on the main page of the discussion forum where the student may open up the message and view it on the screen or even print it out.

ing advantage of synchronous communication. Although this combination is unique and effective, it is certainly not perfect. The next section discusses responses to the center and provides a picture of the current status of the tutoring system at USU.

STUDENT RESPONSES

Although the general buzz about USU's OWL seemed positive, we needed to receive specific feedback from tutors and students, so we posted a detailed questionnaire for students after they completed an online tutoring session. Knowing from our research and conversations with writing center administration and staff that lack of face-to-face communication is one of the main concerns about tutoring in cyberspace, we addressed this concern and others in the survey while attempting to ascertain advantages of the OWL. Forty-six students responded, giving us a glimpse of what they liked and disliked about our OWL.

Face-to-face Interaction
Versus Online Interaction

In general, perceptions of writing center interactions and tutoring dynamics have been rooted in the element of face-to-face contact. OWLs obviously shift this dynamic, so we were curious as to how this affected the overall experience. According to the surveys, some students indeed viewed the lack of face-to-face interactions as a drawback. One student said, "It is kind of impersonal," whereas another student echoed the concerns of many saying, "I would like to meet the person I'm talking to in person. It seems very cold to me over the computer." The comments of these students demonstrate that some felt that the online dynamic, as compared to that of a face-to-face situation, suffers. An OWL, with its lack of face-to-face interaction, is and may continue to be problematic for some people—they might rather meet a tutor in person to discuss writing than go online. What interested us were the benefits students could receive from not meeting face to face, and interestingly enough, several were identified.

Some students mentioned a lessening of intimidation that some would otherwise feel with face-to-face contact. Writing is an inherently personal endeavor, so it is not surprising that students who meet tutors in face-to-face situations do so with some trepidation and may feel intimidated during the tutoring session. Conversely, students who met in our

OWL commented many times that they felt that discussing their papers in cyberspace was wonderfully less intimidating, as can be seen in the following responses: "There's no personal contact so nobody had to feel intimidated or threatened, or worry about other silly stuff like that;" "It is easier to talk to someone over a computer and not feel like they're shutting you out or have bad feelings about you. It's better in some ways to not see the person you're talking to;"and "I like it. I don't feel intimidated by somebody on another computer like I might face to face."

Many students indicated feeling more comfortable in an OWL than in a physical writing center. If so, we wondered what avenues this might open up. One student noted, "There is no nonverbal communication so you have to make sure that your message is clear and understood," whereas another student said, "The way by which we communicated was exact." This is a key link to what can be gained in an OWL; instead of the communication being verbal and nonverbal, ideas and comments are presented in written form, thus enhancing the student's writing and critical thinking skills. Indeed, one student proclaimed OWL tutoring as "Pure, uncluttered communication centered on improving writing." OWLs may have a way to go before the exchanges become "pure" and "uncluttered," but student communication through the medium of writing about writing is a powerful alternative to face-to-face interactions.

Students felt that they communicated their writing needs more clearly in the OWL partially because they felt less intimidated. Many also noted that when they participated in an online session, they were more focused and more apt to stay on task. One student said that working on her paper in an online environment "helped [her] to be more concentrated," whereas another student noted that she "get[s] distracted easily and only having a computer in front of [her] helps [her] keep on topic." In both instances, the students were impressed with their ability to stay focused and attributed that to working on a computer through the OWL.

We wondered if students' ability to focus online might be due in part to the elements of play associated with being online. Because many students perceive computers and the Internet as being fun, some of that enjoyment may seep into discussing their writing. Obviously, we are not interested in wowing people with technology or substituting "fun technology" for learning, but students seem to enjoy working on a computer to discuss their writing. One student said, "It's more fun to 'talk' to someone and this way I don't have to look at them." The synchronous experience of the chat room can be perceived as fun, as another student noted: "Is quite interesting! Like chatting with a friend. But this is more knowledgeable because both of us are chatting with a given topic." Indeed, the word *chatroom* evokes images that are less formal or intimidating than face-to-face meetings, and yet the "given topic"—the student's paper—is intimated by both sides.

THE FUTURE OF THE OWL AT USU

Based on the information gathered so far, USU plans to continue to develop and expand the services offered by the English Department's OWL. In the immediate future, there are plans to experiment with other document -sharing types of environments, such as document uploading. This feature may be slightly more difficult for students to operate, but would allow for more control over maintaining the format of a student's document; such a feature would be particularly effective in tutoring technical writing students. There are also plans to extend services to the entire campus so that any USU student in any course could consult with a tutor about his or her work. This extension has not occurred because of a desire to limit the number of students receiving online consultations.

Down the road, the department's goal is to use video-conferencing technologies so that students and tutors can also interact visually, thereby gaining many of the advantages of both a face-to-face and an online writing conference. Indeed, we see video conferencing as the future of OWL communications, and it is only a matter of time before technology makes this type of writing conference a reasonable choice for OWLs.

CONCLUSION

According to our students, synchronous Web-based communication has been very effective in helping them become better writers. As the evaluations state, they often feel they leave the conference with some concrete tips they can transfer to other writing situations. Despite the reaction to the lack of personal contact, it did not seem to prevent learning from taking place. Researchers and administrators should continue to study and develop Web-based, synchronous, writing lab environments so that students who are beginning to learn via distance courses might have access to the same level of quality academic support services as the students in traditional classrooms. Indeed, even students who find themselves in face-to-face courses might find access to extra help without returning to campus to be a welcome addition. If the goal of a writing conference is to improve a student's ability to write, then synchronous OWLs can help students and tutors accomplish that goal. The lack of face-to-face contact does not keep learning from taking place in a reasonable amount of time with a reasonable level of computer capability.

15

Putting the OO in MOO: Employing Environmental Interaction

Joel A. English
Old Dominion University

While training graduate tutors to conference with writers on the MOO, I emphasize two principles: Let the writers do the talking in conferences, and take time to gain rapport with the students and help acclimate them to the environment. Allowing the writer to maintain authority over the conference and establishing rapport before getting to work are staples of writing center theory and practice. Yet, when writing conferences move to synchronous computer-mediated settings, these guidelines increase in importance.

Our writing center uses a real time, Internet-based environment called the MOO. Computer realms in which multiple users communicate in real time are called *MUDs*. Internet Relay Chat, real time discussion features of classroom software, and talk or phone features on UNIX systems are MUDs. The MOO is a type of MUD that employs command terms so that participants can talk, emote (perform actions and emotions), and manipulate furniture, writing tools, and other objects. In the past 6 years, many writing centers have found MOOs to be viable and valuable environments for writing conferences.

MOO-based tutoring has impressed writing centers by facilitating metacognitive awareness and reflective writing, complicated but important activities in writers' development. *Metacognition* refers to writers' knowledge of how they write or learn. Bartholomae (1987) indicated that a successful pedagogy "directs students in a semantic investigation of how they as individuals write.... [T]he real subject is writing, as writing is defined by students in their own terms through a systematic inquiry into their behavior as writers" (p. 85). Berthoff (1984) agreed that the "capacity for thinking about thinking, for interpreting interpretations, for knowing our knowledge, is ... the chief resource for any teacher and the ground of hope in the enterprise of teaching reading and writing" (p. 743). Furthermore, Raphael (1989) considered metacognition to be fundamental to learning and teaching:

> First, metacognition describes the control process in which active learners engage as they perform various cognitive activities. Second, metacognitive or executive control processes may underlie the very important processes of generalization and transfer of strategies learned. (p. 346)

Metacognition, therefore, helps students describe how and what they have learned about their writing processes and allows them to generalize and apply the process to future writing situations. If writers do not study their writing processes while engaging in them, they may never understand why they have improved as writers, losing any gains soon after walking out of our doors.

How well do traditional writing center conferences confront our students' need for metacognitive thinking and writing? Probably quite well. Keeping North (1984) in mind, face-to-face tutors can help writers focus on what they are learning and how to apply their skills to future writing situations—better writers, not better writings. However, consider the extended potential for metacognitive reflection when each writing conference creates a written transcript that students save, print, and use in further reflection. After the first group of MOO-based conferences in their 1994 Virtual Reality Writing Center, Jordan-Henley and Maid (1995b) noticed that students would "carry around cybertutors' comments for days and read them over and over" (p. 212). Simply moving the writing conference to an online (and therefore "loggable") setting allows writers to continue reflecting on their tutors' advice.

More important than reviewing the tutors' comments is continued reflection on their own online voices. Most writing center tutors understand the value of helping writers assess their own writing. When students read their conference transcripts, they should witness themselves reaching conclusions, understanding discourse conventions, and making writing decisions. A transcript may present a well-intentioned tutor as a dictator rather than a facilitator of the student's learning; such a figure is ultimately debilitating. Although tutors should push writers toward focusing on certain issues and should ask probing questions, they should stop talking and let writers take over the discussion, articulating the knowledge being transacted online. "Keeping the hands off the keyboard" for online writing tutors nearly parallels the suggestion of "not holding a pen in hand" for face-to-face writing tutors. After a successful cybertutorial, the MOO log reflects the student's growing achievement as a writer, plays back what the writer needs to accomplish with the individual writing assignment, testifies to the writer's ability to talk about her learning with another accomplished writer, and illustrates that the writer has maintained authority over her learning and writing processes.

Still, administrators of MOO-based tutoring can attest that not all online tutorials are successful; unsuccessful ones often occur when tutors and writers are uncomfortable in MOOspace. After their first round of online conferences, Jordan-Henley and Maid (1995a) found that successful conferences began with conversation and play; the tutors who failed to do so conducted less productive sessions. Consequently, Jordan-Henley and Maid (1995a) trained tutors to allow time for acclimation:

> One provided virtual fried chicken. Another made good use of the coffeepot on DaedalusMOO. Still another was so good at just putting the student at ease that it seemed as though both soon became unaware that they were working in Cyberspace and not sitting and talking across the table in a real-life writing center. (p. 6)

Writers need practice MOOing before meeting with tutors. Most teachers who encourage cybertutorials bring the writers onto the MOO for practice sessions before asking the students to work with tutors. Eric Crump, then director of the Online Writery at the University of Missouri, Columbia, used "most of the first few weeks of class just hanging out with those classes [that would take part in cybertutoring], helping teachers and students get logged in for the first time, helping them get a handle on the MOO" (personal communication, February 12, 1995). Productive MOO tutorials require that students understand the environment.

The most overt difference between the MOO-based conference and the traditional conference is that talking, emoting, and manipulating objects online require typing words and sentences, as well as using a few programming symbols. The environment of a MOO-based conference depends on what the writer and tutor do—what they say, how they emote, what they do with the objects. The environment depends more on human interaction than on predetermined furniture and objects (although objects are often programmed into meeting rooms). The writer–tutor team controls the on-line world. Such control rarely occurs in a traditional writing center.

The important question, then, is what do the students actually do in this environment? Allowing students so much control over their learning environment can invigorate the learning experience if they take advantage of their newfound authority. Yet, do they? To what extent and in what ways do students manipulate the environment of the MOO, and what good does this do them? To get a sense of how students interact with the MOO environment within tutorials and other learning situations, I systematically studied the logs of my students' tutorials, trying to answer the following questions:

- Do students engage in emoting and controlling objects regularly, or do they simply talk, not taking advantage of the MOO environment?
- What difference does it make to the students who regularly employ objects and emotions? Do those who practice manipulating the environment actually contribute more to conversation? Do they go into more depth in their discussions? In essence, does the authority over environment help students develop comfort, confidence, and learning online?

METHODOLOGY

I carefully reviewed the logs of cybertutorial sessions from my first-year composition course to discover the extent to which students interacted with the MOO environment, that is, how much they emoted and engaged with objects in addition to speaking online. I developed the following scale to calculate the environment interactivity for each tutorial session:

- Low Environmental Interactivity: Student emoted or used objects an average of zero to two times during conference
- Medium Environmental Interactivity: Student emoted or used objects an average of three to six times during conference
- High Environmental Interactivity: Student emoted or used objects an average of over six times during conference

To study the effect of environmental interactivity on the students' online performance, I paid specific attention to the places within the MOO logs where a student or tutor used a programmed object or emoted. I then read the subsequent lines of dialogue to trace the effect of the environmental interactivity: Did the student's engagement encourage the student to be more vocal, indicating comfort in the environment? Did changes in the dynamics follow the environmental interactivity?

To indicate whether there was a correlation between environmental interactivity and online conversation, I evaluated each student's contributions. Comments related to the topic of discussion I named *substantive comments* as opposed to *unrelated comments*, such as chit-chat about personal matters, joking, or other off-the-topic talking. Unrelated comments are not unimportant comments; indeed, students and tutors need to develop rapport by chatting about issues not related to writing. However, unrelated comments focus off of the substance of the writing conference, thus affecting the direction of the tutorial. I compared the students' substantive comments with their unrelated comments, finding a percentage of substantive comments for each student. I then compared the percentages of the high environmental interactivity students to each other, finding whether the percentages were similar; I compared the low environmental interactivity students' substantive percentages with each other, finding whether those figures were similar; and finally, I compared both the groups to each other. This analysis helped discern whether students' levels of environmental interaction correlated with their learning in the tutorials.

FINDINGS

The MOO logs demonstrated that most freshman students did not freely engage in emoting or object manipulation. During the cybertutorials, 80% of students had low levels of environmental interactivity, and 20% had high levels. When tutors did not specifically push for interactivity, the writers did not manipulate the environment as can be seen in the following encounter between Dave, the writer, and Word, the tutor:

Dave has arrived
Word has arrived
Word sits yoga style on the table
Dave asks, "Where shall we start?"
Word asks, "did you get the comments over the e-mail? maybe you had some thoughts on them?" (personal communication, September 17, 1996)

Word begins by creatively sitting down, which could open a short session of play before diving into the work. However, he does not ask Dave to join him in manipulating the environment, and Dave immediately brings up the business of the writing conference. Word follows him into discussing the paper rather than attempting to postpone the work and acclimate the writer to the environment.

The logs clearly demonstrate that tutors who do not purposefully lead writers in early interaction with the environment do not usually establish a comfortable relationship between themselves and the writer nor between the writer and the learning environment. In an encounter between tutor Ash and writer Missy, for example, Ash does not offer any prework play or emoting; she begins immediately by addressing Missy's paper. Consequently, Missy never feels comfortable in the environment, severely hindering the communication and learning. While talking about the paper on the effects of abortion on women's lives, both participants seem uncomfortable in the environment:

> missy asks, "I guess I should probably mention death rates now,
> too, along with the effects?
> Ash says, "definitely side effects, both short term and long term"
> Ash asks, "just thought of another source any idea if there is a
> local chapter of the National Organization for Women?"
> missy says, "I don't really know what to say. I feel kinda stupid."
> Ash says, "if there is, they are probably in the phonebook - maybe
> even on campus I know that they will have recent info"
> Ash asks, "what to say about what?"
> missy says, "no, but is there a Planned Parenthood in Muncie? They
> would probably have really good info."
> Ash says, "I think I have heard of one"
> Ash says, "to tell the truth, I have only lived here since August, so
> I'm afraid I don't know much about the area"
> missy says, "what to say about anything. I'm just sitting here trying
> to think of questions, but can't think of much." (personal communication,
> September 19, 1996)

The odd timing of the conversation and Missy's inability to think of anything to say indicate her lack of comfort with MOOspace. She would have benefitted from some time at the beginning of the conference invested in acclimation and language play.

When tutors pay careful attention to acclimating the writers to the environment, the conferences progress smoothly and benefit the writers. In fact, those first several minutes of MOOtime should be used for establishing rapport. When tutors lead writers in interacting with the environment and engaging in dialogue, the conferences usually prove clear and communicative for both participants, helping the writer learn much about her writing. For example, cybertutor Gable, in conference with writer rmwilson, opens by teaching some tips about the environment and suggesting that she join him in engaging it:

> Gable asks, "Do you know about the dot-dot-dot deal? Like ... that?"
> rmwilson asks, "actually, i think i use it too much. I seem to use it instead of a ",". I think it keeps the reader more on the edge of their seat."
> Gable says, "Well, I spoze that's true. But if you use it here on the MOO, it means you have more to say, but you're ... "
> Gable says, "still typing ... "
> Gable says, "and when you get done ... "
> Gable says, "you just use a period or other punctuation."
> rmwilson says, "that sounds ... "
> rmwilson says, "wonderful."
> Gable says, "it's really helpful when we get to typing longer sentences ... "
> Gable says, "especially when dealing with El Pokey, my modem."
> rmwilson exclaims, "i guess i never thought of the ... thing that way, but you are right!"
> Gable opens his book bag and pulls out two cans of Coke. "Want one?"
> rmwilson says, "sure! Thanks"
> Gable says, "careful. It got shaken up when my modem wend down."
> rmwilson opens the coke very carefully making sure the contents don't spill out.
> rmwilson gulps.
> rmwilson "aaaaaggggggggggghhhhhhhhh" (personal communication, September 18, 1996).

In the conferences in which the tutors encouraged environmental interactivity, more object and emotion engagement occurred, and more productivity was made possible.

Environmental interactivity almost always occurred at the beginning of the sessions. Emoting and object manipulation seemed to help students feel grounded in the environment. The tutors sometimes began by offering writers a virtual drink or snack, by suggesting they sit and make themselves comfortable, or by explaining features of the MOO. As tutors and writers began discussing the writing, they usually traded emoting and object play for straight dialogue. Again, this progression seems logical; just as traditional writing center tutors ease into discussions about writing, so do cybertutors.

Once in a while, a well-intentioned environmental focus hindered a tutoring session. During one of his conferences, Gable used emoting from time to time to pet his cat, which was physically at his feet: "Gable reaches down and rubs his cat on the ears.... Gable's cat is eating his eraser.... Gable's cat carried the eraser into another room. Bizarre." Gable thought this was a clever way to make himself seem more real and connected to Alicia, the writer; upon reading the log, I agreed. However, Alicia found the references distracting: "Having the online session with Gable helped a little, but not a lot.... When we got on the MOO, I felt like he was kind of rambling. He spent more time talking about things that didn't even relate to my paper." Gable's exuberant emoting disrupted Alicia's concentration. Despite occasional overuse, we should encourage environmental interactivity in MOOspace because the logs indicate that such activity, especially at the beginning of conferences, helps students gain control and comfort online.

CONCLUSION

Programmed objects and emoting are innate features of the MOO environment, separating it from other synchronous communication forums. Engaging in these aspects can help students become comfortable communicating online. However, online environmental interactivity is not innate or natural; most students do not spontaneously emote or engage programmed objects. Consequently, students may remain uncomfortable with the online environment rather than interact with it.

Tutors must attend to writers' need for acclimation by leading them in environmental interactivity at the beginning of writing conferences. Students need practice manipulating the environment and taking full advantage of its possibilities during their first visits online. Tutor and writer must establish both interpersonal rapport and comfort with the environment before productive work is possible on the MOO.

The MOO provides the tools needed for first-year writers to become confident, capable, and authoritative in online writing. In order to take advantage of the environment, tutors, teachers, and writers should embrace the environmental features, using them like they use the physicality of the traditional writing center to become grounded in their surroundings and prepared for productivity. Upon accomplishing such grounding, a tutor–writer team can make the most of the cognitive and metacognitive learning that the MOO can facilitate.

16

Ethics, Plugged and Unplugged: The Pedagogy of Disorderly Conduct

Jane Love
University of Florida

Once upon a time, there was a MOO, an educational MOO, where litera-ture and film classes met to discuss projects and assignments and where tu-tors met students to discuss writing. A teacher in this MOO happened, one day, to fall into conversation with a student from another teacher's class. The conversation was unusually relaxed and genial, as MOO conversation often is, and the student volunteered that a class presentation earlier that day had not gone very well. The teacher wondered why, and the student ex-plained that the presentation had taken place in the Purple Porpoise, the MOO equivalent of a local drinking establishment. The student said that everyone had been drinking and carousing, paying little attention. Hmmm, wondered the teacher, so she asked if the student saw anything wrong with virtual drinking during real classtime? "No," said the student. "Of course not, how could there be anything wrong with it—it's virtual?!"

Thereby hang a question and a possibility that interest me very much. The question concerns the ethical dimension of a distinction between real and virtual actions. The possibility is that the MOO may prove to be fertile

181

(albeit virtual) ground for exploring this question with students, both in one-to-one tutoring interactions and in larger, class-based interactions. MOO scholarship necessarily works across these differing modes of pedagogy and resists being restricted to a single type of forum or site. It is this very resistance that sprouts dangling questions and possibilities for MOO tutors and teachers to explore.

MOO misbehavior is a fairly common, and usually mundane, occurrence. I quickly learned to expect a barrage of crude, rude, and sometimes lewd comments and gestures within the first 20 minutes of introducing a tutee or class to the MOO. Particularly popular are acts that involve superhuman feats or the spilling of guts, along with suicide (very popular among young men). The virtuosity of virtuality intoxicates all by itself, even without virtual drinking.

This initial flush of excitement tends to fade, however, under the weight of assignments, logged discussions, and group projects, efforts that serve as the centerpiece of tutor–tutee interaction. Like many instructors, I discovered that the best way to deal with the problem of virtual misbehavior was to be sure that tutees always have a task to complete, preferably one sufficiently challenging to absorb any (potentially problematic) excess student energy. Yet, as the incident previously mentioned suggests, this strategy does not always work—sometimes the frustration incurred by a task tempts a tutee to let off a little steam. As tutees refine and develop their building and programming skills, they often delight in putting these skills to mischievous or subversive uses—a kind of hacker mentality. Of course, sincere confusion exists about what constitutes misconduct in the MOO, where everything that happens is, we might say, just so much verbiage.

Yet, there is another reason for having second thoughts about keeping tutees on-task as a way of managing their behavior (there obviously are compelling reasons to do so pedagogically): Tutees need to explore and test the agency that they experience in the MOO. They do this instinctively and passionately. Disruptive behavior is but one of the avenues available for this exploration, but, as I will explain, I believe it may well be one of the most important. Disorderly conduct in the MOO just might be a potent tool for teaching, both one-to-one and in classrooms.

Return to the opening scenario. The student could not see how there could be anything wrong with virtual drinking because it is not real. My answer to the student (because I was the instructor-half of this exchange) was simple: Virtual drinking might not be real, but it had had real effects on the student presentation, which did not, as my partner in MOO conversation informed me, go well. Although he did not respond, I suppose the student I was speaking with could have replied that the presentation was just as virtual as the drinking and as such did not deserve or warrant the kind of respect and attentiveness it would command as a real life event. I suspect that something like this notion might also be lurking in the backs of many students' minds about the serious academic work and intellectual engagement that many instructors and tutors believe is possible in the MOO.

Instructors do, indeed, believe that such work is possible, and we expend tremendous effort and a great deal of time to realize this possibility, often battling the resistance of colleagues and administrators to do so. Making the case for using MOO to teach writing, however, is not the whole story because even the most convincing argument can fail to assuage the fears of some. Like students, faculty and administrators can also harbor a background suspicion that anything that takes place in a MOO is not quite real and therefore does not deserve the status of serious academic work. Could it be that disorderly conduct among students and resistance to MOO among administrators arise from the same set of assumptions about what constitutes real work and its value?

I do not intend to address the questions of virtuality or of the relationship between the virtual and the real here, at least not in any sustained way. However, it does seem as though this distinction between a virtual MOO and real life lies at the root of both resistance to and misuse of the MOO. Dibbell (1993), in his now legendary *Village Voice* piece, "A Rape in Cyberspace," convincingly demonstrated the untenability of this distinction for synchronous multi-user environments such as MOO. The victims of Mr. Bungle's aggression and sadism experienced very real emotional responses, and the entire community of LambdaMOO was shaken in a way that can only be assessed as real, as real as the community itself. Dibbell, in fact, argued that Mr. Bungle operated not just from a faulty understanding of the virtual–real relationship in the MOO, but that his actions were quite literally sociopathological—not virtually so, but really so, where the measure of the "really so" is the real effects of Mr. Bungle's virtual actions.

Interestingly, when I discussed Dibbell's essay with students, the responses followed a predictable pattern. The men were uncharacteristically quiet during class discussion, oddly so given the enthusiasm they had displayed for the essay based on its title ("How can you rape someone in cyberspace?" one of them asked me, a bit too eagerly to conceal his unspoken and more urgent question: "Do I have a penis I don't know about?"). The women in the class, however, were both vocal and vehement: Nothing had happened, nothing at all, and whatever did happen would not have happened if the two victims had simply, as one young woman put it, "unplugged their computers." For them, the crime, if it did occur, happened with the full complicity of the victims. Yet, they were most emphatic that it had not really happened.

There are many reasons that would predispose young women to adopt an aggressively dismissive posture toward what these students perceived as specious claims of sexual harassment (although they neglected to point out that the notion of cyber-rape arguably trivializes real rape). The analogy between their comments and the chauvinistic "She got what she asked for" response to claims of harassment broke down, for them, along the fault line of the computer cord: that cord, and the plug at the end of it, were the decisive delimiters of what was to be taken seriously and what was not. Pulling the plug represented, for them, the ultimate power play in any question of cyber-violence. These young women felt that they had located the Archimedean point of leverage between the virtual and the real—and it has three prongs on it.

The plug, like the sword of discretion or even the lowly *copulae* of conjunctions, cuts—or works—both ways. Yes, one may at any moment yank the plug on the computer to be swiftly and safely rescinded into … what? Reality? Then what of lessons and learning? Is not learning itself a form of virtuality, a speculative endeavor predicated on the wholly unsubstantiated possibility of there being something inside the tutee to be drawn forth ("education" derives from the Latin *e-ducare*, to draw out), to be rendered real rather than virtual (or vice versa, depending on where one falls with respect to the viability of the subject)? For tutors in particular, who so frequently work one-on-one, the Platonic resonances are difficult to evade: The plug is precisely the conduit, the catalyst, for the illuminating spark that travels from tutor to tutee. Networked technologies strip this quaint figure of its metaphoricity, and in doing so they focus much of our interaction with tutees within the tiny yet so-very-fertile locus of the tip of the prong, a physical location of immense metaphysical import. We can choose whether or not to plug in, whether or not to remain plugged in. Yet, once plugged in, *contra* my female students, I believe we sacrifice a measure of our freedom to unplug. I would not have it otherwise, for this is the absolutely necessary ground of gravity—of seriousness and efficacy of purpose as we tutor and teach—in the MOO.

The plug establishes a connection that is real, even though the mode of that connection, because of its allusiveness to such physical orientatia as space, time, objectification, agency, and causality, is virtual. By demetaphorizing the Platonic spark, the plug allows reality to seep through in the form of such highly human and ethically laden acts as recognition, familiarity, community, mutual regard, antagonism mitigated by mutual regard, curiosity, glee, expression, testing of limits, and—yes—teaching and learning. Because these real connections take place in an environment of virtuality, their reality is not compromised but highlighted, piped all around in the neon of extreme significance by virtue of their seeming insignificance as mere virtualities.

The rape that took place in LambdaMOO—far from trivializing rapes that take place in the real world—highlights the very real emotional and communal consequences of those real world rapes. The truth is that whenever we connect with each other via networked connections, but particularly via synchronous connections such as MOO, the virtuality of that connection is nothing more than the medium for the real and regular stuff of human contact. That things can happen in MOO that cannot or does not happen in real life is indisputable. Yet, I believe this argues more for the extraordinary breadth of range needed to give expression to our regard for each other than for the triviality of MOO.

A pedagogy of disorderly conduct is, like much disorderly conduct, one of opportunity rather than agenda: It opportunistically explores the tensions of MOO as presented by and through tutees themselves and not as part of a syllabus. It seeks not so much to eradicate disorderly conduct as to illuminate it—or, more properly, to use it to illuminate what passes for orderly conduct. It requires of tutors and instructors that they shift a disciplinarian focus on obedience to one of sensitivity to tension and that they deftly shift to the tutee the burden of responsibility for how to respond to such tension. Obviously, such a pedagogy is anything but programmatic, and so, what follow are suggestions shot from the hip, as it were, to the hip, to be transported via the hip and communicated to other (tutee) hips. I recommend a snazzily designed MOO powercord belt for your MOO character, sporting the requisite three-pronged plug (with two-pronged adapter for those recalcitrant cases) as the sole instrument for negotiating this difficult territory. Thus equipped, tutors and instructors may gently (perhaps even humorously) engage tutees and students in the following ways:

1. Because most disorderly conduct takes advantage of the assumed gap between reality and virtuality ("How could it matter? It's not real!"), the most effective response is one that questions this assumption. Ask the tutee

to enumerate the real consequences of eir[1] action in terms of academic performance—distraction and disruption for the tutor or other tutees; loss of instruction for the tutee; wasted expense of time online for tutee and/or tutor; undermining of the productive relationship between tutor and tutee, with consequent slowed progression toward degree; trivialization of the chosen medium of education, with consequent trivialization of education itself; and, of course, many more. It is important that the tutee be engaged as an equal on this question because the point is not so much to instruct but to redirect eir attention to questions of value and consequence without which eir tutorial would be meaningless. Recalling eir goals and purposes enables tutees to assess the consequences of eir MOO behavior in very real terms. In this case, Plato is right: Education is achieved through memory.

2. Because much disorderly conduct takes advantage of the gap between reality and vitality for the sake of exploring agency in the MOO, another response (complementary to the previous one) is to encourage the tutee to describe the appeal of acting out in the MOO. Vitality and intoxication are arguably closely related states of mind (a point which would interestingly beg the question of vitality's relation to intoxication)—acknowledging the appeal of MOO agency provides a powerful entry into the necessarily linked questions of both expression and responsibility. People want and need to express themselves, but what are the constraints on and the responsibilities accompanying that expression? The first suggestion previously mentioned can help outline the consequences of uninhibited self-expression in the MOO, but here the object is to identify the benefits that tutees find in the MOO, whether it be the privilege of addressing eir instructor or tutor by a MOOenym as opposed to a title, enhanced familiarity with other MOOers, or the freedom to design and build outrageous MOO contraptions—some of which, of course, may cross the lines of what would be legal in real life. In these cases, I suggest that tutors and instructors apply the consequence evaluation in the previous suggestion.

3. Because MOO tutorials and instruction presuppose by their intent and purpose a continuity between virtual environments and the real and because tutorial and instructional practices in the MOO also presuppose this continuity, capitalize on it! Use MOO logs of sessions as a stimulus for reflection about MOO behavior. Ask explicitly about how tutees perceive the difference between conventions of the MOO and conventions of the face-to-face writing center. Discuss the advantages and detractions of both.

---

[1]In this essay, pronouns that refer to tutees and tutors specifically in their MOO interactions take the gender neutral forms suggested by Gayatri Spirak and used by default in most MOOs.

Consider how the advantages meet the purposes of tutoring and how they do not; do the same for the disadvantages. If distributed synchronous connectivity is an advantage, then is that solely because it duplicates the local synchronicity of the writing center, or does synchronicity assume a different flavor in the MOO? If the synchronicity of MOO is not (as is the case for many of us) quite synchronous enough, does the lag contribute to a sense of disorder that invites disorderly conduct? Encourage tutees to be aware of the ways in which technology disrupts the vitality of the MOO environment, and encourage em to relate these disruptions to eir purposes in being tutored online.

MOO is inherently hierarchical in its administrative organization (e.g., wizards, archwizards, players, etc.) and so is vulnerable to hacker mentality, as well as classroom mentality: Many standard, default MOO messages convey an autocratic authority that for many tutees and students can be difficult to countenance ("You can't do that;" "I don't understand you;" or "Permission denied"). In my experience, as many tutees find the MOO offputting and stultifying as find it utterly beguiling and liberating. Use discussion to identify which is the case, and why, for each tutee—but more importantly, with each tutee. Do not pretend that MOO is a utopian educational environment—the writing center is not either. Yet, the more you can assist students in identifying their own relation with MOO technology, the more they will be able to optimize the time you spend together.

4. Because much disorderly conduct in the MOO is a consequence of sheer intoxication with MOO, go with it! One must first be sure that true MOO ardor inspires the disorderly conduct, and not some other cause, but this is easily ascertained by the size and nature of the tutee's MOO-building Personalization, often to a disconcerting degree, is the usual characteristic of such intoxication (unless it is of the Star Trek variety, in which case nothing more need be said), and intoxicants are usually pestering and perfectionistic in eir MOO behavior and manifestations. Deploy the intoxicated on other tutees or students. Enlist eir help in teaching others how to program verbs. Draw em into the community by helping em help build it. Once students who are intoxicated with MOO realize that it has tapped into communally valuable skills and characteristics ey possess, ey can easily transform eir ardor into dazzlingly constructive-yet-subversive devices that fully realize the ethical power of MOO to both stabilize and revise the making of a voluntary community.

5. Because some disorderly conduct in the MOO results from a larger antipathy that is not specific to the virtual environment, one may easily

take advantage of the plug to render it ineffectual. Do not unplug your computer. Instead, deploy your spiffy MOO-plug belt to alert the tutee to the limitations to eir presumed omnipotence. (Note: In some MOOs, this may involve recourse to gagging, booting, or otherwise suppressing unwelcome conduct—a recourse that should, of course, itself be scrutinized alongside the tutee, and which otherwise is of nonexistent pedagogical value.) Recommended are the following:

- Retain a log of the disorderly conduct in question.
- Return it to the disorderly tutee, as if returning a lost sweater (i.e., correcting an oversight, not an infraction) to a friend.
- Suggest that said log is, like a sweater, of personal significance.
- Suggest that personal artifacts are best not left around public places—for the tutee's personal protection, of course.

MOO induces a heady conflation of public and private for many participants, and many are unpleasantly caught within eir conflation, too late for extrication. One might argue that this is the (in)felicitous consequence of the MOO's capacity to generate logs of activity, yet this capacity also generates logs of tutor–tutee discussions, assignments, presentations, and other pedagogically pertinent activities, all of which benefit vastly from having available a printed record for examination and discussion. The repercussions of such records sound with only the softest knelling: Do you really want to show yourself in this way? We are not, in general, sensitive to the lingering effects of our self-representations, particularly in this late-capitalist consumer economy that encourages us to indulge fantasies of self inventive and reinventive freedom.

The intimacy and reinventive freedom of MOO is not like any other, and so it speaks closely to that longing for a new self, for a self with no consequences, with total or zero acceptance. Tutors are only incidentally involved in the business of personally accepting tutees, yet we are deeply involved in the business of convincing our tutees that they are capable of constructive, articulate self-expression. We must be willing to assist them in this effort, and we must be willing to utilize both the virtuality of MOO and the real connectivity it fosters, to both enable and challenge tutees in eir encounters with not just technology but also language, representation, and human relations—those most daunting disciplines that underlie all others. The power of the tutor lies precisely in how e is able to occupy a central reflective position in all these areas, simply as a matter of pragmatics. The tutor enables the tutee to connect to the MOO via the Internet. E works with em on grammar, composition, and the conventions of exposition and expression through language. E invites em to consider how ey represent emselves, and in so doing, e focuses eir attention on the ethics that make human relations possible. There is no work that is more essential, nor is there any environment in which it is rendered more essentially.

The hand that yanks the plug rocks the cradle—and perhaps rules the world? A terribly tenuous analogy and one that I, for one, do not believe. Power is far more intricately diffuse and specifically allocated than any given charmed prong will allow for. Yet, anyone who teaches in a MOO knows already that all gifts of agency—all multipronged utility belts, ready for action—come with a heavy and specific responsibility for the entire well-being of the MOO itself. Given thoughtful attention and not just a quick fix, disorderly conduct in the MOO may lead to the realization that the notion of orderly conduct is itself a virtual creation and that reality itself is the ethical result of what people recognize as their virtuality, their capability for choosing actions and values. There is no surer way of bringing on the real than by embracing the virtual, the possible, the imagined, the felt wholeness among us that the MOO softwarily only begins to suggest.

V

Looking to the Future

17

Making Up Tomorrow's Agenda and Shopping Lists Today: Preparing for Future Technologies in Writing Centers

Muriel Harris
Purdue University

Although the use of technology in the writing center might be seen as a choice to make, there is compelling evidence that it is no longer an option. Electronic communication in writing courses and in WAC programs is not a trend or alternative that will fade from the scene. As is evident in the varied uses of technology in the chapters of this book or in the case studies of educational programs and projects such as those described in *Electronic Communication Across the Curriculum*, a 1998 collection of essays edited by Reiss, Selfe, and Young, technology has permanently changed the environment for writing in post secondary education, both in English departments and across campus. In her forward to *Electronic Communication Across the Curriculum*, Selfe (1998) traced the growth and intertwining of writing in writing-across-the-curriculum programs with computers as a technology for communication, culminating in what she describes as "a series of important sea changes in computer-supported writing pedagogies" in the early 1990s

(p. xii). The result, noted Selfe, was the development of a variety of writing-intensive learning environments represented in communication by e-mail, listservs, and, eventually, the Internet and the World Wide Web.

The curricular development described by Selfe continues at a rapid rate, and for writing centers this means a clientele of students who are composing texts on personal computers, in computer labs, in e-mail discussions, in multimedia presentations, on Websites, in distance-learning projects, and so on. Computers as a technology interwoven in communication is a given, as is electronic communication across the curriculum. Writing centers without the technology or staff to work with these students will find themselves no longer in sync with how writers write and with what writers need to know about writing processes as they are affected by technology. Thus, because this introduces new dimensions in the ways that tutors and students collaborate and interact, there is an accompanying need for research that studies how these new tutorial environments impact writing center theory and practice. We need to know much more about how technology changes the nature of tutorial collaboration, we need to know much more about how to train tutors, and we need to study what we must do to prepare for future technology entering the writing center. What we need, finally, is a research agenda and a shopping list that adequately prepares us for what lies ahead.

A major item on that agenda, because it affects what tutors and students do together in tutorial collaboration, is to consider the profound impact technology has had on the way we communicate, on the way we live and work, and on the way we think. Technology has changed our lives in ways that we are just now beginning to understand and come to grips with. Comprehending what these changes mean and considering how to make the best educational use of them is, in the larger sense, the real challenge of the future. The impact of technology is being studied in a variety of ways and as multilayered descriptors of the world we now live in, but all are based on the realization that—for better or worse—we have entered and cannot retreat from the information age in which handling, producing, and relaying information will engage much (if not most) of our time. A portrait of the consequences of this phenomenon is Shenk's (1997) *Data Smog: Surviving the Information Glut,* an extended study, as his subtitle indicates, of how to survive the information glut that has overwhelmed us. The challenge, noted Shenk, is to adapt so that we are "empowered by information instead of bring smothered by it" (p. 16). Information is being produced faster than we can process it, and just dealing with it in terms of information processing now accounts for more than half of the U.S. gross national product (p. 29). Information overload is such a national problem, noted Shenk, that it has strained our ability to comprehend, much less evaluate and make sense of, this morass of data, and it is constricting moral thinking. For example, as Shenk noted, given over 100,000 studies of depression (p. 93), how does one gain a clear sense of what is known, much less come to any well-informed conclusions? The challenge for those of us who assist in educating the future producers and users of so much information is to contemplate how we can help them think about and compose the communicative texts that deal with the vast amounts of information that bombard them. From the first-year composition course research paper to the graduate student dissertation proposal, the texts that students are bringing to writing centers present challenges we must learn more about.

How, then, do we plan for the future? To complicate the problem even more, how can we plan for a future whose shape we cannot necessarily predict? Less than 5 years ago, before the advent of the Internet browser, the "killer app" of the mid-1990s that brought the World Wide Web into our lives, communication online was confined to lines of text. Given the very few years that took us from Gopher to the World Wide Web, what will technology bring us in 10 years? How will it reshape electronic communication? Predicting the shape of tomorrow's advances with any degree of accuracy is, as the aphorism goes, "like nailing jelly to a tree." For example, when I proposed this chapter some months ago, I cited push technology as a promising direction for the future. (*Push technology* would allow information providers to proactively send out information to subscribers without their having to request it.) Within months, push information has become both a reality and a dead-end technology with diminished prospects. Although the February 1998 issue of *Internet World*, a widely read Internet magazine, featured an essay by Calishain on push technology and its promise, an article by Flynn in the February 16, 1998, edition of the *New York CyberTimes* was entitled "Why 'Push' Got Shoved Out of the Market." Technology moves forward at an accelerated pace we can barely catch up with. However, although it is almost impossible to make well-informed plans for future uses of technology in the writing center, it would be irresponsible not to plan. A case study of efforts to plan and develop the OWL at Purdue University and what was learned in the process of reflecting on that development is offered in Harris and Blythe's (1998) "A Discussion on Collaborative Design Methods for Collaborative Online Spaces."

Preparing and planning for the future also means dealing with the tension between pressure to adopt technology and the time needed to consider its uses. In academia, it is too often the case that funds suddenly become available and must be allocated in a very short time, sometimes with an institutional vision that may or may not be an appropriate fit with the writing center's goals, methodologies, and instructional theories. An institution moving toward distance learning might see its writing center as a place to institute writing courses online, to do community outreach, or to serve as the writing component for distance learning programs. In addition, the institution might see advantages to bringing technology into the writing center so that it also becomes the self-study center where remediation software will assist at-risk students or learning-disabled students or ESL students. If the center is committed to interactive, nonevaluative, collaborative learning, such programs cannot be imported without some effect on the center's theory and practice. Given all the potential problems, realities, and the importance of technology in the writing center—in addition to its advantages and the need to draw some blueprints somehow—what, then, can we do to plan for the future? One way to proceed is to segment the various areas in which technology can and should impact the work of writing centers; these are the areas of instruction, administration, institutional mission, and research. Defining the needs and potential within each of these subcategories can help us draw up both an agenda of work that lies ahead and a shopping list for the future.

WHAT USES OF TECHNOLOGY
SHOULD WRITING CENTERS FOCUS ON?

Instructional Uses of Technology in the Writing Center

As the studies of computer-mediated composing indicate, technology is both enabling and disabling for writers. Writers need to acquire basic computer literacy in how to word process, send e-mail, engage in online interaction, and navigate the World Wide Web, and they also need to learn strategies for composing online and for conducting searches online for research papers and reports. Although the Internet has opened doors to vast amounts of information, writers are also even more overwhelmed than they were when doing library searches by the information overload that new technology is tossing at us.[1] They need search strategies and cognitive tools to find, process, evaluate, organize, and integrate the information they collect into coherent pieces of discourse. When freed from linear progression as they engage in hypertext writing, students need new modes of organization and presentation, and as the visual literacy of document design continues to grow in importance, students need to discuss presentation, document segmenting, and formatting as well as content. Tutorials that focused on working with the student in traditional writing processes will need to move through new processes during writing.[2] Tutors trained to assist with the rhetorical and grammatical priorities of text written in hard copy need to acquire new skills and insight into how to help writers with these concerns, and tutors who were once able to deal face to face with writers will need guidance in interacting online, either in text-only situations (such as e-mail), on the Web in various configurations, or teleconferencing. Continued tutor training and ongoing communication among the tutoring staff can also move online in the center.

The research questions that accompany these concerns have to be formulated so that we can proceed in well-informed ways. What are effective tutorial strategies and approaches in these new environments? What other kinds of communicative skills will tutors need to replace traditional ones so important in face-to-face interaction, such as listening and using body language? Are there new ways to listen and extend phatic cues online? How will the nature of interactive communication change when talk as the medium of exchange disappears or when communication is asynchronous?

---

[1]As an example of how overwhelmed students can be when confronting the World Wide Web, I offer the case of Kristen, an undergraduate in our writing lab who is somewhat new to using the Web. As a graduate student tutor and I sat at a computer in the lab developing an online tutorial on how to search the World Wide Web for our OWL, we were considering various visual formatting alternatives we might use. To get some insight into how students plunge in using search engines, we asked Kristen if we could look over her shoulder as she started a simple Web search. When she first encountered the YAHOO! home page, she sat quietly for a bit while we watched and wondered how she would begin her search. Finally, because Kristen continued to scan the page and do nothing, we asked her to talk about what was happening, and she explained that she was bewildered by the screen, not able to discriminate between the advertising in the banner across the top, the information in the frame to the left, the relevant search engine section, and other kinds of information on the page. Clearly, Kristen was experiencing information overload and inadequate visual literacy. How could a tutorial on searching the Web begin without backtracking to help her sort out and understand the contents of the different sections of the Web page?

[2]To illustrate this, see the comparison of Tutorial A in a writing center without an OWL and Tutorial B in a writing center with an OWL in Harris (1998, pp. 3–4). As the student and tutor attempt to talk about the student's research paper, the tutor in Tutorial A cannot assist the student with search strategies, source evaluation, and so on while the student moves through these processes. In Tutorial B, the tutor watches, asks questions, and suggests strategies at the time that the student is engaging in her searching, adding dimensions in tutorial collaboration not possible in Tutorial A.

What new tutoring concerns become relevant? For example, the invitation to students to engage in e-mail tutoring seems to bring with it the student tendency to ask a grammar question that reduces tutoring to grammar fixing, the Band-Aid approach to healing wounded grammar that writing centers battle against. Equally prevalent in having an e-mail service is the tendency for students to e-mail a paper with no accompanying contextual information about the assignment or the student's concerns. In addition to traditional instructional handouts that fill the cabinets of most writing centers, what new topics should be presented in these handouts? What other materials should be on hand for tutors and writers to consult? Without the closer look that research and hard thinking provide us, how can writing centers offer theoretically sound, effective tutorial assistance in this new environment?

Administrative Uses of Technology in the Writing Center

With computer-assisted data gathering in the writing center, directors can gather and sort data on student use and study the writing center's populations in a variety of ways, both for their own insights into their center's needs and effectiveness and for purposes of reporting to administrators how the center is being used. With some minimal use of push technology, writing center directors can also send out notices of workshops, updates on available services, and even publicity notices and reminders to interested students and teachers, ideas suggested, for example, by Crossland (1998) in an essay offering an extended list of administrative uses of e-mail. Various tasks, such as signing up students for tutorials can move online, and notes to teachers can be sent by e-mail, as Stahlnecker (1998) reported is already being done in Creighton University's writing center. Stahlnecker also argued for this type of online communication as a means to "clear up misconceptions and gain appreciation among their campus colleagues" (p. 2). An added advantage to this paperless reporting, she noted, is that e-mail notifications are getting responses from colleagues to those notes, that, as we know, more often tend to disappear into black holes and produce little or no interaction with instructors.

With all the information that can be collected into data-sorting programs, writing center directors face the potential of the kind of "data smog" that Shenk (1997) described, finding themselves so overloaded that much of the information is no longer useful. Included on the list of research questions directors will have to ask themselves is one that asks which data are useful for which purposes and how it can be collected, sorted, and used. With networked connections to institutional databases on the student population, what sorts of studies can be done on students who use the center? Will there be new ways to consider the effectiveness of the center? The use of such data in studies done by Lerner (1997) and Newmann (1999) on the results of student use of their centers already provides one new way for data to show writing center effectiveness as well as new questions that can be asked.

What kinds of other information will be useful for the director's own administrative needs and for the reports to the administration about the center's work? How will writing center administration be affected in terms of the responsibilities of the director? How will interactions with teachers be affected as, for example, Stahlnecker's (1998) encouraging findings that online communication can result in more interaction with instructors? What sorts of training methods will need to be added in tutor training courses? How will the tutorial skills needed affect the selection process in deciding on a new staff? Because the whole body of literature on tutor selection has not yet addressed this matter, despite its being of great urgency already, the question about skills to look for has to be addressed.

Institutional Uses of Technology in the Writing Center

Because technology can open doors for distance learning and outreach, institutions can benefit from Internet sites in writing centers, and writing assistance can be provided across campus where students are writing online. The institutional advantages for a writing center making innovative uses of technology place the center at the heart of writing instruction in ways that can benefit the center—if it does not let itself become overwhelmed by too many programs that dilute its mission. Yet, what place does tutorial interaction have in coursework online? If distance learning becomes central to (or, at least, part of) an institution's mission and practice, as is evident already in the rapid growth of the number of distance learning courses presently available, teachers and students in distance learning courses in a variety of fields of study are going to need new ways to interact. Instead of the traditional question-and-answer exchanges in classes and the office conferences where further discussion occurs, instructors will need to rely on technology to interact with their students. For those new to online interaction, writing centers can become leaders in helping colleagues across the campus learn how to meet students online, either in Web-based courses on campus (where faculty invite students to communicate with them and other students on-line) or for distance learning courses offered to off-campus students. Draw-ing on the experience they have gained with their OWLs, writing center staff can suggest design features, can offer advice and training in methods for effective interaction, and can share their research into what has worked for them in the writing center. Writing centers do not and should not exist primarily for the purpose of course and faculty development for the rest of the institution, but they can step in and lead the way. Institutional funding of technology in the writing center will be seen as a wise investment. Writ-ing center specialists, who advocate among ourselves the effectiveness of writing center theory and pedagogy, will have opportunities to extend our influence beyond our traditional roles in writing programs by inviting col-leagues in other fields to consider the principles for learning that we have built our programs on. The more we come to learn about how to use tech-nology effectively in the center, the more we will have to share.

Research Uses of Technology in the Writing Center

Just as writing center research looks at individual writers and the place of collaborative learning in tutorials, the writing center is a logical place to study the interactions of individual writers and technology. Investigations of online tutoring, writing with computers, online research, and so on are topics for serious study as is the development of Websites in centers. For ex-ample, Blythe's (1997) doctoral dissertation work, researching the OWL at Purdue, is reported in his *Writing Center Journal* essay, "Networked Com-puters + Writing Centers = ? Thinking About Networked Computers in Writing Center Practice." Blythe's work introduces us to the field of design-ing technology for the user by studying the interface of user and technology. How technology changes or enhances individual differences in student writing needs to be the focus of much future research. Writing centers, al-ready focused on individual writers, will be the natural center for such study.

WHAT WILL BE ON OUR SHOPPING LISTS AS WE PLAN FOR TECHNOLOGY IN OUR WRITING CENTERS?

If we agree that technology will need to be studied in terms of its impact on writing center theory and practice, then we should also acknowledge that this expansion requires some shopping lists for the future. The act of planning itself will have to be budgeted into a writing center director's responsibilities—time to think about the questions raised here, time to do the research needed to make decisions, time to draw up shopping lists for which forms of technology to add to the center, and time to seek the funding that will be needed. Funding itself is a highly complex question because it becomes necessary to convince administrators that adding technology means adding personnel, not decreasing it. Technical assistance is an absolute necessity, so basic to the writing center that incorporates technology that no center director should let the first computer in the door without assurances that there will be ongoing technical help in developing and maintaining any and all forms of technology in the center as well as ongoing funding to maintain, upgrade, and further develop all the hardware, software, and instructional materials that will be part of the center's work. Yet, what kinds of hardware, software, and instructional materials might a center director put on a shopping list?

The suggestion here is to have a shopping list for the future that plans for various uses of technology:

- If the center plans to have a Website with resources for writers, then it needs to have a computer that is the server, and it needs accompanying hardware and software to support the Website and to act as a fileserver for a networked writing center. Also needed are a back-up system for the server's hard drive, software for data gathering on Web use and assisting in keeping the site from crashing, and a scanner for turning documents and graphics into computer files.
- If the center plans to have technology for professional development of the staff, then adequate computer access is needed for listservs, document preparation for the Website, research projects, and so forth.
- If the center incorporates technology for administrative purposes, then adequate computer access is needed to enter data, to run data sorting and scheduling programs, to send reports, and for publicity.
- If the center incorporates online tutoring, either synchronous or asynchronous, there has to be computer access for tutors to respond to the students interacting with them online.
- If the center uses its OWL for on-site tutoring in the center, it needs computer access for tutor and student to sit together and use the OWL as an entry to the Web. This would be for face-to-face tutorials with writers who come in for assistance with writing research papers.
- If the center also intends to provide programmed learning on computers, there will need to be sufficient computer access for students to use software and CD-ROM materials for writers working on their own.

The number and type of computers that will be on this shopping list depend on all the researching and planning that must be done in advance. However, the future is already here, and new OWLs are being hatched along with those already flying. It is imperative that we recognize that we cannot just wing it.

18

Centering in the Distance: Writing Centers, Inquiry, and Technology

Gail Cummins
University of Kentucky

> The central problem in literacy theories is the problem of change—when, how, and why do people shift from one literacy to another.
>
> —Miles Myers

Continual reflecting, critical thinking, and active learning are the hallmarks of pedagogy in the University of Kentucky (UK) writing center community. Because our writing center work is based on individual needs, learning is conducted one-on-one, group-to-group, and case-by-case. We promote a contextual and flexible process of active education. In moving from a print to a technological culture, pedagogies must be multiple and adaptable. Unfortunately, many institutions of higher education are arranged as passive learning environments that favor depositing information—what Freire (1997) called the *banking method of education*—as a teaching strategy. Writing center directors, therefore, need to claim and name active pedagogies and to apply them to local technologies and the literacies these technologies enable—both inside and outside of our own institutions and communities.

203

No matter how much technology writing centers use, they stand poised to lead institution-based movements toward technology for learning. Writing center directors need to know how, as Grimm (1996) posited, to articulate our readiness to help transition faculty and students to the new thinking, learning, and teaching technology has forced on us (p. 542).

Certainly, the need to develop active learners who understand that the cultural contexts of any given speech or written event requires some use of knowledge is not novel (Bartholomae,1985; Bizzell, 1992; Rose, 1989). Novel, however—because unnoticed—is the fact that writing centers have been doing this kind of teaching for a long while. Because writing center tutors work with new students, texts, and contexts with every tutorial, good writing center practice teaches a critical literacy—an ability both to observe and interact in any given tutorial.

In addition, writing center work involves a community of teachers and learners across a broad spectrum of grade levels, institutions, learning and teaching styles, and social contexts. Therefore, writing centers are sites of various constructions of literacies: reading, writing, talking, and socializing. Heath (1997) recommended community-based literacy work for true, active learning:

> Community literacy activities are public and social.... On some occasions, they [people in a community] attend to the text itself; on others, they use it only as a starting point for wide-ranging talk. On all occasions, they bring in knowledge related to the text and interpret beyond the text for their own context; in so doing, they achieve a new synthesis of information from the text and the joint experiences of community members. (p. 312)

Writing centers have been engaged in community-based literacy for quite some time. Now that technological literacies are required of community members, writing centers are ready to lead in the transition. Serving as a model of such leadership, the UK Writing Center uses active learning pedagogies in a variety of community literacy partnerships, via e-mail, on the Internet, and through interactive television video (ITV), both at our own university and throughout our state.

To become instructional leaders with technology, we must understand what literacies are required. In his book *Changing Our Minds: Negotiating English and Literacy*, Myers (1996) chronicled the shift in the United States' expression of literacy from an oral to a print to a technological culture. Myers called the literacy that is forced by technology *translation/critical literacy*. According to Myers, fundamental to translation/critical literacy are knowledge values that exist in *event-based discourse*—discourse that alternates between participation and observation, or the use of language and the study of its forms. Participating in event-based discourse, students must become active learners, aware of the metacognitive processes and interpretative strategies they use as they critically translate information transmitted through specific cultures and technologies (pp. 137–138).

At the UK Writing Center—both physically in the center and in cybertutorials—we are constantly involved in event-based discourse. We find out what student assignments are by a method of question and answer, help students identify problems, and then move through the terrain of student text, constantly probing, analyzing, and suggesting. Our writing center consultants guide students with problem-solving questions, while pointing out the metacognitive processes that the solutions require. As Myers (1996) stated:

> Knowledge must be negotiated through social construction, cognitive processing, and concept construction.... Knowledge, in order to be knowledge, must have a design or structure which distinguishes it from information and which connects it to the codes of social formation. (pp. 137–138)

For example, by discussing the structural logic in a student essay, a tutor can help a tutee understand not only the way he or she thinks on paper, but also the formal patterns in writing that help make sense of the thinking. Through such guided discussions, tutees see patterns in how they structure their ideas, allowing them to recreate and change such patterns in future writings.

Negotiating these complex literacies, tutors demonstrate critical literacy. In "Why Writers Need Writing Tutors," Harris (1995) wrote:

> When meeting with tutors, writers gain kinds of knowledge about their writing and about themselves that are not possible in other institutionalized settings.... Tutors can attend to individual differences ... tutors work with [students] in ways that enable and encourage independent thinking and that help them see how to put their theoretical knowledge into practice as they write. Moreover, tutorial interaction helps writers gain confidence in themselves as writers by attending to their affective concerns and assists them in learning what academic language about writing means. (pp. 27, 40)

Continually helping students negotiate various academic discourses, writing center tutors have always been instructors in both the content and process of learning.

Because technology allows for greater access to information, how to process it—or as Myers (1996) would say, translate and critically analyze it—is a daunting task. In addition, this type of learning requires change, and most societies—and their respective institutions—resist change: "During periods of transition from one dominant form of literacy to another, the usual stable tension among different forms of literacy turns into an open struggle. Now is such a time" (Myers, 1996, p. 280). Given that writing centers excel in navigating students—both undergraduate and graduate—through the labyrinth of multiple-discourse communities, we are well suited to guide the journey into the bumpy land of learning with technology. The job for writing center directors, therefore, is to articulate the intersections between our tutoring pedagogies and the technologies that enable them and to find ways to use these intersections productively on our campuses.

One way to articulate our technological literacy pedagogies is to use them in community literacy partnerships. How do writing centers create community literacy partnerships, and how do these partnerships impact relationships within the home community? By adapting technology to serve the literacy needs of different groupings of learners, writing centers can create models for using active pedagogies via technology. One illustration of this is the Kentucky Writing Center Association (KWCA).

The KWCA provides support and information to the faculty, staff, and students of the writing centers in Kentucky (http://www.uky.edu/ArtsSciences/English/wc/kentucky.html). After creating the organization, we established the following goals:

- To collect and disseminate the results of a survey of Kentucky writing centers. This survey will help current writing centers share information about structure, training, funding, and the use of technology. In addition, schools that do not have a writing center now can use the data to strengthen the case for starting one.
- To conduct discussion groups about writing centers at various conferences.
- To participate in the National Conference on Peer Tutoring in Writing at the UK in October, 1997.

Through sharing literacy information across state writing centers, we are all better informed about the individual contexts students bring to their educations and can serve them better in their literacy journeys. Understanding the individual contexts that students bring to their studies in higher education improves our abilities to help them learn, particularly when the idea of literacy is in flux. Myers (1996) wrote:

For the individual student who comes to school with different forms of literacy from family and neighborhood, the literacy challenge in school is an accommodation between local forms of literacy in neighborhood and family and the dominant form of literacy in the national culture. (p. 137)

By disseminating writing center information across the state via technology, the UK Writing Center demonstrates varied active uses of technology. For example, the KWCA hosts its annual meetings via ITV, as an attempt to meld theory and practice in a technological environment that promotes translation/critical learning. Although ITV is not new, it is not always used interactively. At the fall of 1997 KWCA meeting, writing center directors and consultants were in ITV rooms at Northern Kentucky University in Covington, Kentucky; Murray State University in Murray, Kentucky; Hazard Community College in Hazard, Kentucky; and at the UK in Lexington, Kentucky. Posing and answering questions about writing center theory and practice, all attendees engaged in translation/critical literacy work while using a technology available at most higher education institutions in our state.

Many UK Writing Center consultants attended the meeting, which was an excellent training session. The ITV tape now resides in the writing center library, available for viewing. Because the tape is a multilogue of voices dissecting issues of literacy via interactive technology, it models the use of critical literacy, technology, and community. Furthermore, this project demonstrates the UK Writing Center's leadership in using technology in interactive ways—crucial to translation/critical literacy.

Through the KWCA, we share our multiple literacy philosophies, bring the information back to our home institutions, and create models for diverse teaching strategies. Because writing centers approach literacy differently, we need to share our methods for adapting to new technologies. Lunsford (1991) reminded us that writing centers may be "Storehouse Centers" that "view knowledge as individually derived and held," "Garret Centers" that are "informed by a deep-seated belief in individual 'genius,' in the Romantic sense of the term, " (pp. 4–5) and the "Burkean Parlor Center," a collaborative center designed to

engage students not only in solving problems set by teachers but in identifying problems for themselves; not only in working as a group but in monitoring, evaluating, and building a theory of how groups work; not only in understanding and valuing collaboration but in confronting squarely the issues of control that successful collaboration inevitably raises not only in reaching consensus but in valuing dissensus and diversity. (pp. 8–9)

Imagining how to use technology in an active manner forces writing centers to understand our different approaches to event-based discourse and to use this knowledge in the constantly changing approaches technological literacy requires.

It is important, therefore, to network actively beyond our own locations—through e-mail, Internet, ITV—to find out how to use technology within and without our own locations because we, too, must improve as translation/critical literates. As Murphy (1994) pointed out in her article, "The Writing Center and Social Constructivist Theory," we need to remain in a dialectical process:

> Blair states that social constructionism is the latest in our discipline's searches for a "meta ideology" (1989, 21). If so, perhaps the greatest value of "meta ideology" should reside in its capacity to respect philosophical differences and to find merit in both "Garret Centers" and "Burkean Parlor Centers." As James Phillips points out, "the consequence of a multiplicity of models is not chaos and capriciousness" but "a dialectical process" in which, no matter what theory we espouse, we must be sure not to use it "to foreclose rather than to continue inquiry" (1991, 377). (p. 36–37)

It is possible to aid both students and instructors in the shift to technological pedagogy by providing models of different uses of technologies and student groupings to aid inquiry. The Appalachian Partnership of Peer Tutors (APPT), a community literacy partnership, demonstrates an attempt by the UK writing center to use technology to promote active learning. The APPT shares resources and information about peer tutoring, consulting, and directing writing centers across geographies and institutions. In the spring of 1997, APPT created its first collaboration between the UK and Southeast Community College peer tutors. Peer tutors in both places shared information via e-mail, read articles, and discussed them. Next, they met via ITV before meeting in person at Southeast Community College. In the fall of 1997, both groups gave presentations at the National Conference on Peer Tutoring in Writing in Lexington, Kentucky. Although the community college students initially felt ill prepared to present at a national conference, they gained confidence through the community partnership.

Central to the mission of APPT is to forge community partnerships to promote translation/critical literacy and to revise the roles of writing centers and technology. So far, the partnership has accomplished just that. New groupings of writing center consultants are forming across institutional boundaries, and writing center consultation strategies are being exchanged via e-mail. This partnership lets us see how knowledge is negotiated through social construction and return home to see anew how knowledge is shaped in our own context. Technology allows for such a move.

Through a willingness to create community literacy partnerships and experiment with new technologies, the UK Writing Center has paved the way for several partnerships within its own institution. For example, the UK Writing Center provides technology workshops such as "Researching on the Internet" and "Critical Evaluation of the Web"—individually, by small group, or by class. Because students need technological literacies, the university demands these workshops, yet again establishing our writing center as central to university services.

Another partnership occurs with the Office of Distance Learning. The UK Writing Center offers a cybertutoring service to the Office of Distance Learning (http://www.eku.edu/~gscumm1/tutoring/tutoring.htm). Moreover, the UK Writing Center director piloted an online course for the Office of Distance Learning (http://www.uky.edu/~gscumm1/Eng363), learning much in the process about how students negotiate time in cyber-education. The director is using this information to conceptualize the UK cybertutoring service and a forthcoming UK commonwealth virtual writing center with synchronous discussion groups. Offering services late at night comes from careful scrutiny of the online course.

Learning how to articulate the kind of translation/critical pedagogy we apply to technology is central for writing center survival in a technological world. Central, too, is finding out who is in charge of distance learning and technology programs at our institutions and partnering with them. Simpson (1995) reminded us in her article, "Perceptions, Realities, and Possibilities: Central Administration and Writing Centers":

> The kind of information that writing center directors will need to gather and distribute will not be as closely related to the philosophy and daily functioning of a writing center as it will be to larger, institutional issues. Directors need to be sophisticated enough in their own administrative activities to balance the two levels of knowledge and expertise—theoretical and managerial, pedagogical and budgetary—effectively. (p. 52)

Writing center directors must find out how technological decisions are made at our institutions and what literacies the institutions are fostering.

Individualized technological services that writing centers have to offer can be important to administrators because it is still unclear how to make technological changes across institutions:

The university operates in ways similar to Bakhtin's description of the epic. The epic has a strong authorial presence and limited open spaces for contact and responses. Its values and truths are located in traditional forms and pro-tected from contact with the present. The centrifugal forces that institutions suppress are the forces that have the potential to revitalize the system ... writing centers expose the centrifugal forces, the multi-voicedness that the system seeks to contain; they make space for contact with the present and the personal. (Grimm, 1996, p. 543).

By forging community literacy partnerships, writing centers can revitalize pedagogy and personalize literacy, and, in the creation of these external partnerships, we can sculpt new technological terrain in our home institutions.

How we provide our literacy expertise and through what technological media are our next challenges. Writing centers have always been inventive literacy promoters. The core of teaching one-on-one is charting real learning. It is just time to name and claim what Myers (1996) called our translation/critical pedagogies and, as Heath (1997) stated, create community-based literacy partnerships within and without our institutions. By doing so, we can demonstrate what Harris (1995) reminded us that we do so well: Give writers writing tutors ... of a translation/critical kind!

19

The Near and Distant Futures of OWL and the Writing Center*

Barbara J. Monroe
University of Michigan
Rebecca Rickly
Texas Tech University
William Condon
Washington State University
Wayne Butler
The Daedalus Group, Inc.

The name *writing lab* has always sounded too much like a place where white-coated scientists conduct experiments on unsuspecting students; *writing center,* although broader in scope, often does not live up to its name, being hidden away in the recesses of the English Department and not at the center for anyone. What to call those staffing the lab or center is problematic as well: *tutor* sounds too directive; *consultant* seems better, but no one knows exactly what a consultant does. When the writing center becomes

---

*The authors wish to stipulate that, at the time of this writing, all information contained in this chapter is correct. In addition, the authors request that readers who wish to cite this article use all four names in recognition of the role each author has played, both in the development of this chapter and, even more, in the development of the programs and initiatives profiled here.

211

wired, the name game only intensifies: *OWL* has become the ubiquitous acronym for *online writing lab*. Although the reference to the bird is fortuitous (being the pet bird of Athena, goddess of wisdom), this acronym often seems to our faculty colleagues to be a little too cute to take seriously. At the UM, we struggled with these names as well, rethinking what we had done, what we wanted to do, and how best to describe both of these in an accurate yet inspiring manner. We liked the notion of OWL, but did not want to be limited by the terminology, *lab*. We tried various acronyms (*COW*: Center for Online Writing; *OIL*: Online Interactive Learning; *COL*: Center for Online Literacies; and so forth), but none of them had the powerful graphic symbolism of the acronym OWL. So we kept the acronym but reassigned the letters to mean *online writing and learning* to refer to our online tutoring service, in an effort to foreground the human interactivity over the place or even the technology. In other words, we wanted students and writers—and ultimately, administrators and funders—to think of OWL not as a specific place but as any site where distant learners worked together.

This redefinition of OWL has proven prophetic, for the OWL at the UM has flown beyond the writing center, leaving behind its relatively limited purpose of helping Michigan students become better writers. The history and near future of the UM OWL indicate one possible future for OWLs, which might suggest other ways for writing centers to extend their reach not just to students on and off campus, but also to schools, businesses, and communities. In expanding its scope, OWL also holds out the potential to relocate the writing center, politically as well as physically, within the university.

BUILDING THE NEST

The centrifugal trajectory of the Michigan OWL perhaps suggests the future direction of OWLs and writing centers generally. Launched in the fall of 1994, the UM OWL aimed to extend our face-to-face peer tutoring services by making a tutor available to anyone, on campus or off, who had access to e-mail. We began only with an e-mail address, advertising to students in several basic writing classes. As our staff, experience, and confidence grew, OWL was given a home on the Web (winter, 1995) where students could e-mail their papers via the World Wide Web. Once again, we initially did not advertise beyond basic writing classes, but our online presence made itself known: People surfing the Web stumbled on the OWL and sent papers or comments from the very beginning. During our first semester as a Webbed OWL, we received queries from Japan, Missouri, Wisconsin, and, of course, the UM. Suddenly, peer tutoring services were not limited to student writers who walked into the computer lab where tutors were housed; we were now interacting with college students, teachers, high school students, and business people worldwide.

This open-door policy to serve all comers presaged the next stage in our OWL's development: taking OWL off campus as an outreach tool, working with individual schools, rather than exclusively with individual writers. We launched two pilot OWLs, the first with Detroit in 1996 and the second with Bay City in 1997. Actually, our very first high school OWL was piloted with UM's main feeder school, Pioneer High School in Ann Arbor, back in 1992–1993. The two new OWLs in Detroit and Bay City, taken together, allowed us to experiment further with different administrative models—with an eye toward scaling out across the state in a major public relations move by the university.

This shift from individuals to institutions, of course, represented another turn of the screw in terms of difficulty because this kind of OWL required an institutional commitment at both ends of the connection. In order to gain approval from our own institution for the OWL pilot to Detroit, we convincingly argued that such a venture would address the university's own priorities at that time: the push for a richer, more practice-based undergraduate experience, and the *Michigan Mandate*, which called for a concerted effort to increase minority enrollment. We successfully proposed that OWL might be used to broaden our admissions pool beyond the major all-black feeder schools in Detroit by working with the students, meeting them "upstream" (to quote one of the funders of the project), to assist in preparing them for college, both academically and culturally (Monroe, 1997).

To that end, we launched the Detroit OWL pilot in the fall of 1996. Our peer tutors were paired with students at Murray-Wright High School, and the pairs worked together via e-mail for the school year. Because our peer tutor program is a two-semester course sequence, tutors participated in this cybermentoring project as part of that curriculum. Like most outreach projects, this OWL was built on a model of mutual benefits to both institutional partners, UM and Detroit Public Schools; for example, Murray-Wright students received point-of-need instruction from trained UM writing tutors; for the tutors, this OWL experience allowed them to connect classroom theory with real world application—a community-service connection that meshed well with the university's renewed attention to its undergraduate program and that implicitly countered criticism that the university was out of touch with the real world.

Although this OWL was billed as a minority-recruitment strategy and a preemptive strike against the rollback of affirmative action programs nationwide, that goal has not been realized. Yet, the technological viability and the high visibility of the project met the university's implicit public relations goal and in ways consistent with its desired image. First, the Detroit OWL was not just a do-good, feel-good outreach project, as detractors often associate with outreach and with community service, but an academic outreach project, one with instructional content, delivered at low cost (albeit after the enormous startup costs of getting this inner-city school online). Second, it was a distance learning project, which made it alluring. At the same time, the concept played well with the public generally and alumni specifically because it was low-tech, high-touch—that is, it had all of the sex appeal, but none of the perceived impersonality of technology: In the words of one alum, the project had "technology with a heart." Nor was it a technology-for-technology's-sake project, but rather one where technology was actually necessary to reach these students on a regular basis, in a cost-effective and physically safe way—two factors that always stymie outreach efforts to inner-city Detroit. Finally, the model could scale; that is, it could be replicated statewide, in a systemic, programmatic way that could attract major funding from private foundations and/or corporate partners.

The public relations success of the Detroit OWL inspired the launching of a second OWL pilot, to Central High School in Bay City, Michigan, in the fall of 1997. This pilot differed from the Detroit OWL in many respects, most obviously in terms of the race and class demographics of the two constituencies. The community that Central High School serves is primarily White and middle class; the school has traditionally produced many National Merit Scholars. The target students—an eleventh-grade American Literature class—were neither college-bound nor at-risk; they had varied career aspirations, most of which did not include plans to attend college, much less the UM. Unencumbered with the politics of race-based admissions and the concomitant notion of outreach pejoratively perceived as a free handout, the Bay City OWL more prominently foregrounded the public service role of the university. Like other large research institutions in the country, the UM has often been accused of "ivorytowerism," failing to give back to the state and local communities whose taxes support public education—an argument that always comes up on the floor of the state legislature during the annual appropriations battle in very local terms (e.g., "What has the university done for my constituency lately?"). The cultural and intellectual riches of the university—state-owned resources—needed to be distributed; the OWL gave the university the medium and method—distributed learning—to do just that. And the pinpoint precision with which an OWL can be targeted makes it an exceptionally low-cost, high-impact way to make a public relations point in a specific area of the state.

The administrative design of the two pilots also differed greatly. Because the tutors enrolled in our program were already fully booked with cybermentoring the Detroit students, we hired two former tutors to work with the 27 students at Bay City, each tutor working with 13 to 14 students for the year. Unlike the Detroit OWL, the Bay City OWL entailed operational ongoing costs for tutors' wages, a cost that was initially picked up by the UM's academic outreach for this 1-year pilot.

The Bay City OWL pilot not only gave us another opportunity to develop a scalable administrative design and an online pedagogy that would support and invigorate the existing classroom curriculum, but it also gave us a track record with the school itself, which, after that pilot year, wanted the OWL to continue badly enough to share the cost for tutors' wages in the future. With a proven product in hand and with the cost-sharing commitment from the school, the UM's academic outreach brokered an arrangement with Ameritech (the Midwest's Baby Bell that delivers telephone service to the state of Michigan) to fund the project another year. More important, Ameritech was eager to seed more OWLs in other schools around the state; after the 1-year trial funded by Ameritech, schools would bear the cost of continuing OWL services if they chose to continue. Schools would also have greater control over the scope of services to suit their own needs and priorities. For example, they might target at-risk students in English or college-bound students in math, or they might choose to use the OWL to assist all their ninth-grade teachers. They may use the OWL as a tool to integrate technology into their curriculum, having all teachers use the OWL services at least once.

Following the rationale that successful outreach work is mutually beneficial to all partners, what then are the benefits in a state-wide, higher education, high school OWL for all concerned?

First, for the high school, besides the more obvious benefit of the one-to-one instruction to students, teachers are relieved from having to comment on hundreds of papers, which, in turn, encourages them to assign more writing and more revision. Even though only one or maybe a few teachers are involved in any given OWL, they and their students print out the tutors' conferences or share them with others on screen, creating occasions for sharing with other teachers and other students an outside, higher education perspective on writing. Simply put, an OWL incites interest in writing in the schools.

Second, the university can distribute its intellectual property and resources in a cost-effective, instructionally sound way. OWL's high impact and high visibility in the schools make an OWL a highly effective public relations tool. The university gets the good publicity and public good will that accrue from playing a leadership role in leveraging the funding and partnerships.

Third, to funders—in this case, Ameritech—OWL is attractive, in part, because the company has a longer-standing public service record and earmarks significant funds to such efforts—e.g., $26 million last year to more than 3,800 nonprofit organizations ("Ameritech Learning," 1998). Distance learning projects, like OWL, are especially good fits because they groom future consumers for the telecommunications industry. After the seed-year funding runs out, schools might look for business sponsors, most potentially alumni and local professionals who want to contribute to both their homes—their alma mater and their home communities—at once. That potential vision realized, OWL's centrifugal path will have created a centripetal force that draws together partners from both public and private sectors (see Fig. 19.1).

When OWL comes full circle, our writing center also benefits. Although our high school OWL is a not-for-profit enterprise, it will create job opportunities for certified tutors after they have gone through our training pro-

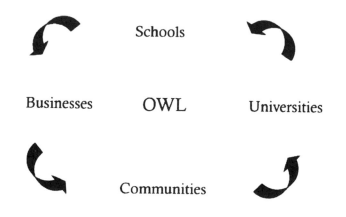

FIG. 19.1. The Centripetal Force of OWL.

gram and have tutored for academic credit. Paid tutors can work the high school OWL as a distance-independent job, even after they have left Ann Arbor for graduate school or elsewhere. This prospect of long-term, interesting, flexible, part-time employment, in turn, helps the writing center recruit new tutors into the program. More important, an outreach OWL allows the writing center to extend its mission beyond the university's walls.

LEAVING THE NEST

The idea behind OWL—collaborative, cooperative distance learning—is one that is now being capitalized by many broad-based partnerships involving the university, business, and K–12, in various combinations. Unfortunately, writing centers have not been very successful in seeing a return in their early investment in OWLs, as distance learning initiatives head for other departments and divisions within the university. For example, the Ameritech Learning Initiative at the UM, a 5 year, $1.5 million grant from Ameritech, will develop learning collaboratories to be used by business and education partnerships in three pilot projects: One will link UM Dearborn College of Engineering and Computer Science faculty and students to engineering practitioners and high school students; another will link students and faculty from the School of Art and Design with small start-up businesses; and a third will link UM Flint's School of Management with local school systems. All three *collaboratories*—meaning the electronic environment as a product as well as the pedagogy—will be developed by the School of Information ("Ameritech Learning", 1998).

Although the future of OWL (aka *collaboratories*)—conceived as any site of active learning and teaching, with public–private partnerships, variously configured—is on the rise, the role of the writing center in the distance education future is much less secure. Even though technorhetoricians in the writing center were among the first to recognize the transformative potential of technology, we generally have not led the way in turning that potential into political and cultural capital, an alchemy that can move the writing center to the center of institutional politics, where the real battles with real life consequences are being waged—battles not just for the writing center's programs, but for the future of the university itself.

Traditionally, the university has been a place where knowledge is made, transformed, consumed, disseminated, and revised. Students entered the walls of the university to learn from someone with enough education to be considered an expert in a particular field. The university had an obligation to these students to provide superior teachers and resources, with the goal of producing educated, responsible citizens in a participatory democracy. The university's duty extended no farther than its own students; universities educated 18-year-olds to 22-year-olds, and what happened to those outside of the ivory tower was no concern to the university.

Today, however, that traditional university is fading away. Although the university may look the same on the outside, education is in the midst of a true shift in operations. What used to be a hierarchical, mentoring relationship is now flattened out and networked. Students entering into a degree program are less likely to take classes where they learn only specific skills or information; emphasis is placed instead on broad competencies. Students are encouraged to model professional communication, working more in cooperative groups than as competitive individuals. This emphasis on community-based learning puts newfound value on lateral communication, collaborative knowledge making, and distributed knowledge as opposed to the more traditional vertical, competitive scenario where knowledge is dispensed in increments by the university to the individual. Many classes today rely less on formal lectures and more on conversation: Active learning is stressed over passive consumption. The pressure for these changes is coming, in part, from students themselves, impatient with the traditional classroom experience. According to James Duderstadt, former UM president, young students are a new breed who "approach learning as a plug-and-play experience, unaccustomed and unwilling to learn sequentially—to read the manual—and inclined to plunge in and learn through participation and experimentation" (cited in Tobin, 1998, p. 41). Returning students—often times their employers paying for their tuition, books, and fees—want "practical, career-oriented instruction. They'd rather learn from experienced practitioners—real engineers, real business people—than research-oriented scholars" (cited in Tobin, 1998, p. 41). In an age where only change is assured, the university seeks to create expert learners who can continue to think critically and learn after they leave.

The future of education lies, then, with the online, networked university, with its flattened hierarchy and collateral human and electronic networks, connecting schools, universities, businesses, and communities. In a way, the writing center of today, with its face-to-face and online components, may be a fleeting Kodak moment of the university in transition, where students attend campus-based classes but with online support systems. Technology integration in campus-based education might be seen as a way of seeding the future, acclimating students for working and learning online, a sample of the anytime, anywhere university to come, where a student may return so often as to render the term *alumnus* obsolete. As brick-and-mortar institutions compete with the anytime, anywhere university for students, education will become a for-profit commodity that can be marketed and sold (Tobin, 1998).

To view the near and distant future of education in market terms is, of course, the consumerist approach, but we have to enter this discursive arena and enter it with entrepreneurial spirit to fulfill our mission as a writing center—that is, to promote a cohesive, highly visible writing program across the curriculum and within the disciplines; to infuse distance learning projects with pedagogical expertise and academic quality; and to instill and maintain the public service values of the university. If we do not get involved, we can look forward to "a market-dominated future in which higher education suffers the same fate of mediocrity that has characterized other market-driven, media-dominated enterprises, such as television and journalism," in Duderstadt's words (cited in Tobin, 1998, p. 43).

FEATHERING THE NEST

To move the writing center to the center of things, we have to build alliances—in effect, practicing what we preach and working collaboratively with other institutional entities. Before seeking (and in order to secure) financial support, writing centers need to look for political support internally rather than externally. Traditionally, this kind of support has come directly from the English Department, and traditionally, it has been scant. Writing centers can build alliances across the university, rather than just with or within English Departments, by appealing to a common agenda: implementation of instructional technologies both within campus-based courses, some of which have town-and-gown distance learning initiatives that link college students with businesses and schools. When a writing center becomes wired, its image as a remediation center tends to get upgraded to "university center for learning assistance" (Wallace, 1998, p. 164). This image shift can mean a place at the table where decisions are made and plans are drawn up and money dispersed about university-wide technology initiatives—if, and perhaps only if, the writing center has an OWL with a flight record, for example, cybertutoring as well as other wired services and resources developed in-house.

For instance, the Texas Tech University writing center, once completely under the auspices of the English Department, is now the university writing center, as Lady Falls Brown discussed earlier in this collection. Although the center is still housed in and partially funded by the English Department, the university writing center director reports directly to the Vice Provost for Academic Affairs. Because the writing center now has greater visibility (and, consequently, a greater responsibility to legitimize its work), it currently operates on a substantially larger budget than when it was housed in a single department. With the expansion online in the form of an OWL, which enables more students to take advantage of writing center services, the director will be able to request additional funding for the online tutors, facilities, and so forth. Brown argued that she is now running the writing center "as it should be rather than as it is funded," and because she has backed up all requests with concrete data, she asked for and received two budget increases in as many years. By the year 2001, the English Department is scheduled to move to a new building, and the university writing center will become a separate entity.

Writing centers with WAC mandates also have the opportunity to go golden by reconceiving their WAC initiatives in terms of electronic communications across the curriculum (ECAC)—a natural "convergence of technologies—that of WAC as a technology supporting teaching and learning of content matter in a variety of disciplines and that of computers as a technology supporting the teaching of writing in a variety of contexts—was not difficult to understand or predict" (Selfe, 1998, pp. xi–xii). ECAC offers numerous and various models for integrating and strengthening established WAC programs with ECAC. As the editors point out in their introduction, ECAC increases a writing center's responsibilities, but with those comes a greater institutional impact. For example, Colorado State University renamed its WAC program to Communication Across the Curriculum when it took that initiative online with a dramatic Web presence. With the increased visibility and impact came a new tenure-track line with a graduate assistant and programmer for the writing center (Palmquist, Kiefer, & Zimmerman, 1998).

Aside from building alliances with other disciplines, wired writing centers can also find partners with other departments and units. Gail Cummins (chap. 18), in this collection, describes the successful partnership with the Office of Distance Learning, which uses the cybertutoring services of the UK writing center. One survey participant, quoted in Mark Shadle's chapter (chap. 1, this volume), describes how the writing center's technology workshop ultimately became added to all the university's summer institutes, including "our national writing project institute, our high school students summer institute, and our faculty writing project summer institute" (p. 8).

Finally, writing centers can forge corporate partnerships, most especially with educational publishers, who may want to use or adapt or link to a writing center's online resources, including perhaps the center's tutoring services. The university's technology-transfer office would conduct these transactions (i.e., negotiate the licensing terms and collect the royalties), with part or most of the proceeds going back to the writing center (see Fig. 19.2).

As the writing center develops these extensive collaborative partnerships, then it will begin to live up to its name as *center*; but without OWLs as sites of cooperative learning, the writing center will remain decentered and perhaps even further marginalized. To nest the futures of the writing center and OWL and to couple their fortunes, we have to have a vision, conceived within each institutional context. If we continue to see the writing center only in traditional terms, we will fail to see what it can become, and the same holds true for OWLs. At the same time, we need not discount all that we have learned in our efforts to expand our services and scope. Russian theorist Mikhail Bakhtin (1981) described dialogic interaction as two competing forces: one that dissipates and confuses (*centrifugal*), and one that unites and combines (*centripetal*). The unity of a group will not be challenged, however, by these two seemingly conflicting forces; in fact, the group will stagnate without both. So goes it for writing centers and OWLs:

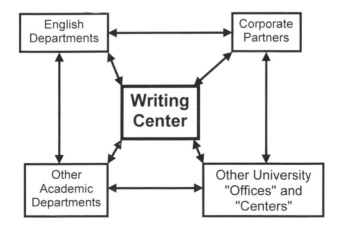

FIG. 19.2. Corporate Partnerships and the Writing Center.

We must move outward, with all the responsibility that comes with increased visibility, but we must continue to look inward as well, examining our goals, our mission, who we are, and who we would like to become.

20

How Many Technoprovocateurs* Does It Take to Create Interversity?

Eric Crump
National Council of Teachers of English

Some ideas are reeled into our mind wrapped up in facts; and some ideas burst upon us naked without the slightest evidence they could be true but with all the conviction they are. The ideas of the latter sort are the more difficult to displace.

—Kevin Kelly

Some things don't have much history, but a whole hell of a lot of future.

—David Hopes

Near the end of *Jurassic Park* (the book, that is), Ian Malcolm lies dying from injuries sustained in a run-in with a tyrannosaur. (We subsequently learn that he is only mostly dead at the end of *Jurassic Park* and manages to re-

---

*A reference to a presentation I gave at the 1995 Conference on College Composition and Communication, "Writing Centers as Technoprovocateurs," in which I argued that writing centers needed to stop playing subservient roles in composition programs and start putting forward their pedagogical practices as viable primary methods of helping writers learn (http://www.missouri.edu/~cccc95/abstracts/crump2.html).

cover enough to star in the sequels, both book and film.) In a semicoma, Malcolm whispers, "Everything … looks different … on the other side" (Crichton, 1990, p. 383). Those of us who develop online writing environments may be in a similar state: ensconced in a dying system but able to glimpse a new and very different world beyond it.

In a sense, of course, we are continuously moving to the other side (the future)—which immediately becomes this side (the present)—and it always is different there (here) than it was back there (the past, 5 minutes ago or 5 years ago). The difference, though, is usually not big enough to make much of an impression. Change appears to be a slow, incremental phenomenon, occurring in continual baby steps. For developers of online writing centers, it may seem we are simultaneously taking baby steps in the process of adapting to a new environment and emerging on the other side in a whole new world. It is almost like driving a car by stomping on the accelerator and the brakes at the same time. In this case, the vehicle is the myriad new technologies that have recently emerged, particularly the Internet. We are propelled forward by our vision of new possibilities enabled by the net, whereas political constraints prevent us from fully exploring these new realms. Unfortunately, the brakes usually win the contest. Even if they cannot contain the energy of the accelerator, they cause wheels to spin.

A quick, informal survey of OWLs in September 1998[1] reveals what I would call the stymied state of affairs, a simultaneous accelerating and braking. If such a list had existed in 1993, you could have counted the number of entries on one hand. Now, there are more than 250 links. The wild growth of writing center presence on the Internet is unremarkable, taken in the context of the times, of course. Everybody is getting on the net these days, after all. Writing center folks are doing their bit to explore the new terrain, to see what the Internet can do and what implications it has for the future of writing centers. It looks like this is the acceleration part, but if it is, it is acceleration from here to the corner. There are exceptions, of course, but for the most part we are not out on the open road yet, I am afraid, and our wheels, in fact, are mostly spinning.

---

[1]I perused the sites listed on the NWCA Web directory of OWLs (http://departments.colgate.edu/diw/NWCAOWLS.html). The page listing e-tutoring resources is more focused, but I thought the OWLs page would reflect the general state of the field better. I paid more attention to those sites that portray themselves as OWLs or online services by some other name because many of the sites listed in the directory are more writing centers online rather than online writing centers. That is, they are Web pages offering information about face-to-face writing centers rather than places that offer writing assistance in online venues.

A closer look at the sites in the list shows that the majority are not really true OWLs, by which I mean writing centers that offer their services in online venues. Many of those that do offer online services are still very limited in terms of scope and shape. Some provide an e-mail address where writers can submit queries. I am sure, in many cases, e-mail exchange is the best available tool. The absence of various and more sophisticated online tools, however, suggests that institutions have not yet opted to apply serious resources to creating online learning environments. Whether that is due to lack of vision or simply lack of funds is hard to say. Some are a combination of both, in many cases. Some sites invite questions about grammar and mechanics. There is nothing wrong with that per se—grammar and mechanics, after all, are important matters and the chief concerns of many writers—but foregrounding those concerns definitely situates the purpose of the service in entirely conventional terms. Most sites explicitly restrict access to the service to students of the local institution, which sounds very reasonable at first, probably politically necessary in most cases, but also limits the possibilities that exploration might reveal.

This stymied state is temporary, I like to think, but we will not break free of it without taking initiative. The conditions are right for it now. The steady crawl toward (but never into, obviously) the future has, throughout history, been punctuated by sudden, disconcerting lurches. When that happens, we may all feel as if we are experiencing the kind of fever-and-morphine-induced delirium Ian Malcolm endured, and perhaps during those times, like Malcolm, we become more inclined to make dramatic, often cryptic, proclamations about the significance of the events we are witnessing, rhetoric that outstrips the real life around us. The hyperrhetoric may cause both raised and furrowed brows in our wise and cautious colleagues, but it also serves as inspiration and perhaps even as catalyst for those who are willing not only to glimpse the world beyond this one, but also to set foot there. Hype is the flying elbows of rhetoric. It makes room for new thoughts to occur. Hype is rude, insistent because courtesy is too easy to contain and control. Do not be too leery of it. Conventionality would have you scoff at grand claims because conventionality is served by suspicion of grandiosity. We need hype because it describes for us the possibilities that do not exist in the realm of the status quo. Without that description, our stymied state might devolve into stasis and death.

> Harding sighed. Despite all efforts, Malcolm was rapidly slipping into a terminal delirium. His fever was higher, and they were almost out of his antibiotics.

"What don't you care about?"

"Anything," Malcolm sighed, "Because … everything looks different … on the other side."

And he smiled. (Crichton, 1990, p. 383)

Mr. Kurtz meets Mona Lisa? Apocalyptic visions and hyperbolic rhetoric sprout like daisies throughout the field of public discourse. Traditionally, key dates like an approaching new millennium inspire more than the usual assertions, whispered and mysterious, that inspire terror and joy quite at the same time. Some may decry the hype as being, well, hype (the term is generally pejorative). As Marvin (1988) conveyed so vividly in *When Old Technologies Were New*, the technological changes clustered around the most recent previous turning of the temporal odometer, the shift from the 19th to the 20th century, also shook the societies of the time, producing hype and horror: "The more any medium triumphed over distance, time, and embodied presence, the more exciting it was, and the more it seemed to tread the path of the future" (p. 194). Although Marvin was talking about the reaction to the electric light, the telegraph, and the telephone, that same sentiment is at work today as emerging technologies seem to be making the same triumphs again.

Marvin's portrayal of the hype at the close of the 19th century appears, just as today's hype does, to be the product of arrogance, inflated expectations, grandiose dreams and visions, and a human habit of stating fantasy as fact, wishful thinking as inevitability. So might skeptics have once dismissed the wild claims that electric light would allow us to write in gigantic letters on the clouds and thereby defeat distance. They might dismiss claims that the telephone would increase the sense of intimacy and empathy among people long separated by distance and custom. They might scoff at the assumptions that new technologies would usher in an era of unparalleled peace and prosperity. Yet, those technologies transformed society and economy in some very profound ways, and if they did not cause Utopia to bloom, they did, as promised, allow us to do things we could not have done before, things we apparently really wanted to be able to do.

That may be a key factor as we try to figure out how the Internet will reshape technology: The net may be an expression of collective desire as much as an extrinsic force coming to bear on an old institution. Pattison (1982) in *On Literacy* took issue with recent technodeterministic theories (McLuhan, Ong, et al.) that suggest that print was responsible for changing our economies and even our cognition, almost an external event that reshaped society from the outside in. Pattison noted that print did not emerge in any consistent pattern everywhere in the world where the technology was discovered. Only European cultures supported the kind of print adoption that resulted in its emerging as a dominant technology: "Print is first an effect, and later a cause ... " (p. 115). We might say print technology was our way of reshaping ourselves from the inside out. Likewise, the net may be something we have created precisely because it helps us do things we apparently really want to do and cannot with previous technologies.

So it is a cliché to say so, and it is hype, but the emergence of the Internet changes everything for education, changes everything more than the current crop of OWLs might suggest at first glance. Having changed (stomping the gas pedal), we react (naturally) by becoming a bit terrified by what we have done. We want to pause and reflect (hit the brakes!) to treat the new environment as if it allows us to do what we have always done, but in a new and more convenient and efficient way. Having changed profoundly, we seem to want everything to remain the same, familiar. That is, the significance of the Internet has largely been accepted but has barely been acted on. In the writing center world, that means we have leapt into the task of creating online venues for our services, but our services have not yet taken the shape of the new environment.

Kemp (1994) warned against this tendency to move forward two steps then move back a step and a half. In the text of a conference presentation, he said, "You can't try to do with computers what you were doing before computers, or you will probably fail. Tentative, skeptical forays into the techniques supported by networked computers seem to contain the seeds of their own destruction" (online). Those tentative first steps may in fact be necessary to take, but having taken them, we need to very quickly attempt to move beyond. I see this dance at work in the OWL I helped found, the University of Missouri's Online Writery (http://www.missouri.edu/~writery/). When we started the project in 1994, the funding rationale was based largely on the claim that we could use e-mail and the Web to deliver writing assistance to writers when and where they needed it most, at their computers. It was and remains a pedagogically and politically legitimate rationale. However, we quickly found that, in practice, those local students at their computers were not ready to take advantage of online tutoring. Their assignments still required that they produce essays on paper, and they responded by using the appropriate tool for that job: word processors. Only a few pioneering faculty were making any significant use of Internet tools in their classes. As net use has been included in the basic structure of classes, we have seen use of the Online Writery by local students increase.

Yet, in the meantime, we found our real constituency: writers of all kinds out there on the net. There is a segment of society that wants and needs the kind of service writing centers provide, but without affiliation to an educational institution, those people have not had access to the support so many college students take for granted, a writing tutor. Although perhaps relying on informal networks of friends or on published self-help resources, they wanted a reliable and informed community of writers. They found the Online Writery (we did not promote it very aggressively), and they sought our help—housewives, bored bureaucrats, retired professors—anybody writing anything who wanted someone to talk to about the process.

Now that more and more classes are incorporating e-mail, discussion lists, and the Web as integral parts of the course infrastructure, the balance of use at the Online Writery is shifting, with an increase in use by local students, who begin to see how it fits with their work in writing courses. Yet, those distant others are still out there, and they still find the Online Writery, still seek assistance and a community of writers. Understandably, the university's distance learning unit recently expressed interest in the Online Writery, wondering whether it could serve students enrolled in online courses.

Yes, of course it can.

However, the lesson of the Online Writery is not that online writing centers can provide convenient support services for distance courses (though surely they can and will). Rather, the Online Writery portrays just how education on the net differs from education on campus. It shows how geography and socioeconomic context reconfigure access to education. It shows how OWLs may help their institutions discover the difference between the net as a learning environment and the campus as a learning environment and, importantly, may help their institutions figure out how to account for that difference.

Distance education is a turbo-charged bandwagon (careening out of control?), and schools are leaping at it, desperate to avoid being left behind. The mad dash is causing anxiety among the ranks of teachers, however, as concern grows about how educationally sound distance programs will be, about whether administrators will sacrifice quality for efficiency, and about whether there will be a place for them in this new regime.

Perhaps a useful way to approach this apparently chaotic situation is to think in terms of how writing teachers (whether in the classroom or the

OWL) might influence the bouncing bandwagon and in what directions. Many of us (and more all the time) have extensive Internet experience, developing online learning environments and teaching online classes. We are getting a sense for and adapting to the culture of the net, to the ways the net reconfigures authority, power, and knowledge. What difference will that online experience make? What difference will we make it make?

The writing classroom has long been obsolete (it is a relic of the industrial age, after all); Dewey (1944), Illich (1970), and Moran (1992) have made the point convincingly. In his chapter from *Re-imagining Computers and Composition: Teaching and Research in the Virtual Age*, Moran said, "this classroom we inhabit is not an inevitable structure, or even a good one *for* our purposes" (p. 8). Not that anyone has ever bothered to justify it because it has been part of educational doxa, but now it is not only an awkward space for writing education, but also an obsolete, unproductive, annoying place, a poor excuse for a learning environment—to some of us. Yet, prior to the broad accessibility of the Internet, there was no viable and compelling alternative. The convergence of Internet and university is the variable that tips the scales toward new possibilities for writing and writing education. We are not headed toward the online classroom (aka "horseless carriage" of education). We are headed toward interversity.

I bother to mention the impending demise of the classroom (as we know it) because I think the fate of writing centers may be intimately linked to it. The face-to-face writing center is, in some ways, parasitic on the face-to-face classroom. Our students are, after all, doing assignments that emanate from those classrooms. Writing centers (and OWLs) are different from classrooms, too, and our differences may become increasingly more important as the adaptation to a networked culture proceeds.

Many distance education efforts bring with them the structure of the conventional institution, usually in the form of vestigial forms of the classroom. It is an online classroom, but a classroom all the same, and until it yields as the dominant model for learning environments, our opportunities on the net will not be realized.

There is one very compelling reason that I think OWLs should begin developing their native Internet capabilities and resituate their campus-classroom-specific vestigial characteristics: adaptability.

In *Out of Control*, Kelly (1995) extensively dealt with the process of evolution as seen through the perspective of complexity theorists. He cited work by Stuart Kauffman, who identified some very definite characteristics that increase the adaptability of complex systems. Kauffman discovered that adaptability increases when a system's degree of interconnectedness resides in a zone somewhere between the paralysis of fragmentation and the chaos of pervasive interconnection. A "sparsely connected system" will be "flatfooted and stagnant." Yet, an "overly-connected system" will be a "frozen gridlock of a thousand mutual pulls." Adaptable systems reside near the edge of chaos (cited in Kelly, 1995, pp. 399, 401).

Prior to the emergence of the Internet, our hierarchical educational institutions were as well-connected as they needed to be, but the net changes the landscape, changes the measure of connectedness. Suddenly, the institution is sparsely connected. The distance education hypermovement suggests to me that the institution realizes it is underconnected, but the specific shape of distance education programs indicates that it has not quite gotten into that optimal zone. Trying to migrate rigid hierarchical relationships among education's players (e.g., students, teachers, administrators, parents) suggests that the institution understands that it needs to move, but has not yet grasped the fundamental difference between hierarchy and network as defining methods of organization.

That is where OWLs may play a key role in the future of education. Already writing centers and their progeny, OWLs, straddle the line between the conventional and the innovative. They serve the subjects of the industrial, mass-production classroom, but they develop rich relationships with those subjects (who then become people), and they often create the conditions for learning communities. The Internet is, in a fundamental way, a technology for creating fertile conditions for learning communities to form and evolve. All those years on the margins of the institution may pay off now that the center is dissipating, now that constellations of peers will replace rigid hierarchies as the defining structure of our organizations.

I am going to sketch out principles for an emerging alternative to the classroom model, something I think will be rich with possibilities. *Interversity*, of course, is a simple and inelegant neologism, a mooshing of *Internet* and *university*, meant to suggest the convergence of the two social institutions, hopefully to the benefit of both and to the benefit of us! The term also lends itself to some interesting (I think) associations, including *interaction, Internet, interest, interlace, interchange, intercession, interconnection,* and *adversity, university, transversity, multiversity, antiversity, perversity, conversity, traversity, diversity.*

Interversity suggests convergence, a blend of the stability and strength and persistence of the university with the productive chaos and creativity and community of the net. A hybrid institution to support a hybrid literacy that is emerging from shared dominance: written language, oral language, graphic or visual rhetoric—hypermedia literacy, a network literacy.

What the university has to offer the Internet, as an educational institution, is greater access as well (especially if we cite the big land grant universities). Maybe the point of big bureaucracy is (or was) mainly to serve as the means for society to invest in its own future, a way to manage the resources needed to bring education to bear upon the promise of youth (that sounds more chilling to me than it once would have). If there is some infusion of bureaucracy into netland, society can leverage its investment. That possibility worries me, but I suppose it might be a good thing.

What the Internet offers the university is the possibility of deflating the power of distance—both geographic and psychological—to thwart our conversations and communities. Many administrators are infatuated with using telecomputing to bridge geodistances in order to reach new customers. Yet, there are other distances to defeat, like the distance between students and teachers in cavernous lecture halls, the distance between students in those same lecture halls, expected as they are to sit quietly and absorb rather than talking and working with each other. With any luck, the term *distance* coupled with *education* will not be useful for much longer. Education, whether it occurs in physical or virtual environments, will be simply education.

Here are some proposed principles for developing interversity, an emerging institution. These are not quite operating principles, more like transitioning principles. How do we get from here to there? By making a few leaps backward to first principles (refocus on learning, growth, creativity) and forward to new practices enabled by new technologies:

- Shift from credentialing to chronicling. Evidence of who people are, what they have done, and what they can do is much more important than what label someone manages to acquire. Resumés and portfolios replace degrees and grade transcripts and test scores.

  Neither learning nor justice is promoted by schooling because educators insist on packaging instruction with certification (p. 16).

  Most learning happens casually, and even most intentional learning is not the result of programmed instruction (p. 18). (Illich, 1970)

- Shift from evaluation to assessment. Grading is out. Assessment is a matter of apprehending quality in context rather than imposing external standards.

- Shift from teacher as expert to teacher as mentor and colleague. We talk about that a bit, but as long as the classroom structure and culture obtain, talk is all we can do. Untether the roles of teacher and student from designated individuals, and let them roam freely through the complex interactions of a community. We should value in teachers their experience and collegiality as much or more than their knowledge.

> In the mediatrix, you throw yourself to others. You create through others. The media philosopher realizes painfully that she must sacrifice her beloved cogito, her cherished institutionalism, her age-old desire for total control to a communal process-in-the-making. (In Crump, 1999, online)

- Shift from student as apprentice or student as container or even student as customer to student as colleague and partner.
- Shift from class as contained project to class as community with mutual interests and common projects. Education is not well served by being walled off from communities or the world. Service learning, a strong movement but still something of a novelty, might become a foundational form of education.

> A thousand minds, a thousand arguments; a lively intermingling of questions, problems, news of the latest happening, jokes; an inexhaustible play of language and thought, a vibrant curiosity; the changeable temper of a thousand spirits by whom every object of discussion is broken into an infinity of sense and significations—all these spring into being, and then are spent. And this is the pleasure of the Florentine public. (in Oldenburg, 1989, p. 27)

- Shift from local political jurisdictions to boundaries drawn by interests.

What we are heading toward is an institution that cares about learning and has as its infrastructure learning environments rather than classrooms, that has as its basic social unit learning communities rather than segregated professional scholars and amateur students. We use the best technologies at our disposal, old and new; we traverse distances both local and global; we bridge or dodge political boundaries that hem us in; and we create the conditions in which richly various conversations can be engaged.

Deutsch (1994), who once delivered the "Ten Commandments of the Internet," included as one of the net's laws: "Listen to the technology; it's trying to tell you something." If we factor in Pattison's (1982) point about the source of technological innovation, we might amend Deutsch's commandment. Technology is us trying to tell us something—something about evolution, about how to change and thrive.

For OWLs hoping not only to survive but also to lead, it might be good to draw a motto from good old Dr. Seuss (1980):

"You can stop, if you want, with the Z
Because most people stop with the Z
But not me!

In the places I go there are things that I see
That I never could spell if
I stopped with the Z

I'm telling you this 'cause you're one of my friends
My alphabet starts where your alphabet ends!

So you see There's no end To the things you might know
Depending how far beyond Zebra you'll go!"
(*On Beyond Zebra*)

It's time to take our collective feet off the brakes so we can get out beyond
the well-known world of education and into the world on the other side.

References

Ameritech learning initiative promotes information technology use. (1998, September 2). News release. *University of Michigan News and Information Services.*

Arndt, V. (1992). Feedback: What writing teachers can learn from their students. In M. Lau & M. Murphy (Eds.), *Developing writing: Purposes and practices,* (pp. 98–118). Hong Kong: Institute of Language in Education & the Education Department.

Aronowitz, S., & Giroux, H. A. (1993). *Education still under siege* (2nd ed.). Critical studies in education and culture series. Westport, CT: Bergin & Harvey.

Bakhtin, M. M. (1981). Discourse in the novel. In M. Holquist (Ed.), *The dialogic imagination,* (pp. 270–73). (C. Emerson & M. Holquist, Trans.) Austin: University of Texas Press.

Barker, T., & Kemp, F. (1990). Network theory: A postmodern pedagogy for the writing classroom. In C. Handa (Ed.), *Computers and community: Teaching composition in the twenty-first century,* (pp. 1–23), Portsmouth, NH: Boynton/Cook.

Bartholomae, D. (1985). Inventing the university. In M. Rose (Ed.) *When a writer can not write: Studies in writer's block and other composing-process problems,* (pp. 134–165). New York: Guilford.

Bartholomae, D. (1987). Teaching basic writing: An alternative to basic skills. In T. Enos (Ed.), *A sourcebook for basic writing teachers* (pp. 84–103). New York: Random House.

Batson, T. (1988). The ENFI project: A networked classroom approach to writing instruction. *Academic Computing, 2,* 55–56.

Bernhardt, S. (1993). The shape of text to come: The texture of print on screens. *College Composition and Communication, 44,* 151–175.

Berthoff, A. E. (1984). Is teaching still possible? Writing, meaning, and higher order reasoning. *College English, 46,* 743–755.

Birkerts, S. (1994). *The Gutenberg elegies: The fate of reading in an electronic age.* Boston: Faber.

Bizzell, P. (1992). *Academic discourse and critical consciousness.* Pittsburgh; PA: University of Pittsburgh Press.

Blythe, S. (1996). Why OWLs? Value, risk, and evolution. *Kairos: A Journal for Teachers of Writing in Webbed Environments* [Online], *1.1.* Available: http://english.ttu.edu/kairos/1.1/owls/owlfront.html.

Blythe, S. (1997). Networked computers + writing centers = ? Thinking about networked computers in writing center practice. *The Writing Center Journal, 17*(2), 89–110.

Blythe, S. (1998). Technology in the writing center: Strategies for implementation and maintenance. In B. B. Silk (Ed.), *The writing center resource manual.* (pp. II.7.1–II.7.13). Emmitsburg, MD: National Writing Center Association Press.

Bohm, D. (1996). *On dialogue.* London: Routledge & Kegan Paul.

Brock, M. N. (1994). Reflections on change: Implementing the process approach in Hong Kong. *Perspectives (Working Papers of the Department of English, City University of Hong Kong)*, 6.2, 73–91.

Brown, J. L. (1984). Helping students to help themselves: Peer evaluation of writing. *Curriculum Review*, 47–50.

Bruffee, K. A. (1984). Collaborative learning and the "conversation of mankind." *College English, 46.7*, 635–652.

Bushman, D. (1991). Past accomplishments and current trends in writing center research. In R. Wallace & J. Simpson (Eds.), *The writing center: New directions*, (pp. 27–38). New York: Garland.

Calishain, Tara. (1998). Channeling your message. *Internet World*, 9(2), 59–62.

Carlacio, J. (1998, November). *What's so democratic about CMC? The rhetoric of techno-literacy in the new millennium.* Conference presentation at the Convention of the Midwest Modern Language Association, St. Louis, MO.

Casal, E. (1998, May 12). Group E-mail. E-list for tutors at California State University at Fresno.

Chesebro, J. W., & Bonsall, D. G. (1989). *Computer-mediated communication: Human relationships in a computerized world.* Tuscaloosa: University of Alabama Press.

Cheung, W., & Warren, M. (1996). Hong Kong students' attitudes toward peer assessment in English language courses. *Asian Journal of English Language Teaching*, 6, 61–75.

Chun, D. (1994). Using computer networking to facilitate the acquisition of interactive competence. *System, 22(1), 17–31.*

Clark, G. (1990). *Dialogue, dialectic, and conversation.* Carbondale: Southern Illinois University Press.

Clifford, J. (1981). Composing in stages: The effects of a collaborative pedagogy. *Research in the Teaching of English, 15*, 37–53.

Cogie, J. (1995). Resisting the editorial urge in writing center conferences: An essential focus on tutor training. In B. L. Stay, C. Murphy, & E. H. Hobson (Eds.), *Writing center perspectives*, (pp. 162–167). Emmitsburg, MD: National Writing Center Association Press.

Cohen, M., & Riel, M. (1989). The effect of distant audiences on students' writing. *American Educational Research Journal, 26*, 143–159.

Collins, P. (1996). The concept of a cooperative. *The Writing Center Journal, 17(1), 58–71.*

Connecting every pupil to the world. (1995, December 28). *New York Times*, p. A14.

Coogan, D. (1994). Towards a rhetoric of online tutoring. *The Writing Lab Newsletter, (19)1*, 3–5.

Coogan, D. (1995). E-Mail tutoring, a new way to do new work. *Computers and Composition, 12*(2), 171–181.

Crichton, M. (1990). *Jurassic park.* New York: Knopf.

Crossland, A. (1998). Electronic mail and the writing center. *The Writing Lab Newsletter, 22*(8), 5–6.

Crump, E. (1992). Online community: Writing centers join the network world. *The Writing Lab Newsletter, 17(2), 1–5.*

Crump, E. (1995). *Writing centers as technoprovocateurs.* [Online]. Available: http://www.missouri.edu/~cccc95/abstracts/crump2.html.

Crump, E. (1996, June 3). E-mail to wcenter. [Online] Available: http://www.ttu.edu/wcenter/9606/msg00025.html.

Crump, E. (1999). Home page. [Online]. Available: http:\\www.missouri.edu/~wleric

Daiute, C. (1985). *Computers and Writing.* Reading; MA: Addison-Wesley.

Daly, J., & Miller, M. (1975a). Apprehension of writing as a predictor of message intensity. *The Journal of Psychology, 89*, 175–177.

Daly, J., & Miller, M. (1975b). The empirical development of an instrument to measure writing apprehension. *Research in the Teaching of English, 9,* 242–249.

Daly, J., & Miller, M. (1975c). Further studies in writing apprehension: SAT scores, success expectations, willingness to take advanced courses, and sex differences. *Research in the Teaching of English, 9,* 249–253.

Daly, J. (1977). The effects of writing apprehension on message encoding. *Journalism Quarterly, 54,* 566–572.

Daly, J., & Shamo, W. (1978). Writing apprehension and occupational choice. *Research in the Teaching of English, 12,* 119–126.

Davis, K. M., Hayward, N., Hunter, K. R., & Wallace, D. L. (1988). The function of talk in the writing conference: A study of tutorial conversation. *The Writing Center Journal, 9*(1), 45–52.

DeCiccio, A. C., Rossi, M. J., & Cain, K. S. (1995). Walking the tightrope: Negotiating between the ideal and the practical in the writing center. In B. L. Stay, C. Murphy, & E. H. Hobson (Eds.), *Writing center perspectives* (pp. 26–37). Emmitsburg, MD: National Writing Center Association Press.

Deutsch, P. (1994, September). Ten commandments of the Internet. *Internet World.* [Online]. Available: http://www.Internetworld.com/print/monthly/info/oldiss.shtml.

DeVoss, D., Hara, M., & Kik, B. (1997). *The role of the World Wide Web in the writing center: Recent programs and projects in the MSU writing center.* Presentation to the 19th conference on the East Central Writing Centers Association. Pittsburgh, PA.

Dewey, J. (1944). *Democracy and education: An introduction to the philosophy of education.* New York: The Free Press.

Dibbell, J. (1993, December 21). A rape in cyberspace. *Village Voice,* pp. 36–42.

Duin, A. H. (1990). Terms and tools: A theory and research-based approach to collaborative writing. *Bulletin of the Association for Business Communication, 53,* 45–50.

Ede, L. (1989). Writing as a social process: A theoretical foundation for writing centers? *The Writing Center Journal, 9*(2), 3–13.

Eldred, J. C. (1989). Computers, composition pedagogy, and the social view. In G. E. Hawisher & C. L. Selfe (Eds.) *Critical perspectives on computers and composition instruction,* (pp. 201–218). New York: Teachers College Press.

Eldred, J. C., & Hawisher, G. E. (1995) Researching electronic networks. *Written Communication, 12,* 330–359.

Ericsson, P. (1994, October 28). E-mail to wcenter. [Online]. Available: http://www.ttu.edu/wcenter/9410/msg00544.html.

Essid, J. (1996). Training peer tutors with conferencing software: Practicing collaboration and planning for difficult tutorials. *Research and Teaching in Developmental Education, 13*(1), 45–55.

Farrell, P. B. (1987). Writer, peer tutor, and computer: A unique relationship. *The Writing Center Journal, 8*(1), 29–33.

Feenberg, A. (1989). The written world: On the theory and practice of computer conferencing. In R. Mason & A. Kaye (Eds.), *Mindweave: Communication, computers, and distance education* (pp. 22–39). New York: Elsevier Science.

Fitzgerald, S. H. (1994). Collaborative learning and whole language theory. In J. A. Mullin & R. Wallace (Eds.), *Intersections: Theory-practice in the writing center* (pp. 11–18). Urbana, IL: National Council of Teachers of English.

Flynn, L. J. (1998, 16 February). Why "push" got shoved out of the market. *New York CyberTimes.* [Online]. Available: www.nytimes.com.

Fox, R. (1980). Treatment of writing apprehension and its effects on composition. *Research in the Teaching of English, 14,* 39–49.

Freire, P. (1997). *Pedagogy of the oppressed* (20th ed.). New York: Continuum.

Gardner, C. (1996, June 3). E-mail to wcenter. [Online] Available: http://www.ttu.edu/wcenter/9606/msg00031.html.

Garratt, L. (1995). Peer feedback in writing: Is it culturally appropriate for Hong Kong Chinese adult learners? *Occasional Papers in English Language Teaching (English Language Teaching Unit, Chinese University of Hong Kong, 5*, pp. 97–118).

George, D. (1984). Working with peer groups in the composition classroom. *College Composition and Communication, 35,* 320–326.

Gilbert, S. (1996). A vision worth working toward: Refocus on learning and teaching: Educational uses of information for everyone. [E-Mail Draft]. (July 2 1996).

Gillam, A. (1994). Collaborative learning and peer tutoring practice. In J. A. Mullin & R. Wallace (Eds.), *Intersections: Theory-practice in the writing center* (pp. 39–53). Urbana, IL: National Council of Teachers of English.

Grimm, N. M. (1996). Rearticulating the work of the writing center. *College Composition and Communication, 47.4,* 523–548.

Haas, C. (1989). Seeing it on the screen isn't really seeing it: Computer writers reading problems. In G. E. Hawisher & C. L. Selfe (Eds.), *Critical perspectives on computers and composition instruction* (pp. 16–29). New York: Teachers College Press.

Hara, M. (1997). Internet writing consultants survey. [Independent Study Paper]. Michigan State University Writing Center.

Harasim, L. (1989). Online education: A new domain. In R. Mason & A. Kaye (Eds.) *Mindweave: Communication, computers, and distance* (pp. 50–62). Oxford, England: Pergamon.

Harris, M. (1986). *Teaching one-to-one: The writing conference.* Urbana, IL: National Council of Teachers of English.

Harris, M. (1990). What's up and what's in: Trends and traditions in writing centers. *The Writing Center Journal, 11*(1), 15–25.

Harris, M. (1993, February 5). E-mail to wcenter [Online]. Available: <http://www.ttu.edu/wcenter/9606/msg00030.html>

Harris, M. (1993). Voices from the net: Putting out the welcome mat for tutors. *The Writing Lab Newsletter 17*(8), 10–12.

Harris, M. (1995). Talk in the middle: Why writers need writing tutors. *College English, 57,* 27–42.

Harris, M. (1996, June 3). E-mail to wcenter [Online]. Available: http://www.ttu.edu/wcenter/9606/msg00030.html.

Harris, M., & Blythe, S. (1998). A discussion on collaborative design methods for collaborative online spaces. In C. Haviland & T. Wolf (Eds.), *Weaving knowledge together: Writing centers and collaboration* (pp. 80–105). Emmitsburg, MD: National Writing Center Association Press.

Harris, M., & Pemberton, M. (1995). Online writing labs (OWLs): A taxonomy of options and issues. *Computers and Composition, 12,* 145–159.

Hartman, K., et al. (1991). Patterns of social interaction and learning to write: Some effects of network technologies. *Written Communication, 8,* 19–113.

Hawisher, G. E., LeBlanc, P., Moran, C., & Selfe, C. L. (1996). *Computers and the teaching of writing in American higher education, 1979–1994: A history.* Norwood, NJ: Ablex.

Healy, D. (1995). From place to space: Perceptual and administrative issues in the online writing center. *Computers and Composition, 12,* 183–93.

Heath, S. B. (1997). Literate traditions. In T. Bruck, S. Diamond, P. Perkins, & K. Smith (Eds.), *Literacies: Reading, writing, interpretation* (pp. 299–315). New York: Norton.

Hemmeter, T. (1990). The "smack of difference": The language of writing center discourse. *Writing Center Journal, 11*(1), 35–48.

Hiltz, S. R., & Turoff, M. (1978). *The network nation: Human communication via computer.* Reading, MA: Addison-Wesley.

Hobson, E. H. (1993). Coming out of the silence. *The Writing Lab Newsletter, 17*(6), 7–8.

Hobson, E. H. (1994). Writing center practice often counters its theory. So what? In J. A. Mullin & R. Wallace (Eds.), *Intersections: Theory-practice in the writing center* (pp. 1–19). Urbana, IL: National Council of Teachers of English.

Hobson, E. H. (1998a). Straddling the virtual fence. Introduction. In E. H. Hobson (Ed.), *Wiring the writing center* (pp. ix–xxvi). Logan: Utah State University Press.

Hobson, E. H. (Ed.). (1998b). *Wiring the writing center.* Logan: Utah State University Press.

Holsti, O. R. (1969). *Content analysis for the social sciences and humanities.* Reading, MA: Addison-Wesley.

Hopes, D. (1998, September 24). Re: Query. Discussion list. *CREWRT* Available: L@lists.missouri.edu. Ftp://missouri.edu/pub/archive/lists/pub/CREWRTL/crewtl.log9809d

Hulet, M. (1997, October). *Cutting out the middleman: Tutoring with a computer.* Conference Presentation at Rocky Mountain Peer Tutoring Conference, Pocatello, ID.

Hurston, Z. N. (1937). *Their eyes were watching God.* New York: Harper & Row.

Hynds, S. (1989). Perspectives on perspectives in the writing center conference. *Focuses, 2*(2), 77–90.

Illich, I. (1970). *Deschooling society.* New York: Harrow.

Inman, J. A., & Howard, D. (1996, September). *Techno-literacy in professional writing.* Conference presentation at the 1996 Albany State University Educational Technology Conference, Albany, GA.

Jameson, F. (1984, July–August). Postmodernism, or the cultural logic of late capitalism. *New Left Review,* 53–92.

Jennings, E. (1987). Paperless writing: Boundary conditions and their implications. In L. Gerrard (Ed.), *Writing at century's end: Essays on computerassisted composition* (pp. 11–20) New York: Random House.

Johnson, J. P. (1996). Writing spaces: Technoprovocateurs and OWLs in the late age of print. *Kairos: A Journal for Teachers of Writing in Webbed Environments,* [Online], *1.1.* Available: http://english.ttu.edu/kairos/1.1/owls/johnson.html.

Jordan-Henley, J., & Maid, B. M. (1994). Guidelines for Consultations and Introductory Memo to Graduate Cybertutors. *The Cyberspace Writing Center Consultation Project Writing Works.* [Online]. Available: http://www2.rscc.cc.tn.us/~jordan_jj/cyberspace/Gradguide.html.

Jordan-Henley, J., & Maid, B. M. (1995a). MOOving along the information superhighway: Writing centers in cyberspace. *The Writing Lab Newsletter.* [Online]. Available: http://fur.rscc.cc.tn.us/VRWCenter/Mooving.html.

Jordan-Henley, J., & Maid, B. M. (1995b). Tutoring in cyberspace: Student impact and college/university collaboration. *Computers and Composition, 12,* 211–218.

Kail, H., & Trimbur, J. (1987). The politics of peer tutoring. *WPA: Writing Program Administration, 11,* 1–2.

Kelly, K. (1994). *Out of Control: The new biology of machines, social systems and the economic World.* (p. 389). Reading, MA: Addison-Wesley.

Kemp, F. (1994, March). *The limits of proof in writing instruction.* Paper presentation at the Conference on College Composition and Communication.

Kemp, F. (1994/1999, April 18). The Limits of Proof in Writing Instruction. [Online]. Available: http://english.ttu.edu/acw/database/essays/cccc94.kemp.html.

Kiesler, S., Siegel, J., & McGuire, T. (1984). Social psychological aspects of computer-mediated communication. *American Psychologist, 39,* 1123–1134.

Kimball, S. (1994, November 29). E-mail to wcenter [Online]. Available: http://www.ttu.edu/wcenter/9411/msg00454.html.

Kinkead, J. (1987). Computer conversations: E-mail and writing instruction. *College Composition and Communication, 38*(3), 337–341.

Kinkead, J. (1988). The electronic writing tutor. *The Writing Lab Newsletter, 13*(4), 4–5.

Kinkead, J., & Harris, J. G. (Eds.). (1993). *Writing centers in context.* Urbana, IL: National Council of Teachers of English.

Kinkead, J., & Hult, C. A. (1995). Letter from the guest editors. *Computers and Composition, 12*(2), 131–133.

Kivela, R. (1996). Working on networked computers: Effects on ESL writer attitude and comprehension. *Asian Journal of English Language Teaching, 6*, 85–93.

Langston, C. (1996, June 3). E-mail to wcenter [Online]. Available: http://www.ttu.edu/wcenter/9606/msg00024.html.

Lasarenko, J. (1996). PR(OWL)ING AROUND: An OWL by any other name. *Kairos: A Journal for Teachers of Writing in Webbed Environments,* [Online], *1.1.* Available: http://english.ttu.edu/kairos/1.1/owls/lasarenko/prowl.html.

Lauer, J. M., & Asher, J. W. (1988). *Composition research: Empirical designs.* New York: Oxford University Press.

Leahy, R. (1998). The rhetoric of written response to student drafts. *The Writing Lab Newsletter, 22*(8), 1–4.

Leavitt, M. (1993). *Gearing up with technology—A centennial challenge for educators.* [Online]. Available: http://www.gvnfo.state.ut.us/sitc/tech2000/vision/edspeech.htm.

Lerner, N. (1997). Counting beans and making beans count. *The Writing Lab Newsletter, 22*(1), 1–4.

Luchte, J. (1987). Computer programs in the writing center: A bibliographic essay. *The Writing Center Journal, 8*(1), 11–19.

Lunsford, A. (1995). Collaboration, control, and the idea of a writing center. In C. Murphy & J. Law (Eds.), *Landmark Essays on Writing Centers* (pp. 109–116). Dans, CA: Hermagoras.

Lunsford, A. (1995). Collaboration, control, and the idea of a writing center. In C. Murphy & S. Sherwood (Eds.), *St. Martin's Sourcebook for Writing Tutors* (pp. 36–42). New York: St. Martin's Press.

Mabrito, M. (1991). Electronic mail as a vehicle for peer response: Conversations of high- and low-apprehensive writers. *Written Communication, 8*, 509–532.

Mabrito, M. (1992). Computer-mediated communication and high-apprehensive writers: Rethinking the collaborative process. *Bulletin of the Association for Business Communication, 55*, 26–30.

Maid, B. M. (1994, September 28). E-mail to wcenter [Online]. Available: http://www.ttu.edu/wcenter/9409/msg00448.html.

Mangelsdorf, K., & Schlumberger, A. (1992). ESL student response stances in a peer-review task. *Journal of Second Language Writing, 1*(3), 235–54.

Marvin, C. (1988). *When old technologies were new: Thinking about electronic communication in the late nineteenth century.* New York: Oxford University Press.

McLuhan, M. (1962). *The Gutenberg galaxy: The making of typographic man.* University of Toronto Press.

McKenzie, L. (1989). The union of a writing center with a computer center: What to put in the marriage contract. *The Writing Lab Newsletter, 14*(3), 1,2,8.

McPherson, P. (1996). *The MSU technology guarantee* [Online]. Available: http://www.msu.edu/events/techinfo/.

Menzer, M. (1995, March 9). E-mail to wcenter [Online]. Available: http://www.ttu.edu/wcenter/9503/msg00181.html.

Miller, M. A. (1995). Techno-literacy and the new professor. *New Literary History*, [On-line], 26(3). Available: http://muse.jhu.edu/journals/new_literary_history/toc/nlhv026.html.

Monroe, B. J. (1997). The Murray-Wright High School/University of Michigan connection. [Online]. Available: http://wwwpersonal.umich.edu/~bjmonroe/mw.html.

Moran, C. (1992). Computers and the writing classroom: A look to the future. In G. E. Hawisher & P. LeBlanc (Eds.), *Re-imagining computers and composition: Teaching and research in the virtual age* (pp. 7–23). Westport, CT: Boynton/Cook.

Mullin, J. A. (1994). Introduction: The theory behind the centers. In J. A. Mullin & R. Wallace (Eds.), *Intersections: Theory-practice in the writing center* (pp. 172–183). Urbana, IL: National Council of Teachers of English.

Murphy, C. (1994). The writing center and social constructivist theory. In J. A. Mullin & R. Wallace (Eds.), *Intersections: Theory-practice in the writing center* (pp. 25–38). Urbana, IL: National Council of Teachers of English.

Murphy, C., & Sherwood, S. (1995b). The tutoring process: Exploring paradigms and practices. In C. Murphy & S. Sherwood. (Eds.), *St. Martin's sourcebook for writing tutors* (pp. 1–17). New York: St. Martin's Press.

Myers, M. (1996). *Changing our minds: Negotiating English and literacy*. Urbana, IL: National Council of Teachers of English.

Nelson, J., & Wambeam, C. (1995). Moving computers into the writing center: The path to least resistance. *Computers and Composition*, 12, 135–143.

Newmann, S. (1999). Demonstrating effectiveness. *The Writing Lab Newsletter*, 23(8), 8–9.

North, S. (1984). The idea of a writing center. *College English*, 46, 433–446.

Ong, W. (1988). *Orality and literacy: The technologizing of the word*. Boston, MA: Routledge.

O'Donoghue, R. (1992). Entering electronic reality. *The Writing Lab Newsletter*, 17(2), 1–5.

Oldenburg, R. (1989). *The great good place: Cafés, coffee shops, community centers, beauty parlors, general stores, bars, hangouts and how they get you through the day*. (New York: Paragon House.

Oppenheimer, T. (1997, July). The computer delusion. *The Atlantic Monthly*, 45–63.

Palmquist, M., Kiefer, K., & Zimmerman, D. E. (1998). Communication across the curriculum and university culture. In D. Reiss, D. Selfe, & A. Young (Eds.), *Electronic communication across the curriculum* (pp. 57–72). Urbana, IL: National Council of Teachers of English.

Pattison, R. (1982). *On literacy: The politics of the word from Homer to the age of rock*. New York: Oxford University Press.

Pegg, B. (1998, January 22). *National Writing Centers Association home page* [Online]. Available: http://departments.colgate.edu/diw/National Writing Center Association.html.

Pelton, J. N. (1996, November–December). Cyberlearning vs. the university: An irresistible force meets an immovable object. *The Futurist*, 17–20.

Pemberton, M. (1992). The prison, the hospital, and the madhouse: Redefining metaphors for the writing center. *The Writing Lab Newsletter*, 17(1), 11–16.

Peyton, J. (1990). Technological innovation meets institution: Birth of creativity or murder of a great idea? *Computers and Composition*, 7, 15–32.

Phinney, M. (1991). Word processing and writing apprehension in first and second language writers. *Computers and Composition*, 9, 65–82.

Pinney, Pete. (1998, August 12). *English III Problem Paper* [Online]. Available: http://chena.uaftvc.alaska.edu/faculty/ppinney/englishIII/problem.html

Pinney, Pete. (1998). *The Narration Outline* [Online]. Available: http://chena.uaftvc.alaska.edu/faculty/ppinney/essays/problem/proboutline.html.

Postman, N. (1992). *Technopoly: The surrender of culture to technology*. New York: Knopf.

Pratt, E., & Sullivan, N. (1994, March). *Comparison of ESL writers in networked and regular classrooms*. Conference Presentation at Teaching English as a Second or Other Language Convention, Baltimore, Maryland.

Raphael, T. E. (1989). Students' metacognitive knowledge about writing. *Research in the Teaching of English, 23*, 343–379.

Reigstad, T., & McAndrew, D. (1984). *Training tutors for writing conferences*. Urbana, IL: National Council of Teachers of English.

Rice, R. (1987). Computer-mediated communication and organizational innovation. *Journal of Communication, 37*, 65–94.

Rice, R., & Love, G. (1987). Electronic emotion: Socio-emotional content in a computer-mediated communication network. *Communication Research, 14*, 85–105.

Roderick, J. (1982). Problems in tutoring. In M. Harris (Ed.), *Tutoring writing* (pp. 32–39). Glenview, IL: Scott, Foresman.

Rose, M. (1989). *Lives on the boundary: The struggles and achievements of America's underprepared*. New York: The Free Press.

Selfe, C. L. (1989). Redefining literacy: The multilayered grammars of computers. In G. E. Hawisher & C. L. Selfe (Eds.), *Critical perspectives on computers and composition instruction* (pp. 3–15). New York: Teacher's College Press.

Selfe, C. L. (1998). Foreword. In D. Reiss, D. Selfe, & A. Young (Eds.), *Electronic communication across the curriculum* (pp. ix–xiv). Urbana, IL: National Council of Teachers of English.

Selfe, R. (1995). Surfing the tsunami: Electronic environments in the writing center. *Computers and Composition, 12*, 311–322.

Serico, J. G. (1986). Making the computer writing center a reality. *The Writing Lab Newsletter, 10*(9), 5–6.

Seuss, Dr. (1980). *On beyond zebra*. New York: Random House.

Shenk, D. (1997). *Data smog: Surviving the information glut*. San Francisco: HarperEdge.

Simpson, J. H. (1985). What lies ahead for writing centers: Position statement on professional concerns. *The Writing Center Journal, 5*(2)–6(1), 35–39.

Simpson, J. H. (1995). Perceptions, realities, and possibilities: Central administration and writing centers. In B. L. Stay, C. Murphy, & E. H. Hobson (Eds.), *Writing center perspectives* (pp. 48–52). Emmitsburg, MD: National Writing Center Association Press.

Sirc, G. (1988, April). Learning to write on a LAN. *T.H.E. Journal*, 99–104.

Spear, K. (1988). *Sharing writing: Peer response groups in English classes*. Portsmouth, NH: Boynton/Cook.

Spitzer, M. (1986). Writing style in computer conferences. *IEEE Transactions on Professional Communications, 29*, 19–22.

Stahlnecker, K. H. (1998). Virtually transforming the writing center: Online conversation, collaboration, and connection. *The Writing Lab Newsletter, 23*(2), 1–4.

Strand, S. (1994, December 22). E-mail to wcenter [Online]. Available: http://www.ttu.edu/wcenter/9412/msg00567.html.

Sullivan, N., & Pratt, E. (1996). A comparative study of two ESL writing environments: A computer-assisted classroom and a traditional oral classroom. *System, 29*(4), 491–501.

Summerfield, J. (1988). Writing centers: A long view. *The Writing Center Journal, 8*(2), 3(9).

Taylor, M. C., & Saarinen, E. (1994). *Imagologies: Media philosophy*. London: Boston, MA: Routledge & Kegan Paul.

Thompson, D. (1988). Conversational networking: Why the teacher gets most of the lines. *Collegiate Microcomputer, 6*, 193–201.

Tobin, J. (1998, September). The futurist. *Ann Arbor News, 23*(1), 41–45.

Turkle, S. (1995). *Life on the screen: Identity in the age of the Internet*. New York: Simon & Schuster.

Ulmer, G. (1997). *What is electracy?* [Online]. Available: http://www.elf.ufl.edu/electracy.html.

Wallace, R. (1998). Random memories of the virtual writing center: The modes-to-nodes problem. In E. H. Hobson (Ed.), *Wiring the writing center,* (pp. 163–170). Logan: Utah State University Press.

Warnock, T., & Warnock, J. (1984). Liberatory writing centers: Restoring authority to writers. In G. Olson (Ed.), *Writing centers: Theory and administration,* (pp. 16–23). Urbana, IL: National Council of Teachers of English.

Webb, M. O. (1995). Feminist epistemology and the extent of the social. *Hypatia, 10*(3), 85–98.

Wolcott, W. (1989). Talking it over: A qualitative study of writing center conferencing. *The Writing Center Journal, 9*(2), 15–29.

Author Index

Subject Index

CONTENTS

ACKNOWLEDGEMENTS

This book was inspired and motivated by Don LePan, president and founder of Broadview Press. Uncharacteristically for publishing executives, Don loves to visit faculty and discuss books. One day he and I were talking and I suggested that Broadview should publish a replacement for Huff's venerable and remarkably successful *How to Lie with Statistics*. Good as it was, it was now over 50 years old and deserved retirement. Don asked, "why don't you do it?" I answered, "because I am not a statistician." Finally he persuaded me to write the book. Not being a statistician turned out to be a kind of blessing. For one thing, I felt no compulsion to include formulas in the book, but more importantly I aimed at a more general introduction to the use of scientific information. This meant going beyond Huff's admonitions about statistical deception and beyond looking at statistical reasoning alone. It also meant going beyond the limits of most introductory statistics texts, which tend to look at individual experiments and studies, but seldom at the issue of scientific convergence and the more general question of how to assess the state of scientific research on a topic.

While Don was the inspiration, it was my family that enabled me to get the text done. My wife, Diana Davidson, was the key to realizing the project. She encouraged me to keep on with the project, and carefully and helpfully edited the text, teaching me in the process how to write in a non-academic manner. I could not have produced this text without her help.

Other members of my family who helped are my daughter Lupin Battersby, a health policy researcher, who gave me advice about research evaluation and did an extensive edit of an early draft; and my daughter Natasha Davidson, a mathematics professor, who discussed statistical issues with me and contributed a number of the cartoon ideas.

Josh Eiserike produced the cartoons, and I owe a lot to his patience as I learned more than I ever thought I would need to know about cartooning. To contact Josh Eiserike or to learn more about his work, please visit his website at <http://www.josheiserike.com>.

Bob Martin reviewed the initial draft making many useful suggestions and painstakingly checking all my references.

John Burbidge did a careful edit catching all those word processing errors that elude the spell checker, and identifying places where a layperson would need greater clarity.

Alex Sager, my editor at Broadview, guided me through the process, seeing me through to the end, in spite of my distractions and procrastinations, and his new baby.

CHAPTER 1

HOW TO LI(V)E WITH STATISTICS: WHY WE NEED TO THINK ABOUT STATISTICAL AND SCIENTIFIC INFORMATION

> *Through and through the world is infested with quantity. To talk*
> *sense is to talk quantities, it is no use saying the nation is large—*
> *how large? It is no use saying that radium is scarce—how scarce? You*
> *can not evade quantity. You may fly to poetry and music and quan-*
> *tity and number will face you in your rhythms and your octaves.*

Alfred North Whitehead (1861-1947)

In September 1995 my sister-in-law, Gail, received the dreaded diagnosis: multiple-site lung cancer. Fatal, little time left. "Go home and die" the specialist said. "The cancer obviously has metastasized [spread]; an operation is useless, chemotherapy a painful and futile palliative." Gail, a friend, my wife, and I decided not to accept the doctor's opinion without some investigation. We decided to use every critical analytical and research tool that we had. None of us was a scientist or physician. We set out to learn about lung cancer and the problems of diagnosis. We were looking for a cure, but if no cure, we'd settle for more and better time for her.

I knew from my research that such prognoses are at best only averages (or **medians**[1]—see Chapter 6) and that she could easily live longer than the doctor predicted.

---

1 All the technical terms in bold are defined in the Glossary at the end of the text.

My sister-in-law quickly transferred to the cancer clinic from the hospital where the initial diagnosis was done and where the prognosis had been given to her. In the cancer clinic we discussed the diagnosis with doctors who worked together in teams and, to some extent, encouraged patient involvement. The librarian in the clinic's library gave us considerable help. We learned that the diagnostic judgement of whether cells had metastasized was based (at that time) on the visual similarity of the cells in the cancer sites. There appeared to be no objective "gold standard"—no clear means to check the reliability of the judgement until it was too late. Using some of what you will learn from this text, we researched and found that pathologist's eye-based judgements were far from reliable. In addition, we learned that lung cancer with multiple sites in the lung was quite exceptional. No one was sure that such a diagnostic appearance meant metastasization.

Using cancer textbooks, *Medline*, and an article in the *Scientific American*, we came to the conclusion that the initial diagnosis was not well validated. We noted that the pathologists even disagreed about the cell type, though the new pathologist assured me he was "90% certain" that the cells from the different sites were identical and hence had the same source. However, because of our research I now knew that this "90%" figure was just a subjective assessment of confidence and not a real measure of reliability. At this time my wife read in the *Scientific American* about DNA testing in a colon and brain cancer study. We asked why DNA testing wasn't being done in this case. For reasons still unclear, the doctors at the cancer agency had not used such procedures in lung cancer cases. They do now. When they used DNA testing on my sister-in-law's lungs, it became clear (to the amazement of the pathologist) that the separate sites were not from the same source, but independent cancers. The cancer had not metastasized. Therefore, taking the risk of an operation to remove the cancer was justified. The operation was done and my sister-in-law remains cancer free.

While this story is just one case,[1] it does show that a basic understanding

---

1   Throughout the text I advise against putting too much reliance on stories and anecdotes, but here I am giving an anecdote in aid of my argument. Hypocrisy? Not really. Anecdotes are memorable and edifying. They have a role to play in explanation and instruction. Anecdotes are a problem only when they are used as evidence for a sweeping generalization. However, here I am not using the story as evidence of a generalization but as an illustration. The story shows that laypeople, using critical thinking and research, can contribute to medical problem solving. I am not claiming that all patients who take an active and intelligent interest in their illnesses generally have better health outcomes. There may be no solutions. Perhaps blind faith in one's doctors is sometimes the best thing for the immune system! Perhaps. But I believe that thinking critically can aid almost any decision-making process. If your life or the life of a loved one was on the line, would you choose intellectual passivity?

of statistical information and scientific method can be helpful, even life saving. My sister-in-law's family and friends were not cancer experts, but by reading research and using critical-thinking strategies, we were able to make reasonable judgements about the advice of the doctors. Of course there were limits to what we could make of the research and textbooks, but most readers will be surprised and pleased to discover how accessible much research is.

Of course, one is not always so fortunate. In a recent friend's cancer battle, research by his family and friends did not save him, but it did help them make sensible decisions about treatment alternatives. It prevented them from spending useless money on quackery and enabled them make the best decisions they could under the circumstances. They too discovered they could read the research and learn what questions to ask about the risk and benefits of various therapies. Sharing the research meant there was a collective understanding of the situation among all family members who could then work together to make the dying person's last hours as meaningful as possible.

When we did our research about Gail's lung cancer there was limited information available on the World Wide Web. This has changed. Now, anyone with Web access can research almost any issue with ease. What is crucial is being able to critically evaluate and make sensible use of such research. The goal of this book is to enable you to make thoughtful and critical use of statistics and scientific information. What you learn from this book will encourage a healthy scepticism about statistics, but should also enable you to make use of valid statistical information.

To think critically is to have the ability and inclination to assess claims and arguments. You may have heard that the Web is full of garbage since anyone can put information on a Web page. True. But libraries and journals are also full of misinformation, and certainly some garbage. Without the aura of "publication" ("I read it in a book!") perhaps people will be more inclined to think critically about information they find on the Web than they do about the information they find in published material.

The key to thinking critically about what you read or are told is to evaluate the evidence using appropriate criteria. Statistical and scientific claims, like all claims, require evidence and support. They should not be taken at face value, or just because some expert is reported to claim them. We should not be overly impressed because statistical and scientific claims have an aura of precision and credibility (e.g., "79.4% of all users report significant improvements!"). Claims spiffed up with numbers can be used to intimidate people who are unable to evaluate them. In the face of such inability, many either concede ("after all, they say ...") or dismiss ("you can prove anything with statistics").

Such defensive reactions are disabling politically and personally. A person who can't evaluate statistical and scientific claims is like someone lost in the forest amidst a natural abundance of food but lacking the knowledge to distinguish edible plants from the poisonous ones. Since statistical and scientific information pervades our life, we cannot afford to be ignorant of how to sort the good from bad.

Perhaps you are familiar with the most famous description of statistics (attributed, curiously, by some authorities to Mark Twain, and by others to Benjamin Disraeli)—that there are "lies, damn lies and statistics."

It's easy to lie with statistics, but
it is even easier to lie without them.

Why are statistics even worse than damn lies? Clearly people can lie, and lie with great effectiveness, using words alone. They can lie perhaps even more effectively with video and photographs. There are many more verbal lies than statistical lies made every day. Politicians can lie, for example, about having evidence of weapons of mass destruction without using any statistics. Verbal lying is a far more common problem than statistical deception so why all the indignation about the misleading use of statistics? The problem I think is with those who are being taken in. We believe that we can detect and evaluate good old-fashioned verbal lies,[1] but unless we have a critical understanding of statistical claims we aren't confident that we can separate truth from deception. And statistics sound, so ... well, true. Statistics can be used to lie and mislead, but, correctly understood, statistics can also be used to expose lies and help us find the truth. As one statistician put it: "it's easy to lie with statistics, but it's even easier to lie without them."[2] Once we have the critical awareness necessary to separate the informative from the deceptive, once we know what questions to ask, we will reduce our chances of being deceived, and will be free to make intelligent use of credible statistical information.

GOING TO THE SOURCE

"Studies say" is becoming a daily phrase used by all media. To take a couple of examples that I found with a brief perusal of the Web: "Study: Shyness Condition Linked to Shorter Life"[3] or "Study Says Oprah is Driving Us Nuts."[4] Such headlines may grab our attention, but they should also put us on guard. Newspapers love the sensational, and studies can often be exploited to provide such headlines. This book will give you the basic information needed to evaluate such popular sources of (mis)information. It will also provide the minimal understanding of science and statistics that is necessary to make intelligent use of such information in your personal life and in your role as a thoughtful citizen. But popular information sources are often not adequate for making decisions about issues of personal or political importance. The reliability of such information is dependant on the competency and fairness of the reporter. Popular sources of information are often too brief and fail to contain the crucial details necessary for making a careful evaluation of the claims, leaving out information such as duration of study or number of people studied. The example in the box is typical.

---

1   There have been numerous studies on our ability to detect good old-fashioned verbal lies and most people are not very good at it. E.g., *A New Scientist Report,* March 18, 2002, accessed at <http://www.newscientist.com/news/news.jsp?id=ns99992054> June 14, 2004.

2   David S. Moore, *Statistics: Concepts and Controversies*, 5th ed. (W.H. Freeman, 2001), xxiii.

3   Accessed at <http://www.wistv.com> December 9, 2003; the study on which the article was based was published in the Proceedings of the National Academy of Science and used 28 male rats as subjects! S.A. Cavigelli and M.K. McClintock, "Fear of Novelty in Infant Rats Predicts Adult Corticosterone Dynamics and an Early Death," *PNAS* 100 (2003): 16131–36.

4   Josh Shaffer, "Is Oprah Gradually Driving Us Nuts? Well, Maybe," *Houston Chronicle,* November 19, 2003.

Want strong bones? Exercise, study says

The Associated Press June 11, 2004

STATE COLLEGE, Pa. — Got exercise?

A recent study indicates that exercise is more important than calcium in developing strong bones in girls and young women.

Researchers at Penn State University and Johns Hopkins University found that even when girls took in far less calcium than the recommended daily allowance, bone strength was not significantly affected, said Tom Lloyd of Penn State's College of Medicine at the Milton S. Hershey Medical Center.

However, when the girls were asked about their exercise habits, a strong correlation was found between exercise and bone strength.

No one is encouraging teens to stop drinking milk. The researchers said that the young women studied still were getting more calcium than many female American teens.

We are not told the duration of the study, nor the numbers in the sample. What is the significance of "bone strength?" How it is measured?

Lack of access to basic research and detailed information was the fate of almost all of us outside our areas of expertise. But all that has changed. The Web contains many sites that are directed at professionals in the field or informed policy makers—and with some basic understanding, you can use them too. A particular goal of this book is to enable readers to go beyond reliance on media reports of polls and scientific findings and use more detailed and reliable websites that contain the actual studies or information on which news reports are based (see Chapter 11). The Web provides remarkable access to **primary research**—the research published by scientists and researchers in their field. With a little effort you can have access to research and information that once would have required a university library and enormous time and effort. Some free sites, such as the one connected to the *British Medical Journal,* even provide systematic reviews and summaries of research, saving you (and, one hopes, your doctor) the trouble of collecting all the relevant research. (More about this in Chapter 11.) The door to abundant information has been opened. All that is required is the ability to understand and evaluate the information.

The great advantages of using primary research are that it can be the *most current and detailed research available*, it has been assessed by fellow professionals (articles are subject to "peer review" before they are published), and it is not "interpreted" by someone else. If you are willing to put in the effort, you can be "liberated" from the frustration of "I don't know, but 'they say.'"

My sister-in-law's life was saved because a number of laypeople did critical research. We evaluated and used information gathered from professionals, scientific studies, and statistical research; we used critical thinking to make a difference in her life. My intent is that this book will help you become a better and more effective critical thinker who can also make the best use of scientific and statistical information to make a difference in your life.

CHAPTER 2

INTRODUCTION TO CRITICAL THINKING

I think all these claims about smoking being bad for you are overblown. My grandfather smoked all his life and died in his nineties.

Now there's an argument that needs a little critical thinking. You don't need to know the horrifying statistics on smoking-related mortality to show what's wrong with that reasoning. The claim that "smoking being a bad idea is overblown" is both vague and contrary to well-established evidence of the dangers of smoking. Because the claim conflicts with existing scientific evidence we would want some really good evidence before being persuaded. The grandfather's impressive lifespan just isn't enough. This quote is a classic example of the fallacy of **anecdotal evidence** (discussed more fully later in this chapter). One good example or story just can't support a broad generalization. That's why we have research and statistics. That's also why we need critical thinking.

Most of us do think critically now and then. Most often, we think critically about ideas we disagree with. But real critical thinking isn't just about doubting what you don't want to believe. Real critical thinking involves an attitude of reasonable scepticism—a habit of asking questions such as how can they know that? what's the evidence for that claim? are there counter-examples to that generalization?

Thinking critically about statistical and scientific claims involves the same questioning attitude involved in evaluating any other type of claim, and the same basic questions. This chapter will introduce four critical questions that should be asked when evaluating any argument, scientific or not. The chapters that follow will show you how to apply these critical questions specifically to statistical and scientific information.

The main way to study critical thinking is through the study of arguments. By **argument** I don't mean a heated exchange between people. In critical thinking, making an argument means giving reasons in support of a claim. In this sense, an argument is simply a set of claims, one of which, the **conclusion**, is supported by one or more other claims called **premises**. You may have heard the following, one of the oldest examples of an argument. It isn't much of an argument, but it has been used since ancient times to teach students logic, and it does involve a general premise of profound human significance.

1. All humans are mortal.
2. Socrates is a human.
Therefore, Socrates is mortal.

In this argument, the claims that "All humans are mortal" and "Socrates is a human" are the premises that provide the reasons for believing the unsurprising conclusion, "Socrates is mortal."

Arguments seldom come laid out as clearly and simply as this example (and hopefully they are more useful). More often they are like the following letter that was written in response to an article about the need to build more retirement homes.

> In this era, people are living to a healthy and ripe old age. My 85-year-old mother lives on her own, power-walks two miles each day, drives her car (safely), climbs stairs, does crosswords, reads the daily paper and could probably beat your columnist at almost anything.—Anna Jones

Before we critically assess this argument, I want to outline the argument by explicitly identifying its premises and conclusion. Thinking

critically about an argument is often facilitated by laying out an argument in this manner. It might go like this:

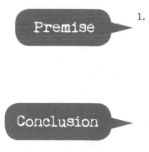

Premise

1. My 85-year-old mother lives on her own, power-walks two miles each day, drives her car (safely), climbs stairs, does crosswords, reads the daily paper and could probably beat your columnist at almost anything.

Conclusion

Therefore: In this era, people are living to a healthy and ripe old age.

Evaluating an argument means evaluating the evidence provided for the conclusion. I recommend approaching this task by using four Critical Questions that should be asked of any claim or argument.

1. **What is being claimed?**
2. **How good is the evidence?**
3. **What other information is relevant?**
4. **Are relevant fallacies avoided?**

The remainder of the chapter will lead you through this set of questions showing how to apply them to simple arguments.

INTRODUCING THE CRITICAL QUESTIONS

Let's use the first two questions to evaluate the argument from Anna Jones.

Critical Question 1: What Is Being Claimed?

It is amazing how often we don't know exactly what we are talking about when we argue. How often do we ask others, or ourselves "So, what is it you are trying to prove?" or "What's your point?" In the argument above, the author makes a number of claims about the health of her mother, but it seems clear that the conclusion is about old people in general. The claims about the mother's health are offered as evidence for this conclusion.

The conclusion is quite vague. When it talks about "people" it clearly does not mean everyone. Does it mean many people? Most people? How old is "old"? What exactly is a "ripe and healthy" old age?

The conclusion is also poorly supported. How did she get to her conclusion? She appears to have thought that "since my mother is healthy, many other old people will be." How well does Anna Jones's evidence support her conclusion?[1] Pretty obviously one healthy mother proves nothing about the general health of our aging population. While that seems obvious, let's do an exercise in argument analysis and take the evaluation process more slowly. To assess the support provided for the conclusion, we need to review a number of different aspects of the evidence.

Critical Question 2: How Good Is the Evidence?

2(A) WHAT IS THE EVIDENCE?

What evidence is presented to support the general claim about the health of the elderly? The evidence is simply the story about the health and independence of one 85 year old—a sample of one.

So how do we go about assessing the evidence? Basically there are two evaluative questions that should be asked.

---

1 When speaking informally I will often use the term "evidence" to refer to factual type premises provided to support the conclusion.

2(B) ASSUMING THE EVIDENCE IS TRUE, HOW MUCH SUPPORT DOES THIS EVIDENCE PROVIDE FOR THE CONCLUSION?

Anna Jones's evidence does not support her conclusion. Whether her mother charges about in her red sports car and dances all night provides virtually no support for any generalizations about the elderly—regardless of whether or not it is true. So we don't have to question or be sceptical of this claim about her mother. Because the premise provides virtually no support for the conclusion, we don't need to check the truth of the premise. We don't need to question Anna about the health and habits of her mother. True or not, Anna's claims provide grossly inadequate evidence for her generalization.

What we'd need here instead is a study of, say, hundreds of elderly people, that concluded that most 85 year olds are quite healthy.

If we believe that the evidence presented would provide good support for a claim, then we would want to ask:

2(C) IS THE EVIDENCE CREDIBLE?

Now imagine that we have a larger study, not just a single example, in support of the conclusion. In that case, we would want to know how the study was done. Was a representative sample taken, or were only people in the geriatric Olympics studied? How long did the study last? How large a number involved? Etc. This book outlines how to use questions like these to assess the credibility of evidence from studies.

THE CRITICAL QUESTIONS

Now let's look at an argument with more than one premise. Suppose someone argues that they are confident that a friend is a "supporter of the Calgary Flames hockey team." They might argue as follows: "John is young, athletic, and from Calgary. He enjoys watching sports and television and drinking beer with his friends. I'm sure he roots for the Flames." Laid out, the argument looks like this:

Premises

1. John is young.
2. John is athletic.
3. John is from Calgary.
4. John enjoys watching sports on television and drinking beer with his friends.

Conclusion

Therefore: John supports the Calgary Flames hockey team.

Critical Question 1: What Is Being Claimed?

The conclusion is "John supports the Calgary Flames hockey team." But what exactly does it mean? What does "supports" mean in this context? Does it mean that he goes to the games, watches the games whenever he can on TV, or merely that when asked, he says "Yeah I support the Flames." If we were really concerned about what was being claimed we would need to know with more precision what "support" means.

Critical Question 2: How Good Is the Evidence?

2(A) WHAT IS THE EVIDENCE?

There are four premises, claims about John that are presented as evidence.

2(B) ASSUMING THE EVIDENCE IS TRUE, HOW STRONG IS ITS SUPPORT FOR THE CONCLUSION?

Assuming they are true, each bit of evidence supplies a small amount of support for the conclusion, though taken together they make a somewhat plausible case that John is *likely* to be a Flames supporter.

2(C) IS THE EVIDENCE CREDIBLE?

We can't really answer this question at least until we know the source of the information. Did it come from John? A friend? Rumours?

So is John a supporter of the Flames? Possibly. There is not really enough evidence for us to be confident of the conclusion, but we are given some reasons to think it likely. What would really persuade us? Finding out he has a season's ticket, or seeing him on television screaming his lungs out for the Flames would probably do it! Asking what evidence would be necessary to convince us, can help us judge the adequacy of the evidence provided.

This is not the end of the questions that need to be asked to evaluate a claim or argument. Things are not that simple. Many conclusions cannot be evaluated with only the evidence provided. Frequently there is other information that is relevant to assessing the credibility of the conclusion or the quality of the evidence provided in support. This is especially true if we are dealing with complex or controversial issues. To make a complete assessment of the credibility of a conclusion and its supporting premises requires considering not just the evidence provided. It requires assessing other relevant information such as the history of the issue, including past research, and the conflicting evidence, counter-arguments, or alternative explanations. If further evidence revealed that John does not like contact sports, for example, then there would be good reason to doubt he was a fan of any hockey team despite the reasons cited in the argument.

In order to illustrate the application of these sorts of further questions, let's look at another typical argument. Suppose Jane told Mary that she thought Mary's boyfriend, Bill, was being unfaithful. Naturally Mary would want to know why Jane thought that. Suppose Jane said she had seen Bill at a party with Sue and that he and Sue were dancing very provocatively. In addition, Mary had noticed that Sue often leaves school with Bill in his car.

Let's lay out the argument as before:

Premises
1. Bill was dancing provocatively with Sue at a party.
2. Bill has been seen often leaving school with Sue.

Conclusion
Therefore: Bill is probably being unfaithful.

Critical Question 1: What Is Being Claimed?

It seems pretty clear what is being claimed.

Critical Question 2: How Good Is the Evidence?

The evidence, as they say in court, is circumstantial. Even if true, it is far from conclusive. Is the informant a reliable person with some personal bias that might motivate her remarks? If reliable, then we can reasonably assume she saw what she saw.

How might we evaluate this argument further? Let's use Critical Question 3.

Critical Question 3: What Other Information Is Relevant?

3(a) What is the history of this issue?
3(b) Does the argument meet the burden of proof or the onus appropriate to its context?
      (i) Is the conclusion consistent with other information we have?
     (ii) If in conflict with previous information, does the argument adequately address the opposing evidence or arguments; is it strong enough to counter previous information?
3(c) Is there relevant information that is missing?

CRITICAL QUESTION 3(A): WHAT IS THE HISTORY OF THE ISSUE?

If Mary knew that the informant, Jane, had a history of causing trouble between partners, that would reduce the weight of her evidence. This same strategy of exploring the history of the issue helps even more when assessing well-known controversial topics.

Most arguments and studies occur in an historic context and are addressing a question that has been studied and debated for some time. Does listening to Mozart make you smarter? Does second-hand smoke cause lung cancer? Are greenhouse gases causing global warming? Questions like these have provoked a history of research and debate. To determine whether a particular argument or study gives adequate reason for believing its conclusion usually requires knowing how this new argument or study fits into the greater context of the debate. For example, a new study that questions the claim that consumption of fat does not contribute to heart problems would be up against hundreds of studies that claim to document its dangers. To decide whether to accept the findings of a new study, we need to look at the strength of the evidence against it. A significant amount of research that points in one direction can only be offset by more powerful and credible work that points in another direction.

CRITICAL QUESTION 3(B): DOES THE ARGUMENT MEET THE BURDEN OF PROOF?

Being suspicious of your partner is a serious issue. Before you move to such a position you should require good, reliable evidence. This means that the informant bears a significant burden of proof in establishing her claim. The idea of **onus** or **burden of proof** is that in most arguments there is an existing default position that might be reasonably held without argument, but those who would challenge such a view have the "burden of proof" on them: they must provide a good argument to counter the assumed default position. The more obviously true the default position seems, the greater the burden of proof. And the more serious a claim is—that is, the more important the consequences of true or false belief—the greater the burden of proof. The evidence provided by Jane would not be adequate to meet the burden of proof required for putting forward such important claims.

Burden of proof is also a very important concept when evaluating scientific research. When we look at scientific research we will see that there is often an existing consensus that establishes an onus, or burden of proof, on any new, conflicting information. A study that makes claims contrary to the existing consensus needs to provide sufficiently strong evidence to meet the burden of proof established by that consensus. Such a study should not only provide evidence for its claims, but also give some account of why the previous position should no longer be accepted.

For example, people who claim there are Sasquatches or that the Loch Ness monster exists a must provide considerable evidence to overturn the current view that there are no such creatures. The onus is on the believer in such curious creatures to come up with evidence, not on the sceptic to "disprove" the existence of such creatures. Often the onus is on the person who claims the existence of something because it is usually much easier to prove that something exists (if it does!) than to prove that it doesn't exist. All it would take would be to find and display an Ogopogo to prove the existence of one; but even a great deal of looking in the right sort of places and failing to find that creature still leaves open some reasonable doubt: maybe we haven't looked enough.

The concept of onus is perhaps most familiar in its use in the legal system. In our criminal justice system, the accused (in nearly all circumstances) is presumed innocent. The *onus* is on the prosecutor to provide enough evidence to prove the accused guilty "beyond a reasonable doubt." The accused does not have an obligation to prove him or herself *innocent*.[1]

CRITICAL QUESTION 3(c): IS THERE RELEVANT INFORMATION THAT IS MISSING?

Relevant Information: Counter Arguments and Alternative Explanations

If Mary knew that Bill and Sue are a competitive salsa dance team, she would have another explanation of why he was dancing with Sue and why they were leaving school together. Until these explanations are eliminated, Mary would not have grounds to accept the offered explanation that Bill and Sue are having a relationship.

With all contentious issues, it is important to know what the counter-arguments are. You can't evaluate the support for a claim by only looking at the positive evidence and arguments. Take, for example, the debate around capital punishment. An argument in favour of capital punishment must do more than make a case for retribution, i.e., that some criminals "deserve to die" because of the heinousness of their crimes. An adequate argument for capital punishment would also need to meet the range of well-known and well supported objections to capital punishment including the evidence that capital punishment fails to

---

1   In civil cases, there is a different burden of proof: proof on a balance of probabilities. This is a burden of proof that is much easier to meet.

deter and sometimes results in the execution of an innocent person. Merely arguing for retribution would be inadequate because such an argument fails to address key existing counter-arguments.

Causal Claims

Another situation in which alternatives must be considered when evaluating the evidence is when someone makes a causal claim. Suppose someone claims that "the plants in Mary's garden grew especially well this year *because* of her new gardener." A sceptic might respond, "That might be true, but we had a particularly mild spring and a sunny and not too dry summer; that too might explain it." We can't accept a causal explanation as THE explanation, until we are confident that other probable explanations could not explain what happened. E.g., "I don't think the weather can explain how well the plants look; we had just as good a summer last year and her garden was not nearly as healthy."

In the case of scientific studies that attempt to determine the explanation of some phenomena, the researchers must always consider alternative explanations to their own and show why *their* explanation is more credible than the alternatives.

Relevant Information: Missing Information

We have already discussed a number of bits of information that were left out in the initial Sue and Bill story. Alternative explanations and counter-evidence are not the only things that may be missing from an argument. Reports of polls or scientific studies often leave out crucial bits of information. The report may not state when the poll was done, or how big the sample was. Reports of scientific studies may leave out how many people were studied, or how long the study was, or who the subjects were, or who paid for it. This information can often be of considerable importance. For example, the headline quoted in Chapter 1 that claimed "Study: Shyness Condition Linked to Shorter Life"[1] failed to mention that the study was done with 28 male rats! As we learn the

---

1 Accessed at <http://www.wistv.com> December 9, 2003; the study on which the article was based, published in the Proceedings of the National Academy of Science, used 28 male rats as subjects! S.A. Cavigelli and M.K. McClintock, "Fear of Novelty in Infant Rats Predicts Adult Corticosterone Dynamics and an Early Death." *PNAS* 100 (2003): 16131–36.

criteria for assessing studies, we will also learn what should be included to make a reasonable judgement of a study's worth.

Lastly, it is often useful to ask if the argument contains any **fallacies**.

Critical Question 4: Are Relevant Fallacies Avoided?

Fallacies are *common arguments that seem persuasive but do not provide adequate support for their conclusion*. There are many such common fallacies that have been identified over the last few thousand years (Aristotle started this project in the fourth century BCE!). Knowing at least some of them helps us guard against being seduced by a persuasive but bad argument.

In the Bill and Sue story, it appears that Jane was guilty of the fallacy of **hasty conclusion**—*coming to a conclusion with too little investigation and inadequate evidence*. She appears to have leapt to the conclusion that Bill was having an affair with Sue without adequate investigation.

A similar fallacy was committed by Anna Jones and the writer who used his grandfather as evidence against the dangers of smoking. They were guilty of hasty generalization since the evidence supplied did not begin to provide sufficient support for the generalizations they made. Many instances of over generalization result from *stories*, like that about the 85-year-old mother of Anna Jones, that paint a vivid and persuasive picture. *The tendency to over generalize from our own experiences or the stories of others is so common it too has a fallacy name:* the fallacy of anecdotal evidence.

There are many common fallacies of everyday reasoning, but there are specific fallacies that tend to crop up in statistical scientific investigations. We will be covering these in detail in the following chapters but an example might be useful. A common problem in sampling done for polls is the fallacy of **biased sampling**. Pollsters and researchers must be careful to get a representative and unbiased **sample** of the population they are studying. You can't make generalizations about Canadians by just studying Vancouverites and you shouldn't make generalizations about Americans based only on a sample of American men or teenagers or city-dwellers. That seems obvious enough, but it is often tricky to avoid getting a subtly biased sample.

While I have listed the question about fallacies last, you probably realize that the identification of fallacies is something that can happen at any stage of the evaluation process. For example, claims and conclusions can suffer from fallacies of *vagueness* ("supports the Flames" or "healthy and ripe old age"). As we saw, evidence can be anecdotal (my 85-year-old mother is healthy), and causal arguments, which we will discuss at length in later chapters, can suffer from ignoring alternative explanations ("The door opened all by itself, there must be ghosts!" Oh? What about the possibility that it was the wind?).

Even though fallacies can show up anywhere in our evaluative process, I put the identification of fallacies as the final question when evaluating evidence because reviewing an argument for fallacies provides a useful, final check.

The Critical Questions are a guide not only to evaluating statistical and scientific information, but any claim or argument. Not all sub-questions are relevant or the same for every kind of subject matter, but the basic four Critical Questions should almost always be useful. The next chapter will demonstrate how to apply and adapt the critical questions that are relevant to the most common type of statistical information: polls.

EVALUATING CLAIMS AND ARGUMENTS
THE CRITICAL QUESTIONS

1. What is being claimed?
2. How good is the evidence?
   a. What is the evidence?
   b. Assuming the evidence is true, how much support does this evidence provide for the conclusion?
   c. Is the evidence credible?
3. What other information is relevant?
   a. What is the history of the issue?
   b. Does the argument meet the burden of proof?
      i. Is the argument consistent with the direction of previous research or evidence?
      ii. If in conflict with previous research, does the argument deal effectively with opposing evidence or arguments; is it strong enough to counter this previous research?
   c. Is there relevant information that is missing?
4. Are relevant fallacies avoided?

CHAPTER 3

POLLING: THE BASICS

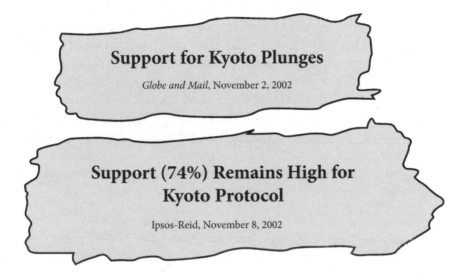

Support for Kyoto Plunges

Globe and Mail, November 2, 2002

Support (74%) Remains High for Kyoto Protocol

Ipsos-Reid, November 8, 2002

THE KYOTO POLLS

Polls are everywhere. From small non-profits to large companies, everyone commissions polls. The media is often filled with reports of polls, sometimes as contradictory as those reported above. What are we to make of these claims? Should we give them any weight or merely dismiss them as more "damnable" statistics? I once heard someone argue, "Never been polled myself; don't see how they could be polling Canadians and not ask me now and again." And it is true that remarkably few people are polled in national opinion polls—little more than 1,000 usually—so how can such polls claim any validity?

Let's begin to answer these questions by looking at the polls referred to in the above headlines using relevant Critical Questions:

1. What is being claimed?
2. How good is the evidence?

Critical Question 1: What Is Being Claimed?

As we will repeatedly learn, newspaper summaries are often misleading and headlines are even worse. So the first thing we have to do is distinguish between what the headlines claim and what the actual poll claims. You may remember the worldwide controversy surrounding whether countries should sign the Kyoto Accord to pledge reduction in greenhouse gas emissions. Most countries did sign, but the US and a few others refused. After the US refused, Canada had to decide whether it would go along. Some of the provinces were opposed on the basis that following the Accord would be bad for their economy. In particular, the Canadian province of Alberta, which produces proportionately more greenhouse gases because of its oil and gas industry, was strongly opposed. So Alberta launched a political effort to convince Canadians that Kyoto would be bad for Canada. Subsequently Alberta commissioned a poll by Ipsos-Reid in an attempt to show that there was nationwide opposition to signing the protocol. The problem for Alberta was that the federal government had been doing extensive polling and found consistently strong support for signing the protocol. No problem, just ask a slightly different question.

COMPARING THE KYOTO POLLS

The poll from November 8, 2002 that supplied the headline "Support (74%) Remains High for Kyoto Protocol" asked:

> As you may know, the Kyoto Accord on climate change requires Canada to reduce its emissions of greenhouse gases to 6% below what they were in 1990 over the next 10 years. This means that Canada would have to reduce its current emissions by about 20% to meet its target. Based on what you have seen, read or heard, do you personally support or oppose implementing the Kyoto Accord?

But the Alberta survey asked:

> Which of the following 3 options do you support?
> 1. Withdraw from the Kyoto Protocol and develop a made-in-Canada plan for reducing greenhouse gas emissions,

2. ratify the Kyoto Protocol, or

3. do nothing?

Given the Alberta choices, 45% of respondents preferred the federal government withdraw from the Kyoto Accord and develop a "made-in-Canada plan." The apparent difference in poll results was clearly the result
of asking different questions. The article in the *Globe* with the "plunges"
headline actually admits that the Alberta poll cannot be compared to
other polls because it asked a different question, but the headline writer
clearly ignored that observation.

Critical Question 2: How Good Is the Evidence?

The way the question is worded is one of the first things to look at in assessing how good the evidence for a poll's claim is.

QUESTION BIAS

Everyone recognizes that the phrasing of questions can influence the answers one receives. This is known as **question bias**. As the Kyoto polls
quoted above show, how one phrases a question ("made-in-Canada plan")
or even the choice of answers given, affect people's responses.

We can see how dramatic the effect of wording can be in an example
from US research. A US survey of attitudes toward welfare found that only
13% of people thought that the government was "spending too much on
assistance to the poor" while 44% believed that too much money was being spent on welfare!"[1] Imagine if they had asked whether the US was
spending too much money on "the dole."

The wording of the actual question asked is one of the most crucial
bits of information we need to know before assessing just what a poll is
claiming. Like the headline in the *Globe*, polls are often reported without
attention to the actual questions asked. Without knowing the wording,
we cannot make a reasonable judgement about the meaning or significance of the poll results. We also need to know how the poll was done. To
evaluate the polling process we need a basic understanding of the theory
behind polling.

---

1   David S. Moore, *Statistics: Concepts and Controversies*, 5th ed. (W.H. Freeman, 2001) 55.

UNDERSTANDING THE THEORY BEHIND POLLING

Critical Question 1: What Is the Poll Result Really Claiming?

One of the most common misleading ways that polling claims are stated is presenting the *percentage of the sample* as if *it were a percentage of the population*. An example of that confusion occurs when the media reported that "74% of Canadians support Kyoto." Such a claim fails to make clear that the percentage supporting Kyoto is actually the percentage of the sample, *those actually questioned*, not a percentage of all Canadians.

A sample is a group of people identified to provide evidence about the **population** the pollster is studying. We are not really interested in just those few who were sampled and questioned. We want to know what Canadians (the population the pollster is studying) *generally* are thinking. The real claim of the pollster is that, based on this sample, *probably about* "74% of all Canadians support Kyoto." As Ipsos-Reid states of one of its Kyoto polls:

> The poll is based on a randomly selected sample of 1,002 adult Canadians. With a sample of this size, the results are considered accurate to within ± 3.1 percentage points,[1] 19 times out of 20, *of what they would have been had the entire adult Canadian population been polled*. (My italics)

What the pollster is claiming is that given the percentage in their sample, the result they would have gotten if they had polled the entire population would very likely be between 70.9% and 77.1% (i.e., 74% minus 3.1% and 74% plus 3.1%). Plus or minus (±) 3.1 percentage *points* (notice, not %) leaves quite a range for variation or error. Similar error ranges apply to other polling results.

How do pollsters get these error range numbers? They use a form of math called "probability theory."

WHAT IS PROBABILITY?

One way of understanding the idea of probability is in terms of what happens over the long run. The **probability** of an event is the rate at

---

1   Note that the plus or minus is 3.1 percentage points, not plus or minus 3.1%.

which the event would happen over the long run. Probability or chance is expressed in two different ways: either as a percentage or a fraction. The probability of flipping a fair coin and it coming up heads is 50% or one half.[1] That means that if you were to flip a fair coin (that is, one not weighted to come up one way more often than the other) a large number of times, it will come up heads close to 50% or one half of the time. In any small number of flips, the percentage of heads may be quite different from 50%. Getting 7 heads in 10 flips is not that rare. Getting 700 flips in 1,000 would be very rare. We intuitively expect to get closer to 50% heads the longer we flip.

Probability is thought of as what happens in the long run because of the amount of variation that is possible in the short run. A short run of heads in a row says nothing about the long run tendency of true coins to turn up heads. Variations from the long run frequency happen in the short run. Variation from the true population value also happens with small samples in polling. If you ask ten people what they think of Kyoto you are unlikely to get a percentage of support and rejection that is reflective of the country's population. It's more likely that you'll get a closer estimate of the whole country's feelings if you ask a larger number of people.

PROBABILITY AND POLLING

To understand how probability applies to polling imagine an enormous well-stirred bowl full of thousands of red and green marbles in equal number. The bowl is the *population* we are interested in. Now *sample* the marbles by reaching in and grabbing 10 marbles. If you got all red you'd be surprised. But if you reached in and grabbed 100 and all of them were also

---

1   You might think it makes little difference how we express the probability of something whether as a fraction or a percentage, but a study from the University of Texas suggests that the form of expression can make a significant difference. I must say the findings agree with my own reactions. We will look at this phenomenon when we think about using statistics to make decisions in Chapter 12. But for now try the following:

You are a juror in a murder trial. The defense attorney presents you with the latest DNA evidence: the suspect has only a 0.1 per cent possibility of matching the DNA purely by chance. Hmm ... it sounds like there's a 99.9 per cent chance that the suspect is the source of the DNA. Accordingly, you conclude that the DNA belongs to the suspect.

Then the defense attorney re-presents the probabilities in a different—yet mathematically equivalent—way: one in 1,000 other people in the population also match the DNA. This time, you and the other jurors are less certain that the DNA came from the suspect. (*Science News* [February 28, 1998] accessed at <http://www.stats.org/newsletters/9804/dna.htm>.)

red you'd be stunned. Even at 70 red out of 100 you'd be very surprised, but not surprised if you got 47 or 55 red out of 100.

As we sample again and again, our intuition is that the larger the number of marbles sampled, the closer the per cent red in the samples will come to the actual percentage of red marbles in the bowl—in this case, 50%. The point is simple: the larger the random sample, the more it tends to get percentages close to the real population value. A **random sample** is an unbiased sample—a sample in which every member of the population has an equal chance of being selected. Using probability theory, statisticians can calculate the likelihood, given a random sample of a population, how close the sample will be to the actual value. They express these calculations in terms of **margin of error** and **confidence level**.

MARGIN OF ERROR AND CONFIDENCE LEVEL

When Ipsos-Reid states,

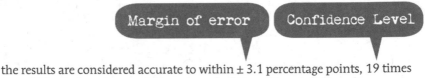

the results are considered accurate to within ± 3.1 percentage points, 19 times out of 20, of what they would have been had the entire adult Canadian population been polled,

Ipsos-Reid is indicating both the margin of error and the confidence level.

Table 1

Margins of Error for 95% Confidence Level	
Sample Size	Margin of Error
100	± 10%
300	± 6%
500	± 5%
1,000	± 3.1%
1,200	± 3%

The margin of error is the range of percentage points around the sample percentage where the true population average is likely. If the pollster gets a sample result of 48% with a sample of 1,200, then the margin of error is ± 3 percentage points given a confidence level of 95%; that means that the pollster can claim that the true population percentage would be somewhere between 45% and 51%, 19 times out of 20.

The likelihood ratio of 19 out of 20 is how likely it is that the true answer is within the margin of error of the sample. This ratio is called the confidence level. The ratio can also be expressed as a percentage: 95% confidence level. What this means is that the pollster believes that 95 times out of 100, the true population percentage will be within the margin of error of the sample percentage. Referring back to the Kyoto example, Ipsos-Reid is saying that they are 95% confident that support for the Kyoto agreement among all Canadians is between 70.9% and 77.1%.[1]

An illustration may help. If we think of a target with the bull's eye representing the true percentage in the population (the target of the pollster), we can think of the margin of error as a circle surrounding the bull's eye. What the pollsters claim when they say their confidence level is 95% is that they will hit inside the circle of ± 3 percentage points 95 out of 100 times (see figure). 95% accuracy is pretty good, though you should remember that the polling companies do a huge number of polls, and 5% of them—not a small number—will give results outside the margin of error.

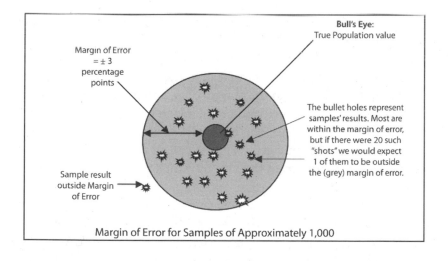

Margin of Error for Samples of Approximately 1,000

---

1   Technically the confidence level is about the mathematical likelihood that a random sample will have a percentage that is within the margin of error of the true population 95% of the time. While most people talk about using the sample percentage to infer the likely range of values in the population, the mathematics is based on calculating the likelihood of a sample having a percentage within the margin of error—as illustrated by the bull's-eye figure. For practical purposes, the distinction is not important.

SAMPLE SIZE

You may have noted the small sample size used by pollsters in order to be 95% confident that their result is within 3 percentage points of the true value. In the news release for one of the Kyoto polls, Ipsos-Reid explained, *"The poll is based on a randomly selected sample of 1,002 adult Canadians."*

1,002 Canadians? Out of 30 million Canadians? Or, just counting adults, out of 23 million? How can that be right? How can the opinions of 1,002 Canadians represent the opinions of 23 million Canadians? After all, 1,002 Canadians is less than .005% of all Canadians. Most people do not believe that such a small number of people can provide any kind of reliable guide to what Canadians on the whole believe. Yet the national polls we read and hear about daily are typically based on just such small samples. (Note pollsters use about the same size samples to survey the US population that is 10 times larger!) How can a sample of a mere 1,000 people tell us anything about the national population?

Let's return to our bowl of marbles. You will note that I never gave a figure for how many marbles were in the bowl. Yet it seemed plausible that the larger the number of marbles sampled, the closer the results would be to the true ratio of red to green marbles. That is exactly how polling works.

People either favour or don't favour Kyoto. They are like red and green marbles in this way. Just yes or no, red or green, Kyoto or not. The key to getting a sample that is accurate to plus or minus three percentage points is to get a random (unbiased) sample of a little more than 1,000 people.[1] If you wanted a smaller margin of error (i.e., a more accurate indication of the population value) you would need a larger sample. Just as with the bowl, the larger the sample, the more accurate it will be—regardless of the size of the population. Because of the cost of sampling, pollsters (and readers) have come to accept the plus or minus 3 percentage points level of accuracy as standard for national polls.

I realize that this might not persuade you. If not, this is one of the "trust me" moments in the text. The problems with polling are numerous, but the mathematics of the theory of sampling is not where the problems lie. *The main challenge in real polling is asking appropriate questions and actually getting a random and unbiased sample.*

Here's how a leading US polling firm, Harris, states the problem at the end of all their polls:

---

1   If you are interested, the mathematics of this is well explained by Jessica Utts, *Seeing Through Statistics,* 3rd ed. (Duxbury, 2001).

In theory, with a probability sample of this size (i.e., 1,000), one can say with 95 per cent certainty that the results have a *statistical precision* of plus or minus 3 percentage points of what they would be if the entire adult population had been polled with complete accuracy.

Unfortunately, there are several other possible sources of error in all polls or surveys that are probably more serious than theoretical calculations of sampling error. They include refusals to be interviewed (non-response), question wording and question order, interviewer bias, weighting by demographic control data ... It is impossible to quantify the errors that may result from these.[1]

As you can see, pollsters occasionally admit that the mathematical precision they claim cannot really be justified.

SAMPLE SIZE, SUB-POLLS, AND INCREASING MARGIN OF ERROR

There is another possible source for error that is sometimes not easy to notice. Even when a poll has a large sample, if the poll is used to produce sub-poll information, the sub-poll information will be based on the smaller sample. A sub-poll samples only a particular selected sub-group. So, for example, the poll sampling 1,000 Canadians may subdivide them into male and female; but there will be fewer than 1,000 (approximately 500), of course, in each sub-sample, so there will be a larger margin of error. In the Ipsos-Reid Kyoto poll, for example, the polling company states:

The poll is based on a randomly selected sample of 1,002 adult Canadians. With a sample of this size, the results are considered accurate to within ± 3.1 percentage points, 19 times out of 20, of what they would have been had the entire adult Canadian population been polled. *The margin of error will be larger within regions and for other sub-groupings of the survey population.* (My italics)

1   Accessed at <http://www.harrisinteractive.com/harris_poll/index.asp?PID=309>.

The fact that a smaller sample results in a larger margin of error has significant implications for comparing groups within a poll. See Table 1 giving the *Margins of Error* earlier in this chapter.

Large polls provide the opportunity to subdivide the information collected into sub-polls on the basis of such obvious criteria as age, gender, and geographic location. Using sub-polls allows the pollster to contrast the views of men and women, young and old, east and west. The problem is that these sub-polls are smaller samples (e.g., women or Albertans) than the national sample and therefore these polls have larger margins of error.

COMPARING SUB-GROUPS

Suppose you wanted to compare the views of men and of women on Kyoto, and suppose you poll 500 men and 500 women. According to the table above, this will result in a margin of error for each group of ± 5%. Now suppose that in the sample 74% of women approve of Kyoto, and 68% of men. Can we conclude that more women than men in the whole population approve of Kyoto? No. Here's why. We can conclude (given the ± 5% margin of error) that between 79% and 69% of women in Canada approve, and that between 73% and 63% of men approve. That means that it could be that only 70% of Canadian women approve, while 72% of men might approve! The fact that there's overlap in the margins of error means that we're not justified in concluding that either is larger in the population than the other.

Graph 1

Question: "Even if there are some problems with the Kyoto Protocol, it should be implemented because it is a good first step."

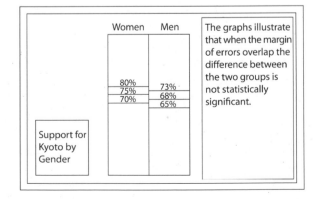

Most responsible journalists and pollsters provide a warning that the sub-polls have a larger margin of error. What is seldom emphasized is that not only do the sub-polls have larger margins of error, but *when two polls or sub-polls are used to make comparisons, we have to take into account two margins of error.* When pollsters compare the percentage of men and women who hold a view on some issue they refer to the percentages *in their sample* (e.g., 74% vs. 68%). Unless the difference in the sample percentages is large, there is not valid statistical basis for claiming that there is a real difference in attitude among men and women in the population. In statistical terminology, the difference is not **statistically significant**—that is, we can't be confident that the apparent difference is not just the result of the natural variation involved in sampling. We can't be 95% confident that there is a real difference in the population.

In their press release, Ipsos-Reid warned about larger margins of error in sub-polls. Nonetheless they contrasted the statistically small differences between views of the 71% of Canadians who agreed with the claim that "even if there are some problems with the Kyoto Protocol, it should be implemented because it is a good first step." They reported the information as follows:[1]

- Quebecers (89%) and those in Atlantic Canada (82%) are the most likely to agree compared to the views of those in Ontario (68%), Saskatchewan/Manitoba (65%) and British Columbia (62%), while Albertans (45%) are the least likely to agree with this view.
- Canadians in lower (78%) and middle (74%) income households are more likely to agree with this position than are those in upper income households (65%).
- Women (74%) are more likely to hold this view than are men (68%).

While the differences between the provinces look statistically significant, those between genders do not. Looking at the gender difference we can see that the 74% figure for women would have a margin of error of ± 5 percentage points i.e., the true percentage is somewhere between 69%-79% and the 68% men in the sample agreeing means that the true rate for men is likely from 63% to 73%. The extensive overlapping of the margins of error as shown means that we can't be 95% confident that the difference in the sample between men and women reflects a real difference in the populace.

1   Notice again how the change in wording of the questions affects people's responses. While 74% of people surveyed initially said that they supported Kyoto, when the question was changed to "even if there are some problems with the Kyoto Protocol, it should be implemented because it is a good first step" the support for Kyoto fell from 74% to 71%. No doubt this small drop occurred because the probe reminded people that indeed there might be some problems!

For all we can tell from this poll, men and women might equally support the claim that "even if there are some problems with the Kyoto Protocol, it should be implemented because it is a good first step" (see Graph 1).

The problem with comparing the provinces is even greater. The size of the sample per province would be between 150-200 with a margin of error of between 8-10 percentage points thus requiring the difference between the samples to be greater than 20 percentage points to be statistically significant. The only reported result that would appear to meet this criterion is the difference between Alberta and the Eastern provinces.

POLLING: A FUNDAMENTAL PROBLEM

In the next chapter I will review the myriad sources of bias that plague polling in the real world. But before that I should point out that even well done polls suffer from a fundamental difficulty: *pollsters are asking people to give "off the top of their heads" answers to questions that are usually about complex issues.* The answers respondents give are seldom a product of careful deliberation, but rather an immediate, often poorly informed reaction to what is being asked.

Often people will give answers about issues about which they know nothing. Studies of respondent behaviour have discovered that on average about 30% to 40% of those polled offer opinions on subjects about which they could not know anything, though it is sometimes even worse than that. For example, when a poll in the US asked about a Metallic Metals Act over 70% offered opinions though there was no such act![1]

---

1   S. Plous, *The Psychology of Judgment and Decision Making* (McGraw-Hill, 1993), 55.

I have some sympathy for people who are being asked to answer questions about issues they haven't really thought about. No one likes to admit ignorance and pollsters often encourage responses despite people's reluctance to answer. I had a personal experience of this when I was phoned years ago by a national pollster about the North American Free Trade Agreement. Knowing that I was one of a mere 1,000 to be asked, I was pleased to have this opportunity to speak out on a major national issue. I was unlikely to get such a chance again. While I had a general understanding and opinion about the free trade agreement, it wasn't adequate for the follow-up questions I was asked. I was repeatedly asked questions about which I knew too little to have an opinion. For example: "What did I think the effect of the agreement would be on Saskatchewan wheat prices?" "Did I think labour unions in the lumber industry would be hurt?" I was never given the option of answering "Don't know"— indeed I was encouraged to have a position despite my proclaiming ignorance. Only reluctantly did the interviewer admit that I could say "Don't know." I assume that pollsters do not want poll results that say "Most people don't know!"

But not surprisingly, the respondents often don't know. Ipsos-Reid in the 2002 Kyoto poll found that "two-thirds (63%, up 4 points since early October) of Canadians agree with the statement that they don't have enough information about the Kyoto Protocol to say whether they support or oppose it."[1]

This result also illustrates the effect of question order. The question whether the respondent had enough information was asked after the question whether the respondent supported signing the Accord. Presumably the number of people willing to have an opinion on the Kyoto Accord would have been reduced after they acknowledged that they didn't have enough information.

The fact that a large percentage of people will answer questions and offer opinions about issues that they then admit to being poorly informed about probably causes you no surprise. For one thing we all do it. But this perfectly natural human failing underlines the very great danger of allowing polls to influence public policy in a representative democracy.

The ideal of democracy is, in principle, to have the citizens make their own political decisions. Representative democracy (as opposed to pure or direct democracy, in which every citizen has a vote on every public matter) is a kind of compromise recognizing the impossibility of such active citizen involvement in a large nation. Some people argue that polling pro-

1   Ipsos-Reid, Press Release, November 8, 2002.

vides a means for more democratic input from the citizens. By finding out the opinions of citizens, pollsters could, in principle, provide a means for greater citizen input to the democratic process.

In principle polls might provide such an input but, as we have seen, there is often a major problem of lack of information. In this age of political cynicism we may wonder just how well-informed our representatives are, but we know that on most issues, we, the people, are usually under-informed. 63% (more or less) of Canadians polled indicated that they did not have enough information about Kyoto. I think we should take comfort from the fact that at least that many were prepared to admit that they were short of information about Kyoto. Something like that percentage is probably true about most complex issues. Since people are often under-prepared to be polled, it is disturbing to see the often cynical role that polling can play in politics.[1]

If politicians really wanted to know what the people thought given sufficient information and time for reflection, there is a method called deliberative polling that has been developed by John Fishkin of Stanford University as a means for getting people's more considered opinions. Fishkin's website (Center for Deliberative Democracy) describes the process as follows:

> A random, representative sample is first polled on the issues. After this baseline poll, members of the sample are invited to gather at a single place to discuss the issues. Carefully balanced briefing materials are sent to the participants and are also made publicly available. The participants engage in dialogue with competing experts and political leaders based on questions they develop in small group discussions with trained moderators. Parts of the weekend events are broadcast on television, either live or in taped and edited form. After the weekend deliberations, the sample is asked the same questions again. The resulting changes in opinion represent the conclusions the public would reach, if people had a good opportunity to become more informed and more engaged by the issues.[2]

1   For example, Dick Morris, a consultant working for Bill Clinton describes the way he and Clinton managed public policy in light of polling results; *The New Prince* (Renaissance, 2000). See also an interview with Morris by ABC accessed at <http://www.abc. net.au/7.30/stories/s127980.htm> July 24, 2006.
2   Center for Deliberative Democracy, Executive Summary, accessed at <http://cdd.stanford.edu/polls/docs/summary/#exec>.

But the media and politicians have evinced little interest in such a pro-cess. There have been only twenty-two such polls conducted worldwide so far. Perhaps there is little interest because politicians recognize that it is the unreflective and uninformed beliefs of many people that determine how they vote.

Since polls usually reflect people's "off the top of the head" reaction to a question, we need to take a poll's claim about what "Canadians *think* ..." with considerable reservation. The role that they often appear to play in influencing governmental decision-making is troubling.

In the next chapter I will review in more detail how polls are actu-ally conducted and the challenges faced by pollsters in trying to get an unbiased poll.

CHAPTER 4

SAMPLING WOES AND OTHER BIASES

SAMPLING IN THE REAL WORLD: HOW GOOD IS THE EVIDENCE?

In the previous chapter I reviewed the basic idea of how polling works and the fundamental problem that people are asked to respond "off the top of their heads." But there are many detailed problems that influence the quality and reliability of polling information. We always need to ask *How good is the evidence?* When evaluating the evidence that the sample provides, we need to look for two sources of bias: 1) bias in the sampling process, e.g., a sample favouring a certain group; and 2) biases resulting from the interview process, e.g., loaded questions, respondent lying, etc.

Selection Bias

The history of polling is replete with famous examples of pollsters failing to get unbiased samples. The problem is not simply one of asking enough people. The most famous biased sample in polling history sampled ten million people! That polling was done for the 1936 US presidential election by the *Literary Digest* magazine. The *Literary Digest* predicted that Landon, a Republican, would beat the incumbent Roosevelt, a Democrat, by a margin of three to two. The *Literary Digest* sent surveys to 10 million people and received 2.3 million surveys back. Nevertheless, the *Literary Digest* made a dramatically wrong prediction—Roosevelt got over 60% of the vote, not the 40% that the *Literary Digest* had predicted!

What went wrong? The *Literary Digest* poll suffered from two kinds of sample **selection bias**. First, in order to find people to send questionnaires to, the magazine used lists that were biased in favour of the wealthy, e.g., they used lists of car and telephone owners, magazine subscribers, etc. Especially in 1936, in the middle of the Great Depression, these lists were very biased in favour of the wealthy in the US, who tend to vote Republican.

Second, even though 2.3 million responses is an enormous number of responses, these were self-selected responses. Those who went to the trouble of responding tended to be those who opposed the incumbent Roosevelt. This form of bias is called **self-selection bias**—the polling bias that results from allowing subjects to chose whether to respond. Typical examples of this kind of bias can be found in mail-in and phone-in polls and now "click-in" web polls loved by TV and radio shows. The possibility of self-selection bias that these polls allow is so great that they should be given no credibility whatsoever.

A well-known example of self-selection bias that underlines the inadequacies of write-in and click-in polls was a 1976 survey conducted by columnist Ann Landers. Ann Landers asked her readers, "If you had it to do over again, would you have children?" She followed with a column headed "70% say they wouldn't do it again!" She had received over 10,000 responses. Seventy per cent said, "No."[1] In response to this column, *Newsday* commissioned a professional poll of some 1,400 people and found 91% said *they would do it again*.

I wouldn't put any faith in the 70% figure nor would I put a great deal of faith in the 91% figure. It's easy to imagine that the circumstances of asking a question like this would result in a high proportion of lying one way or the other. (See the problem of polling and lying known as "respondent deception," below.) The Ann Landers survey asked her readers to respond. Her newspaper column is advice for personal problems, so it's likely that a much larger percentage of her readers are sad or angry about their children than that of the general population. And, among her readers, those who selected themselves for the sample—who chose to respond to her question—are likely more angry or sad than other readers. In general, people who select themselves for polling are frequently motivated by at least irritation, if not anger. Those who were satisfied with their child rearing experiences (or with the incumbent president) tend not to respond. Pollsters know that if they want to get a truly unbiased sample, they cannot allow a self-selected sample. Yet, can they get a truly unbiased sample?

---

1   David S. Moore, *Statistics: Concepts and Controversies*, 5th ed. (W.H. Freeman, 2001), 21.

Representative vs. Random Sampling

We learned in the last chapter that using random samples enabled us to calculate how close our sample is likely to be to the actual population. A truly random sample is (if large enough) likely to give good evidence for generalizing from the sample to the population. But many of us have an intuition that for a sample to provide a basis for generalizing a population, the sample should not be random so much as "representative." The idea of a **representative sample** is that the people in the sample should be like those in the population. So the sample group is carefully chosen to have the same proportion of people in it with relevant characteristics as does the whole population; for example, there should be the same percentage of people over fifty in the sample as in the population if it's supposed that age might be a relevant factor. But what factors should be taken into account?

You might think that factors such as age, geography, income, and gender distribution would do the trick. But actually it is difficult to know all the factors that should be taken into account in order to get a "representative" sample. For example, is the size of town relevant? Is the number of newspapers in the town relevant? We cannot know all the factors that make a sample truly representative. Pollsters have found that trying to construct such a representative sample is fraught with difficulty and error.

George Gallup, the famous pollster, made his name by using a representative sample to correctly call the 1936 US presidential election, the same election that the *Literary Digest* so badly miscalled. Gallup's approach was to create a sample that shared demographic characteristics with the population based on such obvious criteria as age, gender, geography, etc. His sample would have, for example, the same percentage of people over 65 as that of the population.

While such an approach was at first successful, in a later election, using exactly the same "representative" method for obtaining a sample, Gallup was also way off. In 1948, he predicted that Thomas Dewey would defeat Harry Truman by anywhere from five to fifteen percentage points—but Truman actually won by more than four percentage points.

This led Gallup to abandon the notion of trying to create a representative sample. He switched to the other method: random sampling. In random sampling everyone in the population being studied has an *equal chance* of being in the sample, as stated in Chapter 3. A random sample is an unbiased sample—no individual has a greater chance of being polled than any other. Randomness ensures that no group or individual is unfairly favoured and, unlike attempts to get a representative sample, it does not require the pollster to know all the relevant factors that make a sample "representative."

As explained earlier, random sampling also allows the use of probability theory to calculate the accuracy of a sample. The caveat is that a sample must be both random and large enough to provide a relevantly small margin of error. Even genuinely random samples that are too small can produce samples that are biased.

The Reality of "Random" Sampling

Random sampling is the mathematical ideal. In actual practice pollsters use a slightly different technique. Nowadays, the most common way to survey is by telephone. It turns out that even getting a random selection of phone numbers is complicated (see below), but that is just part of the challenge. There is also the problem of who, if anyone, answers the phone. If the pollsters are not careful, phone polls are biased towards people who are at home, have their cell phones turned on, and are willing to answer the phone. Despite Canadian affluence, there are some families (1.3%)[1] who do not have a phone. There is also the problem of language. Few pollsters have interviewers who speak more than one or two languages. Therefore, linguistic minority citizens are very likely to be ignored. *A larger sample would not remedy the problem of selection bias because a larger biased sample is as unreliable as a small biased sample.* In fact, a large biased sample may be even more misleading because we are impressed by large samples. How would you collect a sample that truly gave each person in the population an equal chance of being in it? Hanging around in the mall with a clipboard wouldn't do it: it's easy to see that some sorts of people are more likely to be found in malls than others.

THE KYOTO EXAMPLE

Let's go back to one of the Kyoto polls. How do we know that the sampling of the poll on Kyoto was random or at least unbiased? The Ipsos-Reid media poll claims that "The poll is based on a randomly selected sample of 1,002 adult Canadians." But it also tells us that "These data were *statistically weighted* (my emphasis) to ensure the sample's regional and age/sex composition reflects that of the actual Canadian population according to the 2001 Census data."

---

1   From Statistics Canada, accessed at <http://www40.statcan.ca/l01/cst01/comm03b.htm> July 4, 2006.

Even though they claim the sample was "random" they admit "tweaking" the data to get age, sex, and regional composition similar to (i.e., representative of) the Canadian population! Despite what Ipso-Reid says, it is unlikely that they used a truly random sample.

The method used by most pollsters is not strictly a random sample, but a **stratified sample**. A stratified sample is produced by dividing the population into large groups, often by geography, and then randomly picking some sub-groups within these groupings. Individuals in each selected sub-group are then randomly picked to be polled.

Typically a pollster produces a stratified sample by randomly selecting telephone exchanges and then numbers within these exchanges. The goal is to achieve a sample that is "random" but also geographically and economically representative. Even if they start with a truly random sample of phone numbers, the sampling process is still subject to the other kinds of selection bias reviewed above, i.e., the poll will be biased towards people who have phones, people who answer the phone, and people who speak the dominant languages.

Non-Response Bias

Another key selection problem that is faced by pollsters is non-response bias. Many people aren't home when pollsters call and then those who answer the phone often refuse to answer the questions. Since there is no good reason to think that those who are willing to answer are just like those who aren't willing to, or don't, answer, this creates an important but seldom mentioned form of selection bias called **non-response bias**.

Pollsters seldom reveal their non-response rate. An exception was a US study by the Pew Foundation[1] that found that 33% of those called never answered the phone despite the fact that the survey called back all unanswered phone numbers five times (!) including different times of the day and week. In addition, of those who did answer, 35% refused to talk to the pollsters. A total non-response of 68%! All these problems clearly undermine the claim that the sampling process is random or non-biased.

Pollsters know that their so-called random samples aren't truly random for all the reasons reviewed above, so they "fix them" to make them more representative—for example, by giving more weight in their calculations to responses from people in groups thought to be under-represented in the sample. Whether such "fixing" succeeds in "unbiasing" the sample is difficult to assess, but it certainly makes clear that the sample is not truly random. This leads to the result that the claim of accuracy based on the mathematically calculated margin of error is a bit misleading, because such calculations assume that the sample has been chosen randomly.

OTHER SOURCES OF BIAS

Respondent Deception Bias

A significant challenge to pollsters and people conducting surveys is to get their respondents to tell them the truth—especially if people are being questioned about matters of personal significance.

Many people will not be forthright when asked about how they will vote. Only about 50% of people vote in national elections, but when pollsters are polling they (randomly) call all people—voters and non-voters. Pollsters need to screen non-voters from their sample if the poll is to help predict the election. People will not necessarily admit that they don't plan to vote, so pollsters use various questions to help decide whether a respondent is a likely

---

1   Cited by Moore, p. 49.

voter. They ask where the person voted last time, where the polling station is, etc., in an attempt to sort the voters from the non-voters. This means of course, that, yet again, pollsters will deviate from strictly random sampling and use their judgement as to whether to count a respondent's answer.

Depending on the topic (e.g., attitude towards child rearing mentioned above, race, or worse yet, sex), people surveyed may be tempted to give interviewers answers they think will sound good rather than the truth. This understandable tendency of people to deceive pollsters is called **respondent deception bias**. This bias is even a greater problem for other studies such as marketing studies or sociology studies, which are directed at finding out what people *do* (e.g., recycling, sexual behaviour, car purchasing), not what they say. Asking people what they do is sometimes described as a **proxy**. A proxy is something studied as an indirect way for researchers to get at what they are really interested in. Since tracking people's behaviour is often very difficult, most studies of human behaviour involve collecting information about what people *report*, not what they actually do. Inferring from what people say to what they actually do involves numerous problems including a dubious reliance on people's memory, respondents misunderstanding questions, and people simply not telling the truth. The following example from the famous Harvard University Nurses' Health Study illustrates how questions sometimes involve difficulties of comprehension or memory:

> How often, on average, did you eat a quarter of a cantaloupe during the past year? One to three times a month? Once a week? Two to four times a week? Once a day? Please try to average your seasonal use over the entire year. For example, if cantaloupe is eaten four times a week during the approximately three months it is in season, then the average use would be once a week.[1]

If you know that such a question had been used, you would be (rightly) sceptical about the supposed benefits of melon eating.

Even when people understand the questions, their memory may not be up to the task, or perhaps might be a bit self-serving. An article in a nutrition research journal reports that under-reporting by certain groups of their calorie intake can be as high as 70%.[2] Recent studies of people's

---

1   Quoted by Lawrence Lindner, "Food Surveys Have Wide Margins of Error; Researchers Know that Questionnaire Results Don't Always Reflect Actual Eating Habits," *The Washington Post*, February 1, 2000, Z9.
2   Jennie Macdiarmid and John Blundell, "Assessing Dietary Intake: Who, What and Why of Under-Reporting," *Nutrition Research Reviews* (1998): 11, 231-53.

sexual behaviour found, for example, that men reported 75% more partners than did women in the last five years.[1] It appears somebody wasn't
telling the truth. What is unique about this report is that by comparing
the responses of men and women, the researchers had a means of checking the honesty of the respondents. And it doesn't look good. In most
other cases, all we have is the respondent's word.

Recently Statistics Canada reported that there was a 40% increase in
male participation in housework in Canada.[2] Knowing that such a claim
would be based on a survey of what people said they did, and knowing
the political correctness of men saying that they did housework, I was
sceptical. Nevertheless, on checking the Statistics Canada website for
the methodology involved, I found that spousal reports of activity were
checked against their partner's perception. In addition, the results were
based on people keeping diaries, not remembering what they did. So far so
good. But they also admit to a 41% non-response rate, so it is hard to know
what to infer from the sample to the population at large. So while there
still may be deception, it would have to be on the part of both partners.

Please don't take these observations to be mean or negative about people

1   Richard Lewontin, "Sex Lies and Social Science," *New York Review of Books*, April 20,
    1995. Lewontin was reviewing *The Social Organization of Sexuality: Sexual Practices in the
    United States* by Edward O. Laumann, John H. Gagnon, Robert T. Michael, and Stuart
    Michaels. According to the authors of the book, the most likely explanation is: "Either
    men may exaggerate or women may understate."
2   Statistics Canada, Social and Aboriginal Statistics Division, General Social Survey
    2005, accessed at <http://www.statcan.ca/english/sdds/instrument/4503_Q1_V4_E.
    pdf> July 23, 2006.

being surveyed. Surveys are a big intrusion in people's lives by people they don't know. Who wants to admit to a stranger that you don't vote, or worse yet, how much you eat or drink? I am not criticizing the respondents, just pointing out that given certain sensitive subject matter, it's entirely possible that the information collected is biased and unreliable.

Question Bias Again: Order and Alternatives

QUESTION ORDER

As acknowledged above by the pollster Harris, poll results are not only sensitive to question wording, but even to *question order*. This results in **question order bias**. For example, it is well known to pollsters in the US who survey people's attitudes towards the president, that if their first question is "Do you approve or disapprove of the way that the president is handling his job?" people will usually give a more positive answer than if they ask that question at the end of the survey. It appears that asking the general question after more specific questions causes people to lower their approval rating. Apparently, specific questions remind respondents of issues of which they are critical of the presidential performance and leads to a lower rating of approval. By convention, pollsters ask the general evaluation question first. This seems a bit surprising given that the evaluation at the end of the interview would seem to be a more reflective opinion. But pollsters believe that the opinion offered at the end of the survey would be "biased" by the proceeding questions!

ANSWER CHOICES

As exemplified by the two Kyoto surveys, the alternative answers provided to a question can significantly change the response. As the cartoon illustrates, these can easily be biased towards positive or negative. Another bias is created by not providing alternative answers to the respondent. Compare:

What are the most important issues facing the nation?

Question Set 1	Question Set 2	Question Set 3
A. Environment	A. Environment	No Suggested Answers
B. Economy	B. Economy	
	C. Foreign Relations	
	D. Poverty	
	E. Ethnic Conflict	

It is well-known that people will give different answers depending on the list of alternatives or whether they are simply invited to supply an answer. The latter questioning technique, while free from answer bias, is of course much more difficult to collate into summary results.

Context Bias

Many polls include a general introduction to the survey, which is used by the pollster to create a context for the survey. Such introductions often have a strong influence on how people will answer and therefore create **context bias**. Suppose that a poll on Kyoto began "Many leaders are concerned about the harm the Kyoto agreement might cause the economy." In this case any questions about ratification will obviously tend to be viewed in the context of economic harm rather than long-term reduction of greenhouse gases. *Fully assessing the significance of a poll requires knowing not only the questions and answers, but also any introductory remarks.*

Sponsor Bias

Context and question order can be used to easily manipulate a poll's results. There is a greater danger of manipulation when the sponsor of the poll has an interest in the poll outcome—a situation that can easily lead to **sponsor bias**. For this reason it is important to know not only the pollsters' competence and credibility, but also the bias of the poll sponsor. This form of bias differs from the others in that it is usually the result of a self-conscious effort to skew the results. This is a form of **"prejudicial bias,"** more serious, for example, than the accidental biasing of a sample as the result of sample selection difficulties. This point is dramatically illustrated by the polls cited at the beginning of the previous chapter. Remember when Ipsos-Reid was hired by the Alberta government, they asked which of the following three options respondents supported:

1. Withdraw from the Kyoto Protocol and develop a made-in-Canada plan for reducing greenhouse-gas emissions,
2. ratify the Kyoto Protocol, or
3. do nothing?

And 45% wanted the federal government to withdraw from the Kyoto accord. When Ipsos-Reid was hired by the national media, they asked "Based on what you have seen, read or heard, do you personally support or oppose implementing the Kyoto Accord?" and only 27% opposed the implementation of the Kyoto accord. *Different sponsors, different questions, different numbers.*

While many media reports now report sample size and the margin of error when reporting a poll, they seldom state the exact question(s) asked. Information about the question, context, and funding is equally crucial for assessing the poll results. Some pollsters do post the details of their questions on the Web, though fewer and fewer make this information available for free.

What Other Information Is Relevant?

So far we have looked at how to assess the evidence provided by polls designed to inform us about what people generally think. Before accepting the poll's conclusion about what people really think, we need also to consider whether there is other countervailing information that is relevant. Such information includes the political and social context in which the poll was done. The existence of other polls that may conflict with the current poll should also be considered. The Kyoto poll done for Alberta provides a good example of the relevance of context. Even a superficial glance at the poll's apparently dramatically different results from previous polls should make one suspicious. Short of dramatic political events, we don't expect people's opinions to significantly change week to week.

On the other hand, polls are often taken after major news events, with the consequence that they are likely measuring the influence of a temporary flurry of publicity rather than the more stable views of the populace. As mentioned above, people are usually giving answers to pollsters "off the top of their heads" and their answers are easily influenced by recently publicized events. We can anticipate the results, for example, when there is a poll asking whether young offenders should be dealt with more harshly following a report of a brutal assault by a young offender. Why even pay for such a poll?

FINAL WARNINGS

We need to keep in mind the uncertainty involved in poll results. We also need to recognize that all information involves uncertainty. Polling is better than asking only your friends, but if you are going to give serious consideration to the results you should carefully assess the actual polls using the four critical questions as set out below.

The theoretical margin of error is just that—theoretical. The practical constraints of everyday polling mean that the margin of error is undoubtedly greater than the theoretical ideal. Don't let reporters slip misleadingly precise sample percentages by you as if that was the true figure for the population of the country.

Despite advances in polling techniques, we should remain concerned about sampling bias, especially the exclusion of linguistic minorities, non-responders, and the very poor. Biases resulting from questions, introductory context, question order, or the respondent's tendency to answer without reflection or candour will almost always be at least as problematic as sampling bias.

A Sample Evaluation

Let's try using our critical questions on a poll report. Take this horrific example from USA Today, July 16, 2002.[1]

---

1   From VitalSTATS, August 2002, accessed at <http.//www.stats.org/newsletters/0208/pledge.htm> September 26, 2002.

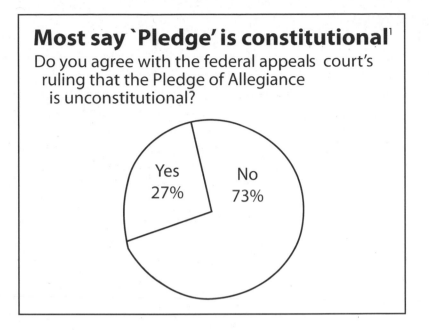

1. What is being claimed? Who is "most?" What population was being sampled?

2. How good is the evidence? If you look at the fine print in the lower left of the picture (which was smaller in the original), the sample turns out to be 235 law students and legal associates *polled over the Internet*. The JD Jungle online survey claimed to have a margin of error of ± 3 per cent. A *random sample* of 235 people would have a margin of error of about ± 6 per cent; but when a sample is a *self-selected* sample such as this one, the concept of the margin of error is completely inappropriate. The results of polls like this one should *never be* relied on.

3. What other information is relevant? We can be sure this poll was done very shortly after the federal court of appeals' decision.

4. Are relevant fallacies avoided? The misleading headline implies a sample of the general population. Selection bias is the obvious fallacy, but even if the sample had been random, the sample size was much too small to justify such a claim.

---

1   Source: JD Jungle online survey of 235 law students and legal associates June 26–27. Margin of error: ±3 percentage points.

SO NOW WHAT?

With so many problems, are polls of any use? Yes and no. As you can see polling is fraught with problems that should limit the amount of confidence we put in their reports.[1] But while polls have problems and need to be taken with the appropriate grains of salt, the alternative—personal impressions—is even more problematic.

Polls are *one* tool for finding out what people, people often very different from ourselves, think and believe. Polls provide us with a source of information about the "off the top of their heads" thinking of a large number of fellow citizens. Used with appropriate care, they provide useful antidotes to our tendency to believe that the opinions of the people we talk to are representative of our community or nation. *Whatever the problems with polls, they involve questioning a larger and more varied collection of people than we would normally come across in our lives.*

EVALUATING POLLS
THE CRITICAL QUESTIONS

1. What is being claimed?
  a. Claims about a population based on a sample always involve a margin of error.
  b. Does the report mistake the information about the sample, for the claim about the population?
  c. Does the report really reflect the questions asked?
2. How good is the evidence?
  a. Was the sampling method unbiased?
    i. If it involves self-selection, stop reading.
    ii. Consider the significance of the inevitable sampling biases resulting from non-response, lack of phone, and minority languages.
  b. Was the sample large enough?
    i. Approximately 1,000 people are needed to generate the kind of margin of error and confidence level that has become accepted as a reasonable basis for claims about national issues (±3 percentage points). 500 is typically used for more local surveys (±5 percentage points).
  c. Is the margin of error allowed for and credible?
    i. The margin of error given is the mathematical ideal; it is reasonable to assume that the actual margin is greater.
    ii. Watch out for claims about sub-polls that have a much larger margin of error. Local polls will usually be smaller and as a result will have margins of error larger than national polls.

---

1   The Appendix contains a table of Gallup's results for presidential elections. As you will see Gallup missed the true electoral results by more than the margin of error more frequently than the mathematical ideal of 1 time in 20.

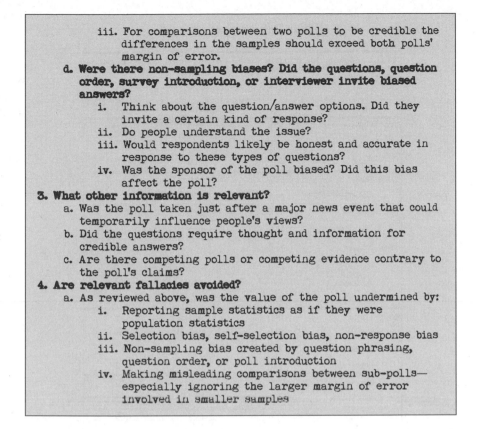

> iii. For comparisons between two polls to be credible the differences in the samples should exceed both polls' margin of error.
>
> d. **Were there non-sampling biases? Did the questions, question order, survey introduction, or interviewer invite biased answers?**
>> i. Think about the question/answer options. Did they invite a certain kind of response?
>> ii. Do people understand the issue?
>> iii. Would respondents likely be honest and accurate in response to these types of questions?
>> iv. Was the sponsor of the poll biased? Did this bias affect the poll?
>
> **3. What other information is relevant?**
>> a. Was the poll taken just after a major news event that could temporarily influence people's views?
>> b. Did the questions require thought and information for credible answers?
>> c. Are there competing polls or competing evidence contrary to the poll's claims?
>
> **4. Are relevant fallacies avoided?**
>> a. As reviewed above, was the value of the poll undermined by:
>>> i. Reporting sample statistics as if they were population statistics
>>> ii. Selection bias, self-selection bias, non-response bias
>>> iii. Non-sampling bias created by question phrasing, question order, or poll introduction
>>> iv. Making misleading comparisons between sub-polls—especially ignoring the larger margin of error involved in smaller samples

APPENDIX

How well do pollsters really do? Elections are one of the few opportunities to check the pollsters results against reality. Below is Gallup's record for some recent US elections, showing (in **bold**) that its results exceed the margin of error of three percentage points on 4 out of 15 elections rather than the theoretical confidence level of 1 out of 20. Also note that on many occasions the differences between the leaders were too close to be statistically significant.

Gallup Poll Accuracy Record

Year	Candidates	Final Gallup Survey	Election Result	Gallup Deviation
1996	Clinton	52.0	50.1	+1.9
	Dole	41.0	41.4	-0.4
	Perot	7.0	8.5	-1.5
1992	Clinton	49.0	43.3	**+5.7**
	Bush	37.0	37.7	-0.7
	Perot	14.0	19.0	-5.0
1988	Bush	56.0	53.0	+2.1
	Dukakis	44.0	46.1	-2.1
1984	Reagan	59.0	59.2	-0.2
	Mondale	41.0	40.8	+0.2
1980	Reagan	47.0	50.8	**-3.8**
	Carter	44.0	41.0	+3.0
	Anderson	8.0	6.6	+1.4
	Other	1.0	1.6	-0.6
1976	Carter	48.0	50.1	-2.1
	Ford	49.0	48.1	+0.9
	McCarthy	2.0	0.9	+1.1
	Other	1.0	0.9	+0.1
1972	Nixon	62.0	61.8	+0.2
	McGovern	38.0	38.2	-0.2
1968	Nixon	43.0	43.5	-0.5
	Humphrey	42.0	42.9	-0.9
	Wallace	15.0	13.6	+1.4
1964	Johnson	64.0	61.3	+2.7
	Goldwater	36.0	38.7	-2.7
1960	Kennedy	51.0	50.1	+0.9
	Nixon	49.0	49.9	-0.9
1956	Eisenhower	59.5	57.8	+1.7
	Stevenson	40.5	42.2	-1.7
1952	Eisenhower	51.0	55.4	**-4.4**
	Stevenson	49.0	44.6	+4.4
1948	Truman	44.5	49.5	**-5.0**
	Dewey	49.5	45.1	+4.4
	Wallace	4.0	2.4	+1.6
	Other	2.0	3.0	-1.0
1944	Roosevelt	51.5	53.8	-2.3
	Dewey	48.5	46.2	+2.3
1940	Roosevelt	52.0	55.0	-3.0
	Wilkie	48.0	45.0	+3.0

CHAPTER 5

THE FACTS MA'AM, NOTHING BUT THE FACTS: GETTING GOOD DATA

You might think that it would be easy to establish the claims that we read and hear about every day. Is unemployment rising? Is inflation steady? What is happening to house prices? Is the population growing and at what rate? What is the **incidence** of AIDS, suicide, crime, and homelessness?

All these topics are discussed every day as if we knew what the facts were and that the big problem was what to do about them. But actually getting some information is quite difficult. People may be reluctant to reveal medical diagnosis such as AIDS, suicide is likely under-reported, crime definitions change, police are more diligent in reporting some crimes than others, and the homeless are by their nature elusive. Even when we have a collection of credible data, having an appropriate and useful way to summarize the data is also a challenge. What does "the crime rate" mean? How do you describe the income of 20 million people? Or the sales of hundreds of houses over a year? Irrespective of how difficult it is to get good data, a credible effort to systematically collect data is almost always better than mere impressions. In this chapter, the Critical Questions will be used for checking data quality. In the next chapter, the Critical Questions will be used to understand and evaluate various ways of describing collected data.

GETTING GOOD DATA

Data can be unreliable for many reasons.

1. The "data" can simply be made up numbers or guesstimates. These kind of data are often called **mythical numbers**, numbers that are widely quoted but are not based on any systematic collection method, e.g., illegal drug sales. Once quoted in the newspaper, figures

such as the value of marijuana sales are seldom questioned, though a moment's reflection would lead one to realize that it would be very difficult to get good data to support these figures. Numbers sound "hard" and objective, but many numbers are quite "soft." Being able to recognize a "soft" number is an important critical skill.

2. Data comparing information from different times or places can often be misleading because apparent differences can result from *changes in the data collection rather than real changes in the world.*

    -   There can be changes in reporting methods; for example, when police begin accepting email reports of property crimes.
    -   There can be changes in diagnostic methods; for example, when improved ways to detect cancer are introduced.
    -   There can be a heightened sensitivity; for example, in reporting school fights to the police.

USING THE CRITICAL QUESTIONS TO EVALUATE DATA QUALITY

Critical Question 1: What Is Being Claimed?

Data claims are often ambiguous or vague. We have all seen headlines such as "Unemployment is down" and Crime rate is up again." You would think that these would be straightforward claims, but they are not.

THE UNEMPLOYMENT RATE

Take unemployment. What is it to be unemployed? If you are retired or taking time off, or staying home looking after children you are not counted as unemployed. If you want a full-time job, but are working only part-time, should you be counted as partly unemployed? What if you live in a depressed region and have given up trying to find a job; are you unemployed? You would think so, but not according to the definition used by national agencies who collect this information. To be counted as "unemployed" you must be seeking work. In the US, if you go two weeks without seeking work, then you are no longer unemployed! Now, there's a solution to the unemployment problem!

This is not to dismiss unemployment figures as useless. The definitions used by governments have been in use for a long time and are similar in many countries. Unemployment trends can certainly be ascertained by using this definition. Nevertheless, the approach to defining unemployment that eliminates those discouraged from looking for work creates a misleadingly positive unemployment rate, ignoring, as it does, many truly unemployed people.

There is another problem with unemployment figures. These rates are based on personal interviews that attempt to determine whether a person really is seeking work, but studies have shown that there is a good deal of variation in how interviewers judge this. After all, what really constitutes looking for work?[1]

CRIME STATISTICS

And what about crime rates? How "hard" are they? What does it mean to say crime rates are up? The media, of course, play a notorious role in creating a sense of violence and danger in our streets. Violence makes news. Headlines never read "No Murders or Violent Crimes Today—Police Chief to Investigate." So what is the truth about crime rates? In fact what Statistics Canada does is literally to take all the police *reported* crimes (which now includes emailed allegations of property crime), adds them up and divides by the population and multiplies by 100,000 to get a rate of crime per 100,000 people. This can result in **misleading aggregation**—combining a wide variety of information into one statistic. For example, in 2004, crime was up by 6%. Lock your doors and windows? Keep the kids at home? Not really. Basically, if you were not a bank, there was no reason to be more concerned about crime that year than the one before. The main reason crime was up was because counterfeiting was up 72%! Homicides were down 7% (homicide has been declining since 1991), abduction was down, sexual assaults, even impaired driving continued to decline, though robbery was up. Even the dramatic increase in counterfeiting reports may be the result of greater vigilance, not more criminal activity. From the point of view of social order and safe streets, this "rise in crime" is not really particularly disturbing. Knowing the details that make up the aggregate crime rate creates a significantly different impression than many people, especially anxious parents, have about the criminal dangers in their environment.[2]

---

1   Moore, p. 129.
2   These are the statistics for 2003 reported in Statistics Canada, *The Daily*, July 28, 2004.

Critical Question 2: How Good Is the Evidence?

MYTHICAL NUMBERS

While crime rates present certain problems, at least there is something resembling hard data (reports of alleged crimes) that can provide a basis for them. But when there is no straightforward way to get reliable data, and where the numbers can serve political agendas, the result is often mythical numbers.

Take figures such as the dollar amount of illegal drug sales. Where do these numbers come from? Not from police statistics and not from the income tax folk. They are guesstimates that are of great political significance to enforcement agencies. Such figures can cut two ways. Claims of increasing drug sales could justify more funding for drug law enforcement or it could show that the police are unable to control drug traffickers. Take your pick, but do not for a minute believe there is much "hardness" to the figures.

DRUG SALES

There are no surveys, random or otherwise, which provide any basis for these claims. Drug statistics are produced by "experts" who give their impressions based on anecdotes and records of drug busts. Because the police do know something about the drug world, they naturally feel some confidence in claiming knowledge about what they really can't know. If they assume that they apprehend 10% of all pot growers a year, then figuring out the amount of pot produced may be as simple as multiplying drug busts by 10. But of course they can't know whether their percentage is correct. Experts in my province of British Columbia have estimated the export of marijuana to be worth variously from $2 billion[1] (by the Fraser Institute) to $6 billion by BC's Organized Crime Agency![2] This despite the fact that the US Border Patrol seized only about $12 million worth of marijuana in 2003! On the basis of some of these numbers, some editorialists have argued that marijuana is BC's second largest export. But this compares carefully counted lumber sales and exports (which are number one) with widely varying drug guesstimates.

Other statistics concerning marginal activities should equally be viewed with great scepticism. Examples of unreliable numbers include the grey

---

1   From a careful study by the Fraser Institute; Stephen T. Easton, *Marijuana Growth in British Columbia* (Fraser Institute Occasional Paper, 2004), accessed at <http://www.cfdp.ca/mj_bc_04.pdf> June 21, 2008.

2   Accessed at <http://www.canoe.ca/CNEWS/Law/Marijuana/2003/04/30/76393.html> June 23, 2006.

economy (income unreported to the tax people), homelessness,[1] and in the United States, illegal abortions and the number of illegal immigrants.

POLITICS AND MYTHICAL NUMBERS

Numbers play a powerful role in public debate and governmental decision-making and are often given a credence and significance they simply do not deserve. While it is commendable to attempt to base decisions on "facts," one should not rely on mythical or even "soft" numbers as if they were well-established facts.

A current example of a debate centring on a "mythical number" is the controversy over whether individuals in third-world countries are receiving any benefit from globalization. Globalization sceptics often mention that the per capita income of people in impoverished countries is about a dollar day, while some economists argue that it is closer to two dollars a day.[2] My first reaction is that this is a difference not worth arguing about—either amount is terrible.

Though the misery of much of the third world is undeniable, the quality of income data cannot support such debates about precise numbers. Deeply impoverished countries, whose governments are often in disarray, do not have the necessary means or inclination to collect reliable data. Even with reliable data, the comparisons across cultures and differing monetary regimes makes the comparisons daunting.

---

1   The widely quoted figure of three million homeless in the US was due to Mitch Snyder, a famous US advocate for the homeless. But he made up this figure. The correct figure is obviously going to be difficult to collect. Reported by Steven D. Levitt and Stephen J. Dubner, *Freakonomics* (New York: Morrow, 2005), 90-91.
2   Benjamin Friedman, "Globalization: Stiglitz's Case, " *The New York Review of Books*, accessed at <http://www.nybooks.com/articles/15630> April 18, 2006.

> [The World Bank] ... *employs a concept of purchasing power "equivalence" that is neither well defined nor appropriate for poverty assessment. These difficulties are inherent in the Bank's "money-metric" approach and cannot be credibly overcome without dispensing with this approach altogether. In addition, the Bank extrapolates incorrectly from limited data and thereby creates an appearance of precision that masks the high probable error of its estimates.*[1]

While it is understandable that the World Bank and other world institutions would like to put precise values on the state of the world, they should recognize the real limitation of their ability to do so. Once we start using these numbers as if they were precise measurements we have slipped into the world of mythic numbers.

Nevertheless, many significant political decisions are based on unreliable data. A well-known example was the CIA's use of very misleading economic data from the former Soviet Union, which led the CIA to miss the impending economic collapse of the Soviet Union. This mis-information was used to encourage military spending to defend against the (collapsing) Soviet "menace."[2]

GIVE ME WATER

Lastly, a mythical number that isn't political but which most people have heard repeatedly quoted is: "You should drink eight glasses of water a day." Dartmouth physiology professor Heinz Valtin was sceptical because he found it difficult to believe that evolution would leave humans with a chronic fluid deficit that needed such significant compensation. His investigations revealed that there is no research that supports this advice. As far as he could tell, the idea probably came from a misquotation of a recommendation from a US Food and Nutrition Board, which recommended 64-80 ounces of fluid a day, but stated that "*most of this is contained in food.*" He does point out that you should, of course, drink fluids if you are thirsty (thirst is a very good indicator of fluid deprivation), on a long airplane flight, when the weather is hot, or if you are engaged in strenuous activity.[3]

---

1   Sanjay Reddy and Thomas Pogge, "How Not to Count the Poor," accessed at <http://www.socialanalysis.org/>.
2   Accessed at <http://www.independent.org/pdf/tir/tir_07_2_roberts.pdf> July 19, 2006.
3   Heinz Valtin, "'Drink at Least Eight Glasses of Water a Day.' Really?" accessed at <http://dms.dartmouth.edu/news/2002_h2/08aug2002_water.shtml> July 19, 2006.

FALSE PRECISION: DOES THE EVIDENCE SUPPORT THE NUMBER?

Numbers have rhetorical power, and precise numbers have even more power. As the cartoon illustrates, precision is often used with mythical numbers to create an impression that data are reliable. Here is how one marketing consultant puts it:

> If you've got around 50 happy clients using the particular product or service, don't tell your prospect, "*I have around 50 happy clients using this system.*" **Instead give them a precise number.** "*We have 53 clients currently using this system!*" The research on this shows that your client is now far more likely to believe you, and your credibility will be much higher than if you had simply said 50.[1]

World Clock 2008
Deaths 44,073,290

Noncummunicable Diseases		Communicable Diseases	
Cardiovascular	12,956,294	STD/HIV/AIDS	2,401,752
Cancer	5,628,904	Diarrhoeal	1,449,094
Respiratory	2,867,651	TB	1,213,674
Digestive	1,523,588	Childhood Cluster	868,898
Neuropsychiatric	860,027	Malaria	706,360
Diabetes	762,481	Meningitis	134,020
Genitourinary	655,670	Tropical Cluster	122,426
Endocrine	187,132	Hepatitis	121,300
Other	520,563	Dengue	14,392
		Encephalitis	10,820
Death by Injury		Leprosy	4,778
Traffic Accidents	922,588	**Other Causes of Death**	
Falls	303,506		
Drownings	296,006	Respiratory Infections	3,116,456
Poisonings	271,396	Perinatal Conditions	1,906,863
Fires	241,504	Maternal Conditions	395,415
Other Accidents	714,379	Nutritional Deficiency	375,510
Suicides	676,852		
Violence	432,729	Abortion	30,056,539
War	132,647	(Abortion is not counted in total deaths)	

---

1   Wayne Berry, "Precise Numbers are Much More Believable than Rounded Numbers: Free Business Tips," accessed at <http://freebusinesstips.com.au/marketing/precise-numbers-are-much-more-believeable-than-rounded-numbers>

I saw a recent headline in a magazine: "Lose 34 pounds by Labour Day." Not a mere 30 pounds but 34! Another example is the website of the "World Clock."[1] The table above is a snapshot of the kind of misleadingly precise data that the site provides. While the date and time on the website are exact, all the other numbers are projections from previous data.

Another interesting example of false precision is the "normal" body temperature, usually given as 98.6°F or 37.0°C. In fact this is an average inferred from a sample. More accurately, but less precisely, the normal range is 36.4-37.1°C (with the usual caveats).

Critical Question 3: What Else is Relevant? What is Missing?

CHANGING MEASURES VS. CHANGING REALITY

Return to crime statistics. Even such a seemingly straightforward category as "assault" is fuzzy in its actual application. In an article describing the costs of crime in Nova Scotia, the author comments that

> ... a substantial increase in common assaults has raised the official violent crime rate in the province above the national average. A substantial portion of the increase in the official crime rate is due to higher reporting rates for *assaults, sexual assaults, domestic violence and other crimes*, a positive sign signifying reduced social tolerance for violent behaviour once considered socially "acceptable."[1]

No doubt the increased intolerance of violence is a social good, but it makes comparison of statistics over time a matter of judgement, not just numbers.

---

1   Ronald Colman, "The Cost of Crime In Nova Scotia," *Journal of Business Administration and Policy Analysis* (January 1, 1999).

DIAGNOSIS AND CHANGE

Increased doctor awareness or improved diagnostic techniques rather than any real increase in the disease can sometimes cause the appearance of an increase in the incidence of a disease. For example, part of the debate over the use of regular mammograms is whether there is a genuine increase in life expectancy of breast cancer patients as a result of the testing or simply earlier detection resulting in longer life while aware of the illness.[1] Another example is thyroid cancer. The incidence of thyroid cancer appears to have doubled in the last 30 years, but in a recent study researchers from the Dartmouth Medical School concluded "that increased diagnostic scrutiny has caused an apparent increase in incidence of cancer rather than a real increase."[2]

---

1   J.P. Bunker, J. Houghton, and M. Braum, "Putting the Risk of Breast Cancer in Perspective," *BMJ* 317, 7168 (November 7, 1998): 1307–09. This study mentions that the reported incidence of breast cancer in the US is 1/8 vs. 1/12 in Britain. The author theorizes that the greater risk in America may reflect the earlier introduction of mass screening, the fact that women are screened at younger ages, and the over diagnosis of tumours of low grade malignancy or of ductal carcinoma in situ—conditions that might never become clinically detectable or life threatening. This illustrates the difficulty of getting reliable data even in this well-studied area.

2   Accessed at <http://dms.dartmouth.edu/news/2006_h1/09may2006_davies.shtml> June 25, 2006.

INFLATION: COMPARING PRICES OVER TIME

Historic comparisons of prices or wages that use values that have not been adjusted for inflation provide completely misleading comparisons. In June 2006, it seemed that the price of oil and gas was at a record high. But if we allow, as we should, for inflation we can see from the graph below the "real" inflationary price of oil was still below the peak of the oil crisis created by OPEC in the early 1980s.[1]

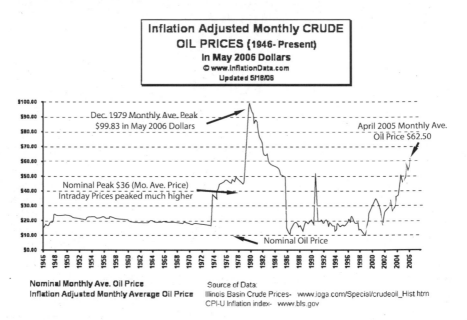

Inflation Adjusted Monthly CRUDE OIL PRICES (1946- Present)
In May 2006 Dollars
© www.InflationData.com
Updated 5/18/06

Nominal Monthly Ave. Oil Price
Inflation Adjusted Monthly Average Oil Price

Source of Data:
Illinois Basin Crude Prices- www.ioga.com/Special/crudeoil_Hist.htm
CPI-U Inflation index- www.bls.gov

KNOW YOUR MURDERER

Another example of the need to ask "what else is relevant?" concerns a number I have often heard and believed: that 50% of murder victims knew their killer. This statistic is often used as one of the arguments against capital punishment since it suggests that at least half of murders are crimes of passion or domestic violence, rather than the acts of malevolent strangers gunning down people on the street. What is missing? A little thought will make that clear. The best we can know is what percentage of *solved* murders are committed by acquaintances; and murders by an acquaintance are much easier to solve than those by a stranger.

---

1   Graph from <http://inflationdata.com/inflation/Inflation_Rate/Historical_Oil_Prices_Chart.asp> accessed June 23, 2006.

When preparing this book I decided to check out these numbers and went to Statistics Canada where I found the latest breakdown of homicides for 1999. As it turns out, in 1999 only about 15% of *solved* murders were committed by a stranger. 35% were done by family members and 50% by other acquaintances. On the other hand only about 80% of homicides were "solved." That means that at least 68% of all murders (solved and unsolved) were committed by people who knew their victim. Even if we assume that a large percentage of the unsolved murders were committed by strangers, the likely rate of murder victims (in Canada) that knew their killer is greater than 50% and probably over 70%. Strangers are not the main perpetrators of homicide.

A related statistic may also provide some reassurance, given the current fear of children being attacked by strangers:

> A total of 36 children under the age of 12 were killed in 1999, down substantially from 55 in 1998 and the average of 53 over the past decade. Of the cases solved by police, almost 80% of these children were killed by a parent, and the remainder by an acquaintance of the family.[1]

Unfortunately, Statistics Canada figures demonstrate the *missing figure* problem: they do not tell us how many of the child murders were actually solved.

Critical Question 4: What are the Fallacies of Data Quality?

Below is a list of the most common errors made in reference to data quality.

Mythical Numbers: These are numbers produced by guesstimation that then take on an unwarranted air of credibility and "hardness."

False precision: Using a level of precision (e.g., a number of decimal points) that cannot be justified by the accuracy of the original data.

Change in *reported* incidence vs. actual change: From crime statistics to health stats, changes in definitions or awareness can create the appear-

---

1 Statistics Canada, "Homicide Statistics," *The Daily*, October 18, 2000, accessed at <http://www.statcan.ca/Daily/English/001018/d001018b.htm> June 21, 2008.

ance of real changes when actually nothing has changed but the reporting. E.g., violence in the Maritimes, thyroid cancer in the US.

Misleading Aggregation: Combining a wide variety of information in one statistic, e.g., crime statistics that lump together everything from disturbing the peace to homicide.

SUMMARY

Using data involves more than just collecting "facts." "Just the facts" is a bit of a myth. Getting good and reliable data is often difficult, especially about taboo and illegal activity. It's tempting to make up mythical numbers that are then widely quoted. It's a good idea to be very sceptical about any statistics concerning illegal activities or any other activities that people would not want others to know about. You should also use common sense when assessing data based on people's recall. No matter how careful the data collection (e.g., the census) there is still room for error and you should not be fooled by a misleadingly precise number into thinking the data is accurate.

CHAPTER 6

MAKING SENSE OF DATA: WHAT DOES IT ALL MEAN?

Having reliable data is just the first step to getting a good statistical picture. Thousands of bits of data aren't useful without some way of describing the whole collection, without some way of expressing what it all means. This section discusses the concepts used to summarize data and how to detect their misleading use.

LOOKING AT THE RAW DATA

SEEING THE BIG PICTURE

USING AVERAGES TO CHARACTERIZE DATA

Critical Question 1: What Is Being Claimed?

Imagine being given a list with the incomes of each and every Canadian family; despite all the data (or because of it) there would be little you could make of it. Collections of data are the basis for making statistical claims, but in themselves they don't tell us much. We need ways of summarizing the data in order to make sense of it.

How we characterize the data depends in part on what we want to know. If we are interested in whether people's incomes are rising we need to know incomes from earlier years (allowing for inflation). We also need to consider whether the *average* would give a good picture of how all Canadians are doing. Perhaps the rich are getting richer and the poor poorer, but the average is staying the same. If we are interested in how wealth is distributed in our country, we need to have ways of summarizing and comparing wealth across millions of households. If we are interested in knowing whether there is still income discrimination against women, we need gender-based information on income and some way of making sure we are comparing the income of the two genders appropriately. An issue that frequently comes up in affluent societies is the question of how many children are living in poverty. To answer this question we need information not only on family incomes and numbers of children but also a credible criterion for "living in poverty." All these questions can be asked using Canadian income data, but they all require different ways of characterizing the data in order to provide an answer.

WHAT CAN THE "AVERAGE" TELL US?

The standard measure for summarizing data, as we all know, is the **average**. Add up all the data (e.g., incomes or grade percentages) and divide by the number of items (wage earners or students) and there you have it: average income or the average grade. (Statisticians call this figure the **mean** but I will follow common usage and call it just plain old average.)

AVERAGES AND THE PROBLEM OF VARIABILITY

The average often gives us a misleading impression of the data being reported. When data exhibits high variability the average can be misleading. For example the average temperature of Phoenix, Arizona—20°C (72°F)—is the same as the average temperature of Orlando, Florida. But Phoenix's temperature varies from a daily average of 12°C (54°F) in the winter to 35°C (94°F) in the summer, while Orlando's much more steady climate varies from 16°C (62°F) in the winter to 26.5°C (82°F) in the summer. Hardly identical climates, but their average temperatures are the same. In general, averages are good ways of summarizing data that has limited variability. But even in cases of limited variability, the average can sometimes obscure what is happening.

Take the following simple example of grades for two students:

	Student A	Student B
Math	90	81
English	89	79
Physics	91	82
French	50	78
Social Studies	80	80
Average	**80**	**80**

Students A and B have the same average grade overall, but student B is a genuine 80% student, while student A appears to be a superior student with a weakness in French. Fortunately with this data we can see the difference, but if we were only given the fact that they had equal averages, we would not have a very accurate impression of their relative scholastic achievements.

Sometimes there really is no "general" tendency or grouping that could be the basis for a meaningful average. The following is from an article characterizing the conflicting research on American leisure patterns:

> Some researchers now argue that the *average* change in the amount of leisure may be the wrong measure to use, because there appear to be two different groups of Americans moving in different directions. One group includes baby boomers, who tend to be workaholics with little leisure time. The other group, which reports increasing leisure time, includes older Americans taking

early retirement, and younger couples who start their families later in life and have fewer children. Simply reporting one overall average misses this story.[1]

"THE OUTLIER" AND THE SOLUTION OF THE MEDIAN

Averages are a poor way to summarize data with high variability such as dramatic differences in income. The average can be very sensitive to exceptional bits of data. Take house prices. In my city house prices are extremely volatile. At one moment you feel rich to be a homeowner and at another you are not sure that you could sell the house for the money you spent on it. What is the actual situation? How can one tell?

The obvious way to tell the value of your house or the current state of house prices is to collect, as realtors do, the latest selling prices. There are different neighbourhoods in even small cities, and large cities have neighbourhoods that are incredibly different in culture and, crucially for our purposes, house prices. This raises a number of questions about what house sales to include in our data. What area do we pick to understand our situation? How do we define its borders? Neighbourhoods are seldom well-defined. For now let us assume that we have a well-defined area and have collected the data of recent sales in the table. What can we conclude about the price of houses?

Sales Ordered by Date	Sales Ordered by Price	
273,000	234,000	
318,000	254,000	
234,000	273,000	
296,000	288,000	
425,000	**290,000**	**Median**
254,000	296,000	
315,000	315,000	
998,000	318,000	
288,000	425,000	
290,000	**998,000**	**Outlier**
369,100	**Average Sale Price**	
299,222	**Average without Outlier**	
290,000	**Median Sale Price**	

1   Janny Scott, *The New York Times*, July 10, 1999, B7.

The average sale price is $369,100, but is that a good indicator of the price of current sales? Notice that one house sold for almost a million, while the others sold for much less. If we take the exceptional house out of the calculation average, then the average is only $299,222. Quite a difference. Which number gives the right impression? Are houses selling for around $299,000 or around $369,000? Suppose we approach the problem differently and ask what was the middle selling price? What was the price at which half the houses sold for more and half for less? That number is $290,000. Notice that this price is much closer to the average we calculated when we excluded the million dollar house.

This middle value is called the median. In cases where the standard arithmetic average is easily skewed by **outliers** (values far from the others), the median is often a better way of representing or summarizing the data. If you want to create an inflated impression of house prices then you would use the average and include the outlier, but using the *median* in this case is a much more accurate way of summarizing the data.

VARIABILITY AND THE MEDIAN: THERE'S LIFE BEYOND THE MEDIAN

Understanding variability is crucial for understanding the significance of summary statistics. Such an understanding can lead us to ask the right questions about crucial information. This point was illustrated by Stephen Jay Gould (a brilliant scientist and popularizer of science) in a powerful and touching article he wrote for the June 1985 issue of *Discover* magazine describing his experience of being diagnosed with mesothelioma—a usually fatal cancer.[1] When he researched the literature on this cancer he discovered that the *median* time of survival after diagnosis was three months! The crucial questions that Gould knew to ask were: What is the range of variability? How long did the "outliers" live? Were there lots of people who lived for many years? Being a cheery and extremely sophisticated scientist, he reflected immediately that while three months was the median—half of those diagnosed were dead by three months—half of those diagnosed lived longer, perhaps much longer; there might be many outliers, people who lived for years after diagnosis. Gould reasoned that given his age, general health, optimistic attitude, and access to the excellent health care, he was likely to be an outlier. And indeed, Gould lived another 20 years and died not of mesothelioma but of another form of cancer in 2002.

---

1 "The Median Isn't the Message," accessed at <http://www.cancerguide.org/median_not_msg.html>.

Just as in the case of my sister-in-law (described in Chapter 1), here it is important to realize that when you are told that a life expectancy is three months, that figure is a median which means that half of those diagnosed live longer, and perhaps many live a great deal longer.[1]

Gould's reflections illustrate the way in which thoughtful consumers of statistical information should think. The danger of not doing so is illustrated by the following story a statistician told me about a relative. The relative, like Gould, was young when he was diagnosed with a cancer, but he was not a sophisticated consumer of statistics and neither was his doctor. He too was told that his life expectancy was three months. Unfortunately he was not told that this was a median time of death from diagnosis and that he might live much longer. He freaked out, left his wife, bought a sailboat and began to sail around the world to live out his last few days. At the end of the first year he was still alive, healthy and sailing, so too at the end of the second year. Maybe this is a happy outcome! But in any case, he should have had better information. The error that his doctor made in telling him his median life expectancy was that he failed to notice or know that most people who were diagnosed with this cancer were old and were quickly killed by the illness; younger people were generally "outliers" and tended to live way beyond the median life expectancy.[2]

THE AVERAGE LIFE: LIFE EXPECTANCY

Speaking of life expectancy, what does the term **life expectancy** mean? For the country as a whole, it is simply the average age of death compensated for by the age distribution of the population. Naturally a generally older population (as Canada is becoming with the aging of the baby boomers) will have a higher average age of death, but life expectancy is calculated in such a way as to offset age distribution. It is well-known that affluent countries have experienced significant increases in life expectancy throughout the twentieth century. What is less well-known is that life expectancy also increases for each individual as she or he ages. Once

---

1   In addition it should be noted that studies show that physicians are not really that good at predicting life expectancy from diagnosis, though in the following study they tended to be optimistic: "Extent and Determinants of Error in Doctors' Prognoses in Terminally Ill Patients: Prospective Cohort Study," BMJ 320, 7233 (February 19, 2000): 469–72..

2   This story also illustrates the issue of using the most appropriate "risk group" (e.g., people your age) when making decisions about life expectancy. This point is discussed at length in Chapter 13.

you are 20 for example, you have already survived a number of years that others haven't so you are likely, on average, to live longer than someone who is only a few days old. This encouraging fact continues on throughout your life so that while the life expectancy *at birth* in Canada (2004) is 74.52 for males, 81.15 for females, the life expectancy of a 65 year old is 81.04 for males and 84.9 for females. Every year you live you can "expect" to live even longer. Of course if you smoke, drink heavily, and sky dive these figures may not apply to you!

These complications, not to mention the changes over time in all these figures, illustrate the deep and general challenge of applying statistical generalizations to one's own case. We will discuss this issue of application in Chapter 12.

Critical Questions 2 and 3 are not really relevant to our discussion of averages, but there are a number fallacies associated with the concept of average.

Critical Question 4: What Are the Fallacies of "Average"?

IGNORING THE SPREAD: USING THE AVERAGE TO CREATE A FALSE SENSE OF SIMILARITY

If the government wants to sell a tax break for the rich it will naturally use the *average* tax savings for all citizens. If the rich save hundreds of thousands of dollars and others save only a few dollars, it may still be technically true that the *average* saving was a $1,000 per taxpayer—whereas the *median* saving might only be a hundred dollars.[1] Generally speaking, when summarizing data with a very great spread (such as income size, tax break benefits, or house prices), using the *average* will be misleading; the *median* (i.e., the number in the middle of the list of data) is more appropriate. The average is fine for class grades because no one can make more than 100%, but incomes can vary from nothing to billions!

---

1 US President Bush's 2003 tax cut was sold on this basis. From ABCNEWS.com: "A Closer Look Behind the Numbers of President Bush's Proposed Tax Plan," January 24, 2003, accessed at <http://abcnews.go.com/sections/business/DailyNews/behindthetaxes_030124.html> May 14, 2006.

   The president said: "92 million Americans will keep an average of $1,083 more of their own money when this tax plan goes through ..." We found: If you look at the average for all taxpayers, this is correct. However, this average is derived from all income levels and all estimated savings. This skews the number upward. According to the Urban Institute-Brookings Institution, 80 per cent of all tax filers would receive less than the $1,083 average the president mentioned. *Meanwhile, half of all tax filers would get less than $100.* [Note the use of median.]

THE PARADOXICAL AVERAGE

There is another situation in which the average is so misleading that it actually produces a paradox. Known as Simpson's Paradox, a classic example occurred when there appeared to be sex discrimination in graduate admissions at one campus of the University of California because the overall percentage of male applicants being admitted was higher than that of women. Surprisingly when the claim was investigated it was discovered that no departments favoured male applicants over women. How could that happen?

I have taken the following simplified example from John Allen Paulo's useful column on mathematics in the news, "Whose Counting."[1] Suppose there were only two departments in the graduate school, economics and psychology. The following chart uses some made up but plausible numbers of average admissions to illustrate the problem.

1	2	3	4	5	6	7
Department	Women Applying	Women Admitted	Percentage of Women Accepted	Men Applying	Men Admitted	Percentage of Men Accepted
Economics	20	15	75%	100	70	70%
Psychology	100	35	35%	20	5	25%
Overall Total	120	50	**42%**	120	75	**62.5%**

Note that in each department the per cent of women accepted from applications was higher than that of men (compare columns 4 and 7 for Economics and Psychology). But the overall percentage of admissions was higher for men than women (compare columns 4 and 7 in the last row Overall Total). The problem is a result of the fact that the department that admitted more students (economics) also had many more male applicants. As a result, the aggregate percentages in the last line give a misleading impression of the conduct of individual departments.

NO ONE IS AVERAGE: MISTAKING THE AVERAGE FOR AN INDIVIDUAL

We should also be careful of confusing the average with the average person. What's the difference? Basically while there are average grades and

---

1   John Allen Paulo, *The Paradox of Averages*, accessed at <http://abcnews.go.com/Technology/WhosCounting/story?id=98444&page=1> June 29, 2001.

average incomes, there is no average person. Huff provides a telling story of how failure to understand this distinction created havoc in a post World War II housing authority. Having done a study and discovered that families were planning to have an average of 2.3 children, the housing authority decided to build only three bedroom homes.[1] This decision was based on a misunderstanding of what the average meant. The average was made up of people whose childbearing plans ranged from not having any children to those that would have six or more. But of course, even though the average number of children is 2.3, no family has that number of children. Each home needs to suit a particular family, not this fictitious average family. No one is average. Nor is anyone fated to be average.

UNDERSTANDING ECONOMIC NUMBERS

An area in which summary numbers have a great deal of importance is economics. Economic policy discussions are dominated by summary

---

1   Darrell Huff, "The Well-Chosen Average," *How to Lie With Statistics* (W.W. Norton, 1954).

numbers such as the inflation index (or CPI—Consumer Price Index), the Gross Domestic Product (GDP), and the rate of unemployment. These and many other measures are all ways of summarizing data that are supposed to reveal the state of the economy and to provide a basis for governmental and central bank decision-making.

Critical Question 1: What Is Being Claimed?

GDP

The most well-known economic number is the **GDP** or **Gross Domestic Product**. Every quarter the government announces how the economy is doing by stating the growth rate of the GDP. The GDP is a measure of a country's total economic output, the value of all the goods and services produced by a country. It is widely assumed that it is good for the GDP to increase and the more it increases the better. For a variety of reasons, including the normal business cycle, the GDP does not increase every quarter. Two consecutive quarters of "negative growth" (= shrinkage) is what economists call a *recession*. A great deal of governmental and central bank effort is directed at avoiding recession and maintaining economic growth as measured by the GDP. A government that presides over a recession has political difficulties. In the worst case a recession can be the precursor to a full-blooded, disastrous depression.

It's difficult to get all the relevant data in a country, and to avoid counting things twice. But the main problem here is not this, or lack of objectivity in the numbers. The main problem is understanding what an increase in the GDP really means.

The GDP really is a "gross" measure. If people spend more on home security because crime rates are up, the GDP goes up. If more money is spent on environmental clean-up because of past neglect, or on disaster repair, the GDP goes up. A country that exports a huge and growing portion of its production can have a large and increasing GDP but a terrible standard of living. If people spend more on health care because of poor lifestyle choices ... you get the idea. The GDP does not measure increasing wealth or well-being, but merely economic output. You might think that two countries with similar per capita GDP (i.e., economic output per person) would be equally well off, but one country could have this wealth distributed extremely unequally or another country with the same

GDP could produce its wealth with two weeks less work per person. Both countries would have the same GDP, but would be clearly very different countries in terms of social well-being. One country would suffer from oppressive inequality, while the other would enjoy more leisure despite having equal economic output. This should remind us that statistics are after all just numbers, and that summary statistics, in particular, always need interpretation.

Concern over the misleading direction encouraged by the GDP has led to a proliferation of indexes that attempt to provide a better measure of well-being than that provided by the GDP. Hopefully such an index can be developed to provide more appropriate information for making good economic policy decisions.[1] The development of an appropriate index of well-being is crucial because of the alarming power that economic numbers have on government decision-making.[2]

INFLATION AND THE CONSUMER PRICE INDEX

Another crucial economic measure is the Consumer Price Index (CPI), which is used to measure inflation. Measuring inflation is far from straightforward. Determining whether prices are rising is not as simple as going to the store every month and comparing the price of oranges and bread.

The CPI is calculated by estimating how much consumers are spending, on average, at a certain time, on a standard "basket of goods," including items in the categories of shelter, food, entertainment, fuel, and transportation. Statisticians measure inflation by first surveying consumers and finding an "average" basket of goods—e.g., how much consumers are, on average, spending on oil, lettuce, and housing. If the basket cost 1% more this month than last month then they project the monthly increase onto a year and say that the inflation rate is 12% or that prices are rising at the yearly rate of 12%.

Of course it is not quite this simple. The price of lettuce goes down in the summer and up in the winter, so fluctuations in lettuce prices do

---

1   The tiny country of Bhutan has recently received some favourable attention for the fact that its leader uses a GNH (Gross National Happiness) measure to guide his development policies.
2   See Andrew C. Revkin, "A New Measure of Well-Being From a Happy Little Kingdom," *The New York Times*, October 4, 2005, accessed at <http://www.nytimes.com/2005/10/04/science/04happ.html?ei=5090&en=a4c0250cf8714dca&ex=1286078400&partner=rss userland&emc=rss&pagewanted=all>, or a more comprehensive article by Alicia Priest in the *Georgia Straight*, June 3, 2004.

not reflect real on-going change in the price of goods. Many commodities exhibit seasonal fluctuation, while other commodities such as oil prices rise and fall because of political unrest as well as ongoing change in the underlying cost structure or supply. Inflation results are frequently published as "seasonally adjusted" rates, which have been altered to allow for these short-term changes in prices.

Critical Question 2: How Good Is the Evidence?

How accurate is the Consumer Price Index? Inflation varies not only from month to month, but also from region to region because prices are different in different places within the same country. Inflation also varies from consumer to consumer since we all have different consumption "baskets" from that used to calculate the Consumer Price Index. There's that problem of variability again.

Perhaps more problematic is the fact that average consumption patterns change more rapidly than the "basket" does. Only a few years ago nobody bought cellphone time, now it's a major cost especially in the lives of young people and any change in the cost of cellphone time would have a significant impact on the inflation rate. How often do the statisticians survey consumption patterns and change the basket? About every five years, though they do now make minor monthly adjustments.[1] So you can see the index may not be that reflective of current consumption patterns.

Among other complexities is change in quality. For many years the nominal price of a basic home computer remained stable at about $1,500, but each year the computer was more powerful, colour monitors were added, storage capacity doubled, etc. So while the price was stable, people who bought a machine in later years actually got more for their money: prices were the same but actually the price of computers was "deflating" because the consumer was getting more for her money. Cars may be more expensive now, but they are also better made. Once you see the problem you can see that measuring inflation is not a simple issue.[2]

And yet inflation rates are of enormous political importance. This is one of the reasons why statistical gathering bodies should be indepen-

---

1   The US Department of Labor explains its calculation of the CPI online at <http://www.
    bls.gov/cpi/cpifaq.htm#Question_6> (accessed August 14, 2004).
2   "... had the BLS [Bureau of Labor Statistics] made no adjustments for quality and merely
    recorded price increases, the CPI would have risen by about 4.7 per cent in 1995 rather
    than the reported 2.5 per cent." Jeff Madrick, *The New York Review of Books*, March 6,
    1997.

dent of the government—otherwise there could be political pressure to make the numbers look good. For example, a few years ago there was a big debate in the US about whether the Consumer Price Index was being correctly calculated. Some politicians and economists argued that the inflation index was "inflated." Because government-funded pensions were pegged to the inflation index, if the index was revised down, the government could save literally billions of dollars. The Bureau of Statistics statisticians won that debate and the way the Index was calculated was not changed. Winning that argument was important for the political independence of the Bureau of Statistics and also good for those who were dependent on government pensions.[1]

The statisticians who calculate the Consumer Price Index must make judgements that go beyond simple measurement or surveys. Yet their work, and the indexes they produce, remain more reliable guides to what is really happening to prices and the economy than the horror we feel when we fill up with gas and see a 10% increase in the price over the previous day!

Critical Question 3: What Else Is Relevant? What's Missing?

One of the most notorious missing numbers in economics is the cost that economic activity imposes on the natural environment. These missed costs, from global warming to the loss of species and aesthetic enjoyment are called **externalities**. Externalities are costs external to the economic system because those who create these costs do not have to pay for them. If a company uses a landfill to dispose of its waste, it must pay for this use, but if it pumps chemicals into the air that may cause global warming and emphysema, it does not have to pay. The health and other costs associated with this kind of pollution escape the pricing mechanism of the market system. If drilling for oil disrupts the caribou and a herd is wiped out, the herd does not go to court and charge the company for this lost. Externalities are important because their absence from costs in the economic system creates a false sense of economic well-being. Externalities are one reason the GDP discussed above is such a poor measure. The GDP counts economic activity such as car sales but not the costs of car usage such as loss of life or air pollution. It's as if you measured your own wealth only by counting your income and ignoring your expenses!

---

1   Jeff Madrick, "The Cost of Living: A New Myth," *The New York Review of Books*, Vol. 44, No. 4, March 6, 1997.

What's to be done about these costs that aren't there? Basically, try to find a way to count them and put them in the equation. In policy making "numbers rule." You greatly weaken your argument that something is harmful (or beneficial) if you are unable to put some numbers to the costs or benefits. The attempt to measure "immeasurables," such as people's sense of well-being or environmental damage, means that these issues are beginning to receive the same detailed attention and weight given to the more easily measurable. For example, entomologists have argued that insects contribute an enormous amount to the economy, but we usually just count them as pests. Entomologists estimate the value of pollination services by bees and other insects at $7 billion in the US alone.[1] The use of statistics can be misleading, but so can the absence of statistics. Numbers have weight, and citizens need to be able not only to criticize their misuse, but to use them effectively to promote good public policy and community well-being.

Critical Question 4: What Are the Fallacies of Data Characterization?

Misleading order: When we use numbers to compare things (for example, cities or universities) a small difference in the numbers can have a much larger difference in the ordering (that is, which one is first on the list, second, etc.). Given the subjectivity involved, slight differences in the numbers can be really meaningless, but the result of moving from first to fourth place on a ranked list can seem like a big deal. Subjectivity isn't the only issue. In 2003, the OECD published results from international testing comparing how countries scored on standardized reading, science, and math tests (see table below).[2] Canadian students tied for fifth on the math test—with a very small difference between Canada and the third and fourth rankings. In fact allowing for the Standard Error (reported in the table in the column labelled "S.E."), which is just the margin of error we learned about in Chapter 3, there was no statistically significant difference between the results from the countries ranked 3-8. Much ado about nothing.

1   David Biello, "Insects Provide Billions in Free Services," *Scientific American* (April 3, 2009), accessed at <http://www.sciam.com/article.cfm?id=insects-provide-billions> April 12, 2009.
2   From the OECD website <http://www.oecd.org/document/34/0,3343,en_2649_392632 38_14152482_1_1_1_1,00.html>, Table A6.1.

Country	Mean score	S.E.
Japan	557	(5.5)
Korea	547	(2.8)
New Zealand	537	(3.1)
Finland	536	(2.2)
Australia	533	(3.5)
Canada	533	(1.4)
Switzerland	529	(4.4)
United Kingdom	529	(2.5)
Belgium	520	(3.9)
France	517	(2.7)
Austria	515	(2.5)
Denmark	514	(2.4)
Iceland	514	(2.3)
Sweden	510	(2.5)
Ireland	503	(2.7)

Missing Measures: This involves leaving out important factors because they are hard to measure. Decisions made without taking costs such as externalities into account will be fundamentally flawed.

Misleading Aggregation: For example, crime statistics that lump together everything from disturbing the peace to homicide (see Chapter 5).

Misleading Average: When there is a large spread in the data or outliers that greatly skew the average, using the average will be misleading. The failure of the average to capture "spread" makes it a useful tool for those who wish to obscure the actual impact of policies such as changes of taxation.

Misleading Comparison: Comparing wages or prices over time without allowing for inflation and other relevant changes.

SUMMARY

When faced with a collection of data we naturally look for a number or numbers that "characterize" or "summarize" the data, but many of these measures are subject to misinterpretation. Unless most of the data such as grades or income are grouped closely together, the *average* can give us a false impression. A common mistake is to misinterpret the average to mean something like "extremely common or typical." Do not mistake the average income for the income of the *average person* who, after all, does not exist.

Also be careful to realize that many measures only appear to measure or only partly measure what we are interested in. The GDP, for example is a very poor measure of even financial well-being. Indexes can often be thought to mean something they don't. The Consumer Price Index is sometimes taken to measure how much more it costs now to live than, say, in 1980. But at best it is an attempt to measure changes in price for "similar" goods. Changes in quality and taste confound the index's use as a cost of living index. The unemployment rate does not really measure what we intuitively think of as unemployment since it excludes the discouraged. Realizing the limits of what reliable measurement can do will lead us to properly appreciate, but not overrate, the value of such numbers. These indexes are another useful antidote to mere subjective impression, but the numbers need appropriate *critical* scrutiny.

CHAPTER 7

THE POWER OF GRAPHS

WHAT TO WATCH FOR: PROPORTION

"Seeing is believing" is an even older cliché than "you can prove anything with statistics" but it reminds us just how compelling visual presentation of information can be. Graphs can be as revealing and persuasive as any picture. Like pictures they can also be powerfully misleading. Our job is to learn to take advantage of the power of graphs while maintaining an appropriately critical perspective. For example, compare these two graphs that track the sales of a fictional company.

Graph 1

Just So Industries Sales in Millions

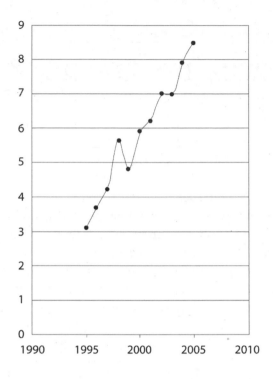

Graph 2

Just So Industries Sales in Millions

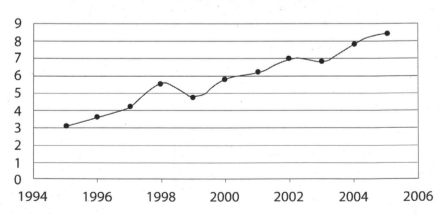

WHAT TO WATCH FOR: VERTICAL SCALE

Which company is more successful? If you looked closely you noticed that the two graphs actually present the same information. They just have different heights and widths. Even the scales are the same. We could also fool around with the scales and create similar impressions. Consider the two graphs below.

Graph 3   Graph 4

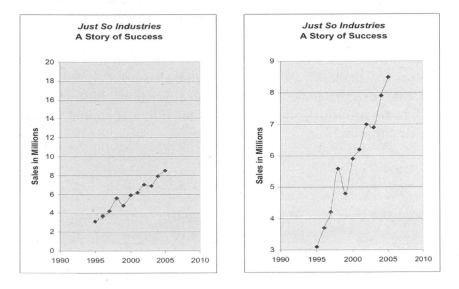

Same heights and width, but the sales axis on the left runs from 0 to 20 million and sales growth appears limited. While the graph on the right shows that we can keep sales growth looking dramatic by having the vertical scale from 3 to 9 million.

WHAT TO WATCH FOR: STARTING VALUE

Even though we know about these tricks, the visual impression of greater growth in sales when the graph is more vertical is powerful and difficult to ignore.

Consider an example of a standard graph showing the value of a stock market composite index:

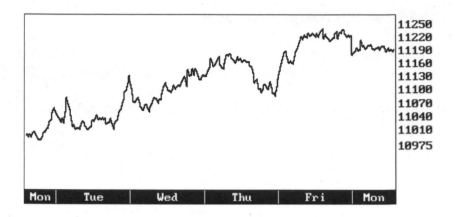

Looks like the market is doing quite well. If you look closely you can see that there has actually been a 2% improvement in the market. Certainly a good week, but the vertical impression of the degree of change is misleading.

Compare it to this graph using the same information and just the daily closing price.

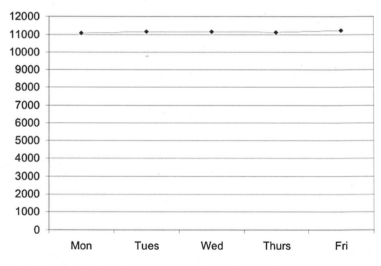

Looks like much less dramatic week on the market.

WHAT TO WATCH FOR: HORIZONTAL SCALE

While the most common manipulation of scales in graphs involves the vertical axis, you should also look out for changes in the horizontal axis.

The following graph from a local paper was meant, I assume, to calm fears about rising interest rates. The change of scale half-way across the horizontal axis was completely deceptive though it supported the reassuring headline (or perhaps the headline writer was also deceived).

Stable for Rest of Year

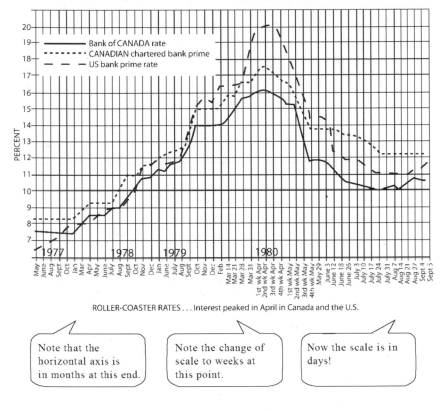

ROLLER-COASTER RATES . . . Interest peaked in April in Canada and the U.S.

Note that the horizontal axis is in months at this end.

Note the change of scale to weeks at this point.

Now the scale is in days!

WHAT TO WATCH FOR: NO SCALE

Sometimes, particularly around the time that people are encouraged to put money in tax-sheltered funds, you have graphs with absolutely NO scales. Just nice upward trending lines.

How do they manage to do this?

Your financial advisor can tell you exactly how well Acme Funds are performing. And why. He or she can also tell you which of Acme's six mutual fund portfolios is right for your investment requirements. Isn't it time to ask the person you trust with your money who they trust?

ACME
MUTUAL FUNDS

WHAT TO WATCH FOR: PICTOGRAMS

Purchasing Power of the Canadian dollar, 1980 to 2000[1]

1980 = $1.00

1985 = $0.70

1990 = $0.56

1995 = $0.50

2000 = $0.46

SHRINKING VALUE OF THE THE DOLLAR

---

1   From Statistics Canada, accessed at <http://www.statcan.ca/english/edu/power/ch9/pictograph/picto.htm> August 1, 2006.

Pictograms are graphs that use pictures instead of bars or lines, and can be used to create misleading impressions in another way. Because pictures of different size must expand horizontally as well as vertically to maintain the same pictorial proportions, the visual impression of change is compounded when the increased height also includes increased width.

The graphic above shows how the Canadian dollar shrank to a value of 46 cents over 20 years because of inflation. But the relative areas of the coins exaggerate the value change. You get the impression that the top coin is several times larger than the bottom one, though the difference is accurately represented by their diameter, not their whole area: the top one is only a little over twice as large as the bottom. Compare the graphic to the bar graph on the right. It is based on the same information but conveys an appearance of a less dramatic decline in the value of the dollar.

The lesson? The proportions, scales, starting values and pictures make the graph. Stretching proportions, shrinking scales, or changing the cut off to a point other than zero can create impressions of greater change.

THE POWER OF GRAPHS

If graphs can so easily mislead should we bother using them? We can see the answer if we consider photographs. We have all seen photos that make someone look like a complete idiot simply because he was caught with his eyes closed for a brief fraction of a second. Photos can lie (and they can be made to lie) but they provide us with information that we just can't get any other way. What did granddad look like as a child? What did I look like when I was born? What did Vancouver look like in 1910? You get the picture!

Graphs have the same advantage: correctly used they can give us an understanding that is difficult if not impossible to get from other ways of presenting the information. Used misleadingly they can deceive.

The Persuasive Power of Graphs: Shark Attacks

Let's take an example. Thanks to *Jaws* and newspaper coverage we are all aware of the dangers of shark attacks. Ever since *Jaws* we are sure to hear of attacks almost anywhere in the world. We can easily get the impression that attacks are increasing and of course they might be. Indeed shark attacks in Florida have gone from less than 20 in the decade 1950-60 to over 180 in the decade 1990-2000. Why? Has the shark population increased so much? Are they getting more ferocious? Perhaps there aren't enough fish so they are turning to humans? Or are there more people swimming in the shark habitat?

I made the following table based on the data from a graph (which I discuss below) supplied by the Florida Museum of Natural History website.

It lists shark attacks by decade throughout the twentieth century. The column on the right shows the population of Florida in millions.

Table 1

Decade	Attacks	Pop
00-10	2	0.6
10-20	3	0.8
20-30	6	1
30-40	5	1.3
40-50	2	2.1
50-60	15	3.2
60-70	41	5.8
70-80	38	7.5
80-90	83	10
90-99	186	16

Just looking at the table, it is hard to tell what the relationship is between population increases and shark attacks. Now look at the following graph that I made from this data. The jagged line shows the number of shark attacks per million of population (not the number of attacks period.) The solid line "averages out" the trend of the jagged line, giving an all-over picture. If there were no increase at all in the number of attacks per million of population, the all-over trend line would be horizontal (represented by the dashed line.)

Graph 5

Shark Attacks Per Million Over Century

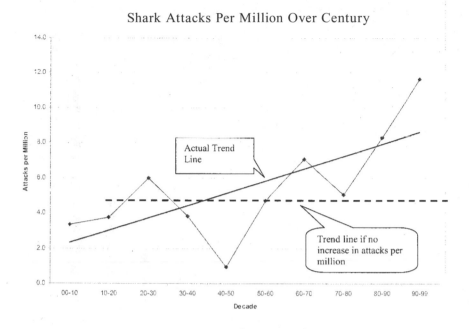

This graph illustrates the advantage that graphs have over simply presenting the data in tables. Yes, graphs can lie, but they can also reveal. Graphs make relationships such as trends over time much easier to see. The actual trend of attacks per population, we can see, is not constant; there is a more complex relationship. For example, there was a drop in attacks/population in the decade 1940-50, perhaps due to the fact that young people were involved with World War II during at least half that decade rather than swimming in the waters off Florida. The graph also shows that while the increase in attacks may partly be a function of the increasing population of Florida, in the last two decades the ratio of attacks to population significantly changed. The graph does not, of course explain this change. Perhaps humans are also swimming more or the increase in population in Florida was primarily along the coast. We would need considerably more relevant data before we knew what conclusion to draw from this info.

Now consider the answer implicit in the following graph from the Florida Museum of Natural History website.

Graph 6

Graphs of Shark Attacks vs. Population Growth over the Past Decade

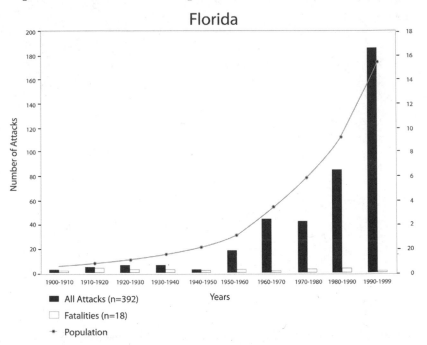

It is interesting to view this graph as a kind of visual argument. We can use our critical questions to evaluate it:

1. WHAT IS BEING CLAIMED?

The bold bars that indicate the number of shark attacks give a vivid impression of dramatically increasing rates of attack. Nonetheless, the overlay of the population line implies that the increase in the rate of attacks is roughly proportional to the increase in population. The graph makes an implicit case for the claim that the increase in shark attacks was largely a result of the increased number of people available to attack, so that an individual's chance of being attacked has not really changed over time.

2. HOW GOOD IS THE EVIDENCE?

Even if we assume that the evidence is correct, the presentation is misleading. One obvious and troubling aspect of the graph is that the scale for the number of shark attacks on the left is necessarily quite different than that on the right for population. By choosing different scales you can make any two sets of data look comparable. As we saw above changing scales can easily give differing impressions. We should be very sceptical of data presented with different scales on the same graph.

3. WHAT OTHER INFORMATION IS RELEVANT?

A better way to graph the data would be the way I did it in Graph 5. That graph shows that the relationship between population growth and shark attacks is hardly as reassuring as shown in the graph supplied by the Florida Natural History Museum. The implicit claim in the Florida Natural History Museum graph that increasing shark attacks was solely a function of population increase is obviously misleading.

4. WHAT FALLACY IS COMMITTED?

The fallacy committed is that of using differing scales on two axes to invite misleading comparisons, which in this case are used to create an appearance of a simple relationship between population growth and shark attacks.

THE ILLUMINATING POWER OF GRAPHS

So yes, graphs can deceive. But the choice of the right graph can also explain and reveal.

Edward Tufte is a renowned graph expert (no, not a *graphologist*—that refers to someone supposed to be able to "read" a person's personality from his or her handwriting). He has written a brilliant study that shows that the failure of the NASA engineers to correctly graph the problem with the Space Shuttle *Challenger*'s O-ring seals meant neither they nor their superiors had a clear idea of the dangerous effects of cold temperatures on the seals.[1] As you may know, it was the failure of these seals that caused the Challenger to explode on takeoff in 1986.

---

1   E. Tufte, *Visual Explanation* (Cheshire, CT: Graphics Press), 39–54. See also his website at <http://www.edwardtufte.com/tufte/index>.

Tufte points out that the information on the failure rate of the seals was presented in such a haphazard manner that a clear case for an association between low temperatures and O-ring failure could not be made. As a result, no one could clearly see the correlation between temperature and failure.

Tufte points out that the engineers presented information about O-ring failures in a table, not in a graph. The following table (Table 2), compiled by Tufte, gives O-ring damage data from tests at various temperatures. Nothing of interest is revealed by this table. But not just any graph would present better information. My Graph 7 illustrates one *useless* way that the information on O-ring damage could have been presented. It reveals nothing about the relationship between temperature and the failure of the O-rings. But Graph 8, showing clearly the relationship between temperature and O-ring failure, would make the danger clear.

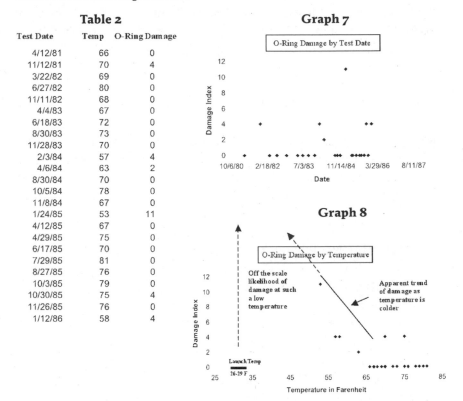

Table 2		
Test Date	Temp	O-Ring Damage
4/12/81	66	0
11/12/81	70	4
3/22/82	69	0
6/27/82	80	0
11/11/82	68	0
4/4/83	67	0
6/18/83	72	0
8/30/83	73	0
11/28/83	70	0
2/3/84	57	4
4/6/84	63	2
8/30/84	70	0
10/5/84	78	0
11/8/84	67	0
1/24/85	53	11
4/12/85	67	0
4/29/85	75	0
6/17/85	70	0
7/29/85	81	0
8/27/85	76	0
10/3/85	79	0
10/30/85	75	4
11/26/85	76	0
1/12/86	58	4

There are many different types of graphs with varying ability to convey information, but the popular media tends to restrict graphs to pie graphs, bar graphs, and line graphs. What you will seldom see outside a text book or journal is a scatter plot. But in this book we will have occasion to use scatterplots. In fact Graphs 7 and 8 are scatter plots.

A scatter plot is a convenient way to display relationships between *any* two variables (not just time) and for displaying a relatively large number of bits of data. Trend lines (see graphs above and below) can be added to indicate the general line of the relationship. They are especially useful therefore when we turn our attention to identifying correlations such as the correlation between smoking and lung cancer discussed in Chapter 8. One of the key research efforts that established this relationship resulted in the data represented in Graph 9.

Graph 9

Correlation between Cigarette Consumption and Subsequent Rates of Lung Cancer for 10 Countries 1930 - 50

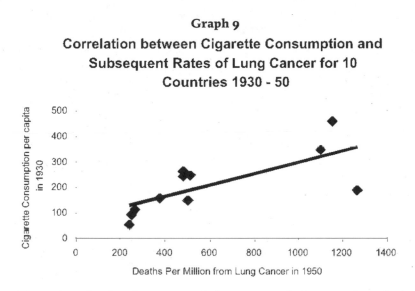

The scatter plot (on the next page) shows per capita income along the horizontal scale and a happiness measure along the vertical scale. The size of the circles represents the relative size of population. The graph illuminates some interesting aspects of wealth and happiness. While a number of very poor countries with incomes on the left side tend to have low levels of general happiness, many rate highly on this scale (e.g., Venezuela and Costa Rica). The general pattern varies widely among the relatively poor though there is a general tendency of a country's happiness to increase as income increases. This recent graph from Gallup[1] contradicts many previous ones that found a much weaker relationship between life satisfaction and income. A possible explanation for this change is that because global communication is now so widespread, people are measuring their well-being or life satisfaction not against local conditions, but against the highly publicized affluence of developed countries.

---

1   Gallup, "Worldwide, Residents of Richer Nations More Satisfied," accessed at <http://www.gallup.com/poll/104608/Worldwide-Residents-Richer-Nations-More-Satisfied.aspx> April 28, 2008.

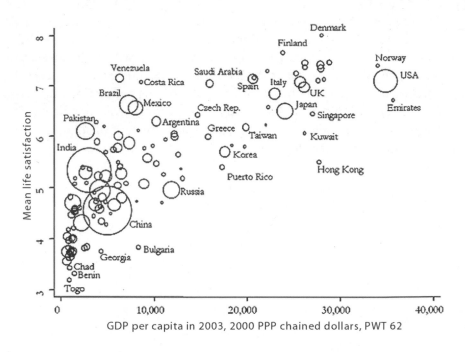

We can compare this graph to a similar one about the relationship between income and life expectancy.

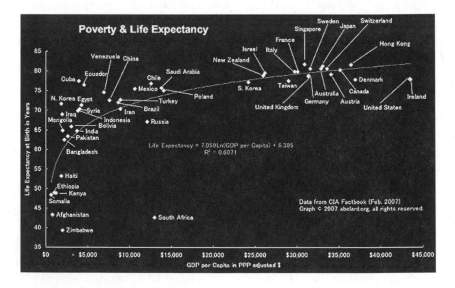

This graph[1] shows that there is a stronger relationship between per capita GDP and life expectancy than there is between happiness and income, though there are still exceptions or *outliers*. Cuba with its relatively low per capita GDP has a high life expectancy and Ireland and the US despite having the highest per capita income have lower life expectancy than many other developed countries with lower per capita GDP.

We will continue to look at graphs throughout the remainder of the text. Graphs can be powerful tools for helping us understand information, but as always, we must remain careful and critical consumers of the information presented.

EVALUATING GRAPHS
THE CRITICAL QUESTIONS

1. **What is being claimed?**
   Graphs often suggest or imply that there is a trend or correlation of some significance.
2. **How good is the evidence?**
   Look carefully at the scale and proportions to evaluate how much the data presented actually supports the appearance of a significant relationship.
3. **What other information is relevant?**
   If the graph attempts to show a trend over time, we need to ask if the relevant period of time is used, or does the graph use too short a period obscuring the real trend.
4. **Are relevant fallacies avoided?**
   - Inappropriate proportions (see Graphs 1 and 2)
   - Misleading scales including *not using 0 at the scale bottom* (Graph 4 and stock market graphs)
   - Varying scales on one axis (interest rate graph)
   - Using differing scales on two axis to invite misleading comparisons (shark graph)
   - Using pictograms that provide misleading visual impressions of change in height by increasing width not just height

---

1   "Oppression, Poverty and Life Expectancy—Briefing Document," <http://www.abelard. org/briefings/oppression_poverty_life_expectancy.php>, based on data taken from the *CIA World Factbook*, February 2007, accessed April 29, 2008.

CHAPTER 8

CORRELATIONS: WHAT GOES WITH WHAT?

INTRODUCTION

"Higher income and education go together"

"Recent studies confirm that women taking hormone replacement are at a higher risk for breast cancer"

"Fat consumption linked to heart attacks"

"Gonorrhoea rates decline with higher beer tax" (A recent favourite)

The media are not only fond of polls, they are increasingly impressed with health-related research. Almost as common as poll reports are reports of associations (statisticians call them **correlations**) between eating some kind of food and getting some beneficial or deleterious effect. And often these reports appear to conflict with one another. Fat gets a lot of blame, but then there is the report that high-fat Greek food—the so-called Mediterranean diet—is associated with reduced heart disease; there is also the "French paradox"— high fat consumption associated with a relatively low rate of heart attack. On the other hand, the apparently healthiest eaters of all are the Japanese, known for their low-fat, high-fish diet and associated very low rate of heart disease. All these well-known associations are statistically based correlations reported over the years by researchers. How valid is their research? What do these associations prove? Why the apparent conflict? Are some claims better than others? This chapter will cover some of the questions to ask in order to evaluate such claims and their supporting research.

Identifying correlations is not something only that researchers do. We all identify correlations ("Whenever I eat Mom's curry I get heartburn," "Whenever Mary knows that John is going to the beach she finds a reason to go to the beach herself," "It never rains when I take my umbrella"). Terms such as "whenever" and "usually" are typically used to express correlations based on informal observations. We use these expressions all the time. Just as humans seem prone to generalize, they seem prone to identify correlations. We are forever "noticing" that something is accompanied by something else—whether it's actually true or not.

Most supposed examples of extra-sensory perception involve individuals noticing connections. An example is that someone calls just when you were thinking about that person. "What a coincidence," we sometimes say. "It must have been ESP." Humorous versions of "noticed" correlations are claims such as "Of course it's raining, it always rains on the weekend." The claim that a particular baseball cap or t-shirt is lucky is really a claim that wearing it is correlated with winning. Frequently one takes such "observed" correlations to imply a cause and effect relationship. Mom's curry causes heartburn and, somehow, the lucky hat actually contributes to winning.

The fact is that correlations abound. Almost every change is correlated with something or other. The growth in the height of children in one country is correlated with the same thing in others; the time on my watch is correlated with the time on yours; summer in the northern hemisphere is correlated with winter in the south. So there are no shortages of correlations. But usually we are interested in correlations because we are interested in causes. We want to know if there is a reason why the Japanese have less heart disease. How do the French survive their delicious but fatty diet?

Identifying a correlation is not all that is involved in establishing a cause and effect relationship, but it is a crucial part. One of the most common errors in reasoning is to leap from evidence that two things are correlated to the conclusion that two things are causally related. In the next chapter we will look at statistical and scientific methods that are used to establish whether an association or correlation is the result of an underlying causal relationship. But for now we need to understand the simpler and more basic issue of what a correlation is and how it is established.

Critical Question: What Does the Claim Mean?

CORRELATION AND COMPARISON

A correlation exists when two factors—for example, smoking and lung cancer, education and income, potato-chip eating and heart attacks—vary together: *co-vary*. Because smoking is associated with a higher frequency of lung cancer, we say smoking and lung cancer are *positively* correlated. Since it appears that drinking red wine is associated with a lower frequency of heart disease, we say that red wine drinking and heart attacks are *negatively* correlated. Because it appears that people who watch violent TV tend to be more violent, we say watching violent television is positively correlated with being violent.

A NEW HEALTH HAZARD

Few people realize the deadly, terrifying ability of the pickle to kill or injure a person for life. Pickles are associated with all major diseases of the body. They can be related to most airline tragedies. Auto accidents are often caused by pickles. There is a positive relationship between crime waves and the consumption of pickles. If you don't believe this, consider the evidence:

- 99.9% of all people who die from cancer have eaten pickles;

- 99.7% of all people involved in air or auto accidents have eaten pickles within 14 days preceding the accident;

- 93.1% of juvenile delinquents come from homes where pickles were served frequently;

- nearly all sick people have eaten pickles;

- of all people born in 1860, who later dined on pickles, there has been 100% mortality;

- all pickle eaters born between 1881 and 1901 have wrinkled skin, have lost their teeth, have brittle bones, and failing eyesight if the ills of eating pickles have not already caused their deaths; and

- even more convincing is the report of a team of researchers: rats force-fed with 20 pounds of pickles for 30 days developed bulging abdomens.

There are two different ways of talking about correlations: categorical and continuous. Most reports of correlations in the media are categorical. "Fish eaters have fewer heart attacks," "Smokers have greater frequency of lung cancer," "Heavy watchers of violent television are more prone to violence." These claims express a correlation between a category of people (fish eaters) and a property (another category) like "having a heart attack." But many of the actual studies made by scientists identify more continuous relationships such as "The frequency of lung cancer increases with the amount and how long you smoke." Or "The height of parents and children are highly correlated."

For now I will focus on the more commonly reported categorical type correlations. I don't wish to constantly repeat the phrase "categorical type correlation," so until I state otherwise, that's the kind of correlation I am talking about.

To better understand how correlations are identified, let's take a familiar sounding but fictitious example."New studies show that 60% of people who eat more than one bag of potato chips a week die of heart attacks." Well chippers, should this result give you pause; should you abandon your favourite vinegar flavoured treat?

Maybe, but not necessarily. Let's see what the result of the study tells us. Does it tell us that people who eat weekly potato chips have a higher rate of heart attacks than non-potato-chip eaters? *No.* No, because there is *no comparison to the rate of heart attacks among those who are not potato-chip eaters*. All we are told is the percentage of heart-attack victims among potato-chip eaters. Such a percentage can only provide part of the evidence for a relationship between consuming potato chips and having a heart attack. *Until we compare the rate of heart attacks of those who are not potato-chip eaters we do not have a basis for claiming a correlation because we have no evidence that heart attacks occur more frequently among those who consume potato chips.*

What is crucial to remember is that we can't tell if there is a correlation by only being told the frequency of a misfortune in one category, e.g., heart attacks in one group with an identified habit like potato-chip eating. This point is brought home in the humorous side bar about the dangers of pickles.

Why do we know that the claims about the dangers of eating pickles are ridiculous? Because although pickle eaters wrinkle up and die, *so does everyone else*—so there is no correlation between pickle eating and dying. How do we tell if there is a correlation? To determine whether being in a particular category is correlated with some outcome, we need a comparison rate of the outcome for people who are not in the category.

Take the example of smoking. We know there is a correlation between smoking and lung cancer because the incidence of lung cancer is much higher (on average about seven times higher) among smokers compared to non-smokers. We can tell that smoking is correlated with lung cancer because we have *compared* lung cancer rates among smokers to rates among non-smokers. Sometimes there is a correlation even though the incidence is small. Just because only 10% of smokers die of lung cancer does not mean there is no correlation between lung cancer and smoking, since only a little more than 1% of non-smokers die of lung cancer.

So here is the crucial rule:

> We can only know if being in a particular category (e.g., being a smoker or a pickle eater) is correlated with some possible effect (e.g., lung cancer, skin wrinkles) by comparing rates of the effect in those who are in the target category with those who are not.

Well, yes that's a mouthful. So let's try this: no comparison, no correlation. Vague, but at least manageable.

Years ago, Maude Barlow, working for former Canadian Prime Minister Trudeau's committee on pornography, announced "It's no accident that 48 per cent of rapists and 14 per cent of child molesters are pornography fans."[1]

---

1   Quoted by Thomas Hurka, "Questions of Principle. Statistics: Time to Update our Brains," *The Globe and Mail* (Toronto), March 6, 1990.

(We might well wonder if these are *mythical numbers*. See Chapter 5.). The implication of her remark was clearly that there was a *correlation* (and a cause and effect relationship but we will get to that) between being a fan of pornography and committing sex crimes. But do her figures provide evidence of a correlation between pornography and sex crimes? Only if the rate of pornography consumption is higher among sex criminals than the male population generally. While I have no information about the general rate of pornography consumption among non-criminal males (or even how it could be measured), neither apparently did Maude Barlow. And without that we cannot know if there is a correlation, to say nothing of a causal relationship.

Another example of a correlation claim without the appropriate comparison was a study done years ago in California that found that over one-third of children of divorced parents were emotionally disturbed. The figure is alarming, but without a comparative study using the same criteria for "emotional disturbance" we don't know whether there is a correlation between divorce and emotionally upset children. And even if there is a correlation we don't know if the one-third figure represents a small increase in emotional disturbance among youth or a large one.[1]

By the way, the concept of correlation sometimes appears with other labels. In many medical studies **"risk factor"** is a common way of expressing correlations between such factors as being overweight and having a heart attack. You have a risk factor for a certain illness if some fact about you, such as your genetic background, your weight, or your life style puts you in a category that is correlated with an illness, i.e., there is a comparatively higher incidence of the illness among people in this category. Again, saying that the rate of heart attacks among those who are overweight is higher than those who aren't overweight means there is a positive correlation between weight and heart attacks. It doesn't mean that being overweight causes heart attacks. More on this later.

Critical Question 2: What Kind of Evidence is Necessary for Establishing Correlations?

Since identifying correlations involves comparing rates between two groups, detecting correlations is often not an easy matter. Using casual (not, by the way, *causal!*) observation we can be easily fooled because of the way we naturally observe the world. For example, we notice the

---

1   Judith Wallterstein and Sandra Blakeslee, *Second Chances: Men, Women, and Children a Decade After Divorce* (Ticknor & Fields, 1989).

weather more on the weekends because it is usually more important to us than during the week. So when it rains on the weekends, we note it. But rain during the week is not as carefully noted. A belief in the correlation between having the weekend off and being rained on is easy to develop without any real basis in the comparative rates of rain. I once heard a weather person explain why people thought we were having a particularly wet July, by pointing out that while the precipitation rate was about normal, a disproportionate amount had, unfortunately, occurred on weekends. The stand-out event of rain on the weekend had led to a false impression of frequency for the whole month.

Informally gathered evidence is, of course, not always wrong. Indeed impressions and hunches of correlation (and possible causal relations) are often the basis for scientific investigation. It was doctors' impressions that there was an increased rate of blood clots in young women using the pill that led to an investigation establishing the relationship. But whether a theory or hypothesis is true or not can be determined only through a more careful and formal process.

Establishing correlations requires comparisons. Researchers sample two groups: one with the outcome or possible cause that is of interest and one without it. They compare the rates in the two samples to see if the differences are large enough to provide good evidence of a correlation in the population.

THE COMPLEXITY OF COMPARISONS: MARGIN OF ERROR AND CORRELATIONS

As in the case of polls, researchers study a sample group in order to make a generalization about the much larger target population. The target population is the entire group that the researcher is interested in, e.g., smokers or potato chip eaters. You may remember that making inferences from a sample to a target population involved margins of error and confidence levels (see Chapter 3). But researchers searching for correlations have a more complex challenge than that of pollsters: they need to compare *two* samples before making claims about the population generally. When the difference between the proportions or averages of two compared samples is greater than the two margins of error, the difference is said to be statistically significant. Differences are said to be "statistically significant" when, in accordance with statistical reasoning described in Chapter 3, we can theoretically be 95% confident that the differences are not due to chance.

STATISTICAL SIGNIFICANCE

It is unfortunate that statisticians chose such a loaded term as "significant" to describe what is merely a probabilistic judgement that difference between the two sample groups is unlikely to be the result of chance. Many results that are statistically significant simply aren't significant or important in any ordinary sense. And sometimes the lack of statistical significance is more medically or humanly important. If, for example there is not a *statistically significant* difference between an expensive and inexpensive form of treatment, this is very *significant* news for medical authorities.[1]

Suppose a large-scale study (involving thousands of students) of different texts designed to teach students to read discovers that 68% of students using the new text were reading at a grade one level at the end of the year while only 64% of those using the old text were reading at grade one level. The researchers tell us the difference was "significant." Oh? How significant? Worth buying millions of dollars of new textbooks? Doubtful.

Whether a difference between two samples is statistically significant (assuming for the moment a random sample) is determined by two factors: sample size and the magnitude of the difference. As we know, the larger the sample, the smaller the margin of error. Small studies have trouble detecting statistically significant differences between the comparison groups unless the difference is very strong; large studies can establish statistically significant differences even with relatively weak and perhaps unimportant correlations.

This can lead to odd results in that large and usually expensive studies are often needed to detect differences that while *statistically significant* (because of the size of the study) may have little or no human or health significance. I'll have more discussion about the importance of statistical significance later when we look at actual studies. But keep in mind that when you read a report that says that a study discovered a "significant difference" between for example the cancer rate of apple eaters and pear eaters, remember that this use of "significance" merely means "unlikely to be due to chance" not "a difference that is of great importance."

---

1   Recent evidence suggests that inexpensive diuretics are as effective against high blood pressure as far more expensive drugs. Lawrence J. Appel, "The Verdict From ALLHAT—Thiazide Diuretics Are the Preferred Initial Therapy for Hypertension,"*Jama* 288 (2002): 3039–42.

P-VALUE

The statistical significance of a correlation claim will often be indicated with a "p"-value. **P-values** are just another way of expressing confidence that the apparent correlation is not due to chance. Stating that the difference between the averages of the two groups has a "p-value" of .05 is just another way of expressing our confidence level of 95%. What it says is that there is only a .05 chance that the measured correlation was the result of chance (i.e., we can be 95% confident it wasn't due to chance). Sometimes you will see "p < .05", which means that the p value calculated was even less than .05, so we can be even more "confident" the correlation wasn't due to chance. As with any kind of sampling, the mathematics by which a "p-value" is calculated assumes the sampling is random. Despite the widespread use of "p-values" to express a correlation, the requirement of random sampling is seldom met. See below about samples of convenience.

CONFIDENCE INTERVAL

Another way of expressing the difference between two comparison samples is by using the concept of **confidence interval**. This term is closely related to margin of error, discussed in Chapter 3. The confidence interval is the range around a percentage observed in a sample, representing the addition and the subtraction of the margin of error. So, for example, if a sample of 500 potato-chip eaters has a heart-attack frequency of 58%, that size of sample indicates a margin of error of ± 5%, so the confidence interval is the range from 53% to 63%—the range in which we can be pretty confident the frequency of heart attacks lies in the whole population of potato-chip eaters. Suppose that a very large sample of eaters and non-eaters showed a rate of heart attacks among eaters to be 1.5 times that of non-eaters. We would then calculate the margin of error, based on the sample size and the assumption of random sampling; we could then say that the confidence interval of the ratio would be (for example) between 1.1 and 1.9. This would typically be expressed as "CI: 1.1-1.9." This CI (confidence interval) tells us that we can be 95% confident that the ratio in the *population* is between 1.9 and 1.1. For there to be a real heart-attack effect of potato-chip eating, there would have to be a ratio of greater than 1. So if the lower bound of the confidence interval is equal to or below 1 then the results would not be *statistically significant*. That means that we could not be 95% confident that there is a real difference between the two groups. In the study we are imagining, the lower bound of the confidence interval is (slightly) greater than 1, so the results are statistically significant, showing a positive correlation between potato-chip eating and heart attacks; though it might just be a very small correlation, if in fact, eaters have only 1.1 times as many heart-attacks as non-eaters.

THE SAMPLING PROBLEM: SAMPLES OF CONVENIENCE

A crucial warning is needed here: *very few researchers use random samples*! More commonly, they use "samples of convenience." A **sample of convenience** is a sample of subjects that one can easily get access to—for example, students or hospital patients, or people who respond to requests for volunteer subjects. These kinds of samples present two obvious problems: they are clearly not random samples, and it is often not clear what populations they are supposed to be samples of. What population, for example, is being studied when a psychologist studies the "convenient" first-year students in her class? Students in psychology? Students generally? Midwest students? Or perhaps, most surprisingly, humans generally! A well-known study by two psychologists, S. Schachter and J.E. Singer, of 180 male (!) students at Minnesota University supposedly "proved" that people's emotions involved their interpretation of their own physiological states.[1] Despite the very limited sample, Schachter and Singer wrote as if they were offering a theory applicable to humans generally! The failure of these samples to be a random sample of any clear population raises serious doubts about the use of the statistical formulae for calculating margins of error and confidence levels. When reading studies we must keep in mind the question of whether, given the typical sample of convenience (i.e., non-random sample), we can reasonably generalize to any population. The mathematical measures of probability and margin of error all assume random sampling of a known population, and are not really applicable to studies that use other sampling methods. We will return to this concern in subsequent chapters, but the example below of research on the correlation between smoking and lung cancer illustrates the kind of problems that can come from using samples of convenience.

---

1   S. Schachter and J.E. Singer, "Cognitive, Social and Physiological Determinants of Emotional State," 1962, accessed at <http://www.holah.karoo.net/schachterstudy.htm> June 15, 2004.

Humphrey Bogart – Died of lung cancer in 1957.

WAYS OF ESTABLISHING CORRELATIONS: TYPES OF STUDIES

During the early 1950s, Humphrey Bogart embodied the smoking ethos of the day while his wife, Lauren Bacall, was legitimating smoking among women—something that was not well accepted at that time.[1]

Even at this time though, medical researchers were noting the dramatic increase in the incidence of lung cancer during the twentieth century: from .8 per 100,000 in 1900 to 34 per 100,000 by 1950.[2] Doctors were reporting their impression that there was a high incidence of lung cancer among cigarette smokers. Research was needed to test whether this impression was correct. What kind of research?

There are two approaches to establishing correlations: observational and experimental. In observational studies the researchers collect data about things like rates of smoking and incidence of cancer. In **experimental studies** researchers actually control possible causal factors, and as a result experiments provide more reliable sources of information about correlations. Most studies of the causes of illness are observational and not experimental, for the obvious reason that researchers do not wish to expose people to harm. An exception was an experiment to test whether exposure to cold caused the common cold; experimenters had subjects

---

1 Picture from "Punch and Nana's Tribute to Bogart," <http://www.geocities.com/Hollywood/Bungalow/6309/BOGEY.html>.
2 J. Cornfield, W. Haenzel, E.C. Hammond, A.M. Lilienfield, M.B. Shimkin, and E.L. Wynder, "Smoking and Lung Cancer: Recent Evidence and a Discussion of Some 'Questions.'" *J Natl Cancer Inst.* 1 (January 22, 1959) 173–203.

jumping into cold water! By the way, there was no evidence that this chilling experience was associated with more colds.[1] In the remaining part of this chapter, I will discuss the evaluation of observational studies. Chapter 9 will address the evaluation of experimental studies.

OBSERVATIONAL STUDIES: PROSPECTIVE AND RETROSPECTIVE

There are two basic kinds of observational studies: retrospective and prospective. Initial studies of causes of illness are typically retrospective. **Retrospective studies** are called that because they look backwards; they're also sometimes called "**case-controlled studies**" in epidemiology. They identify a group of people suffering from an illness (e.g., lung cancer) and attempt to find factors that are different in this group compared to a group of similar people (the **control group**) who do not have the illness. Typically researchers start with a theory based on doctors' impressions that people with a particular illness have a certain typical background (e.g., smoking, or exposure to asbestos). This is a common informal process by which tentative theories or hypotheses are formed. **Prospective** ("forward-looking") **studies** isolate a sample group often called a cohort (these studies are sometimes called "**cohort studies**") and follow the subjects over time, noting differences between them that might be causes of the illness, and recording whether they eventually get the illness or not.

How did scientists study the smoking/lung cancer link? In the early 1950s two retrospective studies of approximately 600-700 cases of lung cancer were done that compared the history of smoking among lung cancer victims and a "control" group. A control group is the comparison group necessary for establishing a correlation. The control group is supposed to be like the diseased group in every *relevant* way (i.e., age, gender mix, social background) except of course people in this group don't have the disease. In this case, the control group was made up of other hospital patients of similar characteristics who did not have lung cancer. This was a study using samples of convenience fraught with all the difficulties that such samples present. Obviously such samples are not random, and therefore are prone to sampling bias such as Gallup found when he used "representative sampling" (see Chapter 4). These early smoking studies dramatically illustrate the problem.

---

1   A famous series of experiments were conducted after World War II, under Dr. Christopher Andrews at the British Medical Research Council's Common Cold Unit. (For information see <http://diseases-viruses.suite101.com/article.cfm/respiratory_viruses>). These and other subsequent experiments failed to show any evidence that the common cold had anything to do with body chilling.

CASE CONTROL STUDY OF LUNG CANCER AND SMOKING

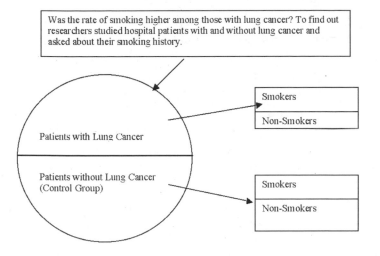

Was the rate of smoking higher among those with lung cancer? To find out researchers studied hospital patients with and without lung cancer and asked about their smoking history.

Patients with Lung Cancer

Smokers

Non-Smokers

Patients without Lung Cancer (Control Group)

Smokers

Non-Smokers

Both of these early studies found a slightly higher rate of smoking among the cancer victims than the control group, but the differences between the rates were *not* great enough to be statistically significant, i.e., the researchers could not be 95% confident that the differences in the rate of smoking between the groups was not due to chance. While researchers still suspected there was a relationship between smoking and lung cancer, their study had failed to demonstrate it. Why? With the advantage of hindsight we can clearly see the problem. While none of the patients in the "control group" had lung cancer, many of them had illnesses to which we now know smoking contributes (such as heart disease). As a result, the patients in the control group were not reflective of the general population—a higher percentage of them were smokers than the general population. The greater percentage of smokers in the control group obscured the actually dramatic difference between rates of lung cancer between smokers and non-smokers. Such is the danger of using samples of convenience rather than truly random samples.[1]

Fortunately researchers did not stop here. The obvious next move was to do a prospective study. Prospective studies can reduce many of the un-

---

1 Ellen Ruppel Shell gives another example of how use of samples of convenience can lead to misleading results. She cites a study that found a correlation between pancreatic cancer and coffee by comparing pancreatic cancer patients to other patients in a ward for digestive disorders. The researchers found a higher coffee consumption among pancreatic cancer patients, but were criticized for ignoring the fact that those patients with digestive disorders probably reduced their coffee consumption (*Atlantic Monthly*, November 1987, accessed at <http://www.theatlantic.com/issues/96jun/cancer/shell.htm> August 2003). Subsequent research has failed to link coffee consumption to pancreatic cancer (*Cancer Epidemiology, Biomarkers and Prevention* 10, 5 (2001) 429–37.

certainties involved in retrospective studies. They can also give us a better idea of the power of a cause (are smokers just a little bit more likely to get lung cancer, or far more likely to get lung cancer?). In prospective studies, sample groups are identified by the input and not the outcome, and then are followed for a period of time to see what the outcomes are. For example, sample groups can be identified by whether or not they are smokers, heavy drinkers, or receiving a new treatment and then they can be followed to see if there is a (statistically significant) difference in the outcomes of those who are smokers, drinkers, etc., compared to those who are not.

COHORT (PROSPECTIVE) STUDY OF SMOKING AND LUNG CANCER

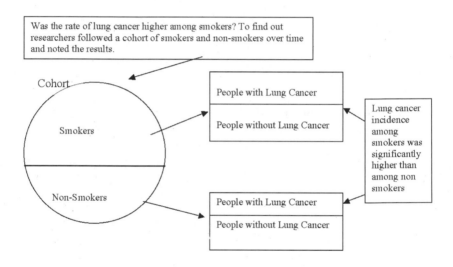

During the early 1950s the American Cancer Society undertook a huge prospective study reporting on the mortality over a period of a few years of 187,783 (!) men aged 50 to 69. In an effort to get a representative sample (but only of men), the researchers used a stratified sample of volunteers recruited from over 400 counties throughout the US. Volunteers were interviewed about their smoking habits. If they died during the study period, the cause of death was recorded. The results showed not only that smokers had a higher mortality rate for lung cancer, but also a higher rate of mortality for other causes of death such as heart attacks.[1]

---

1   The results of this study were published by its organizers, Drs. E.C. Hammond and D. Horn, in "Smoking and Death Rates-Report on Forty-Four Months of Follow-Up of 187,783 Men: I. Total Mortality," *J. Am. Med. Assoc.* 766 (1958): 1159–72. Other 1950s' prospective studies that came up with much the same results were R. Doll and A.B. Hill, "Lung Cancer and Other Causes of Death in Relation to Smoking: A Second Report on the Mortality of British Doctors," *Brit. Med. J.* 2 (1956): 1071–81 and H.F. Dorn, "Tobacco Consumption and Mortality from Cancer and Other Diseases," *Public Health Rept. U.S.* (1959): 581–93.

Establishing a correlation is not establishing a **causal relation**. For example, it is well-known that there is a higher rate of lung cancer among coffee drinkers than those who do not drink coffee, but before you give up your java consider that many smokers love to have a coffee with their cigarette. This mixing of factors that obscures the actual causal factor is called **confounding**. In the next chapter we will discuss the kind of evidence researchers need to supply to make a case that a correlation is evidence of a causal relation, and how they address the problem of the confounding factor. For now, let me just briefly review the advantages and disadvantages of the different types of observational studies.

	Retrospective, Case-Controlled	Prospective, Cohort
Advantages	Especially useful for preliminary research Smaller number of people required Time to carry out study is shorter Can be less expensive Suitable for relatively rare diseases	Less dependent on memory Less likely to have biased data May find associations with other diseases Can establish incidence rates and relative risk More reliable
Disadvantages	Less reliable Dependent on recall for information leading to bias and incomplete information Selection of case and controls presents problems of developing appropriately matched groups	Expensive and time consuming Large number of subjects Can have problem with drop-out rate Subject to confounding associations

Critical Question 3: What Other Information Is Relevant? What Is the History of This Issue?

Some topics—for example, the possible association of TV watching and violence, or of a high-fat diet and illness—are the subject of multiple studies. When evaluating a study that claims an association, we should be mindful, as with any argument, of whether it is supported by other studies or is in conflict with them. A 95% confidence level means that while we expect 19 out of 20 of the apparent correlations not to be due to chance, we also expect that 1 in 20 will simply be a chance result. Therefore, despite achieving statistical significance, therefore an exceptional study could be the result of chance (or also the result of biased sampling!). Samples of convenience are especially vulnerable to bias. Any study that goes against the general direction of research should be viewed with scepticism. Of course, if a report of a correlation is not based on systematic gathering of data but rather reported impressions, then we must remain quite sceptical of the claim until better evidence is presented.

Critical Question 4: Are Relevant Fallacies Avoided?

Most of these fallacies don't have "official names" and I am afraid my names are a bit awkward, but they are a useful checklist:

a. **No comparison**. Is there an appropriate comparison to support the correlational claim? Perhaps I should call this the "pickle fallacy."

b. **Biased sampling**. Is the sampling systematic and unbiased? Just collecting information about events that we notice occur together is not sufficient to establish a correlation. Only the systematic collection of data with appropriate comparisons can really establish evidence of correlation. The mathematical basis for inferring from differences between samples to the population at large is random sampling. Non-random samples such as *samples of convenience* present problems for making any inference to a more general population.

c. **Small sample**. Is the sample large enough to support the correlational claim? Remember that to establish correlations based on small differences in the two groups requires large samples.

d. **Unclear target population**. Have the researchers been clear about the target population of their study? Using samples of convenience means that researchers cannot use statistical inference to infer correlations in the target population. They must identify the target population and make an argument that their sample is a plausible basis for ascribing the correlation to the population.

e. **Fallacy of significance**. Has the reporter or researcher made misleading use of the term "significance"? A "*statistically* significant difference" between two groups means that it's very likely that there's a correlation; but this says nothing about the strength of the correlation or about whether the correlation is of any human, scientific, or personal significance.

AN ILLUSTRATIVE EXAMPLE: DIET AND CANCER

No medical topic has received more press than the relation between diet and various illnesses. Evidence for such connections is, however, often quite shaky. Should we be surprised? Not really, since, as we have seen, this kind of research—retrospective or prospective—is fraught with difficulty. The following account of the effort to establish the relationship between diet and cancer powerfully illustrates some of the difficulties that accompany such research.

> In a 1981 landmark report, Doll and Peto estimated that 35% of US cancer deaths were attributable to dietary factors. This estimate was primarily based on the large differences in rates of specific cancers among countries and observations that these rates were strongly correlated with aspects of national food supplies....
>
> Since the early 1980s many detailed investigations including mechanistic studies, animal experiments, epidemiological observations, and clinical trials have addressed the potential effects of diet on cancer incidence. Although much has been learned, progress has been slower and more difficult than was anticipated. At the beginning of this period, high total fat consumption was widely believed to be the primary reason for the high rates of breast, colon, prostate, and several other cancers.... However, little relation between total fat intake and risk of breast cancer and risk of colon cancer has been found in large prospective studies. Although a weak effect is impossible to exclude, evidence is strong that simply reducing the percentage of energy intake from fat during midlife will not have a major impact on breast and colon cancer....

In other words researchers did not find a reliable correlation.

As evidence to support the dietary fat hypothesis has waned, enthusiasm increased during the 1990s for increasing fruit and vegetable consumption to prevent cancer; the national Five-a-Day program was launched on this basis. Although inverse associations between intakes of fruits or vegetables and incidence of various cancers were reported in numerous case-control studies, the findings from more recent large prospective studies have been far less supportive of a benefit. In a recent report combining large cohorts, no relation was observed between total fruit and vegetable consumption and overall cancer incidence. Randomized trials using high doses of single constituents of fruits and vegetables, and beta carotene in particular, also failed to show benefits.

> Here they failed to find a correlation in an *experiment*. More about experiments in the next chapter.

One lesson from this experience has been that case-control studies of diet, in which patients with cancer and a control group are asked about their diet in years past, can be misleading. Recall of diet might be biased by the diagnosis of cancer, but in typical case-control studies selection bias may be even more problematic. Participation rates of patients with cancer are usually high, but participation of population controls is often only 50% or 60%.

> The problem of memory in retrospective studies

Those who participate are likely to be more health conscious and therefore consume more fruits and vegetables and less fat than those who do not. When cases and controls are compared, this would lead to apparent inverse associations with fruits and vegetables and positive associations with fat.[1]

> The problem of getting appropriate, unbiased controls

---

1   Walter C. Willett, "Diet and Cancer: An Evolving Picture," *Journal of the American Medical Association* 293 (2005): 233–34.

CONCLUSION

We will return to the assessment of numerical study results after we have looked at how correlations are used to establish causal relations. Whether it is mother's curry and heartburn, wearing the lucky hat and winning the game, or food and heart disease correlations suggest that one factor actually contributes to the other. Researchers, like all of us, are interested in correlations as a means to establishing scientifically sound *causal claims*. How such claims can be established is the subject of the next chapter.

Let's use the critical questions to quickly review the material covered in this chapter.

Evaluating Correlational Claims

The Critical Questions

1. **What does the claim of correlation mean?**
   Simply that two events or factors co-vary. They either have a positive correlation and tend to rise and fall together, or a negative correlation and tend to move together but in opposite directions.
2. **How good is the evidence?**
   a. **Are there two relevant groups being compared?**
      Categorical correlational claims require comparison of some rate of incidence between two groups, e.g., the rate of lung cancer in smokers vs. non-smokers.
   b. **Is the difference in rates between the two groups large enough to justify generalizing the apparent correlation?**
      Because of margins of error involved in all sampling, inference to the general population requires that the difference between the groups must be large enough that it is unlikely to be the result of chance sampling variation. Because two groups are involved, the difference must be outside the margin of error of both samples.
   c. **Were the groups being compared appropriately selected?**
      Observational studies do not involve random samples. In case-control studies the question is how well-chosen were the controls. In cohort studies the question is to what extent the groups compared differed in ways other than the factor being studied. Note also, despite the fact that these are not random samples, researchers still use criteria of statistical significance based on this assumption.
3. **What is the context?**
   Have other researchers found similar correlations? Of similar strength? Did other researchers use different types of samples and groups?
4. **Fallacies**
   a. **No comparison.** Is there an appropriate comparison necessary to support the correlational claim?
   b. **Biased sampling.** Is the sampling systematic and unbiased? Non-random samples such as samples of convenience present problems for making any inferences to a more general population.
   c. **Small sample.** Is the sample large enough to support the correlational claim?
   d. **Unclear target population.** Have the researchers been clear about the target population of their study?
   e. **Fallacy of significance.** Has the reporter or researcher made misleading use of the term "significance"? To say a difference between two groups was "statistically significant" does not mean the difference is important.

CHAPTER 9

FINDING THE CAUSE: EVALUATING CAUSAL CLAIMS

THE SEARCH FOR THE CAUSE OF CHOLERA

It was 1854 and cholera was again spreading throughout London. The epidemic of 1849 had killed over 14,000 Londoners. Anxiety was high. John Snow, a leading physician of the day, had studied data from the previous epidemic and already developed the theory that cholera was somehow water borne. Using records produced by the Registrar of Birth and Deaths from the 1849 epidemic, Snow was able to make an initial case for his suspicion that the location of cholera cases was correlated with the location of certain sources of water in London.

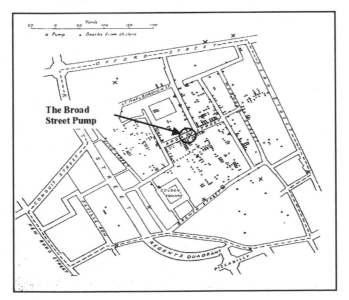

When the epidemic struck again Snow and the Registrar's office worked together to provide a stronger case for the correlation between certain sources of water (namely the Southwark and Vauxhall Water Company whose water contained London sewage) and cholera deaths. They were quickly able to establish that mortality among those consuming water from the Southwark and Vauxhall Company was 5 to 10 times that of those drinking water from other suppliers. Snow produced a famous map (shown above),[1] which graphically illustrated how incidence of the disease was focused around a particular pump. The government immediately moved to close the sources of polluted water and the incidence of the disease declined dramatically. Many lives were saved in this early triumphant achievement of public health. Though Snow did suspect that there was some matter that was being transmitted from those who were sick, the germ theory of illness had not yet been developed. In this early success of the discipline of epidemiology, it was Snow's careful statistical analysis of the geography of the cholera deaths, not biological investigation, that enabled him to identify the cause of the cholera epidemic.

Because the work of epidemiologists focuses on populations, not individuals, statistics are the basic tool of their work. The statistical techniques and arguments used by epidemiologists are used widely by all disciplines. I have chosen to focus on epidemiology for my initial treatment of causal reasoning based on statistical information because this area of research gets a good deal of media publicity, and has seen some of the most successful uses of statistical research. The study of humans and their illnesses is complex, but the study of human behaviour by the social sciences faces even greater challenges. Studying the work of epidemiologists should help you when you look at the use of statistical research in any other science.

An excellent example of successful epidemiological research was the establishment of the causal link between smoking and lung cancer. Later in this chapter we will explore just how this success was achieved.

Correlation and Causality

In Chapter 8 we learned about the complexity involved in identifying and measuring a correlation, but, as John Snow knew, correlations are primarily interesting as the basis for discovering causal relations. Nonetheless, going from a correlation to a valid causal claim is a tricky path full of all sorts of potholes.

1 Accessed at <http://upload.wikimedia.org/wikipedia/commons/c/c7/Snow-cholera-map.jpg>.

For a correlation to be a candidate for capturing a causal relationship one correlate or event (in general—with some exceptions[1]) needs to precede the other. Frequently, people wrongly infer that simply because one event proceeds another that the earlier event is the cause.

Making an inference from mere fact that B follows A to the claim that A caused B is the notorious **post hoc ergo propter hoc fallacy**, or as it is called by its friends, the "post hoc fallacy." "Post hoc ergo propter hoc" simply means "after this therefore because of this." My favourite example involves a wholly surprising factor in climate change: after Canada changed from using Fahrenheit to Celsius the weather has gotten worse.[2] Dionne Warwick claimed numerology helped her succeed because after she changed her name in accordance with numerology theory she became enormously successful. A bit too modest about her singing ability? Correlations abound: the number of churches in a city and number of crimes, increasing beer sales and increasing life expectancy, your watch and my watch, seatbelt signs and bumpy air. But none of these involve a direct causal link.

Humans are constantly on the alert for causal relationships and as a result, often see them where they don't exist. Scientists recognize just

1   Another example of things being not so simple. The moon's rotation around the earth is the primary cause of tides, but the variation is continuous not sequential. Still the change in the tides never *precedes* the changes in the moon's position.
2   Ralph H. Johnson and J. Anthony Blair, *Logical Self-Defense* (New York: IDEBATE Press, 2006), 132-33.

how many coincidences occur that simply have no causal explanation— that are *mere* coincidence. In fact, scientists, despite devoting their lives to finding causes, probably see fewer causes than the layperson. Surprisingly what we take to be remarkable coincidences actually occur rather often and need no special explanation. An event that is so rare it happens on average to only one person in a million per year, will happen to over 500 people in North America in a typical year.

Nonetheless when something of note occurs we look for some antecedent event that can explain it. "That couldn't have happened by chance, there must be an explanation. It's just too weird." Did my new pillow cause my back to ache more this morning, or was it my new workout pattern? Did the new brand of mayonnaise make me sick, did eating oranges cause my acne, and did the moon cause Bill to go crazy (maybe he really is a "lunatic!")? Lots of "post hoc" explanations are available. Superstition is easily maintained by such apparent connections. "Friday the thirteenth, of course, that's why the pipe burst in the cellar!" In those cultures where there is a belief that a variety of gods must be appeased daily in order for life to go well, there is no shortage of reasons for misfortune. If you have lots of ceremonies that need to done correctly to keep the gods happy, you have lots of potential explanations for why the gods are giving you a hard time.

Unfortunately the history of medicine is also full of practices not that different from superstition. Bloodletting was a common medical procedure from ancient times till the nineteenth century. It involved bleeding people to let out the "bad blood" that was supposedly causing the illness. Bloodletting could be maintained as a medical practice because there were undoubtedly people who survived the bloodletting and recovered from both the therapy and their illness. The physician could claim credit for cures, while blaming God or the illness for their failures. "If the patient recovers, the cure worked, if not the patient was simply too ill to be saved." You can't be wrong! The fact that the body has an impressive tendency to heal itself means that many ineffective if not downright dangerous medical practices could be sustained by pointing to successful cures and explaining away failures. Because of the body's own healing processes, scientifically establishing what works and doesn't work is no simple matter.

For medicine to be scientific, a systematic method for discovering causes of illness and for assessing therapeutic effectiveness was necessary. Fortunately epidemiology provided such a method. As the introductory story relates, the containment of cholera was one of the first successes of epidemiology. Have you ever heard of pellagra? If you haven't, it's because an epidemiologist identified the cause of pellagra and public-health measures were taken to prevent it.[1] Heard of any recent cases of the black plague? Another credit to early epidemiology. While it is easy to be sceptical about particular claims of pollsters, we can hardly doubt the benefits of epidemiology. Not only does epidemiology provide the basis for public-health initiatives that prevent infectious diseases, but it is also used to assess the effectiveness of various therapies and drugs. Know anyone who had his or her tonsils out recently? No? Thanks to epidemiological research a generally useless and sometimes dangerous procedure common in my youth has been largely abandoned.[2]

As its name suggests, epidemiology was initially concerned with the study of epidemics such as cholera. The success of statistical investigation into these questions led to a far greater application of statistical methods to all sorts of health problems. One of the great early epidemiologists was Florence Nightingale, who used statistical analysis to persuade the British government to change the way it treated its own soldiers. She used statistics to show that there was higher mortality in the military even in peacetime than among civilian men of similar age. She had earlier documented mortality in military hospitals in the Crimean war where, because of the lack of basic cleanliness, sanitation, and nutrition, more men were killed by their hospital treatment than died on the battlefield.[3]

The great successes of epidemiology should not blind us to the challenges statistical study faces. The results of studies of how diets and lifestyle choices affect people's health get enormous publicity. Unfortunately, as you have probably noted, many of these results are later refuted by subsequent studies. An appreciative but appropriately sceptical understanding is needed for assessing the daily announcements of "studies show." In what follows you should develop an understanding of how epidemiologists do their research and justify their conclusions. Having this understanding will enable you to apply appropriate criteria when assessing the results of their work.

So how do scientists prove that a new drug is effective, or that a substance causes cancer? Let's use the case of smoking and lung cancer to see how scientists first identified a correlation between smoking and lung cancer and then went on to establish that this was indeed a causal relationship.

---

1 Pellagra, largely unknown now in North America, is a disease with various manifestations starting with scaly skin, then diarrhoea, leading to dementia. The discovery that it was caused by a niacin deficiency was made in 1914 by Dr. Joseph Goldberger, an epidemiologist with the US Public Health Service. Paul D. Stolley and Tamar Lasky, *Investigating Disease Patterns: The Science of Epidemiology,* 2nd edition (New York: Scientific American Library, 1998), 45-46.

2 A study done in the 1940s showed that doctors diagnosed the need for tonsillectomy in about 45% of children sent for examination, regardless of their condition! Stolley, pp. 199-20.

3 Stolly, pp. 39-43; see also <http://www.spartacus.schoolnet.co.uk/REnightingale.htm>.

PROVING SMOKING CAUSES LUNG CANCER

Let's start with the first two of our four Critical Questions as our guide:

1. What does the claim mean?
2. How good is the evidence?

Critical Question 1: What Does It Mean To Say That Smoking Causes Lung Cancer?

It does not mean merely that there is a higher rate of lung cancer among smokers than among the non-smoking populace. It means something like "there is some biological process by which the ingredients in inhaled tobacco smoke produce lung cancer in some individuals." Initially such a claim was simply a suspicion. Proving it took many years of study and controversy.

Critical Question 2: How Good Is the Evidence?

FROM CORRELATION TO CAUSAL RELATION

There is much more evidence needed to establish a causal claim than to establish a mere correlation. Some of this evidence is statistical but other aspects of science are also involved. In the last chapter I reviewed some early studies that established a strong correlation between smoking and lung cancer. Many studies followed these early studies and the correlation between smoking and lung cancer became well-established; but, of course, that still left open the question of whether the relationship was one of cause and effect. As I have repeatedly noted: *the correlation of two things does not guarantee that they are causally related.* High-school grades are correlated with university grades, but they don't cause the university grades. Being overweight is a risk factor for a heart attack, but there are some doubts about whether the correlation between weight and the incidence of heart disease is in fact a causal link. Why? Because there could be a so-called **third cause** (or more intelligibly, common cause) that causes both weight and heart attacks such as lack of exercise. People who don't exercise may be both prone to weight gain and to heart attacks. Or perhaps some genetic tendency inclines people to gain weight and to have heart attacks, etc. Establishing a correlation is just the beginning of research into causes, far from the end point.

The question of whether smoking causes lung cancer was also complicated by the fact that smoking was implicated in a number of different diseases besides lung cancer, such as heart disease. In the nineteenth century medical science fought free of the view that something like a "miasma" or (my favourite) "cosmic-telluric changes"[1] could be the cause of many illnesses. At that time these vague general "causes" were invoked to explain a wide variety of illness. The move to the idea of *one disease—one cause* was a great scientific advance. But in the initial investigation of smoking the postulate actually caused confusion and controversy. That something was correlated with a number of diseases, as it appeared smoking was, suggested it was merely associated with these diseases and not a real cause.[2] To understand why this appeared likely, consider again the case of the association of coffee drinking with various illnesses. The explanation could well be that coffee drinkers consume other "drugs" that, unlike coffee, are in fact harmful. This wide range of associations could suggest to a researcher that coffee might be a "marker" for a certain kind of unhealthy lifestyle rather than a real cause. Of course contemporary researchers would never reject the possibility that perhaps coffee was a powerful agent with a variety of unhappy effects. If we suspected that the association with smoking and coffee drinking was the explanation, we could test the claim of coffee's deadly power by comparing the rate of illness among non-smoking coffee drinkers and non-smoking non-coffee drinkers. The current view is that many things can contribute to an illness, and a single thing can contribute to many illnesses. When several things contribute to an effect, none of them is, properly speaking, *the* cause; it's usual to speak of each of them as **causal factors**.

What more evidence is necessary if a researcher is to establish a causal relation based on a correlation? Basically evidence is needed that 1) the causal relationship makes scientific sense, and 2) there is no other explanation that can also account for the correlation.

Scientists test the first criterion (that a causal claim must make scientific sense) by seeing if:

---

1 "Miasma" is *bad air*. The name "malaria" ("mal" = bad) retains the idea that an airborne poisonous vapour or mist can cause disease. "Cosmic-telluric" changes were never very clearly defined. ("Telluric" just means *coming from the earth or its atmosphere*.) You can still find this idea in contemporary quack science: see <http://www.landspurg.com/html/en/o5.shtml>.

2 Stolley, p. 65.

1. There is an appropriate temporal relation—causes (in general) must precede their effects;
2. There is an appropriate dose relation—more cause/more effect;
3. There is an explanatory model consistent with the data;
4. The claim fits with other scientific understanding; and
5. The claim is consistent with relevant testing, for example, on animal models or in Petri dishes.

Let me explain how these criteria work to assess a causal claim.

TEMPORAL RELATIONSHIP

It seems obvious that a cause must precede its effect (though in some cases they do appear to be simultaneous); in any case, the idea of "reverse causality"—in which the effect precedes the cause—does not seem even to make sense. Sometimes the ordering is difficult to determine. Studies on hotel occupancy discovered that when occupancy was down so was spending on advertising. Which is the cause and which the effect? It could of course be a little bit of both and we would have to study the specifics regarding which preceded which to make any reasonable judgement on causality.

DOSE RELATIONSHIP

In medical research one of the most common tests for causality is to check whether there is an appropriate dose relationship—a correlation between the amount of exposure to a supposed cause and the frequency or intensity of the effect. Intuitively we expect that the more that you are exposed to a harmful substance, the more likely you are to suffer the consequences or the more intense the consequences will be. Scientists use this intuition when assessing causal claims and look for evidence that there is a positive correlation (or positive dose relationship) between increased exposure to the cause and increased incidence or severity of the illness. The scatter plot we saw above that related tobacco consumption to rates of lung cancer was a crucial part of the early evidence that smoking caused lung cancer. The graph was important because it showed a strong "dose" relationship between tobacco usage and lung cancer: the frequency of lung cancer in a country was greater when there was more smoking. These data made a good first case for

Graph 1

Correlation between Cigarette Consumption and Subsequent Rates of Lung Cancer for 10 Countries, 1930 - 1950

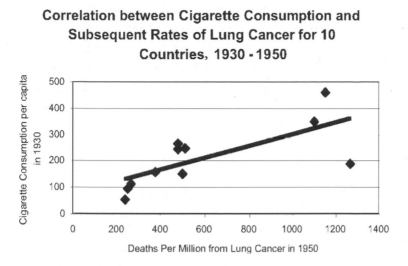

the causal relationship. Later, researchers were able to show not only that smokers had a higher incidence of lung cancer, but also that the more you smoked the more likely you were to get cancer. According to early research, at two packs a day your chance of getting lung cancer was 60 times greater than that of a non smoker versus 7-10 times greater for smokers generally.[1] This result gave additional support to the claim that smoking is a causal factor in lung cancer.

To understand how researchers established a dose relationship we need to move beyond simple categorical correlations. The dose relationship is just a kind of correlation, but one that involves using either continuous measures or at least more than two categories. By using categories such as people who smoke 1-10, 11-20, and 21 and above cigarettes a day, the researcher can group smokers into a number of categories and reveal whether there is a dose relationship that supports a causal claim. The more the correlation shows a strong dose relationship, the more the relationship looks plausibly causal. And of course the contrary is true. If the supposed cause and the illness do not show the typical dose relationship, we then have reason to doubt the causal claim.

An example of this was seen a few years ago when there was considerable controversy over whether exposure to the electrical fields surrounding high voltage power lines caused cancer. Even before

---

1   Jerome Cornfield et al., "Smoking and Lung Cancer: Recent Evidence and a Discussion of Some Questions," *Journal of the National Cancer Institute* 22, 1–6 (January/June 1959): 173–203.

extensive studies failed to find evidence for the causal claim, there was considerable scepticism in the scientific community because in the early experimental studies in which cells were exposed to electrical fields, cells appeared to be affected only at certain mid-range exposures. Higher and lower exposures appeared to have no effect. There appeared to be no proper dose relationship, which suggested a problem with the claim.[1]

EFFECT SIZE

Effect size is a concept related to the dose relationship. What effect size measures is the slope of the dose relationship. Note in Graph 1 above that the line connecting the points clearly slopes up indicating an increased incidence of lung cancer as consumption increases. Had that line been closer to level the effect of tobacco consumption on the incidence of lung cancer would have been much harder to detect and prove. If a relatively small increase in a causal factor yields a relatively large increase in illness (as in smoking and lung cancer), then the effect size is large. If on the contrary doubling a subject's exposure to a causal factor (as in second-hand smoke) only yields a small increase in the incidence of an illness among the exposed, then the effect size is small. Large effects are, of course, easier to detect than smaller ones and are less likely to be obscured or produced by confounding factors. Hence effect size is relevant for evaluating a causal claim and the identification of large effects provides strong evidence for a causal claim.

EXPLANATORY MODELS

As mentioned, we know that coffee drinking and lung cancer are correlated, and might even be dose related because it is likely that the more someone smokes the more coffee they drink. But even if coffee consumption exhibited a strong correlation and an appropriate dose relationship, we would be reluctant to believe the claim that coffee consumption causes lung cancer. Why? Because it does not make biological

---

1   <http://www.mcw.edu/gcrc/cop/powerlines-cancer-FAQ/toc.html#16> is a very detailed review of evidence on the effects of magnetic fields. It also nicely illustrates the complexity involved in assessing such claims.

sense. Unless you breathe your coffee instead of drinking it, it is difficult to see the link between coffee drinking and diseases of the lung. Various kinds of digestive-tract cancer would be plausible products of coffee consumption. But lung cancer? Of course the world is often a strange place and there could be some link, but at the moment any link between coffee and lung cancer is contrary to both common sense and medical understanding. Smoking on the other hand involves inhaling smoke into your lungs. That such an activity could cause trouble in the lungs is hardly surprising even if we don't know the exact process. So the smoking/lung cancer link has medical or scientific plausibility while the coffee link does not.

ANIMAL MODELS

A causal claim is strengthened if we have existing models that would explain the correlation, that is, if we have a biological and chemical account that would link the cause to the effect. Lacking such an account, scientists will often settle for evidence that the causal process in question can be demonstrated by experiments using animals. Since we can't usually experiment on humans to find the causes of illness, scientists use animals for their experiments. Such experiments are not without their own difficulties, including the moral issues surrounding animal experimentation. In addition, animal experiments depend on the assumption that the animal being used (often mice or rats) has the same bodily reactions as that of humans. Of course not all species, not even all mammals, have the same biological reactions as humans. This is hardly the place to go into all this, but it should be remembered that many theories about the cause of illness in humans are based in part on animal experiments. In the case of smoking, researchers were unable to get mice to smoke no matter how many Humphrey Bogart movies they made them watch, but they were able to show that painting the contents of smoke on their skin produced cancer. And while smoking as the cause of lung cancer made sense, we still do not have an adequate account of cancer generally—a point that was often emphasized by the tobacco lobby. What we do have is overwhelming evidence of the link between smoking and lung cancer (including dose relationship) and evidence that the various ingredients in tobacco cause cancer in animals.

We cannot assume that a theory or therapy is wrong simply because we don't have an adequate explanatory model. Consider acupuncture. For a long time acupuncture was dismissed by Western medicine because it did not fit with the medical paradigm of pain. The Chinese explanation of acupuncture's success was that the points of needle insertion were on paths in the body along which qi—a kind of vital energy—flowed. Western medicine has found no evidence of this sort of energy, and no basis in the large-scale or microscopic anatomy of the body for this energy flow. Nonetheless, there is some evidence that acupuncture is effective for some pain and, interestingly, for various kinds of medically induced nausea such as that caused by chemotherapy. Two different explanations that fit within Western medicine have also been offered: one in terms of the release of endorphins (the body's own pain killers) in the brain and the other the activation of a "gate" control system that blocks pain messages.[1]

ELIMINATING COMPETING EXPLANATIONS

Besides providing evidence of an appropriate correlation and a plausible explanation, researchers must show that there is no other plausible explanation that could also explain the correlation.

While this is good science, it is also common sense. When my small grandson was plagued by asthma and congestion, his mother (my daughter) took him to an allergist. The allergist identified many foods that were potential causal suspects. So my daughter eliminated one of these foods

---

1 <http://www.cancer.org/docroot/ETO/content/ETO_5_3X_Acupuncture. asp?sitearea=ETO> and also the somewhat dated "Acupuncture: NIH Consensus Statement," 1997. Accessed at <http://consensus.nih.gov/1997/1997Accupuncture107 html.htm>.

each week and then waited to see her son's reaction. If he did not improve she eliminated another suspect. Finally his congestion disappeared. Now the challenge was to carefully reintroduce foods earlier eliminated until, as it turned out, wheat was clearly (and fortunately not more than wheat) identified as the causal factor. While the problems tackled by science are often not so straightforward, the strategy is basically the same: find what goes with what, assess whether the correlation makes causal sense, and eliminate other possible explanations.

The existence of other possible explanations is often referred to as the problem of the confounding factor—a factor that could also explain the correlation in the study. A confounding factor is any factor (such as age, degree of illness, or some aspect of lifestyle) other than the cause in question that could be part of the explanation for the observed correlation. This factor then "confounds" the researchers' ability to attribute changes solely to the cause being tested. To prove that smoking causes cancer, the researchers needed to show that there was only one important relevant difference—smoking—between those who tended to get lung cancer and the rest of the population: other possible explanations needed to be ruled out (and were). Coffee drinking, while correlated with lung cancer, is not a cause but a confounding factor. The alternative explanation—that is, that coffee drinking is associated with smoking, but it is smoking that is the real cause—must be ruled out before we could conclude that coffee drinking was the cause of lung cancer. But of course it was not ruled out.

ELIMINATING COMPETING EXPLANATIONS: THE THIRD CAUSE PROBLEM

One of the main concerns researchers have in designing their studies is how to eliminate confounding factors. For example, in the case of smoking it was well-known that there was a higher incidence of lung cancer among urban compared to rural residents. In order to ensure that location was not a confounding factor, researchers had to "control" for "urbanity." This was done either by ensuring that the smoking and non-smoking groups had the same proportion of city and country dwellers, or by showing that the incidence of lung cancer was correlated with smoking in both the urban and rural sub-groups.

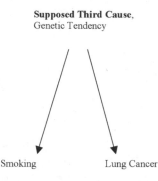

Supposed Third Cause,
Genetic Tendency

Smoking   Lung Cancer

A more speculative objection was raised by the renowned and cantankerous R.A. Fisher who was one of the greatest statisticians of the twentieth century. Fisher was also a smoker and received funding from the tobacco industry.[1] Fisher hypothesized that perhaps there was a genetic proclivity in people both to smoke and to get lung cancer. In which case smoking and lung cancer would be strongly correlated, but not causally related—such a genetic tendency could be a "third cause." A third cause is a cause that produces two different events in such a way that those events are correlated even though they have no direct causal link. Some scientists had a good deal of doubt about Fisher's hypothesis, even though a genetic susceptibility to other forms of cancer had been recognized, but this objection needed to be ruled out in order to show that smoking was the real cause. Fisher's objection was rejected on a number of grounds. For example, people who smoked but quit showed a lower incidence of lung cancer than those who kept smoking. If these people had a tendency to lung cancer and to smoking, but overcame their smoking urge, why the decline in lung-cancer rates? Also, the amount smoked is closely related to incidence of lung cancer. Why would this be true if smoking and lung cancer were the result of some genetic tendency?

It's important to eliminate alternative explanations. Responding to competing explanations is a key part of defending a causal claim. One of the most important research papers during the early days of the smoking controversy was the paper by Cornfield cited in footnote 1, p. 127. Its 30 pages of responses

---

1   D. Salsburg, *Lady Tasting Tea: How Statistics Revolutionized Science in the Twentieth Century* (Henry Holt & Co., 2001).

to the numerous objections of the tobacco industry and sceptical researchers marked a turning point in the debate. The best way to address the problem of confounding factors is to use an experimental approach which can be effective in eliminating them as possible causes.

Experimental Studies

In the previous chapter I reviewed the two different kinds of observational studies: prospective and retrospective. And as mentioned, both these types of studies run the risk of false results because of confounding factors. An alternative research method, the experimental approach, is the best way to control for confounding factors. In this approach, the researcher manipulates the causal factor being tested, so this method can refute hypotheses about confounding factors and provide evidence of a dose relationship. In experiments, the researcher has control of all the potential causal factors and can ensure that only one factor is at work. Mice exposed to smoke in an experiment do not also drink coffee and alcohol, work in asbestos plants, or hang out in polluted urban environments.

But there are still challenges. To avoid selection bias in an experimental study, the subjects (people or animals) must be *randomly* assigned to two different groups. These kinds of experiments are called Randomized Controlled Trials, often referred to with the acronym RCT. In an RCT, one group, the experimental group, is singled out to be exposed to the probable cause (or treatment). The other group, the control group, is not exposed, and is used for comparisons to see if there is a correlation.

To prove that smoking causes cancer, the researcher wants it to be clear that smoking is the only difference between the experimental and control group. Only experiments provide researchers with the kind of control that enables them to eliminate confounding factors. If smoking is the only difference between the experimental and control groups, then any observed differences in the lung-cancer rate between these groups can be attributed to smoking. Of course, it is ethically impossible to experimentally expose humans to harmful substances.

Just as random selection eliminates bias in polling, so does random assignment of subjects to one of the two groups eliminate (in theory anyway) the possibility of bias in the assignment of subjects to the two groups—ensuring that the experimental group and the control group are alike in every possible way (except for the supposed cause, which the researcher imposes on the experimental group only). Selection bias (e.g., putting more healthy people in the control group) would be a confounding factor. We don't want experimenters accidentally (or worse yet intentionally) deciding who, for example, should get the new treatment, and putting the healthier looking people in the experimental group. Subject selection is not the only source of bias; there is also the problem of bias involved in assessing outcomes. The assessment of who got better or worse in a drug trial, for example, and by how much, could easily be biased if the subject or the researcher knew who was in the experimental group and getting the treatment. Both the subject and the experimenter could easily be biased by this information. It's possible that researchers hoping for good results will exaggerate or fake them in an experiment, perhaps only unconsciously; experimental human subjects can imagine, or even experience, good results if they believe they are being treated by an effective drug. For all these reasons the ideal drug experiment is one in which neither the researcher nor the patient knows who is getting the actual treatment. Such a study is called a double blind study, referring to the "blindness" of both the subject and the researchers not knowing who was actually given the active ingredient.

LIMITS OF EXPERIMENTAL STUDIES

Good as they are, even experiments have their problems. For some experiments—for example those involving an obvious treatment, such as surgery—it may be impossible to "blind" anyone from knowing who is getting the real treatment. Furthermore, while random selection into the experimental and control groups eliminates some selection bias, there is still the problem that usually the initial selection of the total pool of subjects from which the two groups are to be randomly chosen is not itself random.

Recruits for experiments on humans are often collected by advertising, or from a sample of convenience like students or patients. The college students in a psychology study who are "randomly assigned" to control and experimental groups are not randomly chosen from the population of human beings! Remember that in order to make a mathematical inference from the experiment to the intended target population, the recruits for the experiment ought to be randomly selected from this target population. Random assignment of the recruits to the experimental and control groups does not address this problem.

A number of human studies are done using patients in large training hospitals; these hospitals are often located in depressed urban areas, with a disproportionately large fraction of patients from poor and ethnic groups, who may differ significantly from other segments of the country's population. Many early studies on the treatment of heart disease involved only men. Even if the men were randomly assigned to experimental and control groups, we would still not know if the results were applicable to women. In addition, certain sorts of subjects may drop out of the experiment, thus biasing the whole group; dropouts might also reduce the sample size, rendering the results statistically insignificant. So even the ideal of the randomized controlled trial has limitations.

Experiments can also have limited value because they are so far removed from what is really the phenomenon of interest. Psychology experiments in the lab create an artificial and controlled environment, and this is a useful way to keep confounding factors under control, but it is difficult in many cases to know how to relate the experimental results to actual behaviour outside the lab, and the question arises how much one can generalize from the experimental results. Studies done in the "real world" may produce different results—either because confounding factors are at work in the outside-world experiment, or because the peculiar biases and extraneous factors introduced by the lab setting are not present. Here's an example. It is easy to see why a study of people's "personal-space needs" (how close people can get to us before we are uncomfortable) done in the lab would yield different results if it were done on people walking down the streets of New York City.[1] Or imagine the difficulty of studying ecosystems. Even if it were possible to study artificial ecosystems built in a lab, this would be quite different from studying them in the wild; the results of such experiments would have to be tested with studies in less artificial environments.

Few studies of the cause of illnesses can be experimental for the obvious reason that it is seldom ethical to randomly assign people to be exposed to a suspected cause of illness. Studies of social and psychological phenomena also face the same problem in that subjects cannot be randomly assigned: how could you, for example, conduct an experiment to see what happens to children who grow up in a one-parent family? We are left with observational studies in which people "select in" to the "experimental" group through lifestyle or other factors, and the problem here is not so much experimenter bias as the possibility of confounding factors (remember the example of smoking and coffee). Consider a common kind of study that correlates people's physical activity and their survival rate. Not surprisingly such studies usually find a correlation between exercise and longevity, but is this a causal relation? Age

1   J. Katzer, et al., *Evaluating Information*, 4th ed. (McGraw-Hill, 1998), 208-15.

is of course just one of the large number of possible confounding factors. Unless the active and inactive groups are identical in age distribution, the possibility exists that the positive correlation between exercise and longevity is due to the fact that those who exercise more tend to be younger, and younger people tend to have a lower mortality rate. And what do couch potatoes eat? Not lots of broccoli, I bet.

THE PLACEBO EFFECT

The **placebo effect** presents a challenge to any testing of humans. The placebo effect occurs when people receiving any sort of treatment—medication or therapy—that they believe is effective tend to improve, even if the treatment is completely ineffective. While this effect is poorly understood by science it is usually thought to be very common—sometimes a quarter or a third of patients receiving a placebo have reported significant improvement.[1] So one cannot test a treatment by simply giving it to the experimental group and doing nothing to the control group, because any relative improvement in the experimental group might be wholly due to the placebo effect. Experimental studies, then, sometimes use three (double-blind) groups: one receiving the treatment being tested, a second receiving no treatment, and a third getting a placebo. The treatment being tested must show a "statistically significant" improvement not only over spontaneous improvement, but also over any possible placebo effect. Recent research has called the effect into question, but still the ideal of studies is that they be double blind so that any effects resulting from the beliefs of either the patient or doctor can be discounted.

SUMMARY

Support for a causal claim should include evidence that:

1. There is a well established correlation;
2. The cause occurs before the effect;

---

1   But some articles question the existence of the placebo effect. See, for example, A. Hrobjartsson and P. Gotzsche, "Is the Placebo Powerless? Update of a Systematic Review with 52 New Randomized Trials Comparing Placebo with No Treatment," *J Intern Med.* 256 (2004): 91–100. Accessed at <http://www.blackwell-synergy.com/doi/pdf/10.1111/j.1365-2796.2004.01355.x?cookieSet=1>.

3. There is a credible explanatory model that links the cause and effect;
4. There is an appropriate dose relationship; and
5. Other competing explanations (confounding factors) have been eliminated.

The ideal method for establishing a causal relationship is the randomized, double-blind experiment because such an experimental approach can eliminate all explanatory factors except the cause being tested. But even controlled experiments have problems with selection bias, limited basis for generalizing, subtle confounding factors, researcher bias, size, statistical anomalies, and just plain errors. Because of these considerations, usually no single experiment is conclusive. Establishing most claims requires repeated testing and peer review. This process is discussed in the next chapter.

Evaluating Causal Research

The Critical Questions

1. What does a causal claim mean?
That an event or treatment or condition is not merely correlated with another, but actually contributes to or produces it.

2. How good is the evidence?
    a. Correlation. Is there good evidence of a correlation between cause and effect (and remember this requires appropriate comparisons)? Were appropriate groups compared or was there bias in sample selection? Statistical significance is the minimal test, but the stronger the correlation the more likely the relationship is *humanly or clinically* important.

    b. Cause precedes effect. With various correlational studies such as cohort studies it is often difficult to make sure that the cause is really occurring before the effect. E.g., whether watching TV violence is the cause or effect of a violent personality.

    c. Fit and Models. Does the cause fit in with our existing understanding? Is there is a causal model or account that provides the links between the cause and its effect?

    d. Dose relationship. Is there a "dose relationship" between the cause and its effect showing that increased exposure results in increased incidence or severity?

    e. Elimination of competing explanations. Showing that other explanations cannot account for the research results is crucial for making a credible claim. *Competing explanations* can range from measurement error and researcher bias to failure to control for *confounding factors*.

        i. Bias. The possibility of bias should be addressed through controls such as double blinding.

        ii. Confounding factors. In all non-experimental studies there is always the possibility that other factors are causally responsible for the studied correlation. Researchers must make credible efforts to control for confounding factors and justify their claim that the studied factor is the appropriate causal explanation.

3. What other information is relevant? What is the context?
The role of context will be addressed in the next chapter. But the key questions are about the direction of other research results and whether the researcher has addressed the onus created by previous research.

4. Fallacies
Post Hoc Ergo Propter Hoc. Has the author simply gone from a correlation or even coincidence to a causal claim without meeting the criteria in #2?

CHAPTER 10

EVALUATING SCIENTIFIC CLAIMS: LOOKING AT THE CONTEXT

In the previous chapter I reviewed the criteria for establishing a causal claim and the processes that researchers use in attempting to prove that a factor like smoking is a cause of cancer. I indicated that the ideal method for establishing such a claim is a genuine experiment where all the confounding factors can be controlled. But often when studying living creatures from bugs to humans, fully controlled experiments are either not possible, not ethical, or of doubtful relevance. For the variety of reasons reviewed before, we should not take the results of any individual study as sufficient evidence to establish a causal claim.

There is a widely quoted study[1] that illustrates the difficulties of experiments with human beings. In a randomized controlled double-blind experiment of the cholesterol-reducing drug clofibrate, 20% of the experimental group and 21% of the control group died, so it appeared clofibrate made no difference. However, many of the clofibrate group failed to take their medicine. Researchers call this the problem of *compliance*. When researchers looked at the clofibrate group according to whether subjects complied, i.e., took the drug or not, they found 15% of those who took the drug died, but 25% of the non-drug takers died. This appears to show that clofibrate is indeed effective. However the study was now confounded by the self-selection of the subjects. So the researchers looked at the placebo group and discovered that in this group 15% of those who took the placebo died, but 28% of those who did not comply (i.e., did not take the placebo) died. What the researchers had discovered is that there is a fundamental

---

1   "Influence of Adherence to Treatment and Response of Cholesterol on Mortality in the Coronary Drug Project," *N Engl J Med.* 303, 18 (Oct. 30, 1980): 1038–41, accessed at <http://www.ncbi.nlm.nih.gov/pubmed/6999345?dopt=Abstract> and Charles H. Hennekens, Julie E. Buring, Sherry L. Mayrent, *Epidemiology in Medicine* (Lippincott Williams & Wilkins, 1987), 206-07.

difference between those who comply and those who don't. This does not mean that taking a pill is good for you; what is more likely is that being "compliant" is associated generally with taking better care of yourself.

The example illustrates that there is often a possibility of error of one kind or another in experiments, as in any study. It is very rare in sciences that any one study is taken to conclusively establish a claim. Most causal claims are established through a process of numerous experiments and studies, each subject to appropriate critical review. This chapter will discuss this process, which is as central to the scientific method as the controlled experiment. Understanding the evaluation process used by science can help laypersons make their own assessments of the research supporting a causal claim.

As we saw with the smoking and lung-cancer example, evaluating causal claims is most appropriately done by evaluating not just one study, but rather the sum and direction of current research. Researchers defending a causal claim do not merely produce a study or experiment; they study research done already, do a series of tests, and respond to the critical remarks of reviewers. One of the most important research papers during the early days of the smoking controversy was the review paper by Cornfield et al. already mentioned in Chapter 8.[1] Much of its substance was devoted to responding to the numerous objections by the tobacco industry and sceptical researchers. Cornfield's review showed that while one could raise objections to any particular study, there was no systematic failure in the studies or experiments that would support rejecting the causal link between smoking and lung cancer. His paper marked a turning point in the controversy about the link between smoking and lung cancer.

Studying the way causal claims are actually established in science means that laypeople trying to find out the latest scientific information must look beyond any individual study to the general direction of research and the views of the greater scientific community. Such an approach is built into the third critical question.

---

1   J. Cornfield, W. Haenszel, E.C. Hammond, A.M. Lilienfield, M.B. Shimkin, and E.L. Wynder, "Smoking and Lung Cancer: Recent Evidence and a Discussion of Some 'Questions,'" *J Natl Cancer Inst.* 1 (Jan. 22, 1959): 173–203.

WHAT OTHER INFORMATION IS RELEVANT?

How Does the Claim Fit with Existing Scientific Research?: Peer Review, Convergence and Quality of Evidence

PEER REVIEW

The preliminary control that science uses to ensure credibility of reported research is subjecting research to **peer review**. This is the process in which experts in the field (the researchers' "peers") examine and evaluate new research. In practice, this is usually done under the auspices of the journal to which the researchers have sent an article giving details of the procedures and conclusion of their research.

While far from a perfect system, the scientific tradition of subjecting studies to peer review is the main way that scientists weed out poorly done studies, and give credit to work well done. Science is a very human enterprise, and it needs the oversight of peer review in assessing causal claims and controlling for experimenter error and bias. And sadly, bias is an ongoing problem, especially in certain fields. For example, recently there have been a number of books and scandals that have called into question the ability of peer-reviewed journals to control the unfortunate influence of studies being funded by drug companies.[1] This sort of prejudicial bias is discussed later on in this chapter.

CONVERGENCE AND REPLICATION

Especially if research comes up with conclusions that are surprising or controversial, it must pass not only the test of peer scrutiny, but also of **replication**. This can involve re-doing an experiment or study, or doing similar studies under slightly different conditions. Because there are so many ways that an experiment or study can go wrong (e.g., selection bias, measurement error, confounding factors, experimenter bias, or just plain statistical anomaly), replication is essential before a novel claim can be credited. Many experiments are themselves forms of either replications of previous experiments or tests of implications of accepted theories.

An interesting example of how multiple experiments are usually required

---

1   Frank Davidoff, MD, et al., "Scholarship, Authorship, and Accountability," *Journal of the American Medical Association* 286 (September 12, 2001), 1232-34. See also Cynthia Crossen, *Tainted Truth: The Manipulation of Fact in America* (Simon & Schuster, 1994).

to establish a claim is illustrated by the supposed "Mozart Effect." A few years ago researchers claimed to have discovered that students who listened to Mozart before taking certain kinds of tests performed better on the tests than those who had not listened to Mozart. The experiment produced "statistically significant" results. The findings were surprising and immediately caught the eye of the media; they were attractive to classical music enthusiasts and seemed to provide a defence of music programs constantly under attack in the schools. Unfortunately, subsequent experiments did not confirm the claim, and a careful review of the data showed only the most limited, short-term effects on certain spatial reasoning tests—effects that also appeared when using stimulation other than Mozart.[1]

This story illustrates again that causal claims cannot be established by one successful experiment even if the results are "statistically significant." As we saw in the early smoking studies, researchers may not know, or think to control for, factors that later turn out to be relevant. Or the results may just be a statistical anomaly. The difficulty of identifying possible confounding factors is one important reason why claims, especially novel claims, must be subject to replication. Experiments take time and money and so the scientific community is usually judicious in choosing claims to re-test. But if an experiment appears to establish a novel or surprising claim, or a claim inconsistent with existing models and understanding, then it is likely to be subject to subsequent testing and sceptical examination in review comments. If such a claim weathers testing by other researchers, we have increasingly good reason to believe the claim in question is credible. The process by which successful theories are supported by numerous studies is often called **convergence**.

For example, as we know, the claim that smoking causes lung cancer was supported by a variety of retrospective studies and a number of large prospective studies. Studies done in different countries using different sample selection processes also showed similar results—adding weight to the smoking argument. There was also striking evidence of a correlation (shown in the graph in Chapter 9) between the incidence of lung-cancer in a country and the amount of tobacco consumed. This latter information was helpful because it was based on *objective* measures of lung-cancer **prevalence** and tobacco consumption, not merely on people's reports of their smoking behaviour commonly used in early studies. It was also international, eliminating the possibility that the increase in lung cancer had causes linked to locality.

Consistent results from cohort studies that follow different groups of

---

1   C.F. Chabris, "Prelude or Requiem for the 'Mozart Effect'?" *Nature* 400 (1999): 826-27. See also <http://www.hno.harvard.edu/gazette/1999/09.16/mozart.html>.

people over considerable time reduce the possibility of confounding, and add weight to a causal claim. On the other hand, if researchers studying a claim are unable to reliably replicate original results, as in the Mozart case or the scandalous case of cold fusion (discussed below), then most scientists conclude the claim in question is not credible.

STUDY QUALITY

The type of study done is also important. As we know prospective large-size cohort studies are better than case-controlled retrospective studies. Experimental studies of an appropriate size are usually even better. Often experimental studies are given so much more weight that they can overturn a history of observational studies. For example, notice in the following editorial from the *Archives of Internal Medicine* that experimental results are taken to *override* previous results from observational studies:

> *Observational* evidence suggests that diets rich in antioxidants may protect against risk of cardiovascular disease, but results from trials have generally been disappointing. The Women's Antioxidant Cardiovascular Study (WACS) examined the effects of vitamins C and E and beta carotene, as well as their combinations, in a *randomized factorial trial* among women at increased risk of vascular events. There were no significant effects on the primary end point of total cardiovascular disease, suggesting that widespread use of these agents for cardiovascular disease prevention does not appear warranted. (my italics)[1]

While we look for scientific consensus and converging research, we need to keep in mind the unavoidable limitations of observation studies and the weight that should be given to more reliable modes of inquiry.

BEWARE OF NEWS

Because peer review and convergence are so important to establishing the credibility of a claim, the claims that emerge from new studies, especially

---

1 *Arch Intern Med* 167 (2007): 1570, accessed at <http://archinte.ama-assn.org/cgi/content/full/167/15/1570> August 24, 2007.

144 IS THAT A FACT?

"preliminary" or initial studies are seldom worthy of any real confidence. When reading newspaper reports of research, especially health research, it is very wise to keep in mind that what makes research news is namely, its *newness*. If the study is *news* then it almost certainly hasn't received the kind of critical scrutiny of peer review and replication that adds weight to its credibility. Initial studies often suffer from being retrospective (since that's where most research begins), small scale (either short duration or small groups), and based on samples of convenience. Sometimes they are based on a study not of humans, but only a few mice! While these characteristics are not true of every new "discovery" reported, it is a good idea to check such reports for sample size and method before giving them any credence. Most scientists reporting on these kinds of results will admit that the "results are preliminary," though this point may not be emphasized by reporters.[1]

A reporter's interest in novelty is often coincident with a researcher's need for publicity. Research costs money and large-scale research costs a lot of money. Scientists testing new claims seldom have access to the kind of funds necessary for large-scale studies. Hence the natural progression in research is from small-scale studies, often retrospective with samples of convenience, to prospective studies of increasing size and duration. Good publicity does not hurt one in the search for research funds. Hence both scientists and news reporters share a common interest in publicizing and perhaps overstating initial results. Reader beware!

A classic case of a causal claim that generated immense publicity but failed to be proven was the famous case of "cold fusion." In 1989, a couple of scientists reported finding a way to unlock the enormous power of nuclear fusion (what's responsible for the energy of the sun and the explosive power of the H-bomb) at everyday temperatures and pressures. Their experimental results were not published in a scientific journal—this would have subjected them to peer review—but were leaked to the media. To make matters worse, there was no explanatory model of how cold fusion could work and no "fit" with the work of other scientists who were attempting to develop fusion as an energy source. While the newspapers played up the news, the scientific community was almost uniformly sceptical and in many cases hostile, because of the improbability of the results and the deviant process through which they were revealed. Subsequent failure of anyone to replicate the results confirmed the

---

1   Marcia Angell and Jerome P Kassirer, "Clinical Research—What Should the Public Believe?" *N Engl J Med* 331, 3 (1994): 189-190; also Gary Taubes, "Epidemiology Faces it Limits," *Science*, 269, 5221 (Jul. 14, 1995): 164-65, 167-69, accessed at <http://www.jstor.org.proxy.lib.sfu.ca/stable/2888429>.

suspicion of the scientific community that the appearance of energy production was probably a problem with the experimental apparatus.

CONFLICTING EVIDENCE

While a uniform failure to replicate an experimental finding is quite damning, conflicting results are more common and require a more judicious assessment. There are seldom uniform results when studying the complexities of the biological and social world. This is why convergence, rather than unanimity or consensus, is the rule for much scientific activity. Because science is often taught at the introductory level as if there is one right answer that all scientists agree on, many non-scientists take the existence of conflicting scientific results as a kind of refutation of a claim or theory. While there are areas of solid scientific consensus (for example, in most of what students learn in first-year science classes), complete consensus is not very common in science in general. *Just because there is some conflicting evidence does not mean that the claim should be rejected.* The cutting edge of all scientific investigations is usually characterized by some disagreement and intellectual conflict. Even in areas of well-established theories there are usually anomalies and experiments that have yielded conflicting results. Given the difficulties of studying complex phenomena, this should not surprise us. Nor should it be the sole basis for rejecting a theory. If there is a reasonable and enduring convergence of results then we have a good basis for believing the theory; in cases where there is more conflict, a different approach is required.

We are all aware of the ongoing conflict about diet and nutrition despite an enormous amount of research. We've explored some reasons why studying people's health and their eating habits is formidably complex, involving many confounding factors. Isolating the influence of particular foods on health is a very difficult task, necessitating separating that influence from other aspects of lifestyle and genetics, and controlling for poor memory or outright lying.

The social sciences generally face this sort of complexity. Experimental study is usually impossible for the activities researchers wish to study, and cohort studies of people in everyday life are fraught with confounding factors. In addition, many of the issues being studied, such as the influence of poverty on crime or health, are of great political significance, so there's a strong political interest in findings, and this sometimes interferes with good science and produces extra friction.

In many social sciences the conflict is institutionalized into "schools" whose views are in fundamental conflict and are unlikely to show convergence in the near future. The Marxist school of economics is unlikely to "converge" with the school of free-market economists. It is unlikely that socio-biologists will come to agree with developmental psychologists. This is not to say that there is no progress in the social sciences. Many approaches to psychology, such as phrenology (the study of the bumps on one's head on the theory that they somehow reveal a person's psychological traits), have disappeared, and others, such as behaviourism (the theory that insisted that all there is to study is observable external behaviour), have had their range of appropriate application reduced. And as we learn more about the workings of the brain, neuroscience may resolve some long-standing disputes in psychology.

The layperson's best strategy when faced with scientific controversy is to withhold judgement. But such a strategy is not always possible. Decisions must be made, and should be based, as much as possible, on the best evidence one has. In these situations of significant scientific controversy the layperson is forced to make judgements between competing theories. In those cases where there is no convergence, the layperson must "weigh the evidence."

THE WEIGHT OF EVIDENCE

The shift from convergence to weight of evidence as our test for credibility can be compared to the difference between making a judgement in criminal cases versus civil cases. When trying criminal cases, the courts require that a guilty verdict must meet the test of "beyond a reasonable doubt." An accused should not be found guilty as long as one can reasonably doubt that the accused did the crime. That an accused is "likely guilty" or very probably guilty is not adequate. In contrast, in non-criminal cases (for example, where someone is suing for damages), the plaintiff or person suing does not have to prove his or her claim "beyond a reasonable doubt." Here, plaintiffs have to prove their cases "on the balance of probabilities." This means that plaintiffs have to prove only that it is more likely than not that their cases are justified. If the "beyond a reasonable doubt" test can be compared to being 99% sure, the "balance probabilities" only requires that we be 51% confident. Such a judgement involves weighing the evidence for or against and deciding whether the weight of the evidence favours one side over the other. And such decisions are inherently less certain than those passing the much tougher test.

So what are the criteria for evaluating a claim supported by scientific research? Before reviewing the criteria that we should employ in assessing the evidence for a causal claim, I need to make a couple of general observations. As you learned above, observational studies, especially retrospective ones, are plagued by numerous problems including subject memories and the difficulty of ensuring that control groups have been appropriately selected. All such studies are also open to researcher bias since the researcher cannot do the research "blind." A claim should be given weight proportional to the number of studies that support it and relative to the credibility of the explanation for the effect. In particular, we should be highly sceptical of any claim that is "news." New findings, not supported by extensive research, and for which there is no credible physical explanation should be given no weight. For example, the recent claim that wireless routers cause health problems should be treated with enormous scepticism as there are neither supporting studies nor a plausible explanation of how such weak radio waves could have any effect.

DETAILED CRITERIA FOR ASSESSMENT OF AGGREGATE EVIDENCE FOR A CAUSAL CLAIM

The strongest evidence for a causal claim is from experiments because experiments provide the best opportunity to control against confounding factors. But experimental studies also need to be evaluated.

How should we "weigh" the evidence?

There are numerous considerations involved in evaluating evidence from experimental studies. (Note: several of the conditions below apply only to experimental studies of effects on humans.)

1. Experiments should be double blinded (neither experimenter nor subject knows who is in the control group and who is in the experimental group).
2. Assignments of subjects should be randomized.
3. Experiments on humans have more weight than animal experiments.
4. Experiments involving larger numbers are more credible.
5. All things being equal, the larger the effect the more credible the causal inference (see Chapter 9, "Effect Size").
6. A variety of experiments involving volunteers from different groups adds weight to the evidence.
7. Consistent results from experiments add considerable weight; conflicting results weaken the basis of convergence unless they are explicable.

8. The more the experiment is a good representative of real world conditions, the more credible the evidence.
9. Generally, the longer the duration of the experiment the better. Not only do repeated experiments with similar outcomes add to the credibility of a claim, but so do more prolonged experiments. For example, when attempting to establish whether a drug is safe, obviously longer experiments are more likely to detect side effects than shorter ones. The recent scandal surrounding Vioxx[1] resulted from limiting the duration from which experimental data was reported to obscure the increased risk of heart attack associated with the drug's use.[2]
10. The experimental results should have a plausible scientific explanation.
11. Where appropriate, the results should reveal a dose relationship.

But since many issues of interest cannot be subject to experimental testing, we need also to make good use of observational studies.

Considerations involved in evaluating observational studies include:

1. Prospective studies (cohort) are generally better than retrospective (case control) studies, but a variety of studies with more or less consistent results adds strength to a claim.
2. A conclusion gets more strength when it (or something close to it) is arrived at by a number of studies—when studies are convergent—especially when they involve different methods and test groups.
3. Studies involving larger numbers are more credible.
4. The quality of the effort to control for obvious confounding factors adds significant weight.
5. All things being equal, the larger the effect the more credible the causal inference. But because observational studies are far more likely to suffer from confounding and bias, many studies are required to support a causal claim that only reveals a small effect. Because of the difficulties involved in observational studies, many epidemiologists recommend giving little

1 Vioxx was a widely touted drug for chronic pain relief that was supposed to be safer than other pain killers used for chronic pain. The Vioxx scandal involved the drug company Merck reporting only a part of the trial. The latter part of the trial showed that Vioxx caused heart problems. By only reporting the early part of the study, the company misled the US Food and Drug Administration.
2 Harlan M. Krumholz, et al., "What Have We Learnt from Vioxx?," *BMJ* 334, 7585 (2007): 120-23.

weight to evidence that does not support a three-to four-fold increased risk.[1]

6. A plausible causal explanation for the results adds weight.
7. Evidence of a dose relationship supports a causal relationship.
8. Generally, the longer the duration of the study the better.

SIMPLIFIED SUMMARY

- Experiments are more credible than observational studies
- Prospective is more credible than retrospective
- Bigger is better
- Longer is better
- More variety of studies is better
- Larger effects are more credible

"Small," "brief," and "few" are all good grounds for scepticism.

The following table provides a way of using the criteria above to make a judgement based on the weight of evidence.[2]

Four-Level Hierarchy for Classifying the Strength of Causal Inferences Based on Available Evidence		
	Judgement	**Evidence Quality**
Strongly Positive	Evidence is **sufficient** to infer a causal relationship.	Extensive studies with appropriate size, duration, and variety, including large prospective studies and if possible experimental studies. A convergence of study results. A credible causal explanation. Large effects or extensive evidence for reported small effect.
Weakly Positive	Evidence is **suggestive but not sufficient** to infer a causal relationship.	Significant evidence of correlations from credible studies with at least some prospective studies. Some experimental evidence if possible. Smaller size and fewer studies than above. Credible causal explanation.

1   See footnote 1, p. 144. Taubes, p. 269.
2   The table categories are from "The Health Consequences of Involuntary Exposure to Tobacco Smoke: A Report of the Surgeon General, US Department of Health and Human Services," accessed at <http://www.surgeongeneral.gov/library/secondhandsmoke>. But the criteria are ones that I have developed.

Inconclusive	Evidence is **inadequate** to infer the presence or absence of a causal relationship.	Evidence is sparse, of poor quality, or conflicting. Credible causal explanation may be lacking.
Negative	Evidence is **suggestive of no causal relationship**.	Extensive studies have failed to reveal a consistent correlation. The causal relationship seems implausible in view of current understanding.

We will show how to use these criteria in the next chapter when we apply them to evaluating the evidence for the claims that second-hand smoke causes lung cancer and cellphone use causes brain cancer. But use of these criteria should not result in a total scepticism about scientific research. Evaluating a scientific theory requires assessing all the evidence and weighing the exceptions and problems against the preponderance of evidence. Some scepticism is healthy and unbiased, but *we should be wary of a scepticism that is really an excuse to avoid any change in one's position*. In assessing the evidence we need not only attend to the prejudicial biases of researchers, but our own biases as well. The manifestly biased attacks on global climate-change research are a current example of how scepticism can be used to serve a bias rather than exemplify thoughtful intellectual scrutiny.

MANUFACTURED DOUBT

Manufactured doubt is an even more disturbing form of prejudicial bias which shows up in current debates regarding high-stake issues with financially powerful interests. This strategy showed up importantly in the debates around smoking and lung cancer. Tobacco companies financed research by scientists who expressed doubt about the tobacco/lung-cancer link. In some cases, tobacco company lawyers rewrote supposedly scientific papers.[1] The history of the tobacco debate is well documented; court cases revealed the way that tobacco companies attempted to influence public opinion and the government through promotion of the idea that the claim that cigarette smoking causes cancer was scientifically undecided.

---

1   S.A. Glantz, et al., *The Cigarette Papers* (Berkeley: The University of California Press, 1996). See also Stanton A. Glantz and Edith D. Balbach, *Tobacco War: Inside the California Battles* (Berkeley: The University of California Press, 2000) accessed at <http://www.escholarship.org/editions/view?docId=ft167nbovq&brand=ucpress>.

Interestingly, one of the leading scientists who was heavily funded by the tobacco industry in the 1960s has now reappeared spreading doubt about the claim that human generated greenhouse gases are causing global warming. Dr. Frederick Seitz, former president of the National Academy of Science and president of Rockefeller University, made $585,000 consulting for R.J. Reynolds and was actively involved in the opposition to the thesis that global warming was caused by human activities. Of course, pointing out that someone is funded by those who stand to gain by a certain position does not prove their argument is wrong. To make such a claim would be to commit the *ad hominem* fallacy. But a track record of such funding is grounds for questioning someone's credibility.

We've said the studies about climate change are inconclusive. But how are we going to explain the fact that Miami is now submerged?

While the global-warming debate is quite complex, nevertheless there is significant convergence in the scientific community that provides strong evidence for humans being the primary cause of global warming. In fact one of the stunning aspects of the study of climate change is the degree of consensus—an impression that you do not get from the popular press. In a 2004 study, Naomi Oreskes of the University of California, San Diego analyzed

> ... 928 abstracts, published in refereed scientific journals between 1993 and 2003, and listed in the ISI database with the keywords "climate change."
>
> The 928 papers were divided into six categories: explicit endorsement of the consensus position, evaluation of impacts, mitigation proposals, methods, paleoclimate analysis, and rejection of the con-

sensus position. Of all the papers, 75% fell into the first three categories, either explicitly or implicitly accepting the consensus view; 25% dealt with methods or paleoclimate, taking no position on current anthropogenic climate change. Remarkably, *none of the papers disagreed with the consensus position.* (my italics)[1]

Assessing the voluminous research about climate change is daunting to the layperson. Looking at its critics, their theories, and their associations can provide an additional basis for the layperson to evaluate their criticism. Look again at Seitz. Seitz is currently head of a right-wing think tank called the George C. Marshall Institute. He is also responsible for a notorious petition circulated supposedly signed by some 17,000 scientists who "oppose" the thesis that humans are the primary cause of global warming. Strangely the list of names does not list the institutional affiliation of the scientists making it hard to check. The letter sent to scientists inviting them to sign the petition was printed to look like a product of the American Association of Science.[2] It all looks a bit tawdry and suspicious. Nor, crucially, do the critics have a credible alternative explanation (other than that the change is "natural") to account for the manifest warming of the planet. So even when there are critics of a view and there *seems* to be a lack of expert consensus (though in the case of global climate change this was a fabricated appearance of non-consensus), a bit of effort by the layperson can usually uncover reasons to credit one view over another.

A complex area of investigation that is characterized by conflicting studies and a lack of consensus concerns the danger of "passive smoking." As you can imagine this is an area of sustained scientific controversy in part because of competing economic and political interests, but also because of the difficulty in getting conclusive evidence of the connection between exposure to second-hand smoke and lung cancer. Nonetheless, a citizen and smoker must make a reasonable decision based on the weight of evidence. We will look at how to do that in the next chapter.

---

1   Naomi Oreskes, "Beyond the Ivory Tower: The Scientific Consensus on Climate Change," *Science* 306, 5702 (2004): 1686.

2   *The Guardian*, September 19, 2006, accessed at <http://72.14.253.104/search?q=cache:VSd74af465EJ:environment.guardian.co.uk/climatechange/story/0,,1875762,00.html+Seitz+petition+global+warming&hl=en&ct=clnk&cd=4&lr=lang_en> February 15, 2007.

Critical Question 4: Are Relevant Fallacies Avoided?

When looking at the big picture, we must check, as we do with individual experiments, that the research has established more than a "mere" association or correlation. Basing a causal claim on evidence of a correlation alone commits that most renowned and common fallacy in causal reasoning, the post hoc ergo propter hoc fallacy. As you may remember, this fallacy involves leaping from a correlation to a causal claim without meeting the criteria for substantiating a causal claim, in particular, ignoring the need for a credible explanation and eliminating other competing explanations. Failure to meet most of the other criteria identified above and in Chapter 9 (e.g., convergence of results) weakens the support for a claim, but does not make the reasoning fallacious.

While evidence of convergence is the primary basis on which a layperson can assess the validity of most causal claims, we should remember that scientists are human. What looks like an emerging consensus based on evidence may just be a result of what might be called the fallacy of **"bandwagoning"**—everyone getting on the bandwagon. This is a familiar phenomenon in human social life and we cannot assume that science is immune to this tendency. The best way for a layperson to detect bandwagoning is to look at the counter claims and studies. Is the counter evidence characterized by bias (see *Manufactured Doubt* section above), as was the objections of the scientists hired by tobacco companies to counter the claim that smoking caused lung cancer? Or does the research seem to be the careful work of unbiased and independent minds? Are the results of the sceptics based on reasonable doubt or large enough studies to give weight to their side, etc.? Is the topic one in which there is a lot of political investment (for example, the issue of global warming), making bias more likely on both sides? These will not be easy calls. Because science is a dependable system, the best strategy is usually to trust scientific convergence unless we have good reason to be suspicious. That does not mean that scientific convergence is always right; it is just our best bet under most circumstances. In those areas of research where there is wide disagreement, there is often little that the layperson can do except wait for a more settled view to emerge.

Another very common fallacy to watch out for in funded research is **prejudicial funding bias**. Funding bias can affect research in a variety of ways: for example, in selection of subjects, skewing of data, or publication of only favourable results. The requirement that studies use random selection and a double blind procedure where possible is meant to control for both intentional and unintentional bias. But even such experiments can be infected with bias if the data is not reported accurately or fully. Recent reports of researchers arbitrarily cutting off the end date of their data in order to put the drugs they are evaluating in a good light is a demonstration of how bias can result in data being manipulated.[1]

EXAMPLE

A recent headline in my local paper illustrates two of these fallacies: *"Public Auto Insurance Causes More Deaths and Damage According to New Study."* Public insurance *causes* deaths? Improbable on the face of it, but who knows? Sceptically, I went to the Web for the source of the information.

1   Thomas Bodenheimer, "Uneasy Alliance—Clinical Investigators and the Pharmaceutical Industry," *N Engl J Med* 342 (2000): 1539-44; also see R. Horton, "Vioxx, the Implosion of Merck, and Aftershocks at the FDA," *Lancet* 364 (2004): 1995-96; A.W. Matthew and B. Martinez, "E-mails Suggest Merck Knew Vioxx's Dangers at Early Stage," *Wall Street Journal*, Nov 1. 2004: A1; l E.J. Topol, "Failing the Public Health—Rofecoxib, Merck, and the FDA," *N Engl J Med* 351 (2004): 1707-09.

The source was a right-wing think tank whose well-known bias against institutions such as public insurance increased my scepticism. And the evidence? Credible statistical evidence that there are "18 per cent more deaths per person and 35 per cent more deaths per kilometre travelled" in those provinces that have public insurance compared to those provinces that have private insurance. Good correlational evidence. But as the author of the study admits after citing the above facts, the real explanation is that public insurance companies do not charge a special high rate for "high risk" drivers (i.e., young males) and as a result there are more young male drivers in those provinces with public insurance. Of course public insurance companies could charge age-based rate differentials so it isn't *public insurance* that is the causal culprit but rather a policy, thought fair by many, that people should not be prejudged for car insurance on the basis of age. Only someone with a bias against public insurance would make the outrageous causal claim contained in the headline.[1] Note that the inference from the data to the headline commits the post hoc ergo propter hoc fallacy and fails almost all our criteria for a good causal argument. While there is a correlation, there is a clear alternative explanation or so-called third cause. To be fair, the report is clear about the actual causal relationships. My criticism is of the inflammatory and misleading headline. This is what comes of mixing ideology and statistics.

Evaluating Causal Claims
The Critical Questions

1. **What does a causal claim mean?**
   That an event or treatment or condition is not merely correlated but actually contributes to or produces the outcome.
2. **How good is the evidence?**
   a. **Correlation.** Is there good evidence of a correlation between cause and effect? Remember this requires appropriate comparisons; were appropriate groups compared? Was there bias in sample selection? Statistical significance is the minimal test, but the stronger the correlation the more likely the relationship is *humanly* or *clinically* important.
   b. **Fit and Models.** Does the cause fit in with our existing understanding? Is there is a biological (or other scientific) model that provides a detailed explanation of how the cause leads to the illness?
   c. **Dose relationship.** Is there is a "dose relationship" between the cause and its effect showing that increased exposure results in increased incidence or severity?

---

1 Mark Mullins, *Fraser Alert: Public Auto Insurance: A Mortality Warning for Motorists* (The Fraser Institute, September 4, 2003).

> **d. Confounding factors.** Is there a credible case made that
> the cause in question and not some other factor is the
> explanation for the correlation? In particular, has the
> possibility of bias been controlled through some kind
> of double blind procedure where appropriate? Do the
> researchers have an inappropriate financial or political
> interest in the outcome?
> **3. What other information is relevant? What is the context?**
> **a. Peer Review.** Were the results published in a peer-reviewed
> journal? Has there been enough time for the scientific
> community to critically review and perhaps even replicate
> the results?
> **b. Convergence.** Have repeated studies controlling for a variety
> of confounding factors tended to support the correlation?
> Are there still other credible explanations for the
> correlation that have not been eliminated?
> **4. Fallacies**
> **a. Post Hoc Ergo Propter Hoc.** Has the author simply gone from
> a correlation or even coincidence to a causal claim without
> meeting the criteria in 2 above?
> **b. Bandwagon.** Is it likely that the apparent convergence is
> a result of groupthink or bandwagoning, rather than an
> emerging consensus driven by careful research?
> **c. Prejudicial Funding Bias.** Have the researchers indicated
> financial or other interests? Has the funder prohibited
> the researcher from publication of results without funder
> authorization? Was the research plainly funded to establish
> an interest of the funder (e.g., oil company funded anti-
> global-warming studies)?

SUMMARY

I've used epidemiology and the study of the smoking/lung cancer link as examples of the strategies that researchers use to establish a causal claim. As you will see when looking at investigations in other domains, the basic approach is the same whether studying the causes of crime, depression, or lung cancer.

In the next chapter we will examine actual research in more detail, looking especially for typical fallacies and unsupported inferences. We will also look at two ways to find out whether there is convergence in support of a claim. There are review articles that attempt to survey all research in a subject to date and evaluate the general direction of the research, and **meta-analysis** that actually combines the data from a number of studies into one large study for better statistical accuracy. If we can find a good review article or meta-analysis, we can usually see the direction of the research, simplifying but not necessarily eliminating the necessity for further checking of the quality of the research.

CHAPTER 11

USING WHAT YOU'VE LEARNED: FINDING AND EVALUATING SCIENTIFIC INFORMATION

PASSIVE SMOKING OR EXPOSURE TO ENVIRONMENTAL TOBACCO SMOKE (ETS): A CASE STUDY OF MISLEADING REPORTING

The media have grown increasingly fond of reporting scientific information, particularly when there are surprising conclusions—results that are inconsistent with the current consensus. As we know now, studies with conclusions inconsistent with existing scientific understanding bear a strong burden of proof and are rightly subject to scepticism and further testing.

Why then do newspapers favour such studies? Sometimes this is just because such reports are after all (new) news; on other occasions there is an ideological agenda. The following example seems to exhibit both these motivations.

In 1998 the *Daily Telegraph* published an article by Victoria Macdonald with the headline:

Passive Smoking Doesn't Cause Cancer—Official

The world's leading health organisation has withheld from publication a study which shows that not only might there be no link between passive smoking and lung cancer but that it could even have a protective effect.

The astounding results are set to throw wide open the debate on passive smoking health risks. The World Health Organisation, which commissioned the 12-centre, seven-country European study has failed to make the findings public, and has instead produced only a summary of the results in an internal report.

Despite repeated approaches, nobody at the WHO headquarters in Geneva would comment on the findings last week. At its International Agency for Research on Cancer in Lyon, France, which coordinated the study, a spokesman would say only that the full report had been submitted to a science journal and no publication date had been set.

The findings are certain to be an embarrassment to the WHO, which has spent years and vast sums on anti-smoking and anti-tobacco campaigns. The study is one of the largest ever to look at the link between passive smoking—or environmental tobacco smoke (ETS)—and lung cancer, and had been eagerly awaited by medical experts and campaigning groups.

Yet the scientists have found that there was no statistical evidence that passive smoking caused lung cancer. The research compared 650 lung cancer patients with 1,542 healthy people. It looked at people who were married to smokers, worked with smokers, both worked and were married to smokers, and those who grew up with smokers.

> Note that this was a case-controlled, retrospective study. The weakest form of evidence

The results are consistent with their [sic] being no additional risk for a person living or working with a smoker and could be consistent with passive smoke having a protective effect against lung cancer. The summary, seen by the *Telegraph*, also states: "There was no association between lung cancer risk and ETS exposure during childhood."

A spokesman for Action on Smoking and Health said the findings "seem rather surprising given the evidence from other major reviews on the subject which have shown a clear association between passive smoking and a number of diseases." Roy Castle, the jazz musician and television presenter who died from lung cancer in 1994, claimed that he contracted the disease from years of inhaling smoke while performing in pubs and clubs.

> An obviously biased source, but they are correct in observing that the results conflict with most other studies

A report published in the *British Medical Journal* last October was hailed by the anti-tobacco lobby as definitive proof when it claimed that non-smokers living with smokers had a 25 per cent risk of developing lung cancer. But yesterday, Dr Chris Proctor, head of science for BAT Industries, the tobacco group, said the findings had to be taken seriously. "If this study cannot find any statistically valid risk you have to ask if there can be any risk at all. It confirms what we and many other scientists have long believed, that while smoking in public may be annoying to some non-smokers, the science does not show that being around a smoker is a lung-cancer risk."

> Another obviously biased source

> He does not *claim* that the study proves there's no connection, but does try to give that impression

The WHO study results come at a time when the British Government has made clear its intention to crack down on smoking in thousands of public places, including bars and restaurants.[1]

What do you think? In the first place the *Daily Telegraph*, while a fairly respectable British newspaper, is (like any newspaper) not a particularly reliable source. We should look deeper, but before doing so, let's take a close look at this report.

---

1 The *Daily Telegraph* (UK), March 8, 1998. Accessed at <http://www.telegraph.co.uk/htmlContent.jhtml?html=/archive/1998/03/08/wtob08.html>.

THE CRITICAL QUESTIONS I

1. **What is the claim?** It appears that this study failed to find a correlation between ETS (environmental tobacco smoke) and lung cancer, although the report suggests that it found there was a possible protective effect from such exposure.

2. **How good is the evidence?** All we have is a newspaper report of one study—a study that used the weakest form of investigative methods—the case-control method. Not very good evidence.

3. **What is the context?** As the article admits, this report flies in the face of most findings that support a link, especially in childhood, between ETS and lung cancer.

4. **Any Fallacies?** There are two obvious fallacies: 1) Inferring (by strong suggestion, if not literal assertion) from failure to find a statistically significant difference to "passive smoking does not cause cancer." As the legal saying goes, "Absence of evidence does not equal evidence of absence"; 2) The bizarre inference from the study that passive smoking could have a "protective effect against lung cancer." This appears to be the result of a misunderstanding of the scientists' use of confidence intervals, but without looking at the study it is hard to tell.

The first strategy when looking at a media report is to try to find the source. As mentioned in the article, at the time of publication of the newspaper report, the actual study had not been published. Since I was looking at the article many years later, I assumed it would be published. But with so little information in the article how was I going to find it?

I simply entered the *Telegraph* headline and date into Google. Because this was a particularly controversial article, the search yielded a large number of citations. One was to an article in the *British Medical Journal* (BMJ) that helped me get the actual name of the group doing the study: IARC (The International Agency for Research on Cancer). I could not find the original article on the IARC website, but I did find a press release that referenced the author of the report whose name I used (Boffetta) on PubMed[1] to find

---

1 PubMed is a web service of the US National Library of Medicine and the National Institutes of Health; it's a very useful source for searching for medical publications (<http://www.ncbi.nlm.nih.gov/pubmed/>).

both the abstract and the free article. Sounds complicated, but it took me about five minutes.

Not surprisingly the newspaper's rendition of the article is misleading. The first thing I did was to review the article's abstract. An abstract is a summary of the research that often gives the crucial details such as method, data, and conclusion. Abstracts are frequently available online, for free, when the article itself is unavailable or not free. They provide a handy and reliable way to get a brief summary of primary sources. In this case, what the abstract actually states is that "The OR[1] (odds ratio) for over exposure to spousal ETS was 1.16 (95% CI = 0.93-1.44)."[2] The increase in lung cancer in the observed sample was not very large: 16%. This is a smaller observed range than many other studies have found, but not "no effect" as reported in the paper. Given the size of the study, the confidence interval (CI)—the range within which we're 95% certain the effect occurs in the general population—is quite large, ranging between .93 and 1.44. That means that based on this study we cannot be 95% sure that there is a positive correlation between being exposed to a smoking spouse and getting lung cancer. Since the lowest end of the confidence interval falls below 1, the claim that there is a positive association between exposure and cancer is not "statistically significant." The abstract claims that the results were "consistent with claim that ETS has some association with lung cancer." The newspaper on the other hand states: "The results are consistent with their [sic] being no additional risk for a person living or working with a smoker." Both are, taken literally, correct, but what the newspaper says can certainly mislead the average reader.

The claim of the representative of the tobacco industry, "If this study cannot find any statistically valid risk you have to ask if there can be any risk at all" is also misleading. Of course, the matter is a serious one, and you have to ask this question, but this study does nothing to raise serious doubts about risk.

---

1 "Odds ratio" is another way of expressing relative risk though it will give figures that appear to increase the risk if the relative risk is high. For most practical purposes you can treat "odds ratio" as another way of expressing relative risk.

2 P. Boffetta, et al., "Multicenter Case-Control Study of Exposure to Environmental Tobacco Smoke and Lung Cancer in Europe," *J Natl Cancer Inst.* 90, 19 (Oct. 7, 1998): 1440-50, accessed at <http://www.ncbi.nlm.nih.gov/pubmed/9776409?ordinalpos=4&itool=EntrezSystem2.PEntrez.Pubmed.Pubmed_ResultsPanel.Pubmed_RVDocSum>.

THE CRITICAL QUESTIONS II

Let's review the critical questions as applied to the actual study:

1. **What is the actual claim in the study?** That there is some evidence, though not enough to satisfy the usual level of confidence required for statistical significance, of an association of ETS with lung cancer. There is no suggestion in the study that exposure to ETS might have some protective effect.

2. **How good is the evidence?** Not great. The study is a case-control study using data from 12 different sites in Europe and the authors admit that different sites used different ways of identifying controls. They also observe that the exposure to ETS of many of the subjects had been reduced in the last few years as spouses gave up smoking.

3. **What is the context?** As the authors of the study acknowledge, the effect level that they calculated is somewhat smaller than many other studies up to this date.

4. **Any Fallacies?** The most obvious shortcoming of the study is that the number of subjects is too small for reliable detection of a small effect. The scientists who did the study, and who published its results, did not commit the outrageous fallacy in the newspaper report of claiming that exposure to ETS could have a protective effect. Nor did they take their failure to establish a statistically significant correlation as evidence of a lack of causal connection.

ETS—THE BIG PICTURE

There are important public-health considerations raised by the possibility of environmental tobacco smoke's possible effects. One study is far from decisive. If we are to have a reasonably informed opinion on the topic we need to do a more thorough investigation. How would we go about getting adequate information to develop such an informed opinion? The first thing we need to find out is the current status of research on this claim, and whether the research is heading towards consensus.

Getting the Big Picture

Our first task then is to look for a summary that reviews the literature with sufficient breadth and currency to give us a general understanding of the issues and a sense of the direction of the research. Ideally this article will have references that enable us to dig deeper when we are ready. Consider the analogy of a map. In a city new to you, you need a large scale map that will give you the big picture: a sense of which streets are the main arterials, which run north and south, east and west. Getting general bearings precedes knowledge of the details. This is as true of learning a new subject area as it is learning a new city. So our first goal is to find such a big-picture map (article). To understand the state of research on a question, even an article from the popular press can be useful. A big-picture map oversimplifies, but that is why it is useful at the beginning. So don't be afraid of articles that simplify, but keep in mind that they are only the beginning and do not provide an appropriate basis for careful and critical decision-making.

Sometimes we can find **systematic reviews** of research literature, which simply attempt to give a summary. But a much more detailed and useful overview is given by the meta-analysis.

Meta-Analysis

Meta-analysis is a method statisticians have developed to bring together the data from a multitude of studies; this results in larger samples and, in principle, more reliable statistical conclusions. Meta-analysis involves sifting through all previous research and collecting the data from high-quality studies into one big sample and then doing statistical analysis on this new "sample." There are difficulties about doing meta-analysis that involve the quality of the original studies, whether the studies are comparable (i.e., are we combining apples and apples or apples and oranges), and what is called the "desk drawer" effect (explained below). While meta-analysis can strengthen a correlational claim, it does not always address the other questions relevant to a causal claim (e.g., is there another plausible explanation of the apparent effect?). Nonetheless such studies are often a good way to assess the state of current research and some do include a non-statistical review of the research which can help address the questions of causal plausibility and research convergence.

DESK DRAWER PROBLEM

The **desk drawer effect** (sometimes called "publication bias") often affects research. This refers to the fact that studies that fail to achieve statistically significant results often do not get published (they stay in the desk drawer). Statistically significant results are much more likely to be published. Studies that failed to get statistically significant results may merely have included samples that are too small; but if they were all added up, they could be significant. Since they are not published, however, a summary meta-analysis will not figure in these negative results. So meta-analyses, which tend not to include negative data, may be biased towards finding a correlation or finding a greater degree of correlation than a total aggregation of the research would justify. In a meta-analysis of the data on second-hand smoke, for example, statisticians J.B. Copas and J.Q. Shi argue that the risk of cancer resulting may have been considerably overestimated for exactly this reason: studies with less than statistically significant results tend not to be published, so summaries of existing published research ignore these, calculating the risk from studies that show large enough positive results to be statistically significant.[1] The article below summarizes their argument.

> LONDON (Reuters) Passive smoking may not increase the risk of lung cancer in non-smokers as much as doctors previously estimated, British researchers say.
>
> Statisticians at the University of Warwick in central England believe earlier studies that estimated second-hand smoke could increase a person's chance of lung cancer by nearly 25 per cent may have overstated the risk.
>
> "The excess risk is likely to be closer to 15 per cent than 24 per cent," researcher John Copas said in a report in the *British Medical Journal*.
>
> Copas and his colleague, Dr. Jian Qing Shi, analyzed the findings of 37 previous passive-smoking trials. They concluded publication bias may have skewed the research and exaggerated the risk.
>
> "The published estimate of the increased risk of

---

1   "Reanalysis of Epidemiological Evidence on Lung Cancer and Passive Smoking," *British Medical Journal* 320 (February 12, 2000): 417–18. For a summary, see <http://www.bmj.com/content/vol320/issue7232/press_release.dtl>.

lung cancer associated with environmental tobacco smoke needs to be interpreted with caution," Copas said.

Publication bias can occur when more studies with positive results are published in medical journals, than those with negative outcomes. So, when a review of all the research is done it includes studies likely to have positive results. Copas and Shi *estimated* the number of studies that were conducted but not published to revise the estimated risk (my italics).[1]

The problem with the authors' estimate is that it appears to be a *mythical number*,[2] since it guesses at unpublished data. While their speculation should not be given much weight, their concern is legitimate. To address this concern, many researchers doing meta-analysis contact researchers in the field and ask for unpublished data and studies.

Finding Summaries of the Literature

Where can we find such overviews or credible meta-analysis? For medical research such as the second-hand smoke issue, the obvious strategy is to go to PubMed, mentioned above, the enormous medical database. I typed "ETS meta-analysis" into their search box, but unfortunately this did not turn up any really recent reviews. So I decided on another strategy. I went to the obviously biased website of the group "Action on Smoking and Health" cited in the article from the *Daily Telegraph* anticipating that, if their site was at all credible, it would have links to up-to-date research. I wasn't disappointed. The site provided a number of links including the 2006 US Surgeon General's report, *The Health Consequences of Involuntary Exposure to Tobacco Smoke*.[3]

The Surgeon General's report is a daunting 700-page review of all the literature on this topic, but there is an executive summary,[4] and the first

---

1   *Nanaimo Daily News*, February 18, 2000: A.9.
2   See Chapter 5.
3   US Department of Health and Human Services, "The Health Consequences of Involuntary Exposure to Tobacco Smoke: A Report of the Surgeon General," accessed at <http://www.surgeongeneral.gov/library/secondhandsmoke/report/>.
4   <http://www.surgeongeneral.gov/library/secondhandsmoke/report/executive summary.pdf>

chapter, "Introduction, Summary, and Conclusions," is a manageable size. This first chapter also contains a table for grading the collected state of research—a variant of which I introduced in the previous chapter.

Four-Level Hierarchy for Classifying the Strength of Causal Inferences Based on Available Evidence[1]

Level 1	Evidence is **sufficient** to infer a causal relationship.
Level 2	Evidence is **suggestive but not sufficient** to infer a causal relationship.
Level 3	Evidence is **inadequate** to infer the presence or absence of a causal relationship (which encompasses evidence that is sparse, of poor quality, or conflicting).
Level 4	Evidence is **suggestive of no causal relationship**.

Below is an example (a small part of the report's conclusions) of how these descriptors are used when stating a finding.

CANCER

1. The *evidence is sufficient* to infer a causal relationship between secondhand smoke exposure and lung cancer among lifetime nonsmokers. This conclusion extends to all secondhand smoke exposure, regardless of location.
2. The pooled evidence indicates a 20 to 30 per cent increase in the risk of lung cancer from secondhand smoke exposure associated with living with a smoker.

BREAST CANCER

1. The *evidence is suggestive but not sufficient* to infer a causal relationship.

Later chapters in the *Report* contain the details of the arguments for these conclusions. Crucially, argument sections in the *Report* point out that the

---

1   US Department of Health and Human Services, Chapter 1, p. 10.

support found for the causal claim is not just statistical. Additional evidence is:

- It is known that smoking causes a variety of illnesses.
- Second-hand smoke contains the same carcinogens as "first-hand" smoke.
- The incidence of disease shows a "dose relationship" to exposure to second-hand smoke.

All this together with the statistical data provide, according to the *Report*, evidence that meets the criteria of Level 1 and is sufficient to infer a causal relationship between second-hand smoke exposure and lung cancer among lifetime non-smokers.

There's good reason to look closely at any research or summary of research in an area as politically charged as ETS. On the one side is intense lobbying and pressure, and more subtle influence by research funding and management from the tobacco companies. On the other side is social pressure on the scientific community to find harmful effects of ETS. For example, the *British Journal of Medicine* received a great deal of virulent criticism after they published a reasonable peer-reviewed study[1] that failed to find a correlation between ETS and lung cancer. The journal's editor remarked, "I found it disturbing that so many people and organizations referred to the flaws in the study without specifying what they were. Indeed, this debate was much more remarkable for its passion than its precision."[2] It may be that the pressures from both sides cancel each other out!

The claims about ETS are based on a plausible causal model (after all we know that smoking causes lung cancer) and considerable research. Nevertheless, there are a couple of obvious problems with establishing the level of exposure to second-hand smoke. First, the amount of cancer-causing substance received second hand is very much lower than what a smoker gets. Where a statistically significant effect is found, it is often a small one. Second, exposure levels are difficult to ascertain and confounding factors abound. These two factors mean that it is not surprising that studies occasionally fail to find a "statistically significant" effect.

Is the evidence sufficient to justify a ban on smoking in public places?

1 James E. Enstrom and Geoffrey C. Kabat, "Environmental Tobacco Smoke and Tobacco Related Mortality in a Prospective Study of Californians, 1960-98," *British Medical Journal* 326, 1057 (May 17, 2003).
2 Richard Smith, "Passive Smoking; Comment from the Editor, " *British Medical Journal* 327, 7413 (August 30, 2003).

Even if the incidence of ETS-related health problems (as well as lung cancer these include heart disease and other respiratory illnesses such as asthma) is small, the benefits of a ban are likely to be considerable. Because there is such widespread exposure (in some workplaces, for example), even a small percentage decline in illness would represent an important public-health benefit. There would also, of course, be the benefit resulting from helping (ok, *forcing*) smokers to reduce consumption, and enhancing the negative public attitude towards smoking.

Applying the Criteria to Other Claims

CELLPHONES AND HEALTH

Cellphone use has increased dramatically in the last few years and this use has raised two safety questions: 1) Does cellphone use while driving increase the risk of accident? 2) Does cellphone use increase the risk of brain cancer?

Let's take a quick look at researchers' attempts to answer these questions.

Question 1: Does Cellphone Use While Driving Increase the Risk of Accident?

The answer seems obvious. We have all seen drivers making driving errors while talking on their cellphone; perhaps we have even done that ourselves.

But all distractions can potentially cause accidents and we have a natural tendency to "confirmation bias"—the collection of evidence that supports our theories and the ignoring of evidence that does not. How many times do we note a person driving using a cellphone and not making a driving error? So research is relevant to determine both the relative magnitude and frequency of accidents caused by cellphone use.

As you would anticipate, research supports the claim that cellphone use does significantly (and not just statistically so) increase the likelihood of being involved in a car accident. Both experimental and observational studies have been done. Experimental studies involving simulated driving situations have shown that people's reaction times are slowed when using a cellphone. This slowing of reactions occurs regardless of whether the phone is handheld or hands-free. The weakness of these studies is that the situations are artificial and the study group, a far from random set of volunteers, is small. So the applicability of these results to the real world is open to question.

In my investigation of this topic, I found a 2005 article in the *British Medical Journal* that describes the current state of research and provides important additional results.[1] Getting good observational studies in this area is not without its challenges. Police reports for example would be woefully inadequate and, at best, give us a per cent of all accidents that involved cellphone use, not the increased risk of an accident while using a cellphone. The method used in the *BMJ* reported research is fairly novel:

> We compared a driver's use of a mobile phone at the estimated time of a crash with the same driver's use during another suitable time period. Because drivers are their own controls, the design controls for characteristics of the driver that may affect the risk of a crash but do not change over a short period of time. As it is important that risks during control periods and crash trips are similar, we compared phone activity during the hazard interval (time immediately before the crash) with phone activity during control intervals (equivalent times during which participants were driving but did not crash) in the previous week.

---

1 Suzanne P. McEvoy, et al., "Role of Mobile Phones in Motor Vehicle Crashes Resulting in Hospital Attendance: A Case-Crossover Study," *British Medical Journal* 331, 428 (July 12, 2005), accessed at <http://www.pubmedcentral.nih.gov/articlerender.fcgi?artid=1188107>.

The study found a fourfold increase in the risk of accident when using a phone regardless of whether it was handheld or hands-free. This heightened risk is consistent with data from previous studies referenced in this study. The care given to verify actual use and the use of subjects as their own controls minimizes the problems of confounding. The fact that this study is consistent with both earlier studies and experimental studies adds weight to the claim. That it is also common sense that phone use would be distracting provides the plausible causal explanation that is required. All and all, there is considerable reason to believe that cellphone use while driving significantly increases the risk of an accident.

Question 2: Does Cellphone Use Increase the Risk of Brain Cancer?

Interestingly this is a more controversial area of research. Partly because cancer develops slowly, getting adequate data for correlations at this time is going to be difficult. Also, there is no common-sense view about the relationship between exposure and brain cancer, but there is considerable common, if not sensible, fear of such a relationship. Governments have been involved in major efforts to determine whether cellphones can cause cancer, but because of suspicion that such studies are unduly influenced by the cellphone industry, I sought out a non-governmental review of the topic and found a 2004 review by M. Kundi. His review notes that at that time, the longest studies had found evidence of some association between cellphone use and benign brain tumours. He concludes:

> Although there is evidence from independent epidemiological studies pointing to a moderately increased cancer risk for subjects using a mobile phone for several years, there remains always the possibility of bias and confounding unless there is supporting evidence from animal and in vitro studies as well as a mechanistic explanation.[1]

In other words, without a biological explanation the inconsistent results from epidemiological studies cannot be given much weight.

But this is such an active research area that I continued my search. I did that by using Kundi's name in a citation index, which lists all articles that

---

1   Kundi, "Mobile Phone Use and Cancer," *Occup. Environ. Med.* 161 (2004): 560–70, doi:10.1136/oem.2003.007724.

have referred to his paper. This method enabled me to find the most recent survey of the topic. I found an article in the *Journal of the National Cancer Institute* from 2006 that involved an enormous cohort (420,095 people) over a long period of time (their first cellphone subscription was between 1982 and 1995, and they were followed through 2002 for cancer incidence), thus avoiding some of the criticisms of the sort raised by Kundi of earlier studies.

The conclusion, as stated in the article's abstract, is:

> We found no evidence for an association between tumor risk and cellular telephone use among either short-term or long-term users. Moreover, the narrow confidence intervals [a result of such a large study] provide evidence that any large association of risk of cancer and cellular telephone use can be excluded.[1]

Contradictory Evidence

These results seem convincing, but once we have found the direction of research and have a sense of the current consensus (or lack of any), it is still useful to check and see if we can find and understand the views of those who are not part of the consensus. Like members of any social group, scientists are subject to subtle and not so subtle social and financial pressure. We all understand that companies funding research may put pressure on researchers to look in a certain direction, but pressure might

1   J. Schüz, et al., "Cellular Telephone Use and Cancer Risk: Update of a Nationwide Danish Cohort," *J Natl Cancer Inst.* 98 (2006): 1707–13.

come from all sorts of other directions. We all know that scientists have held, sometimes with great confidence, erroneous views. On everything from plate tectonics (until the 1960s virtually no geologists accepted this view) to the ever-changing world of nutritional advice, science has had to self-correct. The great thing about science is that it does self-correct. We should be careful not to dismiss dissidents and sceptics whose views may later be vindicated. A review of the arguments of the critics can also give a sense of the strengths and weaknesses of the accepted view. In the above example, Kundi gives reasons for his doubts about the current research on the cellphone/brain cancer link. He held the view that the studies up to that time that failed to find an effect were inconclusive because of small sample size and insufficient duration. As you saw, the newest studies were more comprehensive and based on longer usage.

Using the table introduced in Chapter 10 (and reproduced below) we can say that, given the current state of the research, the appropriate judgement of claim 1 that "cellphone use causes increased risk of accidents" is Strongly Positive (evidence is sufficient to infer a causal relationship). The appropriate judgement of claim 2 that "cellphone use causes brain cancer" is Negative (the evidence is suggestive of no causal relationship).

Four-Level Hierarchy for Classifying the Strength of Causal Inferences Based on Available Evidence		
	Judgement	**Evidence Quality**
Strongly Positive	Evidence is **sufficient** to infer a causal relationship.	Extensive studies with appropriate size, duration and variety, including large prospective studies and if possible experimental studies. A convergence of study results. A credible causal explanation. Large effects or extensive evidence for reported small effect.
Weakly Positive	Evidence is **suggestive but not sufficient** to infer a causal relationship.	Significant correlation evidence from credible studies with at least some prospective studies. Some experimental evidence if possible. Smaller size and fewer studies than above. Credible causal explanation.

Inconclusive	Evidence is **inadequate** to infer the presence or absence of a causal relationship.	Evidence is sparse, of poor quality, or conflicting. Credible causal explanation may be lacking.
Negative	Evidence is **suggestive of no causal relationship.**	Extensive studies have failed to reveal a consistent correlation. The causal relationship seems implausible in view of current understanding.

Using Websites

As I illustrated above, the Web can be an excellent tool for searching for relevant scientific information. Even biased websites, if they provide links, can be useful. But websites are often problematic sources of information: in many cases, they are superficial or just interested in selling you something.

What we need to do when looking at websites is just what we need to do when using any source of information—we need to evaluate it critically. One warning: do not rely on first impressions. Resist the impulse to be persuaded by a reliable-sounding name, by reassuring phrases, or by a professional appearance, let alone a glitzy one. Studies have shown that Web users tend to be overly impressed by the appearance of a site;[1] of course, appearances do not guarantee reliability any more than do fancy fonts or fancy pants. The Canadian Cancer Research Group, for example, had at the time of writing, a very professional-looking website, on which was posted some very well-written text, beginning with the following passage:

> The Canadian Cancer Research Group (CCRG) is a clinical biotechnology company with research, application and development expertise in diagnostics and therapeutics, focused upon immunological disorders. The group is staffed with experts in medicine, laboratory sciences, chemistry, pharmacology, immunology and biotechnology in its clinical and laboratory settings, located in Ottawa, Canada.[2]

---

1   From the Stanford Persuasive Technology Lab. References accessed at <http://www.consumerwebwatch.org/news/report3_credibilityresearch/stanford PTL_TOC.htm> June 20, 2004.

2   <http://www.ccrg.com/index.htm>.

This is a paragraph that breathes reassurance and respectability; the succession of abstract and general nouns and adjectives (*clinical biotechnology*; *research, application and development expertise*; *diagnostics and therapeutics*) fosters a sense in the reader of sound business and medical practice. So too does the company's location (Ottawa being the home of many of Canada's finest technology companies as well as of its government). And the impression is enhanced by the conventionally handsome, highly professional appearance of the website. But if we look again we might notice the degree to which the description here is vague. Who are these "experts"? What are their qualifications?

At the time this text was posted on the site (2004) we would certainly have had reason to ask such questions. The website was promoting a cancer cure that was not medically recognized; the site provided no information as to the qualifications of the people doing the work, and no information on research supporting its claims. It was also listed at the time on the QuackWatch website.[1] But it certainly looked and sounded professional!

So when we get to a website what do we look for? First and foremost, we need to know who is supplying the information. We need to assess whether the information is coming from a trustworthy and reasonably unbiased source. Obviously biased sources such as sites selling a particular product, or politicized websites run by, for example, right-wing think tanks or environmental-activist groups, can, of course, give us a lot of information and leads. But given their bias, we know that we must look for other sources or follow up their references to be sure we are getting an accurate picture. Biased sources can be knowledgeable, but it would be naïve simply to trust them.

Below is a list of critical questions to keep in mind when using information from a website. There's nothing special about websites that make these applicable: they are the same questions you should ask of your doctor, a car salesman, or politician. There are similar ways to assess any claim or argument from a book, journal, individual, or website.

> Critical Questions for Evaluating Websites
>
> **1. Who is supplying the argument or information?**
> Is the supplier a credible source? (Government organizations, academic institutions, reputable publications)

---

1 <http://www.quackwatch.com/>. This website, run by a physician, announces itself as "Your Guide to Quackery, Health Fraud, and Intelligent Decisions." It has received a good deal of praise from mainstream medical and consumer organizations, and a good deal of criticism from herbalists, homeopaths, and other "alternative" medical people.

Is there bias (obvious or not so obvious) because of financial support, or political bias (e.g., right wing, left wing, environmental group, or opponent)?

What seems to be the motivation for this site/study?

Does the site provide helpful information about its sources/authors?

Does the knowledge of the source provide grounds for confidence or doubt?

Does the source have the relevant competencies to support undocumented claims made on the site?

2. **How is the argument or information presented?**

Is the tone of the presentation appropriate?

Is the argument presented in an intelligible and reasonable form?

Does the site depend on testimonials (fallacy of anecdotal evidence) to support its claims?

Are the conclusions/claims expressed with an appropriate level of confidence for the evidence supplied?

In controversial areas, are a variety of positions reviewed and discussed?

Does the site/author provide supporting references from credible sources (e.g., peer-reviewed journals)?

Does the author/site help the reader get additional information both pro and con? Is this easily accessed through links?

Is the information current? Are dates given for the information?

3. **Is there critical information left out?**

The best way to assess this is to find websites with a different or critical point of view (e.g., Quackwatch).

APPENDIX

Where to Look?

In researching a claim, it is useful to consider what level of information you require given your concern, your level of understanding, and your time. I divide credible information sources into roughly three levels.

LEVEL 1

Level 1 is the popular but nevertheless respected media, such as *Scientific American, Atlantic Monthly, New York Times,* and *Globe and Mail.* Another source at this level is websites provided by government or health agencies (cancer societies, for example), supplying responsibly digested information for the layperson. These can be excellent sources of overview articles, usually written by knowledgeable researchers. But this is still the tip of the information iceberg. The information presented by these sources is written by reporters, not scientists; it's a step removed from basic information. Unfortunately, the information at this level is often simplified, assuming that you want to know, for example, how to reduce the risk of colon cancer, not what the latest research is showing. If you want more detailed information, which you can approach critically, you will usually need to look elsewhere. These sources sometimes supply links to more detailed research, but that is not their primary focus.

Level 1 material seldom provides enough evidence to support a well-reasoned and confident belief. A thoughtful person facing important decisions about personal or public-policy matters will need to go to a second level.

LEVEL 2

Level 2 sites and material are written for the sophisticated non-experts such as government policy makers. A classic example of such a site is the website of the Intergovernmental Panel on Climate Change.[1] On this site you can get a variety of information, ranging from fairly superficial accounts of global warming to extensive literature reviews written for policy makers and primary research written by and for researchers in the field. Many UN sites and the World Bank site also have this range of information.

Literature reviews and meta-analysis, while not written for the non-expert, often provide overview discussions that are comprehensible to that reader. Most importantly these reviews provide us with the crucial information about the direction of the research (consensus or dissensus) and how reliable it is. But be sure to evaluate the material critically. Just because you are being supplied much more in-depth information does not mean that it should not be subject to appropriate critical scrutiny and scepticism.[2]

---

1   <http://www.ipcc.ch/>.

2   The Cochrane Collaboration is an organization dedicated to providing reviews of healthcare research through their website <http://www.cochrane.org>. A review of this reviewing service published in the *British Medical Journal*, while quite favourable, nevertheless warns: "Its users should interpret reviews cautiously, particularly those with conclusions favouring experimental interventions and those with many typographical errors." (Ole Olsen, et al., "Quality of Cochrane Reviews: Assessment of Sample from 1998," *British Medical Journal* 323 (October 31, 2001): 829–32.

LEVEL 3

Lastly, there is Level 3 research. This is the level of primary research that is found published in peer-reviewed journals in all fields. Articles in these journals are often technical and filled with jargon; this makes them difficult for a layperson to follow. Do not despair. These articles usually come with an abstract or summary at the beginning and concluding discussion at the end, and these are often understandable. They will usually tell you the kind of study involved and the sample size; these are, of course, key clues for assessing the value of the research. And they may indicate the current state of research and how this study relates to previous work. Abstracts may well be freely available on websites when the full article is not. How much deeper into the article one wishes to delve depends on how important it is to make a decision based on the most thorough review of the information available and one's level of understanding. But since what we are usually interested in is not so much the details of a specific study, but rather where the direction of the research is headed, the detail is usually unimportant. For our purposes, what we need, even from the peer-reviewed journals, are reliable overview summaries that can give us an understanding of the direction of the research and the extent to which researchers feel confident about this direction.

FOOTNOTES

Publishers generally exclude footnotes from popular journals, while peer-reviewed journals often contain an overwhelming number of footnotes. Hostility to the tedium of footnoting when writing the academic essay often leads students to "footnote phobia"—they're too complicated, too tedious, and too academic.

But in research, footnotes are our friends. When we're looking for information, a well-footnoted article is a kind of "open-sesame" into the literature. Footnotes in a recent specialized journal article will often reveal crucial bits of information, for example, a summary or **seminal article**—one that set the direction or changed the direction of the research. Subsequent research will often be in reaction to that article, critical or supportive. By knowing which article is setting the tone or direction of research we are in a much better position to achieve our goal of understanding where the research is going and how well it is getting there.

BOOKS

Because I have assumed that you will be attempting to find both the most easily accessible and most current research, I have emphasized Web-based research. However, depending on the topic and its importance, you may need to go to the library. Textbooks, though usually out of date in highly active fields, often provide the kind of overview that can give you a picture of the current understanding. Just as there are seminal articles there are seminal books, and if your research has revealed a particular book that many people refer to, then you probably need to look at that text. Remember, just because a claim is in print, even in a textbook, does not make it true. You should note when reading scientific textbooks that they have ways of signalling the state of scientific uncertainty though they seldom emphasize it. When they say "Scientists currently believe ..." they are giving you a hint that this is still an unsettled area of scientific controversy. This kind of introductory remark is in contrast to the more typical phrasing used to state claims that are uncontroversial, for example, "The molecular weight of oxygen is...."

CHAPTER 12

PROBABILITY AND JUDGEMENT

A reasonable probability is the only certainty.

E.W. Howe

INTRODUCTION

The first goal of this book has been to improve your ability to think criti-cally about statistical and scientific information. The second goal is to help you make good use of this information in your everyday decision-making. Key to making good use of this information is understanding not only how to asses the "iffiness" of scientific generalizations, but also how to use this information to make decisions in view of the uncertain-ties of everyday life. To understand how to deal with uncertainty, we need to explore the idea of probability a bit further.

Considerations of probability are common but often unnoticed. They are involved in everything from thinking about the chance of getting a sexually transmitted disease to estimating the safety of various modes of travel, from concerns about global warming to the likelihood of career success. Some-times we are almost unaware of this influence. You probably plan your life on an implicit assumption about your life expectancy. But do you really know what it is? Perhaps you are reluctant to marry because you have heard that 50% of marriages end in divorce. But Statistics Canada reports less than 1/3 of marriages end in divorce.[1] Perhaps you are uneasy about going out at night because you believe that there is a high violent-crime rate in your city. But as you learned earlier, such rates are significantly down.

---

1   Statistics Canada, "Divorce in the 1990s," *Health Reports* 9, 2 (Autumn 1997), accessed at <http://www.statcan.ca/english/kits/pdf/divor3.pdf> August 24, 2007.

Are we afraid to walk in the street at night for good reason or have we been unduly scared by stories in the press? Is our belief that there is not an unemployment problem based on the fact that all our friends are working, or is it based on carefully collected statistical information? One of the most common human errors is to overgeneralize from one's own experience. An unwarranted generalization from one's own experience, or from someone else's, is called the fallacy of "anecdotal evidence." Remember, your life is a "bad sample." In this chapter we will enhance our understanding of probability in order to learn how to make better use of statistical information.

Most of us are not very comfortable with thinking probabilistically. We do say things like "it will *probably* rain," "we *might* have to stop work early," "it is *just possible* that they might get back together," but we prefer certainty and speak more often in terms of either/or. Is the new drug safe or not? Is she coming or not? Will it rain or not? Is coffee good for you or isn't it? Do you support me or are you against me?

Actually, practically everything is iffy. Aside from the proverbial taxes and death, the best we can hope for is the highly probable. A "safe" drug is actually one with a very low probability of harm. That carrots are good for you means that they are *generally* good for people, except for those with allergies and unless tainted by human handlers. As we know, the claims of science, even when supported with years of research, sometimes turn out to be false or needing serious revision. One of the great challenges to becoming a critical thinker and making good use of statistical and scientific information is learning how to deal with all this uncertainty. An increased understanding of probability can help us do that.

So what is a critical thinker to do in the face of a universe of chance? Fortunately mathematicians have made considerable progress in formalizing ways of thinking about variability and chance. Interestingly, despite a history of thousands of years of gambling, the mathematics of probability was not developed until Blaise Pascal and Pierre Fermat worked out the basic theory in the 1600s in response to a request for some gambling advice from a French nobleman. Ian Hacking comments that so great was the ignorance of probability in the ancient world, that had any Roman understood the mathematics of gambling he could have easily won the whole empire.[1]

You don't have to be a mathematician to have a basic understanding of probability, but it's difficult to apply this understanding in the face of what seems to be a natural tendency for most of us to think in non-iffy ways. Psychologists have studied how well humans deal with uncertainty and probability, and their research suggests that we tend not to do it very well. But we can learn. My goal is to help you get a "feel" for probabilistic thinking so that you can deal with the uncertainties of life more competently.

PROBABILITY: THE BASIC IDEA

Critical Question 1: What Does "Probability" Mean?

As mentioned in Chapter 3, the easiest way to think about the probability of something happening is in terms of the long-run frequency. Why the long run? Because there is a great deal of variation in the short run. We all recognize that in the short run we could flip, say, eight heads in a row. Such a run would say nothing about the long-run frequency or tendency of the coin—it would simply be a reflection of the fact that the long run is made up of a lot of short-run variability including the occasional surprising run of heads.

Variations from the probable that happen in the short run tend to disappear in the long run. Perhaps you could flip eight heads in a row, but you

1   *The Taming of Chance* (Cambridge: Cambridge University Press, 1990).

would never flip 80 heads in a row. Short-run improbabilities disappear in the long run total. So the fact that the probability of flipping a head is 50% tells us that *in the long run* the frequency of heads will be about 50%.

Critical Question 2: How Good Is the Evidence?

There are two sources of evidence for a probability claim: experience and calculation.

We don't of course always have to do a lot of coin flips to see if the probability of heads showing up is 50%: we already have good reason to believe that each side of the coin is equally likely to come up. In general, if we have good reason to believe that each of two or more possible events is equally likely to come up (for example, each side of the coin being flipped, or each side of a die coming up when thrown, or each card being picked from a thoroughly shuffled deck), then we can *calculate* rather than experiment. For example, there are 4 kings in a deck of 52 cards so the chance of being dealt a king from a full deck is 4/52 (7.7%). So we could expect a king to be dealt about 8% of the time.

In most cases of interest to us though, it is experience, not theoretical calculation that is the source of evidence for the probability claim. For example, about 90 Americans are killed by lightning in any year.[1] Because there are about 300 million Americans, this means that the probability of a an American being killed by lightening in a year is about one in three million. Everything from life expectancy to the chance of getting killed in a car accident can be calculated in the same way.

Critical Question 4: Probability Fallacies

The first classic fallacy is the **gambler's fallacy**. Because probability is long-term frequency, there is a natural tendency (of some gamblers any-way) to think that short-run deviations from the likely long run will be "corrected" by chance. Given a run of say six heads you might think that the chance that the next flip will be tails is better than 50/50. "After all," a gambler might think, "the six head run will have to be offset in the long run by some tails." But the coin doesn't know about its past behaviour. Runs of heads will be offset, but no one knows when. Coin flips are what

---

1   US National Oceanic and Atmospheric Administration, Technical Memorandum, NWS SR-193.

statisticians call *independent events*: one outcome does not affect the probability of any other. Unless we are dealing with loaded coins or clever magicians, there is no reason to think that past behaviour will help us predict what will happen next. There are several websites[1] giving past winning numbers for the LOTTO 6/49 Canadian national lottery; this is depressing evidence of the gambler's fallacy in action: presumably many players will pick different numbers, believing that those that won in the past are thus less likely to come up. (Or maybe some players think these numbers are *more* likely.) This information is of course useless, but it seems to have been put out for those people who believe in the gambler's fallacy—more exploitation of the lottery-ticket buyer's mathematical naiveté.

REPRESENTATIVENESS

So powerful is the belief that short-run behaviour should be representative of long-run behaviour, that studies have shown that people tend to believe that the run

HTHHTHTT is more likely than this one: HHHHTTTT.

They believe this because the first one looks random and the second one suspiciously patterned. But in fact any particular series has the same chance as any other series. We need to be clear here. Getting four heads in a row is less likely than say getting three heads in a row. But any precise and particular run, such as above, has the same likelihood as any other.

Now let's test your intuition. To play Lotto 6/49, you pick six numbers, each between one and 49. Which of the following Lotto 6/49 combinations do you think is more likely?

1,2,3,4,5,6 or 23,19,44,2,16,8

It is quite hard to believe that they are equally unlikely, but they are. Should I ever be foolish enough to buy a lottery ticket I would pick the first set of numbers because should I win (!) I could be quite sure I would not have to share my prize with anyone else.[2]

---

1   For example, <http://www.lottolore.com/lotto649.html>.
2   Or I would try to. I too would have to overcome my deep-seated but wrong-headed feeling that this set was more improbable than another more random looking one.

Summary

Probability theory is a useful tool for thinking about the uncertainty of many events. The probability of a repeated event (e.g., tails on a coin flip) equals the long-run tendency for that event. But despite this fact, and contrary to our intuitions, short-run series may well differ significantly from the long-run tendency. According to psychological research, we expect patterns in the short run to look like patterns that will emerge in the long run. As a result we intuitively underrate the likelihood of exceptional patterns such as eight out of ten coin flips turning up heads. Or we are surprised when a family has six girls. But the average of approximately 50% heads in coin flips and female children in births is made up of a lot of short-run "exceptions." This tendency leads us to misjudge the probability of events that seem to deviate from the long-run tendency, or may lead us to think, when faced with an apparently "deviant pattern" (seven heads in a row) that there is some force that will correct for this oddness—the so-called gambler's fallacy.

SUBJECTIVE PROBABILITY ASSESSMENT

Critical Question 1: What Does It Mean?

Thinking of probability as the long-run frequency helps us understand what a probability statement means and explains a lot of the mathematics involved; it gives an objective meaning to the notion that the odds of flipping a head is 50/50. But often we have a "subjective" impression of the likelihood of an event such as whether it is going to rain on our birthday, or whether we will get the job we just interviewed for, or whether we will be attacked by a bear. These subjective judgements drive a great many decisions. If we feel a desired outcome (like getting a certain job) is likely, we will try to achieve it; if, on the other hand, we fear a bad outcome is likely (like getting mugged on the street) we will avoid going out.

Critical Question 2: How Good Is the Evidence?

Given the significance of these subjective judgements, we need to know how much we can rely on them. Let us first look at those intuitions that can actually be checked. Psychologists and sociologists have studied people's intuitions of the likelihood of a variety of events such as car accidents, lightning hits, muggings and murders, and getting a major illness. What they have found is that many of our common judgements tend to be skewed by a variety of factors.

THE UNRELIABILITY OF SUBJECTIVE ESTIMATES OF PROBABILITY

Experience

Our beliefs about what is safe, a reasonable risk, etc., are based on our impression of probabilities. And our beliefs determine our actions. If we believe that our car has a good chance of being broken into, we take precautions that we wouldn't take if we thought it unlikely. But do we look up crime statistics when deciding the likelihood of car theft? Not likely. We have an impression based on what we have heard (my neighbour's car was broken into last week), perhaps our own experience (never happened to me), and what we hear through the media. But a moment's reflection suggests *that this method for assessing probability and risk cannot be reliable*. How can we trust that what we experience or hear is a representative sample of what is actually going on (e.g., the actual rate of car break-ins)? "If it bleeds it leads" is a notorious cliché about editorial policy in the media. "Bloody" disasters get readers' attention and sell newspapers. So sadly, the media bombards us with tales of misfortune, of child murders, and plane crashes, creating the impressions of a high frequency of such disasters.

Of course it is not only the media that creates false impressions of likelihood.[1] Our own experience is also a powerful influence. This is illustrated by a car purchase I made. Over ten years ago I bought my first new car. I wanted a safe, reliable, and not too expensive car. After studying *Consumer Reports* I decided to buy a Ford Taurus. I noted in my research that Tauruses had a 75% satisfaction rating among owners; this compared favourably to other North American produced cars, but unfavourably to Japanese cars (typically rated above 90%). Nonetheless Taurus had air bags and a good safety rating. So I bought one. I had trouble, especially with the transmission (was it four or five that I had put in? Only three were covered under the warranty!). Of course I knew my odds were one in four

---

1 P. Slovic, et al., "Fact vs. Fear: Understanding Risk Perception" in *Judgement Under Uncertainty: Heuristics and Biases*, E. Kahnman and A. Tversky, eds. (Cambridge: Cambridge University Press, 1982).

of being unsatisfied, but once the breakdowns happened to me, Tauruses in general became "lemons" in my view. I would never buy another one. I collected stories from other disgruntled owners. My subjective sense of the probability of a Taurus being a lemon had risen to almost certainty. Whenever I met owners who hadn't had trouble, I viewed their experiences as minor miracles.

Vividness

Our own experiences create vivid memories that influence our sense of the probable. A common way of arriving at a subjective probability assessment is by doing a reflective inventory of what we can recall happening or what we have heard. Can we easily think of examples of such events? If we can, then they are judged probable, if not, not. The more easily we can bring up similar events from memory, the higher the probability we give it. But it is crucial to remember that *your life is a bad sample.* Your experiences and what you have read or heard are clearly not a random sample and almost certainly not representative of what is really happening in the world.

The problem seems to be that we are strongly inclined to generalize from our own experience as if it were representative. We tend to ignore the fact that each of us come from a certain place, have only lived in a limited number of places, have tended to associate with a limited group of people usually of similar background and education, etc. Our lives are a biased, non-representative, and usually too small sample. We are all too willing to generalize from very limited experience.

It probably made sense for our ancestors on the savannah to decide that all red berries were sickening if they ate a red berry that made them sick. Quick and dirty generalizations were undoubtedly useful in a relatively stable and homogenous environment. If milk poured from a bottle tastes sour you don't have to taste it repeatedly to make sure it's sour. One taste is enough because we know that the sourness is usually spread throughout the bottle.

But life is not a bottle of milk. In the complex and mobile world of today, generalizing from a very small sample is more likely incorrect. Take the berry example again. Berries vary. They are shipped to us from all over the world. Perhaps the berry is from a bad patch, or had too much pesticide applied, or we were sick when we ate it. In the modern world, jumping to the conclusion that red berries are sickening from one experience would undoubtedly be rash and unwarranted.

We don't need statistics to tell us that a very small sample is not a reliable basis for making generalizations; we already know that. But nonetheless, we seem powerfully prone to overgeneralize. "Canadian are ..." "New Yorkers are ..." "Serbs are ..." "Blacks are ..." "Whites are ..." "Men are ..." "Women are...." In some cases these claims involve sweeping generalizations about literally billions of people. If such generalizations have any basis they are usually based on small and biased samples that do not provide a reasonable basis for such claims. Many such beliefs are, of course, just prejudices handed down from generation to generation, often with terrible human consequences.

So our first lesson for thinking critically about subjective judgements of probability is to recognize that *subjective probability impressions may well differ from true likelihood*. Unless we've done some research, our information sources (including our own experiences) are bound to have been unrepresentative or biased. For example, the crime statistics cited in Chapter 5 are a surprise for most people and counter to their impression that violence, child abductions, etc., remain high and are even increasing.

Memory

The unrepresentative and biased nature of our own experience is not all that misleads us when estimating (or guesstimating) probability. Our memories are also a problem. Even if by chance, our experiences were representative of the actual frequency with which events happen, our memories are unlikely to provide a reliable ratio of likelihood. We tend to remember particularly outstanding events (or frightening ones) and events that accord with our prejudices, and to forget or ignore others. Men who believe women are poor drivers will note each driving error they see made by a woman but will not note those made by men, and more importantly, will not notice good driving by females. In fact, men are considerably more likely to be involved in accidents than women.[1] So the problem is not just that we experience an unrepresentative sample; it's also that we have natural tendencies to collect unreliable and prejudiced information. Because our subjective probability judgements are biased by our own prejudices and experiences, it's difficult to be a good intuitive assessor of probabilities.

---

1   Data from Idaho Department of Highways is relevant: "In 2001, males were 1.4 times more likely than females to be involved in any collision and 2.4 times more likely than females to be involved in a fatal collision." <http://www2.state.id.us/itd/highways/ohs/2001Data/Drivers2001.pdf>.

The Challenge of Combining Probabilities

One of the well-documented areas where our subjective impressions often let us down is when we are combining two or more probabilities. For example, we all make estimates of how long a project will take, like writing a paper or repairing a faucet. We recognize that the success of a project requires that a number of events fall into place. How is the probability of the whole project being finished related to the probability of each event?

Consider, for example, a building project. Estimating how long it will take involves estimates of the probability of such things as the material arriving on time, the workers showing up, getting through city hall red tape, the weather being ok, etc. In order to get an estimate of the likelihood of the project being completed on time, we can assign a probability estimate to each of these events and *combine* the probabilities to get an estimate for the whole project. How do we do this?

The good news is that you already understand most of what you need in order to understand the basics of combining probabilities.

Everyone understands that when flipping a coin you have a 50% chance of getting a head—one chance in two. And if you flip a coin twice the chance of getting two heads is 25% or one chance in four. How do we know that? The simplest way to see it is to imagine all the possible outcomes of flipping two coins. In the one-coin flip there are two possible (and equally likely) outcomes (H and T), and we are interested only in one, hence 50% (1/2), chance of our head. When flipping two coins there are four possible (equally likely) outcomes (HH, HT, TH, TT), and we are interested only in the HH outcome; this is one out of the four equally possible outcomes, so there is a 25% chance of getting it. The general idea here is that the chance of two events happening equals the probability of the first event times the probability of the second event. So the probability of two heads is 50% x 50% = 25%, or ½ x ½ = ¼.[1]

| H | H | H | T | T | H | T | T |

For more than two events, you multiply the probability of each, so the probability of three heads is ½ x ½ x ½ = ⅛.

---

1   This is true when the two events are independent—that is, when getting or not getting the first event has no effect on the probability of getting the second event. Flipping a coin twice fits this requirement, but picking coloured marbles out of a jar *without replacing them* does not. Your chance of getting a second red marble is affected by your success or failure to get a red marble on the first pick.

One of the implications of the rule is that the more events that need to turn out the way we want in order for a project to be a success (i.e., the more probabilities that we multiply), the lower the chance that everything will work out.

This observation helps explain a lot of failed predictions because almost all projects require a number of events to come together for successful completion (e.g., you are fixing a leaky faucet, you have to find the tool, you have to have the right washer, the inside of the faucet can't be rusted out ...). While each event may have a relatively high probability, as you start to need a series of events to work out, the chance of all doing so becomes increasingly remote. The implications of the rule "the probability of a series of events equals the probability of each event multiplied by the others" is that no matter how carefully we plan, when we plan complex projects (e.g., the space shuttle) it is almost certain that something will go wrong. Murphy was right (see below).

A well-known expression of human frustration is Murphy's Law, usually expressed as "If something can go wrong, it will." Examples typically cited are toast falling butter side down and the fact that whatever line we queue in always ends up the slowest. Some of these perceptions have genuine statistical validity; others, of course, are based on our tendency to remember the perverse. Quickly now, how many times have you not been in the slowest line?

But some of these perceptions do have a scientific basis. In a charming article in *Scientific American*, R.A. Mathews shows that many of these frustrating phenomena are just what probability theory would predict. An example: "Probability theory ... holds the key to another notorious example of Murphy's Law: If odd socks can be created, they will be." [Why?] Imagine you have a drawer containing only complete pairs of socks. Now suppose one goes missing; ... Instantly you have an odd sock left behind in the drawer. Now a second sock goes missing. This can be either that odd sock just created or—far more likely—it will be a sock from an as yet unbroken complete pair, creating yet another odd sock in the drawer. Random sock loss is always more likely to create the maximum possible number of odd socks than to leave us free of the things.

Scientific American 276, 4 (April 1997): 88.

Compound Probability and Imagination

While most of us are aware of the reasoning described above, we often forget to apply it. This is where our intuitions and more careful probabilistic reasoning tend to part company. Here's an example.[1]

Suppose you are asked to guess the probability per year of an earthquake occurring in California killing 10,000 or more people. Guess some plausible number: one in 1,000? Now estimate the probability of an earthquake occurring in California that causes a dam to break and the resulting flood kills over 10,000 people. Is this more probable, say, one in 500? Does the idea of a dam bursting change your assessment of the probability of thousands being killed? Many people would assign a higher probability to the second scenario than to the first, because they find it *easier to imagine* that many people could be killed by a breaking dam. But by adding the breaking dam to the story, we have increased the number of events that have to happen so we have actually *decreased* the probability.

Here's a way of thinking about this that may sharpen your intuitions. Imagine that the chance of a large-scale fatal earthquake is X%. There are several possible ways this could happen: by causing building collapse, by

---

1   Kevin McKean, "Decisions, Decisions," *Discover Magazine* (June 1985): 22–31.

causing huge fires, by breaking a dam, etc. Each of these possibilities con-tributes a fraction to the total possibility X, so the probability of each must be less than the total. Using the multiplication rule referred to above the probability of a 10,000 death earthquake must be greater than the chance of such an earthquake *multiplied by* the probability of the dam breaking given the earthquake. Just as in the coin-flipping example, the chance of three heads coming up in a row must be less than two heads.

But stories speak to our feeling of the possible, a good story makes the events seem easy to imagine, makes them seem plausible and probable. This example underlines how ease of imagining can influence our sense of the probable—and not in reliable ways. It appears that along with using ease of recall, we seem naturally inclined to make intuitive judgements of the probable on the basis of ease of imagining. Plausible stories make an event easy to imagine and enhance the impression of probability. In the face of such stories, we need to keep in mind the diminished probability of a sequence of events. The tendency of stories to make events seem likely helps to sell commercial projects. Ignoring the enormous number of events that must fall into line to make a project work leads the vast proportion of projects (from home renovation to skyscrapers) to finish over-time and over-budget. The story may be plausible, but the math often is not.

Daniel Kahneman, who did much of the research on people's weak-nesses in using imagination as the basis of time estimates, recommends not even trying to figure out the probabilities, but rather asking someone with similar experience (or using your own experience: how long did the last paper take you to finish?). In support of this observation he related a story of his own. When he and a number of writers were planning to write an introductory book about probability they discussed how long it would take them. About two years, they estimated. Then someone asked them if they have ever been involved in a similar project. Yes, they replied; and how long did that take? Six years, was the answer. So guess how long the projected book took. Right, six years.[1]

Practical Note

Remember when planning any complex project discount the plausible story in view of the problem of compound probabilities. See how long it took others to complete similar projects. And, of course, don't forget Murphy's Law.

1   Ibid.

CALIBRATION

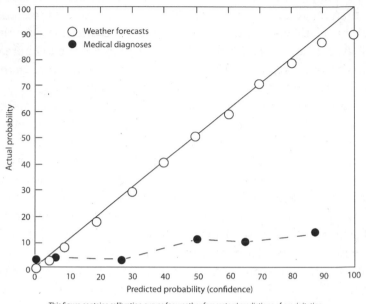

This figure contains calibration curves for weather forecasters' predictions of precipitation (hollow circles) and physicians' diagnoses of pneumonia (filled circles). Although the weather forecasters are almost perfectly calibrated, the physicians show substantial overconfidence (i.e., unwarranted certainty that patients have pneumonia). The data on weather forecasters comes from a report by Allan Murphy and Robert Winkler (1984), and the data on the physicians comes from a study by Jay Christensen-Szalanski and James Bushyhead (1981).

Fortunately it appears that we can learn to improve our probabilistic assessments. People whose estimates of likelihood agree with measured long-term frequency are said to be well **calibrated**. It should not surprise us to learn that few of us are well calibrated. Despite the seemingly poor predictive power of weather forecasts, one of the best calibrated groups of people is weather people. Apparently, being frequently wrong (and having that information brought to your attention) produces an appropriate self-awareness and humility. Plous gives an interesting chart[1] comparing the calibration of doctors and weather people. The 45 degree line represents perfect calibration. That means that when you say you are "50%" certain about a prediction, you are right about 50% of the time. The jagged line along the bottom representing medical judgements shows that despite increasing confidence (measured by the horizontal axis), a doctor's likelihood of being correct shows only limited improvement. According to Plous, people's confidence in their judgements appears to have little to do with their actual reliability. Generally speaking, a high level of confidence is a

---

1   S. Plous, *The Psychology of Judgment and Decision Making* (New York: McGraw-Hill, 1993), 228.

sign of being poorly calibrated. Disturbingly, this is as true for those whose decisions have profound consequences, such as doctors and murder witnesses, as it is for most of us. What can we do about our poor calibration?

Critical Question 3: What Other Information is Relevant?

Plous recommends a good technique for judging probability—indeed, for making any judgement: be humbler. Downgrade your confidence by stopping to consider reasons why your judgement might be wrong.[1] Consider alternative explanations and counter-evidence. Nothing chastens the mind like other possibilities.

Critical Question 4: Are Relevant Fallacies Avoided?

We covered many of the fallacies of probability estimation above. Unfortunately this is an area where most of us are not very good at making accurate estimates. Here is a brief summary of some of the typical fallacies.

1. **Overgeneralizing (Anecdotal Evidence)**: We all love to generalize, but seldom do we have the kind of systematically acquired information that would warrant our generalizations. Sometimes this is a result of the fallacy of Representativeness.
2. **Representativeness**: The often unconscious assumption that short-run experiences will be like, or are *representative*, of long-run probabilities. It can also be due to prejudice—racism, sexism, etc.
3. **Gambler's Fallacy**: Reasoning based on the assumption that future events will compensate for past non-representative runs.
4. **Overconfidence**: This is the fallacy of having confidence in a belief that is not proportional to your evidence.
5. **Availability**: This is the fallacy of estimating probabilities on the basis of our ability to recall events ("No one I know has ever been bitten by a dog, so dogs present no dangers.").
6. **Vividness**: This is the fallacy of allowing powerful personal experiences to influence our assessment of probabilities ("Those Tauruses, they are terrible cars. I should know. I owned one and it was a lemon.").

1 Ibid.

7. **Good Story Fallacy**: This is the fallacy of allowing a plausible story to make an event sound probable even though the sequence that the story describes would be more implausible than just the event (e.g., the story about the earthquake).

EVALUATING JUDGEMENTS OF PROBABILITY
THE CRITICAL QUESTIONS

1. What exactly is being claimed?
A probability judgement assesses an event as likely or unlikely. With repeated events the probability judgement is a claim about how often the event will occur in the long run. Objectivity in probability judgements can be obtained through good observation and correct calculation; sometimes subjective expectation is, however, quite divergent.

2. How good is the evidence?
- Have you used systematically gathered evidence, or just impressions from your own experience or the media?
- Is your impression based on your ability to imagine the event occurring? This is not a reliable source.
- Are you overconfident given the evidence you actually have?

3. What other information is relevant?
- Have you considered counter-evidence or counter-examples?
- Have you carefully considered past examples—e.g., other projects undertaken?

4. Are relevant fallacies avoided?
- **Overgeneralizing (Anecdotal Evidence):** We all love to generalize, but seldom do we have the kind of systematically acquired information that would warrant our generalizations.
- **Representativeness:** This is the fallacy that presumes that short-run experiences will be like, or are representative, of long-run probabilities.
- **Overconfidence:** This is the fallacy of having confidence in a belief that is not proportional to your evidence.
- **Gambler's Fallacy:** Reasoning based on the assumption that future events will compensate for past non-representative runs.
- **Availability:** This is the fallacy of estimating probabilities on the basis of our ability to recall events.
- **Vividness:** This is the fallacy of allowing powerful personal experiences to influence our assessment of probabilities.
- **Good Story Fallacy:** This is the fallacy of allowing a plausible story to make an event sound probable even though the sequence that the story describes would be more implausible than just the event.

CHAPTER 13

STUDIES SHOW, BUT SO WHAT?

DECISIONS, DECISIONS, DECISIONS

"The studies say" that even moderate drinking increases a woman's chance of getting breast cancer. On the other hand, studies say that moderate alcohol consumption reduces the risk of heart attacks and increases life expectancy. What's a person to do?

You are offered an extended warranty on your new LCD television for a mere 10% of the purchase price. Should you buy the warranty?

Evidence discussed in Chapter 11 shows that using a cellphone while driving increases the risk of accidents. Should you stop using your cellphone in the car? Up to now, we have been concerned with what we should *believe* as a result of studies and polls, now we want to know what we should *do*. That means that the questions we ask, the critical questions, are different. When we evaluate claims we look at the evidence, but when we are deciding what to do, we need to look not only at the evidence, but also at the probable costs and benefits of the action. How should we make use of statistical information to make good decisions? One way to do this is to look at a decision as a kind of bet.

Good Bets

What makes a good bet? Thinking about the long run can help answer this question. A **good bet** is one that if made repeatedly will result in a positive payoff.

Let's take a simple example. Suppose someone offers to make the following bet: you pay $1 to flip a coin, and collect $3 if you call it correctly. Since you have a 50% chance of winning, in the long run you will win half the time. So for every two plays you will pay $2 and win $3 (on average). This is a good bet. But suppose you were offered to play a dice game: you pay $1 and chose a number, and if you win you get $5. In the long run you would win one out of six, paying $6 for every $5 you won. A bad bet—in the long run you will lose money. If, on the other hand, the payoff were $6, then this would be a break-even bet—neither a good bet nor a bad one.

The basic method for figuring out if a bet is a good one is to multiply the payoff by the probability and subtract the cost of playing. If the number is positive, it's a good bet. The coin-flipping example from above, "$3 × 1/2 = $1.50 - $1= $.50," a good bet. The first dice bet is, "$5 × 1/6 = $.83 – $1 = - $.17," a bad bet. The second dice bet is, "$6 × 1/6 = $1 – $1 = 0," breaks even in the long run, and is neither a good nor a bad bet.

Warranties

Let's take a practical application of the principle of a good bet. Many of us have been offered extended warranties when we buy electronic equipment. Should we take these warranties? Many products come with a one-year warranty. The store typically offers to extend the warranty for two more years for a "mere" 10% of the purchase price. The question is, is that a good deal, in other words, is that a good bet? For the extended warranty to be a good bet, you would have to assume that more than one in ten of the gizmos need replacing during the second or third year. Let us say you are purchasing a TV that costs $1000. The extended warranty would cost an additional $100. Naturally, for the store to make money on its extended warranties, the warranty has to be a bad bet for the buyer. For sellers to break even they should replace about one in ten machines. That way they get $1000 of warranty payments for ten TVs and replace, on average, one of them, worth $1000. If they only have to replace 1 in 20 TVs, they get $2000 in warranty purchases and only have to pay out $1000 in replacements. So by buying the extended warranty you are betting that there is at least a 1 in 10 chance of the TV breaking down in the extended warranty period. Is it reasonable to assume that the TV will break down at this rate?

Consumer Reports states:

> Most big-ticket items are very dependable. For example, only eight per cent of analog camcorders, electric ranges, dishwashers, and top-freezer refrigerators were *repaired* in their first three years, according to 38,000 *Consumer Reports* readers surveyed in 2000.

Note the 8% includes repairs in the first year already covered by standard warranties; so the rate for the second and third years is lower. The items cited by *Consumer Reports* all have moving parts and are therefore more likely to break down. Since a TV has no moving parts, it seems likely that the repair rate for TVs is even lower. *Consumer Reports* adds:

> The odds are heavily stacked against your collecting on an extended warranty. In fact, the operating profit margins on such warranties are nearly 70 per cent, vs. 10 per cent on the products they cover, says Laura Champine, a consumer-products analyst at Morgan Keegan, a Memphis investment bank.[1]

So extended warranties are generally a bad bet. But, as with any aggregate data, there are likely to be sub-groups to which the average does not apply. Data from laptops suggest that extended warranties might be a good buy because of their relatively high failure rate.[2]

Insurance generally, of course, is a bad bet. If it weren't, the insurance companies would go broke, just as a casino can only have slot machines that are bad bets for the players—good bets for the casino—or they would go broke. What you have to decide is whether the "peace of mind" that comes from owning an insurance policy makes up for your probable long-term financial loss involved in the bad bet. When considering insurance such as home fire insurance, being protected against the catastrophic costs of a fire provides a "peace of mind benefit" that, for most people, offsets the long-

---

1 *Consumer Reports*, December 2003, p. 9. Accessed at <http://www.ca.uky.edu/hes/fcs/HSFP/updates/2004/update0083.htm>.
2 Ibid; also <http://www.macintouch.com/reliability/laptops.html>, which reports warranty claims of 18% in the second and third years on early iBooks.

run financial costs. Extended warranties on small purchases with their generally relatively high premiums are a much more dubious purchase.

Framing

There is an additional consideration involved in the purchase of a warranty. Psychologists have done research that shows that our choices are significantly influenced by how we **frame** a decision—how we see the decision and its consequences, which is partly a matter of how the choice has been presented to us, and partly determined by our own personal habits, attention, and dispositions. The store that offers you extended warranties at a "mere 10%" of the cost is using the fact that we tend to think of costs in percentages rather than absolute values. To most of us, a "mere 10%" sounds less than $100. To illustrate the power of framing consider the following example used by Kahneman and Tversky.[1] Suppose, while you are shopping, you are told that you could get the laundry detergent you were about to purchase for $10 down the street for 50% less (i.e., $5 less); would you be tempted to go down the street to make the purchase? Now suppose you are out shopping for a diamond ring with a value of $500 and you are told that you could get the same ring down the street for $5 less. Would you be tempted then? Even though there is the same level of inconvenience in making the purchase "down the street," and you save the same amount of money ($5), most people are tempted by the first bargain at 50% off and not by the second bargain—though it's the same $5 savings. Once someone is committed to spending five hundred or a thousand dollars on a major appliance, the "small" percentage added to the cost by the extended warranty is all too easily accepted. So when stores offer you extended warranties you need to keep in mind not only that they are offering you a bad bet, but also that they are likely "framing" the decision to make it seem less costly than it really is.

COST/BENEFIT ANALYSIS

What we have been describing is **cost/benefit analysis**. In cost/benefit analysis we look at the probable benefits (pay offs), subtract the costs, and then see if we are ahead.

---

1   Mckean.

Example: Ginseng and the Common Cold

Let's take a practical example. Some research has supported the claim that ginseng can help prevent the common cold. A recent study was done on a particular commercial version of ginseng called COLD-fx. According to the study, those on the therapy had 25% fewer colds during a four-month period when catching a cold is more likely. The average number of colds in the placebo group was .93 and the average in the treatment group was .68. Leaving aside for the moment possible side effects and assuming that these figures are representative of the effectiveness of the treatment, is COLD-fx worth it? The current cost of a month's supply of COLD-fx is approximately $25. Remembering that to assess whether something is a good bet we should think in terms of the long run. To do that, let's compare using COLD-fx to non-use over ten years. This will illustrate how the monetary value you place on getting a cold determines whether COLD-fx is a good bet.

At $25 a month for pills during the four months of the cold season, you would be paying about $1000 in ten years. The benefit (assuming their results are valid) would be a 25% less chance of getting a cold during the so-called flu season. Seem worth it? If you value having a cold at about a negative $100, you can see from the table below that the medication is not really worth it. Though if you value a cold at minus $400, then it might (just) be worth it. I notice that the ads for COLD-fx often feature professional athlete testimonials. This makes sense. The players are being paid well over $400/day, so even a small reduction in the frequencies of colds would be a net benefit for the team. For others? You decide.

	A	B	C	D Valuing Colds at -$100	E 10 year Net Benefit	F Valuing Colds at -$400	G 10 year Net Benefit
	Cost of Treatment for Four Months	Cost of Treatment for 10 Years	Chance of Getting a Cold/Year	10 Year "Cost" of Having a Cold @ $100/ Cold/Year	Cost of Meds Minus Residual Cost of Colds	10 Year "Cost" of Having a Cold @ $400/ Cold/Year	Cost of Meds Minus Residual Cost of Colds
Use Nothing	0	0	.93	$930		$3720	
Use COLD-fx	25 × 4 =$100	$1000	.68	$680		$2720	
Difference				$250	-$430	$1000	+$80

This method seems to work pretty well for simple issues like that above, but cost/benefit analysis has earned a bad reputation when evaluating issues of significant human or environmental harm. The idea of weighing costs and benefits when making a decision is both common-sensical and reasonable. But economists who make use of this concept, insist on using the monetary value of all costs, even the loss of human life. This allows them to calculate which decision will produce the most expected value. If the monetary benefits exceed the costs of acting, then it is a good decision to proceed with an action. The difficulty with this approach is that many considerations such as species loss or loss of life do not lend themselves to monetary evaluation. As a result decisions based on a purely monetary-value approach to cost/benefit are frequently troubling.

Many years ago, Ford had a problem with the gas tank of their Pinto. Using cost/benefit analysis, Ford decided out that it would be cheaper to pay court-imposed liability damages for burn deaths and injuries caused by their Pinto's poorly designed gas tank than to call back the Pintos and fix their tank.[1] This example shows a second problem with this approach to cost/benefit analysis: it ignores the fact that one group may receive the benefits, while another suffers the costs.

A recent example of the kind of problems involved in using strict cost/benefit analysis is provided by its application to the dangers of cellphone use while driving. There seems to be no doubt that such use increases the risk of an accident. Because of this, some governments have banned such use and many others are considering a ban. But the authors of a recent article used cost/benefit analysis to argue against such regulations. They estimated the monetary value (benefit) of car cellphone use to owners based on how much consumers were willing to pay for cellphone use and the percentage of use in cars. They then subtracted the estimated costs of accidents resulting from cellphone use in the car including repair bills, medical bills, and lost wages of crashes, and even death. They argue that the benefits exceed the costs, and since benefits exceed the costs, the authors contend cellphone use in cars should not be banned![2]

As we all know, neither all benefits nor all costs are monetary. The idea that a good decision generally is one in which benefits exceed costs in the broadest sense seems simply sensible—but only if we include non-

---

1   This story is reviewed in an article on the website of The Center For Auto Safety <http://www.autosafety.org/article.php?did=480&scid=96>.

2   R.W. Hahn and P.C. Tetlock, *The Economics of Regulating Cellular Phones in Vehicles.* (Washington, DC: American Enterprise Institute-Brookings Joint Center for Regulatory Studies, 1999), accessed at <http://aei-brookings.org/admin/authorpdfs/redirect-safely.php?fname=../pdffiles/working_99_09.pdf>. For a critique of the cost/benefit analysis see Frank Ackerman and Lisa Heinzerling, *Priceless: On Knowing the Price of Everything and the Value of Nothing* (New York: New Press, 2004).

monetary costs and benefits. To use considerations of costs and benefits sensibly we must keep in mind three things:

1. It seems difficult or impossible to value many important costs and benefits in monetary terms. On the other hand, it seems that in some circumstances we do. For example, suppose that putting a guardrail on a mountain highway would prevent an average of one auto fatality a year. The guardrail, which would last for ten years before needing replacement, would cost $10 million dollars. That's a cost of a million dollars per life saved. If the government decides to make such a decision, aren't they saying that each life saved is worth at least a million dollars? These are the kind of decisions frequently presented to institutions such as governments and hospitals. Whether we assign an exact value to human life as economists do, or just face the costs of saving lives as in the above example, we are using cost/benefit analysis.

2. Almost all benefits and costs are uncertain. When making a decision we must look both at the costs and benefits *and* how likely they are to occur. That brings us back to how to use statistical information and probabilities to make decisions.

3. When using cost/benefit analysis to make a decision, it is important to consider not only the costs and benefits, but also the distribution of the costs and benefits. For example, a recent installation of rapid transit in my city meant the closing down of a major retail street for over two years while the subway route was installed. The result was that most stores on the street went bankrupt. Perhaps those losses will be offset by the benefits we all receive from improved transit, but it seems manifestly unfair to the stores that were ruined, and to date the government has refused any appropriate compensation.

USING STATISTICAL INFORMATION TO MAKE LIFESTYLE DECISIONS

Innumerable studies are now published that estimate the probable risks and benefits involved in all sorts of lifestyle decisions, from smoking to the consumption of alcohol, from napping to exercising. There are other activities like skiing and snow boarding (and as mentioned, using a cellphone while driving) whose risks have also been studied. What use should we make of these studies? Should they influence our dietary and lifestyle choices? If so, how?

As an example, let's look at a summary of a report on the influence of drinking on the incidence of breast cancer:

> CBS News reported last night that a new study from the UK had demonstrated a link between drinking and breast cancer. Although CBS claimed that the study "analyzed 150,000 women around the world" it was actually a re-analysis of 53 separate studies. These "meta-analyses" are always questionable because different studies generally apply different methods, and accounting for differences may be difficult. Nevertheless, the study is reputable. It does not claim to show that drinking causes breast cancer, but it does demonstrate that the risk of the disease increases as more alcohol is consumed daily (a "dose-response relationship"). It also postulates a credible biological pathway—a damaged liver hinders the metabolization of estrogen, increasing breast cancer risk.
>
> *Note the study was a meta-analysis*
>
> *The author notes the dose relationship*
>
> *The author notes the biological model*
>
> Yet the actual risks of drinking in itself are pretty small. It is only when one drinks heavily that the risk becomes appreciably large. A woman who has, on average, one alcoholic drink a day, suffers only a 3% increased risk of breast cancer. Two drinks implies a 13% increased risk, three a 20% increased risk, and so on (six drinks a day gives a 46% increased risk).[1]

The author is right to note that the report does not "demonstrate" that alcohol causes breast cancer because the biological mechanism relating alcohol consumption and breast cancer is still uncertain, and the increase in risk is quite small. The report rightly warns that this study was a meta-analysis and subject to the concern of whether good and bad data are being mixed together (chapter 11). The aggregate numbers are large, but we are

---

1 From STATS weblog, "Shock News: Heavy Drinking Bad for You: A New Study has Reputable Results, but they Shouldn't Surprise Anyone," 14, 10 (November 13, 2002), accessed at (<http://www.stats.org>). The article summarizes the study from the Collaborative Group on Hormonal Factors in Breast Cancer, "Alcohol, Tobacco and Breast Cancer—Collaborative Reanalysis of Individual Data from 53 Epidemiological Studies, Including 58,515 Women with Breast Cancer and 95,067 Women without the Disease," *Br J Cancer* 187, 11 (Nov. 18, 2002): 1234–45.

not told whether the results are from prospective or retrospective studies. Nor are we told how the confounding factors of age or lifestyle were addressed. How many women who are heavy drinkers also eat their broccoli? So of course, I went to the abstract of the original research to see if these factors had been addressed. The abstract does mention controlling for age, but there is no indication of controlling for lifestyle factors other than tobacco consumption. As the article mentions, the relative risk identified by the study is quite small and therefore, given the difficulties of doing these kinds of studies, appropriately subject to considerable scepticism.

But suppose, for the purpose of this chapter, we accept the study results as credible. What is the significance of these results for a woman's decision about alcohol consumption? In order to answer this question we need to review a few crucial concepts.

Absolute and Relative Risk

The first point to notice is that the report cites an increase in **relative risk**. There are a number of ways of reporting risk. As I mentioned in Chapter 12, the chance of being killed by lightning in any year is about 0.25 in a million.[1] This is the yearly **absolute risk** of being killed by lightning. But risk is often reported as a **risk ratio**, or relative risk. For example, people living in Kansas have twice the risk of US residents in general—a much higher relative risk (compared to the broader group). The absolute risk of being killed by lightning in Kansas is 0.57 in a million. Still a pretty small risk compared to say being killed in a motor vehicle accident in any year, which is about 120 in a million. Being killed in a car accident has a relative risk that is about 400 times greater (or 40,000% greater!) than being hit by lightning in Kansas.

As you can see from these examples, describing risk in terms of relative risk can often sound very scary even when the absolute risk involved is still very small. Making sensible life decisions using statistical information about risk requires we keep in mind the *crucial distinction between relative and absolute risk*. Cancer agencies and pharmaceutical companies are all too attracted to using *relative risk* numbers because they are almost always larger than *absolute risk* and if you want to scare people into changing their lifestyle, or buying your drugs, bigger numbers work better. There are of course also legitimate reasons for reporting relative risk when testing a therapy or pharmaceutical or the results of differing consumption patterns. As we saw with the COLD-fx example, we needed to

1   <http://www.nsc.org/lrs/statinfo/odds.htm> US National Safety Council.

know the relative advantage of taking the medication versus not taking it in order to decide if the benefit was worth the cost. But to make use of the information we almost always need both *relative* and *absolute risk* values.

The relative risk of a smoker getting lung cancer compared to a non-smoker is somewhere between five and 15 times depending on amount smoked. But not all smokers get lung cancer. In all the discussion about the dangers of smoking we hardly ever hear what the absolute risk of lung cancer is. What is the absolute risk of lung cancer for a smoker? Based on a recent study[1] it is about 40/1000 for all smokers. The absolute risk of a smoker dying from coronary heart disease is much greater at 177/1000, though the relative risk of dying from heart disease for a smoker is only about one and a half times greater (1.5) than that of a never-smoker. The figure on death from heart disease illustrates the importance of knowing both relative and absolute risk. While smoking "only" increases a smoker's chance of dying from heart disease by 50%, the smoker is still four times more likely to die from heart disease than lung cancer.

This shows why, as consumers of information, we need to know not only relative but absolute risk. I am not particularly interested in living in Kansas, but the doubling of my risk of being hit by lightning is not one of the reasons that would influence my decision. To put the Kansas-lightning risk (0.57 in a million) in perspective: the chance of a person drowning in the bath in any year is about two in a million. I certainly would not consider that a reason to give up bathing.

---

1   James E. Enstrom and Geoffrey C. Kabat, "Environmental Tobacco Smoke and Tobacco Related Mortality in a Prospective Study of Californians, 1960-98," *BMJ* 326 (May 2003): 1057.

Knowing Your "Risk Group": Do the Figures Apply to Me?

> "I don't think our brains have evolved to think about risk statistically," Dr. Slovic said. "One of the first things we think about is: well, is this relevant to me?"[1]

While I would agree with Dr. Slovic's remark that we have not evolved to think about risk statistically, I think asking whether a statistic is relevant to oneself is quite "evolved" and sensible. The problem is that statistics arc always about groups, tendencies, and averages. If we are going to make use of statistical information we need to know the extent to which it applies to us or at least to a group of people like us in relevant ways. Remember the difference between the likelihood of being struck by lightning in Kansas versus the US generally. Where you live makes a difference in terms of all kinds of risks (e.g., lung cancer caused by urban air pollution): so does your age, gender, and ethnicity. If you are going to make good use of statistical information you need to make sure that the probabilities apply to people most like yourself, what is called your **risk group**. And while statistics can never apply to just you (unless you're a baseball player), the closer the risk group "fits" you, the more useful the information for decision-making.

Know your risk group.

1 Gina Kolata, "Experts Strive to Put Diseases in Proper Perspective," *The New York Times*, Late Edition, July 2, 2002: F5.

In Chapter 6 I discussed the reflections of the famous palaeontologist S.J. Gould when he was diagnosed with mesothelioma. He noted that there was wide variability beyond the median life expectancy of three months, and he argued that he was likely to be in the outlier (risk) group who lived the longest because he was young, cheerful, and had access to the best health care. He was right and lived into his sixties, dying of a different cancer.[1]

LIFE EXPECTANCY

To illustrate the value of using the right risk group for statistics that are relevant to you remember our discussion of the concepts of life expectancy in Chapter 6. I noted that not only is our life expectancy a function of gender and geography, but it is also a function of age. The longer you live, the more likely you are to live longer because once you have lived, for example, to age forty, you have avoided a number of death-dealing events. As one expert put it, we gain about five hours of life for every day we live.[2]

While many factors that determine our life expectancy are beyond our control, many are not. We make choices about how to travel, what sports to play, and what to eat, among other important and somewhat risky decisions. Let's take a couple of examples to see how we might use statistical information as a basis for our decision.

Putting Risk in Perspective

FLY OR DRIVE?

Most people have heard that travelling by commercial airlines is the safest way to travel. The data certainly supports that, in part, because the danger of air travel is unrelated to how far you travel, i.e., whether you are flying 5,000 km or 500 km the danger is virtually identical because the most dangerous time is during the takeoff and landing. What is the risk of dying in a commercial plane crash? In terms of *fatalities per flight*, it is about one in seven million—a virtually irrelevant risk. To see how

1   "The Median Isn't the Message," accessed at <http://www.cancerguide.org/median_not_msg.html>.
2   Misty Harris, "We're Gaining Time as We Get Older; One Expert Says People Today Are Adding Five Hours of Life Expectancy for Every Day They Live," *The Vancouver Sun*, May 9, 2007: A11.

irrelevant, consider that if you took a flight every day of the year, on the average it would take 19,000 years before you were a victim of a fatal crash.

Suppose you were deciding whether to drive or fly the 1,000 km to grandma's house. Which would be safer? Motor vehicle fatality rates, which have declined significantly in the last 20 years, are approximately 1/100 million kilometres travelled. So your chance of a fatal accident in 1,000 km is approximately one in 100,000, which is significantly riskier than one in seven million for flying. The relative risk of dying going by car is about 70 times that of taking the plane. In addition, your chance of being involved in an injury resulting from a car accident is much higher than in planes—approximately 100 per 100 million kilometres. But the rate of injury for flying is essentially the same as that of fatalities. If you think in terms of lifetime risk, driving is not all that safe. If you drive, say, 20,000 km a year, in an 80-year lifespan that is 1,600,000 km; so you have a *lifetime risk* of about 1.6/1,000 of dying in a car accident. How significant a risk is that?

John Paling, a "risk consultant," has made the following useful graph that can help us think about risks by comparing the risks of a variety of activities with which we are familiar (I have added two more risk benchmarks).[1]

Risks with which we are all "At Home"

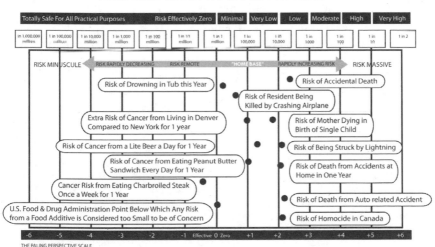

1 <http://www.riskcomm.com/pdfdocs/PPS04HomeBaseBW.pdf>.

As you can see, Paling classes the one in a million annual risk as virtually zero. Everything from the risk of drowning in the tub to being murdered (in the US) is above this minimal risk. Given you drive 20,000 km per year, the average risk of a fatal accident is about 2/10,000, which puts it a bit above being killed by an accident in the home, but it is three times higher than your chance of being murdered (even in the US).[1]

Risk assessment is not of course all about probability. The kind of misfortune associated with the risk—the way in which harm is caused—is also an important consideration. For example, we fear terrorists and plane accidents in part because they are well-publicized horrors. Terrorism is greatly feared despite the fact that an individual in North America has more of a chance of drowning in the bath than being killed by a terrorist—even if a terrorist attack of the magnitude of 9/11 occurred every year.[2] We also fear terrorism because it is a risk over which we have no control. While the risk of travelling in a car is greater than that of travelling by plane, many fear flying not only because of the high publicity given to plane crashes, but also because they have no control over their situation when they are in a plane. When you are driving you can think, "Well yes, there is a risk, but I am a good driver and can minimize that risk." And to some extent you are right. Safe drivers have a fatality rate of 1/billion miles[3] as compared to the US national average of approximately 1,500/billion miles.[4] Familiarity is also a significant factor in our risk assessment. We are more fearful of the new risks than the old. No doubt when people first started driving automobiles many were (justly) fearful of driving in a car, though we now take that risk for granted. But sometimes the familiar is far more deadly than the new. For example, the SARS outbreak that paralyzed Toronto in 2003 killed about 50 people, while the ordinary flu kills about 1,000 Canadians every year.[5]

---

1   While Paling's chart is useful, some of his data is dubious or misleading. Note his figure for being struck by lighting: it reflects "lifetime risk" not yearly risk while other figures are for yearly risk. The basis of some of the other figures is unclear. What is useful is being able to see the kind of risk with which we are normally comfortable so that we can contrast this risk level with other risk information.
2   Jeffrey S. Rosenthal, *Struck by Lightning* (Toronto: HarperCollins, 2005), 80.
3   Arnold Barnett, Chance Lectures, Dartmouth College, 1997, accessed at <http://www.dartmouth.edu/~chance/ChanceLecture/AudioVideox.html#Videos97>.
4   Bureau of Transportation Statistics, Research and Innovative Technology Administration, United States Department of Transportation <http://www.bts.gov/publications/national_transportation_statistics/html/table_02_17.html>.
5   Rosenthal, pp. 80-81.

RISK AND SPORTS

What about sports? Participation in sports is widespread, and by and large a healthy, life enhancing activity. But there are risks. Getting good risk information about sports is not that easy since most sports do not keep careful records. When Sonny Bono and Michael Kennedy were both killed in 1998 in skiing accidents, there was considerable focus on the dangers of skiing. Information available at that time suggested that the approximately 35 people who die each year from skiing represent less than one death per million skier days. Not surprisingly most of those dying (85%) were young males. Of course death is not the only negative consequence of a skiing accident; it is just the easiest data to find. On the other hand, if you are not a young male your chances of dying while skiing are significantly less than Paling's "o" risk. While bowling is undoubtedly safer than skiing, the risk associated with risky sports such as skydiving is far greater. Such figures as I can find claim that the fatality rate for skydiving is about 8.5 per million jumps (850% more risky than skiing!).[1] Is it foolish then to sky dive? That depends on your "risk budget" and your "risk group." That is, it depends on how you view the pleasures of skydiving versus the risk of being killed, and also how safe a skydiver you are.

Comparison of the Frequency of Annual US Emergency Department Visits for Injuries Associated with Selected Activities and Products

Selected Activity	Estimated Annual No. of Emergency Department Visits
Baseball/softball*	404 364
Dog bites	333 687
Playground*	266 810
All-terrain vehicles, mopeds, etc.*	125 136
Volleyball*	97 523
Inline skating*	75 994
Horseback riding*	71 162
Baby walkers †	28 000
Skateboards*	25 486

* Data from US Consumer Product Safety Commission.

† Data from US Consumer Product Safety Commission.

1 <http://theblueskyranch.com/sta/tb7.htm> accessed September 18, 2008.

Of course death is not the only risk we take when we play sports. Interestingly enough a seemingly benign sport like baseball results in numerous injuries serious enough to send people to the hospital. The above table is from the US. Of course, without knowing how many people are playing baseball we cannot tell what the rate of injuries per game is. But obviously even non-extreme sports like baseball and volleyball have their level of risk—a risk level with which we are generally comfortable.

Risk, Breast Cancer, and Alcohol

So far we have discussed the concepts of absolute and relative risk, risk group, and how to put risk into perspective. Let's apply these concepts to the issue (introduced above) of the relation between breast cancer and alcohol consumption. As noted, there is some evidence that moderate drinking increases a woman's lifetime chance of getting breast cancer. But first let us deal with the highly publicized risk of breast cancer that all women face.

LIFETIME VS. YEARLY RISK

If you are a woman you are probably quite aware of the well-known claim that one in ten women will get breast cancer (actually the published figures vary from one in nine to one in eleven). What does this mean? Be careful: this is lifetime risk, not the yearly risk which we were discussing above when talking about lightning and skiing. The *lifetime risk* of being killed by lightning is pretty small—about 20/1,000,000—but it is approximately 80 times greater than being killed by lightning in any one year. However, unlike being struck by lightning, a crucial determinant of the likelihood of breast cancer is age.

A woman's chance of getting any cancer in a particular year increases with age. Let's look at some typical figures for breast-cancer incidence.[1] Note in the introduction to the table that there are other factors beside age that are also relevant to determining the appropriate risk group.

---

1 Breast Cancer Action Saskatchewan, attributed to National Cancer Institute, accessed at <http://bcask.ca/index.php?option=com_content&task=view&id=13&Itemid=37>.

Incidence by Age

This risk model is based on population averages. Each woman's breast cancer risk may be higher or lower, depending upon several factors, including family history, genetics, age of menstruation, and other factors that have not yet been identified.

A Woman's Chances of Breast Cancer Increase With Age

From age 30 to age 39   0.44% (1 in 227)

From age 40 to age 49   1.49% (1 in 67)

From age 50 to age 59   2.79% (1 in 36)

From age 60 to age 70   3.38% (1 in 26)

Source: National Cancer Institute, <http://www.cancer.gov>, 2004.

Scary, but a bit misleading. The table *does not mean* that during your sixth decade (from 50 through 59) you have one chance in 36 of getting breast cancer. The numbers given here are cumulative. (The number means that one in 36 women will have been *diagnosed* by 59.) The actual chance of a woman getting breast cancer during the five-year period from age 50-54, for example, is about 2.4 per 1,000.[1] Putting this in a more positive perspective, that means a woman has a 99.75% chance of *not* being diagnosed with breast cancer in that period, quite different than one in ten. It is also crucial to note that *these are not mortality figures*.

Thanks to advances in treatment and perhaps screening, survival rates have improved enormously. Survival rates are measured usually on the basis of five-year survival, so that a woman who survives five-years from diagnosis is usually treated as cured of that cancer. The five-year survival rate for breast cancer is about 88% for women age 50-54, meaning that the risk of dying from breast cancer in the period 50-54 is 12% of the risk of being diagnosed with breast cancer. In other words, the risk of a woman *dying* from breast cancer during this period is .12 × 1/400 or, approximately 3/10,000. Putting this another way, 99.97% of woman aged 50-54 are *not* likely to die of breast cancer in that year.

The following chart prepared by British researchers demonstrates the relative impact of various kinds of illness on life expectancy. The chart, showing the number of deaths per 100,000 women, indicates very few deaths from the identified diseases until about 50, and thereafter cardiovascular and smoking-related deaths greatly exceed that of breast cancers.

---

1   "Breast Cancer Incidence," accessed at <http://seer.cancer.gov/faststats/selections.php#Output>, September 18, 2008.

Lifetime Risk[1]

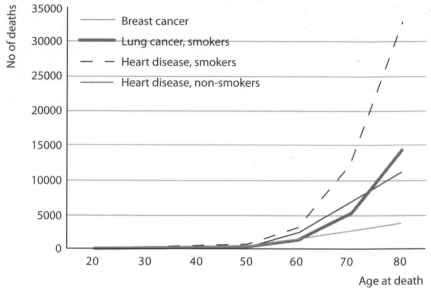

USING THE INFORMATION

So, does the claimed increased risk of breast cancer associated with alcohol provide a good reason to not consume or limit alcohol consumption among women?

According to the article, moderate drinking may increase the likelihood of breast cancer by somewhere between 3-13%. Because of the nature of this kind of research, we know that these numbers have considerable uncertainty. But for the moment let us assume they are correct.

The increased risk identified with moderate drinking is a shift from a risk of 25/10,000 to 27.5/10,000 for a woman being diagnosed with breast cancer during the five years from 50 to 54 (an increase of approximately .3/10,000 chance of *dying* of breast cancer at current cure rates). Is this a sufficient reason for an individual not to have a glass of wine a day?

There are basically six issues involved when thinking about this information:

1 J.P. Bunker, J. Houghton, M. Baum, "Putting the Risk of Breast Cancer in Perspective," *BMJ* 317, 7168 (November 7, 1998): 1307-09. I mentioned this study in Chapter 5 because the figures from Britain and the US on breast-cancer incidence are dramatically different: US is 1/8 vs. 1/12 in Britain. This illustrates the uncertainty involved in the underlying data for risk assessment, even in this well-studied area.

- How reliable are the risk estimates?
- Which risk statistic (which risk group) is relevant to me?
- What are the relative and absolute risks involved?
- Are there also health benefits associated with wine consumption?
- What non-health benefits are lost in changing my consumption habits?
- How should the risk be "framed"?

As suggested by Paling above, a way to think about this decision is by comparing it to other "risk" decisions that seem acceptable. So let us compare moderate wine drinking to driving. To do that, we need to focus not on breast-cancer incidence but actual mortality. Comparing 100,000 moderate drinkers to 100,000 non-drinkers in the cohort of 50-54-year-old women, there are about 33 deaths per year from breast cancer in the moderate drinking group versus 30 in the non-drinking group. In that same period approximately 12 people per 100,000 will die from traffic accidents. In other words, the increase in risk of dying from breast cancer as a result of wine drinking is one quarter of the risk of dying that results from driving a car.

So what should a woman do? Let's review the questions:

- *How reliable are the risk estimates?* While the research has been extensive, there is significant variation in results. Control for lifestyle factors is difficult and the size of the increased risk is too small to establish much credibility. The statistics are not particularly reliable.
- *Which risk statistic (which risk group) is relevant to me?* While risk is clearly age related, it may also be that moderate wine consumption is a risk just for a vulnerable sub-group.[1] The medical profession seems to take this view; doctors sometimes take special care to caution women with high-risk family background against alcohol consumption.
- *What are the relative and absolute risks involved?* See discussion above.
- *Are there also health benefits associated with wine consumption?* Most research suggests that moderate alcohol consumption is

---

1   Mary Beth Terry, Marilie D. Gammon, Fang Fang Zhang, Julia A. Knight, Qiao Wang, Julie A. Britton, Susan L. Teitelbaum, Alfred I. Neugut, and Regina M. Santella, "ADH3 Genotype, Alcohol Intake and Breast Cancer Risk," *Carcinogenesis* 27: 840-47. Abstract available at <http://carcin.oxfordjournals.org/cgi/content/abstract/bgi285v1>.

associated with lower incidence of heart disease, but some recent research has called this association into question. This is a
hard question to answer at this point.

- *What non-health benefits are lost in changing my consumption habits?* Depends on how much you enjoy your wine.

- *How should the risk be framed?* Typically these facts are "framed" as
risk or loss. But framed more positively, a 50-54-year-old woman
has a 99.97% of *not* dying of breast cancer and a moderate drinker
of the same age has a 99.88% of *not* dying of breast cancer during
that year.

THINKING MORE GENERALLY ABOUT RISK

But perhaps you are not a 50-year-old woman. How does this way
of thinking about risk apply to you? What worries about risk and
health might a 20 year old have? What about going out for a walk at
night? Or perhaps using a cellphone? Being 20 years old means that
you are in a low-risk group for most ailments. The main source of
serious harm and fatalities in this group is accidents, especially car
accidents.

The first rule for the sensible use of risk information is to use this
information to identify significant risks and then avoid these risks.
That may mean focusing on risks that seldom get much publicity
nowadays.

For example, auto safety. The solution is simple: put on your seat belt
and don't be in cars that are driven recklessly by either you or others
(e.g., don't drink and drive). Don't drive when you are tired. On the
other hand, do go for walks. It is very safe to walk in most places in
Canada (e.g., two robberies[1] with a weapon per 10,000 persons),[2] so walk
and don't worry.

What about cellphones? As you know from our research in Chapter
10, despite a considerable number of studies there is currently no evidence
that cellphone use causes cancer.[3] A review of the studies suggests that

---

1 I cite robbery with a weapon because this is usually a "stranger" crime. Assault and
homicide include the unfortunate rate of domestic violence.
2 Warren Silver, *Crime Statistics in Canada, 2006* (Statistics Canada, 2006) accessed at
<http://www.statcan.ca/english/freepub/85-002-XIE/85-002-XIE2007005.pdf>.
3 Chapter 11 of this work; but see also the editorial "Brains and Mobile Phones" by Michael Maier in *BMJ* 332 (April 15, 2006): 864-65, available at <http://www.bmj.com/
cgi/content/full/332/7546/864>.

it is unlikely that cellphones cause cancer, not only because there is no statistical evidence, but also because there is no biological mechanism given the low level of radiation involved.

On the other hand, common sense and statistical evidence support the claim that talking on a cellphone while driving does increase the chance of having an accident. It seems obvious that juggling a cellphone, dialling, and talking can detract from one's concentration on driving. For one thing you only have one hand on the wheel. But as we saw in Chapter 11, two recent studies found that there was about four times the risk of an accident when drivers use a cellphone regardless of whether the phone was handheld or hands-free. That's relative risk of course. This suggests that the risk is from the loss of concentration caused by the conversation, and not the fact that one's hand is occupied. This also suggests that the cellphone risk may be similar to what you get when talking to someone in the car, thinking distractedly, or "rubbernecking."

There is evidence that young people in particular have an increased risk of accidents when there are others in the car. Talking on a cellphone can add one more distraction to managing a cup of coffee, changing the CD, and staring at passing people. Is the additional risk involved worth the advantage of talking while driving? While accidents happen no matter how careful you are, obviously the more care and attention you are giving to your driving the less likely you will be to have an accident. Should you drive when overtired or while not paying attention and looking out the window? Obviously not. Have you had an accident? About one person in 50 is involved in a traffic accident in North America every year. Quadrupling your chances of an accident to four in 50 by talking on a cellphone seems a pretty significant increase in both relative and absolute risk and does suggest that pulling over when using a cellphone is a good idea.

What about eating? Everyone believes that what you eat can affect your long-term health. But how much increase in risk, say of heart disease, is associated with eating french fries? A recent extensive review of the studies on trans fats and their effects on health claims that a "two per cent increase in energy intake from trans fatty acids was associated with a 23 per cent increase in the incidence of CHD (congestive heart disease)."[1] Of course this is lifetime risk. Not too many 20 year olds get CHD.

---

1   Dariush Mozaffarian, et al., "Trans Fatty Acids and Cardiovascular Disease," *N Engl J Med* 354 (2006): 1601–13.

What about unprotected sex? There are numerous sexually transmitted diseases that can be transmitted by unprotected sex, with AIDS the best known. What are your chances of getting AIDS from unprotected sex? Depends on you and your partner's risk group. Here's a table provided by the reliable Center for Disease Control and Prevention in the US. It breaks down by cause of transmission the 37,000 new AIDS cases in the US during 2006.

Transmission Category	Estimated # of AIDS Cases, in 2006		
	Adult and Adolescent Male	Adult and Adolescent Female	Total
Male-to-Male Sexual Contact	16,001	-	16,001
Injection Drug Use	4,410	2,385	6,795
Male-to-Male Sexual Contact and Injection Drug Use	1,803	-	1,803
High-Risk Heterosexual Contact*	4,558	7,196	11,754
Other**	217	220	437

*Heterosexual contact with a person known to have, or to be at high risk for, HIV infection.
** Includes hemophilia, blood transfusion, perinatal exposure, and risk not reported or not identified.[1]

The population of the US in 2006 was about 299 million, and since there were about 37,000 new AIDS cases, that means that there were 12 new AIDS cases that year per 10,000 people. A large majority of these resulted from male-to-male sexual contact and injection drug use. There were 12,191 new cases of AIDS from other causes (for example, sexual contact with someone who is high risk), that is, less than four cases per 10,000 people. This is a rather small risk. And if your heterosexual contact (like most) is not with high-risk people, then your risk vanishes down to very close to zero. On the other hand, the risk of acquiring one of the many other sexually transmitted diseases is considerably higher. The number of young people in the age group 15-24 in 2000 was 39.2 million, giving an incidence rate of 22/100. That is, about 22% of people in this category for this estimate had contracted an STD in the US in 2000. Of course some may have contracted more than one, but the figure is still alarmingly high.[2]

---

1   <http://www.cdc.gov/hiv/topics/surveillance/basic.htm#exposure>.
2   Berman Hillard Weinstock Stuart, "Sexually Transmitted Diseases Among American Youth: Incidence and Prevalence Estimates, 2000," *Perspectives on Sexual and Reproductive Health* 36, 1 (2004): 6-10.

Estimated Incidence and Prevalence of Selected STDs Among 15–24-year-olds and Strength of Evidence, United States, 2000

STD	Incidence	Prevalence	Strength of evidence
Total	**9.1 million**	**u**	
Chlamydia	1.5 million	1.0 million	II
Gonorrhea	431,000	u	II
Syphilis	8,200	u	II
Genital herpes	640,000	4.2 million	II
HPV	4.6 million	9.2 million	III
Hepatitis B	7,500	u	II
Trichomoniasis	1.9 million	u	III
HIV	15,000	u	II

In contrast, the latest study by Statistics Canada, based on a large survey of 15-24 year olds who were sexually active only found a reported STD incidence of 4%, though the authors suggest that the true figure is likely higher than reported because of a lack of symptoms, awareness, or candour.[1]

Going Beyond the Personal: The Public-Policy Perspective

Should trans fats be banned? Should using cellphones in your car be prohibited? What about having all women tested for breast cancer?

These questions illustrate one of the dilemmas of using statistical information. While a small increase in risk might not be significant to an individual, the same increase in, say, breast-cancer rates may be a public-health problem. A 1% increase in the incidence of (female) breast cancer means approximately 18,000 additional new cases per year in the US.[2]

TESTING

One obvious public-policy method for reducing health risks is early detection through widespread testing. Mammograms, for example, have

1 "Early Sexual Intercourse, Condom Use and Sexually Transmitted Diseases," *The Daily*, May 3, 2005, accessed at <http://www.statcan.ca/Daily/English/050503/d050503a. htm>.
2 Based on information from the American Cancer Institute <http://cancernet.nci.nih. gov/cancertopics/types/breast>.

shown that early detection can save lives.[1] But surprisingly there are some dangers with such testing. The most obvious is the danger of **false negatives**, i.e., the danger that a test will miss detecting an illness or a tumor. Such false negatives give a person an incorrect sense of security. This problem can be reduced by designing the test to produce the absolute minimum of false negatives. The mammogram currently depends on a trained radiologist examining x-rays to detect tumors. X-rays produce pictures with black and white images that need to be interpreted to decide which white spots are just normal tissue and which are tumors. To reduce false negatives, the radiologists can "err" in the direction of interpreting difficult-to-decide white spots as tumors and refer the patient for biopsy.[2] You would think that such a tendency to err in the direction of caution would be an entirely good thing. But not necessarily. Being told that you might have breast cancer is troubling and a biopsy is not a particularly pleasant experience. Additional procedures, of course, cost money. We don't, in other words, want to have too many **false positives**, i.e., false judgements that a woman might have breast cancer. Nor do we want to have too many false-negative judgements—that a person is cancer free when she is not. There is not, unfortunately, an absolute resolution of this tension. Reducing false positives usually increases false negatives and vice versa.

There is a connected concern with health testing that is sometimes called the paradox of false positives. Because of the great value of early detection in most illnesses, it is tempting to assume that public health could be improved by various kinds of universal testing such as the encouragement that all women over 50 get bi-yearly mammograms. Why not mammograms for women under 50, or universal testing for AIDS for example? Here is the problem. If a disease is relatively uncommon universal testing will produce a horrific number of false positives. Take a disease with a prevalence rate of one in 10,000. And let us say that we test 10 million people. Among the 10

---

1 But primarily in women over 60, in whom (as discussed here) breast cancer is far more common.

2 A recent study noted that false-positive rates vary considerably among radiologists: from 3.5% to 7.9% in this particular study, though the average in the US is closer to 10%. This same study found that false-positive rates were climbing among US radiologists as they became increasingly afraid of being sued for false negatives. The study report suggests that such a high rate of false positives is acceptable because it minimizes false negatives—as long as women understand that false positives are common and being called back for another test (usually another x-ray) does not mean that one has cancer. See American Cancer Society, "False-Positive Mammogram Results Vary Among Radiologists," accessed at <http://www.cancer.org/docroot/NWS/content/NWS_1_1x_False-Positive_Mammogram_Results_Vary_Among_Radiologists.asp> September 8, 2002.

million there will be 1,000 people with the disease. If we use a test that is 99% accurate, we will detect 990 of those with the disease. But we will also have a 1% false-positive rate. That means we will wrongly identify 100,000 people as having the disease. 100,000 false positives to catch 990 real cases. The personal and public-health costs of such an error rate are enormous. And few tests are as accurate as 99% (see table).

Test with 99% Accuracy 1% False Positive Rate	People with Disease	People without Disease
Population = 10 million, One in 10,000 has disease	1,000	9,999,000
Identified as Having Disease	990 (Correctly)	99,990 (Wrongly)
Identified as NOT Having Disease	10 (Wrongly)	9,899,010 (Correctly)

This is another illustration of the difference in perspective between the personal and the public. An individual may wish to get tested for breast cancer or prostate cancer, but any universal testing for these diseases would simply generate too many false positives.

To demonstrate the danger of false positives consider a device actually being designed to enhance airport security. The company making the devices claims that they will miss only 10% of terrorists and only identify 4% of innocent people for further investigation. But about 750 million people fly through North American airports every year. That means that 30 million (!) innocent people a year will be detained as suspects at airport security.[1] Universal testing, even a test with significant accuracy generates way too many false positives if the group being tested has a very low incidence of whatever is being tested for, whether cancer or terrorists' plans.

STATISTICS AND THE LAW

So should cellphone use while driving be made illegal? A number of jurisdictions have done so already, including New York State. The evidence is compelling that using cellphones increases the risk of accidents, though the magnitude of the risk increase seems similar to other distractions, e.g.,

---

1   "Airport Biometric Station Screens People for 'Hostile Intent'—Boing Boing," accessed at <http://www.boingboing.net/2006/08/14/airport-biometric-st.html>, September 21, 2008. Thanks to Bob Martin for bringing this example to my attention.

putting CDs in the changer and "rubbernecking." The risk appears to be less than that for fatigue and alcohol. We have already looked at one cost/benefit analysis that concluded that banning cellphones would not be a good idea, but another study, using a different way of estimating costs, concluded that costs about equalled benefits. In any case, as we have seen, the uncertainty of estimating risks and of measuring costs and benefits make the use of cost/benefit analysis a questionable tool for developing public policy. In addition, it has been found that in one district where cellphone use was made illegal, rates of use did not diminish.[1] People seem to want to use their cellphone while driving even if it is illegal.

Trans fats have also been banned in a number of jurisdictions, with Denmark leading the way. There appears to be not much cost to producers or consumers in abandoning the use of artificial trans fats, though many governments prefer to provide new warning labels rather than banning a product. Reliability questions arise in all diet research, but there is considerable consensus at the moment that trans fats are dangerous.

The questions of whether an issue like cellphone use or trans fats should be treated with legislation is a complicated one with issues such as freedom and practicality that extend far beyond consideration of statistics. But citizens who understand the strengths and weaknesses of statistical information at least have some basis for making a rational decision.

LIVING WITH UNCERTAINTY

Many of life's activities have both potential risks and benefits. Focusing on risk avoidance can be stultifying, but clearly in genuinely risky cases—for example, skydiving—it's foolish to ignore the dangers. Risk perception is justifiably subjective, reflecting the fact that individuals have different levels of aversion to different dangers. Even when they know the same facts, reasonable people will make different judgements about the appropriateness of a risk. Most people fear dying of cancer more than they do dying of a heart attack even though heart attack fatalities are the most common cause of death. Debilitating illnesses, even if they do not result in death, are also intensely feared (though studies show that we tend to overrate how badly we will feel if such illnesses befall us).[2] On the other hand, the pleasure we take in activities should

---

1   A.T. McCartt and L.L. Geary, "Longer Term Effects of New York State's Law on Drivers' Handheld Cell Phone Use," *Injury Prevention* 10 (2004): 11–15.
2   G. Johnson, Book Reviews, *Scientific American* 94 (2006): N. 6.

not be ignored. People like to ski, drive their cars, and have a drink. Each of these activities has risks associated with them, but so does taking a bath. As Paling's chart shows, many daily activities have a yearly fatality risk level of somewhere around one to five in 10,000. It would appear that this is a level of risk that we can more or less ignore. That said, not jay-walking, driving carefully, and putting on your seat belt can all reduce the risks of our everyday activities. Risk probabilities are not fate and we have the ability in many cases to minimize them if we wish.

Our society has been described as increasingly risk averse and safety conscious. Perhaps we are. One of the benefits of affluence is that we can afford to drive safer cars on safer roads, and provide more protection to our children. Safety is a benefit that many people appreciate, but it is not the only good in life. Doing almost anything inevitably involves some risk. While being able to avoid risk is a benefit, being fearful, an attitude much encouraged by the media, is obviously not healthy. Getting the facts about risks can help reduce fears that are based on false impressions. After we know the risks involved in a choice, it is up to each of us individually to decide if the benefits of an activity are worth the risk. Those who get considerable pleasure from relatively high risk activities are no more unreasonable than those who avoid them. Denying that skydiving is a risky sport is unreasonable, but being willing to take such risks can be reasonable given the value a person places on the experience. Not taking a plane because it is "too risky" is unreasonable. But taking the more "risky" car can be reasonable if you want to stop and see the scenery. Living a good life involves engaging in those activities whose value exceeds the reasonably anticipated risks; it involves using information wisely.

JUDGEMENT AND RISK:
USING STATISTICAL INFORMATION TO MAKE REASONABLE DECISIONS
THE CRITICAL QUESTIONS

1. **What are the relevant statistics?**
   When looking at risk, you want to make sure that you are
   asking the relevant question. E.g., is it deaths per mile,
   fatalities per year or lifetime?
   You also need to use data on the most relevant risk group.
   Are those studied like you in important respects such as age,
   lifestyle, and geographic location?
2. **How good is the evidence?**
   Have you used systematically gathered evidence or just
   impressions from your own experience or the media?
   Is your impression based on your ability to imagine the event
   occurring? This is not a reliable source.
3. **What other information is relevant?**
   Decision-making should take into account benefits, not just risk.
   What are all the benefits and risks involved? E.g., the benefits
   and side effects of drugs.
   You need to consider all relevant alternatives, not just one or two.
4. **Are relevant fallacies avoided?**
   Subjectivity: Rather than using the best data, you make a
   decision based on your impression of likelihood.
   Framing: How we frame a consideration, whether as a
   percentage of purchase or loss of life vs. life saved,
   significantly influences our decision. But some frames lead
   us to downplay or exaggerate consideration. E.g., we downplay
   the cost of a warranty or exaggerate the value of a loss
   leading to overly risky behaviour to avoid it.
   Horror: Some risks are very unlikely but because of publicity
   or intrinsic horror they loom large in our consideration.
   But sometimes given the low probability, these fears are
   given too much consideration. E.g., fear of flying for some,
   fear of terrorism.
   Erroneous Risk Group: If we are to make the best use of
   statistical information we need to use the most relevant
   risk group. E.g., life expectancy depends not only on your
   location but also your age. The longer you live, the higher
   your life expectancy.

GLOSSARY

Absolute risk See **Risk ratio**

Anecdotal evidence Stories and casual observations that are offered as evidence. Fallacy of anecdotal evidence is the fallacy of basing a generalization on our own experiences or the stories of others. The problem with anecdotal evidence is that people find it persuasive as a justification for a generalization even though it usually relies on only one or two cases. Anecdotal evidence is contrasted with the systematic evidence typically collected by scientists. It is not credible scientific evidence, though it sometimes provides the impetus for scientific research.

Argument Making an argument means giving reasons in support of a claim. An argument is a set of claims, one of which, the **conclusion**, is supported by one or more other claims called **premises**.

Association One of the common ways of expressing a correlation. E.g., obesity is associated with diabetes. See **Risk factor**

Availability This is the fallacy of estimating probabilities on the basis of our ability to recall events. ("No one I know has ever been bitten by a dog, so dogs present no dangers.")

Average See **Mean**

Bandwagon fallacy When the apparent convergence in the research is a result of groupthink or bandwagoning, rather than an emerging consensus driven by careful research.

Biased sampling Sampling a population in a manner that fails to ensure that all members of the population have an equal chance of being sampled. See **Random sample**

Burden of proof In most arguments there is an existing default position that might be reasonably held without argument, but those who would challenge such a view have the "burden of proof" or "onus" on them; they must provide a good argument to counter the assumed default position. The more well-established the default position is, the greater the burden of proof. And the more serious a claim is—that is, the more important the consequences of true or false belief—the greater the burden of proof.

Calibration This term, as it is used in decision theory, refers to how good a person is at estimating the likelihood that a claim he believes is true. People whose estimates of likelihood are accurate are said to be well calibrated.

Case-controlled study A retrospective study that isolates the experimental and control groups on the basis of the presence or absence of the studied outcome. E.g., A case-controlled study of smoking and lung cancer would isolate a group of lung-cancer patients and then compare their rates of smoking to that of another similar (control group) group that did not have lung cancer.

Causal factor When several factors can contribute to an effect, none of them is, properly speaking, *the* cause; it's usual to speak of each of them as causal factors.

Causal relation Two events or kinds of events (e.g., smoking and lung cancer) have a causal relation when one event actually contributes to the frequency of the other event.

Cohort studies A prospective study that isolates a "cohort" or sample and follows it over time to detect the incidence of certain events. Sometimes cohorts are identified by their having the possible cause. So a cohort study might follow smokers and non-smokers over a number of years to detect incidence of lung cancer. Other cohort studies simply follow a large group over time and then use statistical methods to detect correlations between exposure (e.g., smoking) and outcomes (e.g., lung cancer).

Conclusion The claim that is the point of an argument.

Confidence interval The range around a percentage calculated from a sample, representing the addition and subtraction of the margin of error. See **Margin of error**

Confidence level Expresses how likely it is that the true value for the population is within the margin of error of the sample. See **Margin of error**

Confounding factor A causal factor associated with an outcome that masks or distorts the effect of the cause being studied. For example, early studies found that there was a higher rate of lung cancer among coffee drinkers than non-coffee drinkers. The correlation between coffee drinking and cancer resulted from the high rate of smoking among coffee drinkers, confounding the study of whether drinking coffee contributed to the incidence of lung cancer.

Context bias Bias that results from a pollster's general introduction to the survey. Such introductions often have a strong influence on how people will answer and, if not neutral, will create context bias.

Control group The comparison group created to provide the basis of comparison necessary for establishing a correlation. The control group is supposed to be like the studied group in every *relevant* way (i.e., age, gender mix, social background, etc.) except of course people in the control group don't have either the cause or effect being studied (e.g., they are non-smokers or they don't have lung cancer).

Convergence A criteria that is used to evaluate the state of research on a claim. If numerous studies tend to get similar results, it is said that the studies are converging. That different researchers using different methods are reaching the same results provides strong support for the claim in question.

Correlation A correlation exists when two factors—for example, smoking and lung cancer, education and income, potato-chip eating and heart attacks—vary together, i.e., co-vary. Because smoking is associated with a higher frequency of lung cancer, we say smoking and lung cancer are positively correlated. Since it appears that drinking red wine is associated with a lower frequency of heart disease, we say that drinking red wine and heart attacks are negatively correlated. A correlation is part of the basis for a causal claim, but saying two things are correlated is not to say one causes the other.

Cost/benefit analysis In cost/benefit analysis we look at the probable benefits (pay offs), subtract the costs, and then see if we are ahead. Cost/benefit analysis is typically done by assessing dollar costs, the probability of outcomes, and the negative cost of these outcomes. Having assigned dollar values then the expected costs and benefits of a decision can be calculated. The presumption of this analysis is that if cost exceeds benefits it is a bad decision, but if the projected benefits exceed costs it is a good decision.

Desk drawer effect This refers to the fact that studies that fail to achieve statistically significant results usually do not get published (they stay in the *desk drawer*).

Experimental studies Experimental studies involve dividing a sample into a control group and an experimental group and subjecting the experimental group to a cause to see if the outcomes of the experimental group differ from that of the control. The advantage of experimental studies is that in theory the two groups being compared differ in only one respect—the experimental factor—so a resultant difference in outcome can be confidently ascribed to the experimental factor.

Externalities Costs external to the economic system because those who create these costs do not have to pay for them. Some typical examples of these missed costs are global warming and health costs that are the result of emissions.

Fallacies Common arguments that seem persuasive but do not provide adequate support for their conclusion.

False negatives A negative result from a test indicating non-incidence of a disease when the subject has the disease.

False positives A positive result for a test indicating incidence when there is none.

False precision Using a level of precision (e.g., a number of decimal points) that cannot be justified by the accuracy of the original data.

Framing effect The effect on decisions and beliefs that results from how a choice is presented (e.g., focusing on positive outcomes or negative outcomes).

Gambler's fallacy The belief that if there has been a short-term run of unlikely outcomes (e.g., flipping four heads in a row) then it is more likely than usual (i.e., better than 1 chance in 2) that tails will come up "to correct the deviation." There is another form of this fallacy when the gambler believes that having flipped four heads in a row the coin is "hot" and will turn up heads again. Both these fallacies involve a failure to realize that each flip is independent and does not "know" about earlier flips. The first form involves the common belief that short series of events should be like long-run series. This belief is called the **representativeness fallacy**.

GDP or **Gross Domestic Product** The GDP is a measure of a country's total economic output, the value of all the goods and services produced by a country.

Good bet A bet that if made repeatedly will result in a positive payoff.

Hasty conclusion The fallacy of coming to a conclusion with too little investigation and inadequate evidence.

Incidence The number of people acquiring an illness during a year per population, e.g., the incidence of AIDS is five per 1,000 per year. See **Prevalence**

Life expectancy For a country as a whole, it is simply the average age of death adjusted for the age distribution of the population.

Margin of error In polling, the range of percentage points around the sample percentage within which the true population average is likely. If the pollster gets a result of 48% with a sample of 1,200, then the margin of error is ±3 percentage points given a confidence level of 95%; that means that the pollster can claim that the true population percentage would be somewhere between 45% and 51%, 19 times out of 20. The likelihood ratio of 19 out of 20 is how likely it is that the true answer is within the margin of error of the sample. This ratio is called the **confidence level**. The ratio can also be expressed as a percentage: the 95% confidence level.

Mean The statisticians' word for the standard arithmetic average. What most people just call "the average."

Median The middle number in a set of data used particularly in cases where the standard arithmetic average (or **mean**) is easily skewed by **outliers** (values far from the others). The median is often a better way of representing or summarizing the data than the mean because it is less sensitive to outliers.

Meta-analysis A method statisticians have developed to bring together and use data from a multitude of studies. Meta-analysis involves sifting through all previous research and collecting the data from high-quality studies into one big sample, and then doing statistical analysis on this new "sample." This method results in larger samples and, in principle, more reliable statistical conclusions.

Misleading aggregation Combining a wide variety of information in one statistic, e.g., crime statistics that lump together everything from disturbing the peace to homicide.

Mythical numbers These are numbers produced by guesstimation that then take on an unwarranted air of credibility and "hardness."

Non-response bias A type of **selection bias** created by the fact that many of those sampled are either not home or will not agree to be questioned.

Odds ratio Another way of expressing numerically a correlation (very similar to **risk ratio**).

Onus See **Burden of proof**

Outliers Values in a set of data that are far from the others.

Peer review This is the process in which experts in the field (the researchers' "peers") examine and evaluate new research before it is published. In practice, this is usually done under the auspices of the journal (a so-called peer-reviewed journal) to which the researchers have sent an article giving details of the procedures and the conclusion of their research.

Placebo effect The placebo effect occurs when people receiving any sort of treatment (medication or therapy) that they believe is effective tend to improve even if the treatment is completely ineffective biologically.

Population The group being studied by researchers or pollsters. Often called the target population.

Post hoc ergo propter hoc fallacy Inferring from mere fact that B follows A to the claim that A caused B. "Post hoc ergo propter hoc" simply means "after this therefore because of this."

Prejudicial funding bias Bias intentionally created by the sponsor of the poll or study who has an interest in the outcome. This bias differs from the accidental biasing of a sample as the result of sample selection difficulties. The sponsors' influence can affect, for example, the phrasing of questions as in the Kyoto polls discussed in the text, or the termination date of a study as in the Vioxx scandal.

Premise A claim in an argument intended to support the conclusion.

Prevalence The total number of people in a population with a disease. E.g., 10% of the population has cancer. Cf. **incidence**, which is a time-bound measure of frequency.

Primary research The research published by scientists and researchers in their field.

Probability The probability of some event is the rate that event happens over the long run. Probability or chance is expressed in two different ways, either as a percentage or a fraction. The probability of flipping a fair coin and it coming up heads is 50% or ½. That means that if you were to flip a fair coin (that is, one not weighted to come up one way more often than the other) a large number of times, it will come up heads close to 50% or ½ of the time.

Prospective studies Prospective studies follow sample group(s) forward through time noting interested events (e.g., death rates among smokers and non-smokers).

Proxy Something studied (e.g., people's reports) as an indirect way for researchers to get at what they are really interested in. For example, using people's reports of what they eat instead of actually measuring what they eat. Since tracking people's behaviour is often very difficult, most studies of human behaviour involve collecting information about what people *report, not what they actually do.*

P-Value The probability that the difference between the control and experimental group is due to chance. A p-value of .05 means that there is only a 5% chance that the difference was due to chance. P-values are typically given in terms of "less than or equal to," e.g., $p \leq .05$, meaning that results meet or better the usual criteria for statistical significance, which is having a p-value better than or equal to .05.

Question bias A bias introduced into polling by the phrasing of the questions.

Question order bias A bias introduced into polling by the order of the questions.

Random sample The method of sampling in which every member of the population has an equal chance of being selected. A random sample is therefore an unbiased sample—no individual has a greater chance of being polled than any other. Randomness ensures that no group or individual is unfairly favoured and, unlike attempts to get a **representative sample**, it does not require that the pollster know all the relevant factors that make a sample "representative." Randomness also provides the sampling basis for the mathematics that determines **margin of error** and **confidence level**.

Relative risk See **Risk ratio**

Replication The re-doing of an experiment or study, or doing similar studies under slightly different conditions as an additional test of a causal claim.

Representative sample A sample created to have the same proportion of people with relevant characteristics as the whole population; for example, there should be the same percentage of people over fifty in the sample as in the population, if it's supposed that age is a relevant factor.

Representativeness fallacy Believing that short series of events should be like long-run series, or more popularly, believing that your experience is "representative" of the experience of others.

Respondent deception bias A bias in studies created by the understandable tendency of people to deceive pollsters when questioned. This bias is even a greater problem for studies that are directed at finding out what people *do* (e.g., recycling, sexual behaviour, eating), not what they believe. Especially common if the topic is one about which people do not necessarily wish to reveal their true views (e.g., sexual behaviour).

Retrospective studies Retrospective studies identify people who have exhibited some aspect of interest (e.g., lung cancer, criminal behaviour, extraordinarily long life) and attempt, usually through interviews, to determine past experiences that are correlated with the aspect of interest (e.g., did the extraordinarily long lived drink more than others?).

Risk factor One of the common ways of expressing a correlation. Something is a risk factor for an illness if it is positively correlated with it. E.g., cancer in your parents is a risk factor for your getting cancer. As with correlations, risk factors may or may not be causal factors.

Risk group The group (population) that provides the basis for risk assessment claims. E.g., the risk of getting lung cancer depends on whether you are in the risk group of smokers or non-smokers. While statistics can never apply to just you (unless you're a baseball player), the closer the risk group "fits" you, the more useful the information for decision-making.

Risk ratio A risk ratio expresses the increased likelihood that someone will suffer a particular outcome based on his or her having an associated risk factor (very similar to **odds ratio**). Risk ratios can be measured in two ways: absolute and relative. Your absolute risk is the chance of having a particular misfortune typically given in yearly terms (e.g., the yearly risk of being hit by lightning). Relative risk is risk expressed in relation to some other, typically less risky, activity or a control group (e.g., the relative risk of lung cancer is based on comparing the rate of lung cancers among smokers to the rate among non-smokers). For example, the chance of being killed by lightning in any year is about 0.25 in a million. This is the absolute risk of being killed by lightning in a year. But people living in Kansas have twice the risk of US residents in general—a much higher risk ratio or relative risk (compared to the broader group). The absolute risk of being killed by lightning *in Kansas* is 0.57 in a million. Still a pretty small risk compared to say being killed in a motor vehicle accident in any year, which is about 120 in a million. Being killed in a car accident has a relative risk that is more than 400 times greater (or 40,000% greater!) than being killed by lightning.

Sample The group of people selected to provide a basis for making an inference about the **population** the pollster is studying.

Sample of convenience A sample of subjects that one can easily get access to—for example, students or hospital patients, or people who respond to requests for volunteer subjects.

Selection bias A sampling method that results in some members of the population (e.g., the poor) having a different probability of being selected for a sample. Such a bias means that the sample does not provide a good basis for inference to the population.

Self-selection bias The polling bias that results from allowing subjects to chose whether to respond. Typical examples of this are "phone-in" and "click-in" polls.

Seminal article A research article that set the direction or changed the direction of research. You can usually identify a seminal article by noticing which articles are widely cited on a particular topic.

Sponsor bias The result of a sponsor of a poll using their influence to bias the kind of questions asked, the introduction to the poll, or the question order. Because all these aspects of polling can easily be used to manipulate a poll's results, assessment of the poll requires checking that such influence did not occur. Polls done by news agencies or other disinterested parties are usually more free from this kind of bias than those with clearly interested sponsors such as oil companies or environmental groups.

Statistical significance A difference between two statistics that is unlikely to be due to chance, i.e., a difference that is likely to be true of the population as a whole, sometimes abbreviated as SSD (statistically significant difference). Such a difference is evidence of a correlation, but should not be taken as evidence that the study is showing anything "significant" in the sense of *humanly important*.

Stratified sample A sample produced by dividing the population into large groups, often by geography, and then randomly picking some sub-groups within these groupings. Individuals in each selected sub-group are then randomly picked to be polled. Typically a pollster produces a stratified sample by randomly selecting telephone exchanges and then numbers within these exchanges. The goal is to achieve a sample that is "random" but also geographically and economically representative.

Systematic review A review article that is based on the extensive and systematic collection of all related research. Unlike **meta-analysis** it does not involve aggregating the data from various studies, but does attempt to assess the direction of the research and the degree of support for the claim in question.

Third cause A cause that produces two different events in such a way that those events are correlated even though they have no direct causal link.